AF600180

HU FENG

SUNY series in Global Modernity

Ravi Arvind Palat and Roxann Prazniak, editors

HU FENG

A MARXIST INTELLECTUAL IN A COMMUNIST STATE, 1930–1955

RUTH Y. Y. HUNG

Published by State University of New York Press, Albany

Printed in the United States of America

For information, contact State University of New York Press, Albany, NY
www.sunypress.edu

Library of Congress Cataloging-in-Publication Data

Names: Hung, Ruth Y. Y., author.
Title: Hu Feng: A Marxist Intellectual in a Communist State, 1930–1955 / Ruth Y. Y. Hung, author.
Description: Albany : State University of New York Press, [2020] | Series: SUNY series in Global Modernity | Includes bibliographical references and index.
Identifiers: ISBN 9781438479538 (hardcover : alk. paper) | ISBN 9781438479552 (ebook)
Further information is available at the Library of Congress.

10 9 8 7 6 5 4 3 2 1

CONTENTS

Acknowledgments		vii
A Note on Translations		ix
I	Introduction	1
II	Foolishness and Consciousness	19
III	In the Path of Lu Xun	43
IV	Criticism as Contest	65
V	The Problematics of Literary Subjectivism	89
VI	Time Has Begun	109
VII	The Hu Feng Incident Revisited	133
Epilogue		153
Chronology of Hu Feng's Life: 1902–1985		163
List of Chinese Names and Terms		177
Notes		183

Bibliography 239
- Works by Hu Feng 239
- Biographies of Hu Feng 240
- Periodicals 241
- Works Cited 242

Index 269

ACKNOWLEDGMENTS

Two papers of mine served as earlier versions of chapters VI and VII of this book. I cite " 'Time Has Begun': Hu Feng's Poiesis in Socialist China, 1937–1950," *Canadian Review of Comparative Literature* 44, no. 3 (September 2017), and "The Politics of Modern Literary Criticism in China: The Hu Feng Incident Revisited," in *Writing under Socialism Past and Present*, edited by Meesha Nehru and Sara Jones (Nottingham: Russell Press, 2011). I am grateful to the editors and publishers for their assistance. Cordial thanks to the four anonymous readers, whose constructive suggestions I wisely followed. I also want to extend my appreciation to the acquisitions editor, Andrew Kenyon, for his support in putting this book in print.

I could not begin to thank individually all the people from whom I have learned and through whose life and work I strive to become the person and critic I aspire to be. But foremost among the individuals I must mention is the late Arif Dirlik (1940–2017), whose struggle for the conditions for democracy compassed my scale of criticism. Arif was moreover a great mentor, one of the rare models of critical consciousness not in any degree disparaged by "authority" outside of himself. Arif gave this book its current title. I owe special thanks to Paul A. Bové, whose *Poetry against Torture*, a seminar series delivered at the University of Hong Kong, taught me criticism's capacity for poiesis and what remains valuable in the provision of poetry. Wlad Godzich encouraged my work and taught me to stay focused on what matters most in criticism. Liu Tao Tao, my advisor at Oxford University, spent a generous amount of time and mind instructing me and commented on the manuscript. Wendy Gan, Elaine Y. L. Ho, Douglas Kerr, Wang Aihe, and Wang Xiaoying contributed to my education in ways I always cherish and remember. I would also like to thank Catherine Li and Julie Ma, under whose tutelage I crossed the line between ignorance and knowledge without losing the space for wonder.

This book had taken close to a decade to finish, witnessing the formation of my ever-growing family. During this time, my two Japanese Spitz dogs—Bai Bai and Xiao Xiao—flourished into their senior years and became my next teachers after Hu Feng. They, along with Sasha Hua Tong, made more expansive and inclusive my radar of love and understanding of humanity. Finally, in reflecting on the process of my constant search for the right ethics and clarity of mind within my writing, I came to realize that I had written a tribute to Q. S. Tong.

A NOTE ON TRANSLATIONS

Wherever possible, I used a readily available English translation for all translations from Chinese, and the references for those translations are provided in the endnotes. Where no translation is specified, the translation is mine.

1

INTRODUCTION

> Beautifully simple himself, he loved everything simple, genuine, sincere, and he had a peculiar way of making other people simple.
>
> In order to live well and humanly one must work—work with love and with faith.
>
> —Maxim Gorky[1]

The purpose of this book is to make a statement on critical literature's humanistic aims and methods by inserting into the archives of global modernity a historically significant case of intellectual engagement: the dilemma of Hu Feng (1902–85). Hu was a believer in the Chinese Marxist cause, but, as an intellectual, he could not accept its takeover by an apparatus of repression. In his career as a Marxist literary critic and a fellow traveler of the Chinese Communist Party (CCP), Hu practiced and called for thinking that eventually became an intellectual force critical of the CCP's authoritarian control over cultural and ideological matters. In 1955, the CCP, under instructions from Mao Zedong, mobilized a nationwide campaign to demonize Hu as an ideological enemy and a counterrevolutionary element. The Hu Feng Incident (hereafter the Hu Incident) was the first and the most revealing political onslaught against a critic and his associates in the history of the People's Republic of China (PRC). Unprecedented in scale and exceptional in its intensity, the Hu Incident implicated more than two thousand people, ranging from Hu's closest family members, associates, and colleagues to remote literary correspondents. In the end, the CCP charged seventy-eight people with the crime of being "elements of the Hu counter-revolutionary clique," many of whom were driven mad or died in prison. Among the surviving "elements," most were imprisoned for more than two decades. Despite apparent facts, the Hu Incident was not an entirely straightforward case of state coercion, nor was it symmetrically related to political violence. Hu's literary and political career, especially as it overlapped with the period in which Marxist literary criticism had transformed from a motivated sociopolitical force into an oppressive establishment following the CCP's political ascendancy, affords a unique entry point into the study of China's journey toward modern authoritarianism.

Today, Hu's status as a modern intellectual remains representative because, over time, his revolutionary experience and overall aesthetics have provided cherished lessons on the politics of Marxist critical engagement. For instance, by epitomizing such intellectual events as the Hu Incident and the Cultural Revolution, historians have demonstrated the vicissitudes of Marxism in China. What did Marxist criticism in China under Mao mean? Specifically, what did it denote to the "committed writer" who seemed to have found in it a resolution to the paradox of literature and politics? Did Chinese "New Literature" emerge from the negotiations between the CCP's revolutionary politics and the intellectuals' revolutionary aspirations? At what point did realpolitik and radical visions walk separate paths, and to what extent was "literature" a *praxis*, an expression, a statement of "revolution"? Did Hu, in his role as an intellectual critic, really "practice" Marxism as he "practiced" literature and criticism? If not, how did he exploit the chasm between ideology and practice? These questions did not solely belong to Hu, as their significance converged at a growing scope of intellectual discourses on a socialist commitment that was self-critically tinged.

In terms of Mao, the Marxist intellectuals' questions oscillated between assumed objectivity in self-assessment and a visible effort to remain politically active. By charting and analyzing Hu's developing relationships with historical figures from what Mao called "the mass of revolutionary intellectuals,"[2] and by showing the fundamental conflicts and agreements between them, this book intends to confirm the necessity of Hu's brand of intellectual impulse. Hu's intellectual life and career, I believe, revealed much of what was essential to the era's revolutionary spirit, Chinese modernity's historical goals, and the critical humanist's aesthetic aims.

To get a better idea of my perspectives on Hu, one notes first that my focus will be on Hu as a Marxist intellectual and CCP fellow traveler, not as a victim of the CCP's revolutionary scheme. For instance, I am less interested in asking whether Hu had been treated fairly by Mao and in the political movements that persecuted him than in exploring how Hu's literary criticism exemplified a case of modern literary criticism and its contribution to international revolutionary politics. Hu, a protégé of Lu Xun (1881–1936) and a member of the Japanese Communist Party, came into his own in the 1940s during a series of debates with his fellow left-wing writers. He participated in historical events that strengthened state authoritarianism and used these momentous events to think through criticism and poiesis's enduring importance in modern society, especially within the context of the modernization and transformation of the PRC. In the first days of the Chinese Revolution, Hu and his generation of literary critics began a lifelong collaboration with institutions of power to build a socialist democracy. Not satisfied with acting just as respondents, they were anxious to create, interact, and negotiate with these institutions. They embraced Marxism's morality and code of critical acts and accepted the political demand to subscribe literary subjectivism to a unique form of collectivism—one that eventually subsumed all subjectivities to itself.

Another way to understand this book is through its presentation of the disturbing history of early modern China's relationship with Western colonial powers and its reexamination of Chinese Marxism's ties to global modernism. Apart from the former Soviet Union, the PRC was the only major Communist country where literature and criticism were a direct conduit to such events as the Chinese Revolution and the Cultural Revolution, both of which were historically significant in modernity's global expression. By direct participation in politics, Chinese intellectuals helped guide the PRC's initiatives during the long course of its ideological advancement in global politics. Hu's critical intellectual work, which followed Lu Xun's and outlived his as it also crossed the crucial threshold of 1949, offered an antithesis of the PRC's modernization values. The PRC indoctrinated these values not only within the nation but also globally in the wake of its much disguised "peaceful rise" at the turn of the twenty-first century. From this perspective, this book aims at enriching the cultural and intellectual history of modern China as well as informing a collective understanding of the "rising" PRC, both ideologically and politically.

Finally, this book will add to the archive of this committed literary intellectual in that it documents Hu's decades of thought and action—his development as a revolutionary, his critical mode of practice, and his resistance to the demands of self-erasure and self-critique within the Party. The book follows the career of Hu as a Marxist writer and critic, from his emergence as a prominent figure in left-wing literary politics within the Party to his becoming a target in the first Party-led critical campaign after the PRC's founding. Two events of historical significance bracket this period: the establishment of the Chinese League of Left-wing Writers (hereafter the Left-league) in 1930 and the arrest of Hu in 1955. This time frame overlaps with the crucial period of modern criticism's development in China, which witnessed the sinicization and "Maofication" of Marxism from a framework for revolutionary thought to a schema of intellectual neutralization. The major intellectual-political events that took place in this period defined not only Hu's life but also the PRC's state and national history, from the time the PRC fought for survival to the time it consolidated power beyond measure. Studying Hu's revolutionary experience during this period will provide a better understanding of the left-wing politics of intellectual engagement, as well as the genealogical formation of Marxist critical practice and its language in China under Mao and the CCP. For instance, in the collaboration between state intellectuals and the structure of power, Hu, having sealed his political fate with the CCP's road to statism, found himself spiraling down into a set of conditions that he helped forge, through which a revolutionary movement gained ground even after it became a significant force against human freedom.

MARXIST CRITICISM AND THE MAKING OF MODERN CHINA

In the first half of the twentieth century, when the Sino-Japanese War made urgent the need to address the question of a national crisis, Chinese intellectuals embraced Marxism as an apostle of human liberation and emancipation. The Marxist "materialistic and anti-metaphysical" interpretation of human society provided the intellectuals with "a program of action, definite goals and a so-called historically determined role for themselves."[3] In this spirit of populist Marxism, those who came of age after the May Fourth Movement (1915–21) recognized the *practical* aspect of literature and criticism. Qu Qiubai, whom T. A. Hsia called a "tenderhearted Communist,"[4] declared in a famous essay, "There is no reason to stop at 'May Fourth.' China's cultural movements must obey the revolutionary demands. The step we are going to take has nothing to do with 'May Fourth.' "[5] Notably, Qu's statement of radical politics regarding May Fourth embraced a radical pragmatism over such ideas as "democracy," "science," "freedom," and "human emancipation."

Despite his attraction to Enlightenment ideals, Qu typically sought to create the conditions of possibility for ideas to acquire social and personal realities. The pressure of the Sino-Japanese War compelled him to join the CCP and participate in China's modernization, believing that the Party was the key to individual and national survival. Regarding the relationship between Marxism and the modern Chinese intellectual, Richard Solomon wrote: "The personal uncertainties of an era of social upheaval almost instinctively lead a generation alienated from discredited or ineffectual social organizations to establish associations of their own, through which they seek personal meaning in collective action."[6]

It is evident that Marxist criticism played an attractive role in grooming a generation of intellectuals that Mao called "the class of the petty bourgeoisie."[7] The intellectuals' sense of self was founded on institutional power, and they came to equate revolutionary romanticism with political pragmatism. The writer was as competent as the soldier and, to repeat Mao's two-army theory, was part of one of the two armies in wartime China. Mao's March 1926 article "Analysis of the Classes in Chinese Society" emphasized the significance of creative works, proclaiming that they were direct material evidence of writers' contribution to radical politics and that they revealed the sociopolitical orientations of the writer:

> *The petty bourgeoisie.* Included in this category are . . . the lower levels of the intellectuals—students, primary and secondary school teachers, lower government functionaries, office clerks, small lawyers. . . . This class deserves very close attention. . . . In normal times [different] sections of the petty bourgeoisie differ in their attitude to the revolution. But in times of war, that is, when the tide of the revolution runs high and the dawn of victory is in sight, not only will the left-wing of the petty bourgeoisie join the revolution, but the middle section too may join, and even right-wingers . . . will have to go along with the revolution.[8]

Indeed, in times of war, artists and writers willingly joined forces to propagate a culture of national resistance, fostering a revolutionary collectivity that entailed the loss of intellectual autonomy. Decades after the revolution, when recalling the conditions of the 1930s in a speech in 1977, Zhou Yang (1908–89) emphasized the "little opportunity" that critics and writers had in knowing "the profound meaning of Mao Zedong Thought."[9] Hence, "the flag of international socialism was the flag of the CCP," and the "belief in communism" was "almost religious."[10] When asked why she remained committed to the Party despite imprisonment and manual labor for over a decade, Ding Ling (1904–86) replied, in the same mystic tone, "We have our own ideology."[11] What did "our own ideology" mean? How did Mao Zedong Thought become divine to these left-wing writers whom Zhou represented? What turned the May Fourth brand of critical awakening against Chinese traditionalism into revolutionary politics? What were the forces that motivated literary critics and writers to form associations as power bases from which to launch ideological battles? Despite the CCP's politicization of literature, suppression of creative subjectivity, and reform of intellectuals, why did Hu and the intellectuals of his time continue to develop a relationship with the political, ideological, and powerful?

Hu's life and case are remarkable for the intensity with which they adumbrated the answers to those questions. In 1965, Mei Zhi visited her husband in Qincheng Prison for the first time in a decade. As Mei Zhi went to "hug him and weep," Hu very calmly approached her and gave her the same old smile, assuaging and convincing his wife that standing in front of her was "the same man"—full of strength and resolute.[12] Extraordinarily, the long years of separation and confinement had not clouded Hu's mind, which testified to his faith in the CCP and his belief that personal fate was inseparable from the national course. At their third meeting, Hu insisted that his approach to Marxism had no "big problems," and that he would bet his life on the correctness of his ideological outlook: "I couldn't think of anything worse," he said to Mei Zhi.[13]

> It would have been fine had they persecuted me because it wouldn't have been my mistake. . . . I'd neither acted out of personal interest nor chased after fame. I responded as any Chinese should, harboring no evil intent. I will accept the Party's ruling whatever.[14]

In the same vein, Hu rejected the advice of Xiong Zimin (1897–1980), who urged him to take advantage of the political turbulence in the early 1970s that brought down his enemies. He wrote in reply, "My state of mind is as it has been for the last decade or so. I confide unshakably in Chairman Mao and the Party Central Committee's leadership."[15] Ultimately, Hu founded his sense of self on his understanding of the historical vocation of Marxist Communism in modern China and on his assumption that the Party shared with him that same understanding.

Of the models of political and ideological commitment that surrounded Hu, his choice of engagement was archetypical, as it articulated the revolutionary politics and romanticism that galvanized a generation of Marxist intellectuals under Mao and, along with them, a catalog of moral and intellectual dilemmas that was to recur among these intellectuals for over half a century. Hu was not only one among these Marxist revolutionaries but also characteristic of how these committed intellectuals typically behaved under the circumstances. Like most in interwar China, Hu saw the CCP's revolutionary ideology as a noble vocation that could unify the country and as a potent political force that could transform social uncertainties into political possibilities. However, as the reality of the war brought together writers with similar outlooks, it also created internal conflicts within the same ideological camp. Within this camp, one was more likely to be a poet or a scribbler or a master of ideas than a slave of dogmas.

Studying Hu requires vigilance against two reductionist views. First, the left-wing intellectuals were no more than transmitters of the Party's ideology and instruments for class struggle. Second, there was no possibility of true intellectual agency or activity under the authoritarian rule of the CCP.[16] Following these two views, Hu's participation in the Chinese Revolution, for example, might have been either a "logical conclusion" of the Chinese nationalist movement or a result of his passionate belief in Marxism. In either case, Hu did not seem to be different from other ideological functionaries, as he entered into what David Kelly called a "contractual obligation" to the CCP without knowing what it would mean for him.[17] In the former case, Hu was a passive historical product; in the latter, his political passion blinded him. If Hu's historical consciousness and political commitment were indeed nothing more than revolutionary impulses, one could hardly justify the fact that the Party singled out Hu's literary views for criticism. The Party even made a case—the first one after 1949—of Hu as a "counterrevolutionary." Although a revolutionary intellectual himself, in the early 1940s Hu emerged as one of the most vocal critics of the corrupt practice of left-wing critical discourse.

How and why Hu differed from his generation of left-wing intellectuals is a significant subject of Hu studies. From the outset, Hu's critical practice called forth the role of the intellectual's agency and power in the Chinese Revolution and the events thereafter; it also formed a living process that required a review, reexamination, and reflection at each historical juncture. Given the close link between Hu's personal life and the vicissitudes of the PRC's founding, perhaps the first step in the approach to this reassessment is to identify several stages of Hu's career and how they corresponded to some of the most important political, cultural, and historical events in modern China. These stages in Hu's life included the years of active engagement in radical social movements (1925–29), the years of ideological enlightenment and identity formation (1930–36), the years of the creation of his critical consciousness (1937–48), and the years of disillusionment and disturbance (1949–55). Collectively, these stages were characteristic and consequences of the turn of events that punctuated the intellectual and literary history of modern China: Sun Yat-sen's death in 1925; the establishment and dissolution of the Left-league in 1930 and 1936, respectively; the outbreak of the Sino-Japanese War in 1936; the establishment of the PRC in 1949; and the arrest and imprisonment of Hu in 1955. The different stages of Hu's life exposed an engagé writer's changing experience of Chinese socialism: from the call to arms to the task of promoting socialist ideology; and from the struggle to maintain critical consciousness in the face of political orders to the day-to-day conflict with the ideological state policies of literature and criticism. To reassess Hu's intellectual, social, and political activities at various historical junctures is to avoid the pitfall of confusing Hu as a political dissident of an authoritarian regime.[18] The path between revolutionary romanticism and Marxist ideology depended on objective trends that constituted and defined the content of intellectual responsibility and the form of political commitment.

THE POET IN THE MARXIST CRITIC

Scholars generally recognize Hu's historical importance, especially in the context of Communist China's intellectual persecution, but they tend to underplay his revolutionary romanticism, literary status, and legacy. Today, half a century after the end of the Cultural Revolution, the Hu Incident that foreboded this global ideological event scarcely needs further rectification, as the CCP rectified it in the 1980s.[19] For Hu, the relationship between individual practice and political power was a dynamic process that involved the interaction of multiple forces and determinations, with an important one being the writer's subjectivity. For instance, a close reading of Hu's 1949 *Time Has Begun* 时间开始了, a book-length eulogy to the PRC's founding, offered a glimpse of the practice of a literary subjectivism and a poetic form that frustrated the CCP's wartime politics. Studies on intellectuals and Marxism in modern China should, accordingly, recognize that Hu and his generation of left-wing writers and critics were not merely prisoners of political power but modes of being in the same power structure. Hu was a Marxist critic, editor, poet, and exile who struggled precariously in the ideological homeland that he helped build, and these aspects of his persona made him a well-rounded figure. Playing these different roles, Hu called forth a critical biography of a set of radical intellectuals, with Hu as the central figure and with close reference to his poetry and critical writings.

I do not deny the importance of the political system in the development of some of the most significant cultural and political events that took place in Mao's China. However, the widely accepted reading of the politics of Chinese intellectual life, in both the PRC and abroad, is as limited and limiting as it is useful.[20] Take Peter Benenson's *Persecution 1961* as an example. The book is about nine individuals who share the tragic fate and experience of persecution and, in some cases, are tortured for holding opinions divergent from their respective governments. Hu is one of them. Without showing overt sympathy, Benenson defined the significance of the Hu Incident in terms of Hu's political dissidence and indicted the CCP for political terror. Although largely ignored by scholars, *Persecution 1961* interests me because it is among the earliest critical studies of the Hu Incident in the West. Furthermore, the response to the book reflected what Western readers understood about intellectual life in Mao's China. A review of the book in the *Times Literary Supplement* expressed some difficulty in understanding the way Benenson presented his subjects. While the review released Benenson from the task of "righting such wrongs in the world," it suggested that the book injected pathos into history and offered an account of some "tragic stories of brave and lonely human beings for whom the author feels passionate sympathy."[21] "His book is so cool and dry that . . . it reads like a counsel's brief drawn up by a somewhat *unimaginative* solicitor. . . . This desperate endeavor to be detached and aloof prevents Mr. Benenson . . . from giving us vivid accounts and developing them dramatically."[22] Yet if Benenson elicited "passionate sympathy" for political dissidence with imagination but without dramatizing the "tragic stories of the brave and lonely human beings," would it still be possible to understand the complex experiences of the Chinese Marxist intellectuals? After all, Hu and his generation of writers were among the original forces and determinations that drove modern Chinese literary and intellectual life to a tragic climax and finale. Were commitment to mean anything, it is "surely conscious, active, and open: a *choice* of position," said Raymond Williams.[23] As much as the Marxist writers and intellectuals of revolutionary China were "brave and lonely human beings," they were also *historical agents.* They searched for and found meaning in the practice of epoch-changing politics and contributed to the formation of the CCP's revolutionary discourse and ideological apparatuses. In that sense, the portrayal of Hu as merely oppressed does not represent him adequately but rather eclipses his struggle to be at once within and without political and institutional power.

Kirk A. Denton's 1998 book *The Problematic of Self in Modern Chinese Literature* is, at present, the only full-length work in English devoted to the study of Hu's literary theory, specifically his concept of literary subjectivism in socialist realism. Denton crystallized Hu's literary criticism into a formative idea within a more stringent space of national literature and literary history. The elaborate, influential study showed that while Hu's theory of literary subjectivism provided Lu Ling, his protégé, with a theoretical foundation,[24] it in turn descended from traditional Chinese thought, especially the Confucian paradigm of "Great Learning."[25] The argument that tradition played a role in what was a very modern conflict provided a unique point of entry into understanding the modernity of Hu's creativity. Denton's contribution to the study of Hu is not limited to practical criticism. In his 2008 essay titled "The Hu Feng Group: Genealogy of a Literary School," Denton analyzed the literary activities of Hu's group, in particular its editorial work that launched and published the important literary journals *July* and *Hope* in war-torn China.[26] "Can we look beneath these politicized representations and arrive at a more historically accurate view of the group's collectivity?";[27] Denton's essay followed from that premise, but it also conveyed that the creation of Hu's group was a political, not a historical, act. Fundamental questions like "What was the Hu Feng group?" and "How was the Hu Feng group . . . constructed for political purposes?" were articulated most forcefully in Denton's painstaking efforts to reconstruct history.[28]

My study of Hu sought to shift the perspective from Denton's intramural one to an extramural one of Hu's concerns and readings, including his critical work and poetry, by telling Hu's story along more disciplinarily broader and historically complete lines. Outside of the PRC's intellectual history and political context, the career and case of Hu have much to enrich and deepen the history of the modern intellectual and global Marxism, for example, his conviction in the creative subject's unique function in left-wing literature and its comprehensive intellectual history. Hu learned, mostly via Lu Xun's translation work, from a broad spectrum of radical writers and critics, such as A. P. Chekhov, Maxim Gorky, Georg Lukács, Aleksey Nikolayevich Tolstoy, Kuriyagawa Hakuson, Arishima Takeo, and Romain Rolland, to name just a few. The theater of Hu's intellectual genealogy and critical genesis included literary, philosophical, psychoanalytical, and sociopolitical influences. Moreover, the major intellectual-political events that defined Hu's life against the CCP's socialist history were comparable to those that confined such intellectuals-in-exile as Antonio Gramsci, Romain Rolland, and Primo Levi—all of whom experienced some of the same struggles and crises in their encounter between power and the individual. In this respect, the literary and political career of Hu as a Marxist literary critic at work is an apt example, not just in the study of the national history of China but also in efforts to continue to expand the concept of the "committed critic." The study of Hu, in this sense, is an attempt to explore the parameters in which creative freedom and political commitment negotiate with each other.

Euro-American scholars have had the most active voice in the discussion of Hu's literary and political career, until now. This book has a great deal to add to the discussion, which should include modern Chinese writing and criticism in the context of global realities. In practice, this book is limited to a single body of literature in which Hu's life and corpus are central to the global exchange in question. Moreover, it makes a central figure available to readers along with much of the critical, political, and creative geography through which he moved, addressing other key figures and events in the broader field and drawing them into historical and critical view.

The story of Hu as a Marxist literary critic throughout one quarter of a century is an instructive case, as it augments incipient critical discussions of modern Chinese writing in the full scholarly and cultural sphere of global literatures and advanced criticism.[29] In this book, the chapter on Hu and Lu Xun will exemplify this potential. Although existing studies on Lu Xun have made a notable exception to the general rule that modern Chinese literature is a mere example of "third world" writings in the hinterland of world literatures, Hu, who worked closely with Lu Xun, was arguably the most important figure after Lu Xun regarding critical consciousness. Ironically, Fredric Jameson's influential notion of national allegory, based on his reading of Lu Xun's "Diary of a Madman," univocally directed Western criticism's study of the experience of Chinese modernity even as it attempted to "liberate" it from Sinological studies, which rarely engage in critical work outside of its area.[30] The revision or emendation of these successful and substantial efforts requires not only new studies on more writers from the same theoretical framework, but it must also loosen its theoretical grip and make the subject of investigation viable in its own right.

Paradoxically, as a sociohistorical force under the ideology of the PRC, a state apparatus that defined literature and criticism in predetermined terms, the Chinese experience of Marxist literary criticism and socialist realism was dictated by the interactions between intellectual practice and institutional forms of power, between "marginalized writers" and "core writers," and between fellow travelers and Party representatives. A remarkable galaxy of individuals, under specific circumstances, fought hard within and without to bring about, first, the ascent of "Marxist socialist realism" as a contender for generations of practice, and then its division into power cliques and discourse. Lu Xun brought modern Chinese literature (i.e., May Fourth literature) to the pinnacle of its development, but his sympathy for socialist Communism and his complex relationship with the Left-league was a major reason for its branching off and out into the ideological straitjacket of "revolutionary literature." Meanwhile, it was Hu's defiance of what he called "formalism"—the mechanical application of Marxist schemata in literary works—that first suggested to the literary arena that orthodox socialist realism offered no magic formula for the May Fourth project of mass enlightenment, and thus for laying the foundations of Chinese modernity.[31] Without Hu, "modern Chinese literature" may have entered into the Cultural Revolution without warning, and much earlier, and thus may not have drawn so stolidly the later generations' attention to the importance of intellectual responsibility and consciousness.

THE STRUCTURE OF THIS BOOK

Following the introduction in this chapter, the next six chapters will present Hu's formative years, his literary and political career, and the tragedy of the Hu Incident, ending with some closing thoughts in the epilogue. Hu's revolutionary impulse began with his raison d'être for social revolution. For much of the time in his formative years, Hu wandered around like most raw youths, but his extensive exposure to social reality through encounters with circles of people from diverse backgrounds began to educate him. By the late 1920s, Hu's wandering soul began to settle down, residing in the camp of left-wing revolutionary writers. The transition of Hu's antifeudal sentiment, from an "instinctive discontent" to a political consciousness, occurred under the influence of two intellectual sources: Japanese Marxism and Lu Xun. These forces, in their different ways, empowered the historical subject with what Hu called the "subjective combative spirit 主观战斗精神," a term that marked Hu's position in Chinese Marxist thought.

In Japan, Hu was a political activist more than he was a student of language and literature. He became a member of the Anti-Japanese War Alliance, the Japanese branch of the Left-league, and the Japanese Communist Party. Partly for practical reasons, and partly because of his deep attraction to the everyday life of Japanese toilers, Hu spent much of his time studying their letters, correspondences, and translations of their literature. In an essay written in 1933, the year of Hu's expulsion from Japan for being an "anti-Japanese Communist," Hu reflected on his years in Japan:

> It's been more than ten years since I first got in touch with literature and art. . . . Literature and art retained in me some passionate desires at a time when I found life most monotonous and cold, and gave me power when the future was completely blanked out by the feeling of hopelessness and desperation. Yet, before the year 1931, in which I encountered a few friends who enlightened me with [Marxist] literary theory, my relation to literature and art was limited to some personal needs, to my aspiration to discover and cultivate myself.[32]

The way Japanese writers and Communists practiced Marxist criticism had instructive and instrumental value to Hu, who understood Marxist theory and its application in Japanese literature as the very embodiment of the most politically progressive form of life.

In 1933, Hu returned to Shanghai and began working for the Left-league. Anxious about losing his intellectual self to the call of Party solidarity and the grip of revolutionary ideology, Hu chose to be a fellow traveler and worked for the CCP under the guidance of Lu Xun. In Japan, Hu learned about revolutionary collectivism and praxis; and from Lu Xun, he learned about critical consciousness, a virtue that tore open the rift between Hu and the Party intellectuals. In the three years before Lu Xun's death in 1936, Hu participated in the disputes and literary debates that Lu Xun fought with such Party representatives as Zhou Yang. Despite his "loyalty" to the CCP, conflicts with Party leaders marked his life and jeopardized his career. Hu's layered relationship with the CCP, concretized by his self-regard first as a poet and critic and second as a fellow traveler, had significant implications for his future.

At this point, two historical moments deserve attention: first, the emergence of "a public sphere"[33] in the 1930s, an "ideal speech situation" in which "the force of the better argument" alone may have prevailed;[34] and second, Japan's surrender in 1945 and the Chinese Civil War (1937–50), which defeated the kind of intellectual liberalism that had characterized and molded the public sphere. In the early 1940s, particularly after the publication of Mao's "Talks at the Yan'an Forum on Literature and Art" (hereafter "Talks") in 1942, many writers entangled themselves in institutional politics, distancing themselves from what in Europe Gramsci called "the elementary passions of the people."[35] These "left-wingers," Hu felt, fed their political appetites slavishly by leaping to empty dogmatism, and in so doing, impaired criticism's purpose and function as a weapon against what Lu Xun called "intellectual servitude."[36] As Zhi Kejian observed perceptively, revolutionary writers in the 1940s did not have "the ability to perform their two tasks simultaneously: first, that of maintaining the fundamental principles of literature; second, that of solving concrete problems in literary thought and creative practice."[37] In other words, having practiced socialist discourse in the 1930s, these writers indulged in a situation where they were more capable of implementing discursive power than exercising the independent force of mind needed to experiment with "revolutionary literature" or New Literature. Consequently, they built an ideological stronghold by launching themselves into debates against marginal literary groups and in so doing formed a single regiment, an esoteric guild for their institutional rise and security.

After the Yan'an Forum, an ideological stance became almost the sole basis for evaluating a writer's political identity. The life and fate of writers under Mao and the CCP were always inseparable from the politics of criticism; they could make a political fortune or ruin their career by merely producing a novel, a play, a painting, or even a short story. *Time Has Begun*, written amid the long-standing conflicts between Hu and Party writers, conflated many of Hu's mixed sentiments about the arrival of a power regime he at once anticipated and reprehended. Hu's poiesis, which extended beyond poetry to embrace pedagogical and editorial work that nurtured a group of emergent writers (i.e., the *July* writers) of his time, gave the poet-critic a chance to develop a subjectivity and poetic form that tantalized the literary space beyond the confines of the CCP's wartime politics. Reflecting on how Hu's "300,000-Character Report"[38] could so dramatically become a piece of evidence against him, Lu Yuan observed that "under an abnormal condition, normal and productive differences and demands for debate could trigger off an explosion of political problems."[39] What Lu Yuan referred to as the "abnormal" situation of the literary and intellectual scene in Maoist China was a classic example of a modern alignment of literary and critical production with the interests of politics. Under these circumstances, whatever writers produced was no longer an individual's reaction to the external or a personal catharsis of the internal but instead took on public consequences and had lasting political implications.

Although Hu learned much about the Yan'an Forum and was no less conscious of China's wartime reality than his counterparts in Yan'an, his credentials paled in comparison with those writers who had gone through the Yan'an intellectual neutralization movement. The "Yan'an writers," in their strategic use of ideological and institutional power, brought about the 1948 Hong Kong campaign against Hu, evidencing the operation of a political apparatus in the domain of literary criticism. No longer shielded by Lu Xun, how did Hu maintain his sense of self as a Marxist critical intellectual? How should one read Hu, who, out of his apprehension about the development of Marxist criticism into a hegemonic discourse, was a rival to be *the* moral conscience of the Chinese Revolution? What were the practical implications of some of his literary concepts that clashed with the CCP's cultural policies and ideological demands? In his response to the Party's campaign against him, Hu represented an archetype of a committed critic whose aversion to power apparatuses, whose passion for life and literature, and whose allegiance to Lu Xun's "combative criticism" retained in him a character trait and a personal style in criticism. As such, he preserved Marxism as a means to an intellectual ideal rather than employing it as a program of intellectual remolding.

Despite numerous organized critical debates between Hu and Party writers over a sustained period, there was a radical difference in nature between the debates before 1949 and those after that year. Hu's literary and political life—from his first public appearance as a Marxist critic in 1932 to his arrest in 1955—straddled the decisive temporal divide of 1949. After 1949, conflicts between Hu and Party writers were no longer "internal conflicts within the people" but struggled between an individual's convictions and state-ideological power. As the CCP ascended to state power, it had planned some of the most significant cultural events, which included a spelled-out cultural policy and a fully developed system that critics could consistently resort to as a guide for cultural practices. These facts were of fundamental importance, especially for Hu, who had traveled with the CCP in the early years of the Chinese Revolution when the Party was much more tolerant of criticism and still in search of the most ideologically useful literary and cultural forms. Wu Xiru (1906–85), Zhou Enlai's political secretary during the 1930s and 1940s, revealed an important fact about the Hu Incident in his memoir: "During the few months when the Central Committee identified Hu as a counterrevolutionary and thus the target of the national attack, it sent the Party secretary of the Hubei Province a clear message: the problem of Hu began after the Liberation."[40] In other words, Hu's tragedy was in part caused by his refusal to acknowledge and to accept the new political conditions and the historical turning point that the PRC's founding had created.

According to Jürgen Habermas, "Anybody who enters the political public sphere and criticizes other people cannot be a crybaby himself."[41] In the end, to describe the critical conflicts between Hu and his counterparts meant passing political judgment on left-wing intellectuals, including Hu. By all accounts, Hu was not an easygoing colleague, for he could be self-absorbed, relentless, and punctilious. Mao called him an "ambitious careerist."[42] In private, he had moments of unconcealed delight at his enemies' failures—like Zhou being derided and rejected. At such moments, he exploited others' difficulties for his political advantage. Despite being constrained by shortcomings in his personality, Hu was not disqualified as an intellectual who lived to write and speak truth to power, for the very revolutionary romanticism that motivated Hu to collaborate with politics was qualitatively different from that which motivated such "radical intellectuals" as Yao Wenyuan (1931–2005). Yao, the CCP's chief literary critic for two decades, between the mid-1950s and mid-1970s, was a key figure in the Hu Incident. His 1965 article titled "On the New Historical Beijing Opera 'Hai Rui Dismissed from Office' " was one of the most important pieces of literary criticism in the PRC's political history: it launched nothing less than the Cultural Revolution.

Hu's destiny was inseparable from the means-end contradiction that Michel Foucault described in his discussion of what he called "specific" intellectuals. In an interview in 1976, Foucault distinguished between specific intellectuals and traditional or, as he called it, "universal" intellectuals: "What must now be taken into account in the intellectual is not the 'bearer of universal values.' Rather, it's the person occupying a specific position—but whose specificity is linked . . . to the general functioning of an apparatus of truth."[43] What was at stake was the contradiction between means and ends. As Marxist literary criticism provided Chinese intellectuals with "an apparatus of truth" through which they directly participated in politics, it was at the same time a form of power that alienated and limited intellectual power vis-à-vis a specifically institutionalized mechanism. Although Foucault discussed the notion of specific intellectuals in the 1970s, with American academics in mind, Hu was an embodiment of that contradiction about which Foucault spoke. Thus, a study of Hu must adequately address a wide range of issues, including Hu's revolutionary idealism, his critical consciousness, his commitment to the moral and aesthetic qualities of literature, and his political ambitions.

Hu's deeply personal and intellectual claims on the political effects of the Chinese Revolution and the Civil War, as well as his criticism, poiesis, and editorial work, presented theoretical challenges to the conception of the "committed critic." They compelled the literary and intellectual scenes to reflect on the two-way shift between ideological commitment and literary subjectivism. Specifically, Hu's concept and practice of the "subjective combative spirit"—the basis of a theoretical advancement in literary enlightenment in a broad sense—emerged as a language with intellectual, creative, and critical power, offering a bridge between modern Chinese literature and criticism and global discussions on the modern critic and the politics of intellectual engagement. To study Hu's poiesis of criticism, then, is not only an academic exercise in historical revision; it is an attempt to provide a node in current scholarly and critical trends to discuss, reconsider, and further politicize Hu's career and literary ideals.

II

FOOLISHNESS AND CONSCIOUSNESS

> All of a sudden I seem to understand / whoever with a pen in hand wants to become a warrior / must, in front of the people and the struggle, / render the self small, smaller, and still smaller / until nothing except passion was left.
>
> —Hu Feng[1]

In the cartography of the Chinese road to Western modernization, the intellectual power of committed intellectuals was either subsumed under the authoritarian CCP or associated with the all-encompassing term *Chinese* or *China* under colonial capitalism. What was unnoticed was the (emotional) exploitation of and violence against the intellect by not only the orthodox discourse of Chinese nationalism and modernization but also by the intellectuals themselves. As reflected in both his public and private statements about commitment, Hu considered the CCP the ideological instrument of Marxism and, as such, historically unique rather than conditioned. In a piece of self-criticism written in 1955, when the Party's control over the country extended to his personal life, Hu wrote: "Had it not been for the revolution and the Communist Party I would not have a sense of security in life for the past twenty or more years. My belief in the Party and the masses had supported me through the most challenging years."[2] Although Mao later ridiculed, preempted, and appropriated this message, rebutting that "what is false is false; the disguise must be peeled off,"[3] what little of

Hu's true feelings that permeated through his experiences, criticism, private correspondences, and biographies presented a full picture of the psychology of a Marxist intellectual whose commitment was not in any way compromised.

Marxism under Mao was singular. State-ideological power achieved the privileged leverage to destabilize all forms of sociopolitical, cultural, and intellectual agencies. In Hu's case, he vindicated his commitment to the CCP with a kind of "blindness" if not "foolishness," underscoring the convergence of ideological devotion and political action in his participation in the Chinese Revolution. Before serving his fourteen-year sentence of imprisonment as a political exile in Sichuan, Hu wrote to Qiao Guanhua in a letter dated February 14, 1966: "A foolish person always has some blind confidence in or fantasy about the idea of the proletarian movement. . . . For me, no matter how difficult and demoralizing the circumstances have become, the question of 'whether there is a point to live on' never crossed my mind."[4] Any intellectual believing in critical conscience would have found the above claim of mysticism indefensible. Indeed, Hu's intellectual agency demonstrated moments of remission, which remains contested but critical to one's understanding of Marxist intellectuals in early modern China. Intellectuals who were committed to the critical humanist principles and questions of national survival inevitably negotiated their marginalization and dissent with state power. Even if Hu was derisive in considering himself "foolish" for better or for worse, he was sincere in his commitment to what he called "the proletarian movement," which he had internalized, taken part in, and advocated for much of his life.

Rooted in Hu's pessimistic but willful remark about his intention to "live on" under the CCP's direction was a sense of self-sacrifice. How was this achieved? In what ways and at what cost had Hu accumulated evidence of his faith? How would later generations consider Hu's "foolishness" as a compatible part of his praxis? Praxis, in its most general sense, refers to action and activity and, in Marxism, to the free, universal, creative, and self-creative activity through which humans create and change the world and themselves. In the *Economic and Philosophical Manuscripts of 1844*, Karl Marx elaborated his view of man as a free creative being of praxis: "free, conscious activity is the species-character of the human being," and "the practical construction of an *objective* world, the work upon inorganic nature, is the confirmation of man as a conscious species-being."[5] Hu's "foolishness" had to do with his refusal to minimize literary subjectivism's historical role in the Chinese Revolution. He knew that to confront and engage Marxist historicism as he experienced it, he had to take in both its determinism and its particularity.

In writing his memoir late in life, Hu accounted for the beginning of this praxis—namely, his years in Japan and the preparatory years that led him to his perusal of modern education. In his account, Hu reiterated the trope "defeated idealist"—another version of his "foolishness"—to demonstrate how political activism had to be brought about by a series of psychological discontinuities rather than ideological imperatives.[6] This experience of being a defeated idealist remained symptomatic of Hu's career as a Marxist critic. His schooling years were among the first that revealed its expression, the characteristics of which would become evident whenever there was a demand to address doctrinal concerns or remain contingent on political calls.

IN SEARCH OF MARXISM

In retrospect, it is clear that the generation of radical intellectuals to which Hu belonged compromised the historical role of the individual writer-critic—his independence of mind, his critical consciousness, and his literary subjectivism. The impact of this compromise throughout much of Mao's authoritarianism in the second half of the twentieth century was manifest. After the 1910s, some left-wing-oriented figures representative of the May Fourth camp began to search for ways through which literature and art might participate in the cause of Chinese modernity and revolution. The search for Chinese New Literature became paramount to the intellectual agenda of such figures as Chen Duxiu, Cheng Fangwu, Qu Qiubai, and Guo Moruo.[7] Following Chen Duxiu's 1917 essay "On Literary Revolution 文学革命论," which set the tone of the debate on literature's propagandist potential for sociopolitical use,[8] the periodical *Creation Monthly* 创造月刊 published several essays representative of this theme a decade later.[9] During that era, the theme of national salvation and progress determined the subject of modern Chinese literature, and writers and artists prioritized their role in this general historical process over their artistic experiments and adventures. Thus, any aesthetics other than identification with national causes were a digression, and anything other than Chinese modernization was a literary indulgence. Whatever the nuances found in the different formulations of politicized literature, the literary intellectuals' thematic foci remained remarkably constant.

Within the revolutionary camp, Marxist criticism as a theory groomed a generation of writers in the way Marxist literary works, as direct evidence of one's sociopolitical orientations, stamped the writer concerned as an active player of radical politics. The writer was as powerful as the soldier and, to repeat Mao's two-army theory, was part of one of the two armies in the Chinese Revolution. Indeed, by the time Hu came of age and set off for such cities as Wuchang in 1921, and then Shanghai in 1923 to partake in Western learning, he was in pursuit of Marxist criticism, at that time the prime requisite of New Literature and characteristically the locus of modern Chinese intellectual radicalism. Bonnie McDougall's critical survey of the influence of Western literary trends on modern Chinese literature observed that "by 1934 or 1935, it was considered eccentric in literary circles not to be . . . left-wing, and between 1935 and 1939, the Communist Party had an almost irresistible fascination for any writer under forty."[10]

Much as left-wing literary criticism defined the intellectual atmosphere of the time and applied to all, including Hu, one most crucial demarcating qualification influenced Hu: a reverence for the uniqueness of an individual's experience of Marxism. This qualification shall make the problem of praxis recurrent in Hu's political career. For Hu, who was well versed in May Fourth critical discourse, literature had always already emanated from a political, historical, and national conscience. Still, until he participated in the nationalistic and revolutionary movements of the 1920s, his writings were hardly polemical. Reading May Fourth criticism made Hu conscious of the need to combine literature with revolution without telling him how.[11] Still very much a youthful idealist, Hu felt defeated by the political reality of the late 1920s and was confused about his role as a writer in the Chinese Revolution. The question Hu attempted to understand was *how* relevant New Literature was to *him* in inspiring him to participate in the Revolution in a way that would not alienate the self:

> I wanted to write a novel
> about a youth in search of a way . . .
> He was determined
> to use his voice to revitalize old China.
> After a few trials, however
> he felt defeated.
> In the end, he could but lie on the railroad in the evening
> Looking at the approaching train
>   and the robust worker with a flag in hand . . .
> he was lost in the sight of the worker-brother and the little red flag
>   that seemed to sail against the wind
> Suddenly

'Weng!' a thunderous sound
  the iron wheels that went running on his body
    ran past . . .
. . .
I was hopeless
  I threw away that pen
I realized
 love was dreamy
 passion was no fuel
Do I have the power
  to offer the "flag" in my heart?
How could I use the dead body of the youth
. . .
 to destroy the numbed iron wall of ancient China?[12]

With a sense of self-criticism, self-reflection, and self-understanding, Hu set a challenge for the poet: subordinate the self's "love" and "passion" to the cause of radical politics. In the process of stressing the instinctive discontent that Hu felt about the "old China," he found it necessary to "revitalize" and often gravitated to radical acts. For example, in 1923, with revolutionaries like Yang Tianzhen and Yuan Xiyan, Hu declared that "there was still warmth in the world" and that "a certain passion existed in pursuit of truth in the world."[13] This allegiance to radical social causes prepared him for the adoption of Marxism as his literary framework. A year later, he published the story "Two Members on a Labor-Union Sub-committee" in the Shanghai newspaper *National Daily: Awakenings* to commemorate those who were killed by warlords for taking part in the Great Jinghan Railway Strike.

Historical accounts and personal memoirs portraying the youthful Hu as a rebel abound, with some highlighting his emotive streak. Wu Qiru, who once served as political secretary to Zhou Enlai, remembered Hu as a passionate interlocutor with a broad regional (Zhanchun) accent. He recalled how "streams of sweat [came] trickling down Hu's forehead as his nose twitched and as his freckled face looked increasingly intense."[14] Qian Yanbin, Hu's secondary school classmate, remembered his "exceptional character": "He was very studious, fond of learning, knowledgeable, and pugnacious. Always dressed in a peasant-like long-robe made of some coarse-fabric . . . he was truly distinctive when he spoke."[15] Although an apparent crowd-puller, Hu was not one of those fanatics who dreamt, in Lu Xun's words, "romantic dreams about the revolution."[16] In his early revolutionary years, Hu had served as both a stimulus and a model; many of his passionate moments had an effect on the world surrounding him. For example, Ba Jin, albeit somewhat dramatic in his account, provided further evidence of the social significance of Hu's emotional devotion to social activism and revolutionary practice.

Ba Jin's *The Dead Sun* 死去的太阳 (1930) probably sourced inspiration from both Hu the person (the character Fang Guoliang in *The Dead Sun* alluded to Hu's given name Guangren 光人, which meant literally "bright man") and his writings, specifically the one with the same title. Hu's "The Dead Sun," composed in 1925, was an elegy commemorating the death of Sun Yat-sen, the first provisional president of the Republic of China (1912–49). In it, Hu compared the two "Suns" on account of their both being a source of energy and a symbol of hope.[17] Fifty years after Ba Jin published his novel, he remembered Hu as a young activist at school: "Even now, I could still picture him standing there on a stage and giving a speech in great excitement."[18] The occasion Ba Jin was referring to was the 5/30 Incident, in which the British police fatally shot students and workers in Shanghai. That day, Hu stood on a stage to rally and enlist mass support against imperial violence. From above, he shouted and cried; he stamped his feet and spoke at the top of his lungs. Hu was the spirit of a drama, the soul of a moving scene, and a stimulating force for action. "I have not told him," wrote Ba Jin, "that on that day, I joined up with the other audiences to take the little train down to Heji Egg Factory."[19]

Hu's radical expression and idealism were always in good supply, but these sentiments were rarities against the realities of twentieth-century China. Indeed, Hu operated in a revolutionary register that was a willfully humanistic one. His sentiments functioned as a perennial catalyst to the cause that he sought to further within the parameters of what he had come to accept as true. For instance, in late 1965, despite having served a ten-year sentence in jail and facing the prospect of an additional four years of house arrest,[20] Hu confided to Mei Zhi that he was a truly "stubborn" humanist: "They thought the testimony had defeated me, knocked me out. They dictated my food intake, thinking that I, frightened and heartbroken, would have no appetite. I stuck to my meal habit, washing down two full bowls of rice with the soup, regardless of their taste."[21] Hu wanted to show them that he was "solely infuriated and saddened," that "the trial had not defeated [him]," that "they had underestimated humanity."[22] He asked, "Could they have destroyed the human mind and spirit with just this trail?"[23] Hu's humanist convictions underscored the extent to which, no matter what had happened, the strength of the human mind and spirit, acting as the basis of social reconstruction and regeneration, still held for him a position of mastery. Under house arrest and knowing well the impact of his case on his children, Hu asked Xiao Feng, his daughter, to recite an excerpt from Arishima Takeo's (1878–1923) "To the Little Ones":[24]

> I have loved you and will do so forever. It is not because I want any rewards for having fathered you. I seek only one thing, from you whom I have taught to love: accept my gratitude. By the time you attain adulthood, I might have died, or still be working hard, or have aged to a bare nothingness. No matter what happens . . . the older generations must not bog down youth. At best, you should be like those lion cubs who, having consumed and exhausted their mother, leave the pride for life.[25]

To the aged and aging father, the future remained hopeful because the "little ones" could still "leave the pride for life," carrying with them the expectations of those who had nurtured and loved them. Hu succeeded in shifting his attention from his plight to the juncture at which the burdens of the past and hopes for the future converged. This was the difference between being a humanist and being a nihilist. Although Hu battled against Chinese traditionalism, the sentiment appropriate for rebellion had a particular desire for healing and construction. What motivated Hu's revolutionary temperament was not the nihilistic temptation of radical action but a desire to question the sense of social privilege taken for granted by those in power, by those who were often indifferent to the depth of humanity found in the weak, the uneducated, and the poor. A humanist, different from a cynic, raised questions about the condition of human living with an optimism characteristic of an idealist nation- and society-builder.

For Hu, the Chinese Revolution provided the synergy for the May Fourth enlightenment ideals to overturn traditional Chinese society and culture's barbarism and anachronism. His practice of May Fourth spirit and appeal for radical critical theories necessitated his blending of dissonant passions with a constructive synthesis. Unlike such apolitical writers as Lin Yutang and Zhang Tianyi, whom Hu criticized,[26] Hu searched in Marxism for a channel to transform his creative impulse and social discontent into a "raised consciousness." In the context of the Chinese Revolution, "raising consciousness" referred to revolutionary writers' and artists' attempts to portray the process in which an individual experiences a moral transformation, from selfish ignorance to commitment to a formal revolutionary agenda.[27]

Struggling to wake from a "dreamy love," from the listlessness of a consuming "passion,"[28] Hu was anxious to embed himself in the political activism of the everyday and came to realize that literature was an indispensable agent and apparatus of social and individual liberation.

ON FOREIGN SOIL

Hu left China in September 1929. Like many of his peers who studied abroad, he went to Japan in search of solutions to "the problems of China," that is, to "keep step with the spirit of the times" and to reconcile "the contradictory relations between literature and revolution."[29] As Cheng Ching-mao observed, few students "went to Japan with literary studies in mind. . . . Japan's remarkable success in modernization, of which literature was an inseparable part, impressed them. They were eager to follow the successful Japanese experience."[30] Upon arrival in Japan, Hu settled first at the East Asia Language School, Kanda, and subsequently Keio Gijuku (Keio University) in the spring of 1931. Keio Gijuku hosted three Nobel laureate lectures: Rabindranath Tagore (1861–1941) in 1916, Bertrand Russell (1872–1970) in July 1921, and Albert Einstein (1879–1955) in November 1921. Among them, the lecture tour by Russell presented a complex picture of the sociopolitical circumstances of 1920s Japan in general and that of the intellectual atmosphere at Keio Gijuku specifically. For much of his twelve-day trip, Russell stayed with Yamamoto Sanehiko, the editor of *Kaizo* (*Reconstruction*); he also met with the socialist Osugi Sakae (1885–1923) and his common-law wife, Ito Noe (1895–1923). Russell found his stay "very interesting" but "far from pleasant."[31] The English-language newspaper *Japan Chronicle Weekly* reported the event as follows:

> The conversazione arranged by the *Kaizo* office in Tokyo, which . . . caused much alarm and concern to the police authorities on account of invitations being extended to some well-known Socialists, took place at the Imperial Hotel on Tuesday from 11 a.m. Messrs. Osugi, Sakai [Toshihiko] and Ishikawa [Sanshiro] the well-known Socialists, whose invitation to the gathering was the cause of perturbations in officialdom, attended without any positive molestation from the police. *The Jiji*, which is generally trustworthy, says that about a dozen detectives were specially detailed in the neighborhood of the hotel. Among others who

were present were Drs. Anezaki [Shoji, 1873–1949] and Kuwaki [Genyoku, 1874–1946, philosopher], professors at the Tokyo Imperial University, Dr. Kitazawa [Shinjiro], of the Waseda University, Professor Abe [Jiro? 1883–1959, philosopher, critic, and educator], of the Keio University, Dr. Fukuda [Tokuzo, 1874–1930, economist], of the Commercial College, Mr. Suzuzki [*sic*; Bunji], the president of the Yuai-kai, and Messrs. Chiba, Sugimura and Baba [Tsunego], journalists.[32]

On the evening of July 28, 1921, Russell gave a lecture in front of "some 3,600 people . . . mostly intellectuals," as observed by Kitazawa Shinjiro; "the hall . . . was already crowded by 4:00 in the afternoon," and it became "so full that there was no standing room" during the "wonderful" lecture.[33] The Japan scholar William Snell offered a perceptive account of the event, shedding some light on Keio Gijuku as the breeding ground for anarchists, socialists, and Marxists in early twentieth-century Japan:

The greatest mystery, however, concerns the lack of official records or documentation at Keio Gijuku regarding the event, unlike that of Albert Einstein (again at the invitation of Kaizo and on the recommendation of Russell)[,] which is recorded in the published history of the institution. I would hazard a guess that the lecture was not given with the official sanction of Keio, although it may . . . have been arranged by Fukuda Tokuzo, who was a part-time lecturer there.[34]

At Kaizo Gijuku, where politics and culture intersected, Hu published under the pseudonyms Mamoru Nakamura and Gu Fei essays to introduce the Chinese Left-league's activities to cultural circles in Japan.[35] He joined the Association for Art Studies at the Proletarian Science Center (a unit under the Japan Proletarian Culture Federation established by Koreto Kurahara in 1931)[36] and participated in its weekly group reading meetings. Predominant in Hu's reading were periodicals about proletarian cultural movements. Despite his limited Japanese, Hu felt "deeply attracted to the letters written by Japanese writers and peasants."[37] As he found them "full of concrete feelings about everyday life and class struggle," they "absorbed" him.[38] In these semiliterary and semipolitical activities, Hu befriended Kiyoshi Eguchi,[39] a member of the Japanese Proletarian Authors' League (hereafter Authors' League),[40] through whom he also made acquaintances with leaders of the Japanese Proletarian Movement, including the novelist and dramatist Ujaku Akita (1883–1962) and the proletariat writer and Japanese Communist Party member Takiji Kobayashi.[41]

Hu's close connection with Japanese Marxists and Communists played a vital part in his intellectual and personal development. For instance, he saw "the vitality of the Proletarian Cultural Movement," especially in the figure of Ujaku Akita, who, "despite many difficulties," not only "stood firmly in the camp of the Japanese proletariat masses" but also displayed an "*unfailing optimism*" about "the eventual triumph of the proletariat."[42] From this fifty-year-old man, Hu learned how to be "angry" without "indulging in unproductive sentimentalism."[43] Impressed by the Japanese left-wing writers' sense of engagement in actual work,[44] Hu began to understand *how* literature and criticism were inseparable from society, and *how* the practice of Marxist literary criticism could create a strategic base on which writers of similar intellectual temperament, literary tastes, and radical leanings might get together and search for ways to improve reality and the world.

Hu's friendship with Japanese left-wing writers and critics and his participation in their activities constituted a substantial first step in the development of his approach to Marxist theory. As Mei Zhi recalled, based on "the life of the working class as recorded in those letters that the proletariat literary magazines published," Hu began to feel his "compassions thaw out" and "to acquire a clear vision."[45] Increasingly after that, "proletarianism became formative and directional in his critical consciousness."[46] In reaching this realization of an ideologically clear vision, Hu acceded to Marxism as his point of departure and brought critical and creative impulses inside the scope of Marxist historical materialism. A Marxist literary critic was political only in the sense that she was politically committed. "The present is different from the days when you were young," Hu said to Guo Moruo during their first meeting in Japan in 1931,[47] because "we have recognized the class character of literature. It is perhaps difficult for literary associations like the Creation Society that [is] devoted, singularly and entirely, to literature to emerge anymore."[48] At around the same time, in a letter to Zhu Qixia, Hu spoke once again of his "great leap forward" in understanding literature's "essential" relationship to realpolitik and the possibility of imagination reconciling and maintaining a relationship with praxis:

> What progress have I made over the last year in the conceptualization [of literature and art]? . . . In short, all my previous theories on literature and art have completely lost color. Although

> I have not yet had a [critical] foundation and my class origin have been confining me, through searching in the dark, my path [to the revolution] seems to become more evident day by day.[49]

This letter, in general, was a compendium of Hu's past experiences—his rejection of pure aestheticism, his notion of the revolutionary writer incapacitated by the hustle of day-to-day political activism, and, above all, his sense of being a politically ineffective writer consumed by "passions." Revealed thus in the letter was an important moment in the process of Hu's self-transformation from a student of literature to a literary intellectual, taking upon himself the task of writing as both a public act and a cause for consciously affirming certain social ideals. Like many paragraphs in Hu's letters and essays written during his earlier "enlightened" years, the quoted paragraph above articulated a somewhat undigested Marxist view of literature. Yet, notwithstanding its didacticism and determination, the passage documented Hu's cautiousness in his attempt to position himself within the institute of Marxism and to meet the standards expected by the Marxist view of history and social determinism. This cautiousness was also present in an essay written during his Japan years, in which Hu pointed out that politics and literature, though inseparable, were not indistinguishable.[50]

For Hu, revolutionary literature and revolutionary politics were parallel but distinct paths leading to the same historical telos, and there was thus the possibility of aligning literature with politics without conflating the sociohistorical roles of each. Such a possibility was at least a belief held by Marx when he talked about the "brotherhood of fiction-writers" in Victorian England—Charles Dickens, William Makepeace Thackeray, Charlotte Brontë, and Elizabeth Gaskell.[51] In other words, revolutionary literature had opportunities, when it returned to its roots in ethics, to develop itself as a lived politics that could think through problems posed by the bourgeois sentimentalism across and within national literatures, and within the realities of what was increasingly a nationwide plague of wartime lethargy. Marxist views on literature and art appealed to Hu because they were *morally* sound in the specific condition of semifeudal and semicolonial China and because in calling writers to arms they enabled an oppositional discourse. Conscientious of his national and social roles and knowing that individual intellectuals of his time must not "[fail] to be a man of action,"[52] Hu chose to be a revolutionary over and against, for example, the "third-category man" or the "free man." He thus understood the close affinity between literature and politics in 1930s China in terms of their shared task as a repository of social truth.

As Albert Camus pointed out in "L'Homme révolté," possibly one of the most influential essays of the twentieth century, "the revolutionary acts in the name of a value, still inarticulate, but through which he at least senses that he is united with all the people. . . . Every revolutionary act . . . pulls him out of his supposed solitude and gives him a reason to act."[53]

AN APPRENTICE IN "A REPUBLIC OF CRITICISM"

On foreign soil, Hu rediscovered the task of the critic. Before going to Japan, he considered criticism a predator of creative works, dismissing it as "a dishonorable business" that did nothing except find fault with "the products of a writer's heart and mind."[54] Grateful to his Marxist comrades in Japan who "enlightened and taught him about literary theory,"[55] Hu began to see criticism as no longer a game of textual interpretation restoring the goal of criticism—a purposive unity of humanism in practical and imaginative terms. Whereas Hu's experience of classical Chinese criticism (mostly single-author studies) furthered his defiance against dull conformity, his weekly participation in proletariat literature reading groups brought about his assimilation into the rhythms and enchantments of literary criticism. Accordingly, Hu asserted:

> If the purpose of literary creation is to reform life, to discover love and hate in real life, and if one can create from actual life a literary world that can shed light on the future of humanity, then literary criticism positively transforms life. In its task of exploring both the imaginative world and the real world, literary criticism comprehends concrete creative works, helps understand the writers, and identifies the significance of a literary phenomenon by grounding [its subject of study] on lived experiences.[56]

In this account, Hu discussed literature and criticism with similar concerns. By overlapping the space of critical imagination (to improve, discover, and transform life) with that of the creative act (to shed light on the future of humanity), Hu recognized a singularity in criticism's humanistic goals; it thus does not have a "predatory" character, only a reformative and communicative one. Still early in his study of Marxism, however, Hu remained vague about criticism's humanistic goals, falling short of words in his attempt to make clear what R. P. Blackmur, two decades later, did successfully.

Criticism, as defined by Blackmur, is like poetry, in the way it "names and arranges what it knows and loves, and searches endlessly with every fresh impulse or impression for better names and more orderly arrangements."[57] To "name" and "arrange" is to, in Hu's terms, build a "literary world" in which the writer imagines the changes necessary for the creation of a new future having "better names" and "more orderly arrangements." Meanwhile, literary criticism cannot translate directly what the changes are; it can only "identify," "comprehend," and "help understand" them.

Significantly, in Hu's experience of practicing Marxist literary criticism in Japan, the content and form, the substance and manner of debate, were analogous. In this same letter to Zhu dated October 4, 1932, Hu talked about how he wanted to overcome all difficulties and staunchly "combine the personal with the collective."[58] As proletarian critical discourse engaged Hu in radical politics' call to action, the weekly meetings led him into a collectivity, a growing web of personal relationships that became the foundation of what I would call a "republic of criticism." In Hu's experience, the intellectual attraction and emotional appeal of Japanese Marxism lay in the everyday practices—both personal and institutional, individual and collective—that it demanded of its participants. One hot day in the summer of 1932, Hu went to visit Eguchi Kan and chanced upon a meeting of some members of the Japanese Proletarian Cultural Movement. Though the meeting was more of a chat without a fixed agenda, it instructed Hu's search for his place in the revolution as it demonstrated the fruition of open debate, discussion, and knowledge achieved through apperception. In a nostalgic and reverential tone typically found in descriptions of the romanticism of youthful idealism,[59] Hu recollected details of the meeting and singled out the incidents that encouraged him to find the value of criticism in debates and disagreements:

> In the middle of the room, there was an extended balcony table, crowded around which were participants sitting on broken chairs and beer-boxes. Some were passionate, and others were calm, but they all looked genuine and sincere. In a moderate voice, they kept on the discussions and the debates, insisting that the beliefs they advocate would roar in the Japanese literary circle and beyond. In that room stuffed full of cigarette smoke, I began to understand why my idealism was demoralizing. I came to terms with the contradiction between society and art, a problem I had been struggling to solve for the past seven or eight years.[60]

Notably, Hu's description focused on the meeting's formal ambiance. Against time and eroding memory, in addressing what remained vivid, Hu might have revealed a set of conditions or premises that would come to define his ideological and collective conscience: heterogeneity, equality, fraternity, and freedom of expression. The "genuine and sincere" participants rekindled his hope in the future and led him to use criticism as an instrument of the proletarian revolution. The idea of a revolution cultivated by collective life lingered in Hu, who had so far been a solitary voyager:

> At that time I, a deserter,
> defeated even before I got to fight,
> held on to a frail thread of hope for resurrection.
> I crossed the ocean, and
> arrived at your land [Japan].
> I toiled under
> the pain of the country's historical feudalism.
> I was bored with
> the desolate history of ancient [China].
> I felt the passionate spirit of your struggle.
> I was engaged.
> I pursued what was ahead.
> I was completely lost,
> until finally, I discovered Marxism.
> It's sweet like the vast sea.
> I drank a drop of it
> (even if it was merely a drop).
> I felt a swarm of warmth,
> like an affectionate fire,
> circulating in the blood of my whole body.[61]

To be part of a support group was a new experience for Hu, who had thus far been unsuccessful in rallying public support. Notwithstanding the Sino-Japanese War, the legacy of the friendship with the Japanese people, founded on a short but concrete experience of mutual respect, bequeathed Hu a general sense of the strategies applicable to approaching the Chinese Revolution. Many years later, Hu still remembered the affective ties that existed among Ujaku Akita, Takiji Kobayashi, and Nagata Hiroshi, who together created a community of critics in which Hu felt that he had "within a short period . . . lived a whole life":

I have learned
what the rule of the ruling-class means,
what the struggle of the struggling-class means;
I have learned
the qualities of a man as a man!
how some men become a dog!
how some men are God transformed! . . .
I have learned
what partisanship
 means,
what internationalism means![62]

This Marxist partisanship was the key to Hu's success in finding an active mode of action. Hu joined Nihon Kyosanto (the Japanese Communist Party, hereafter JCP) in October 1931.[63] After the 9/18 Incident in 1931, together with Fang Han and Wang Chengzhi, Hu formed the Anti-imperialist League, a Chinese group that read *Sekki* (*Red Flag*).[64] This literary group, later accepted as a Japanese Communist unit, served as a conduit through which Hu became a Communist Party member.[65]

As later chapters will further explore, Hu's literary and political experience in Japan served as a model and a bridge for his future literary developments in several senses. First, it was a blueprint for an integrated community of writers in which participants otherwise divided by boundaries of rank and place could collaborate. The Marxists and Communists, with whom Hu became acquainted in Japan, provided an example of what an organized collectivity could achieve. Hu was excited about the possibility of joining a similar community of left-wing literature and criticism upon his return to the Republic. A young man in his thirties, Hu found a sense of self and achievement in his institutional relationship with such revolutionaries as Zhou Yang and Feng Xuefeng (1902–74). Until he began his executive work for the Left-league in 1933, his acquaintance with revolutionary writers, whether Japanese or Chinese, was informal.[66] Perhaps beyond a certain degree of political consciousness, Hu was better acquainted with individual revolutionary writers than with revolutionary literature as a formative category.

Second, the fact that Hu obtained his Communist Party membership in Japan—an imperialist, class-segregated, "Westernized" nation in which Marxist socialism was in existence in a trajectory different from the way it had developed in China—said something significant about Japanese Marxism's intellectual appeal to Hu. In the late 1860s, attempting to explain the "pre-capitalist" economic properties shared by agrarian Russia, India, and China, Marx and Engels made a clear distinction: "The revolution sought by modern Socialism is, briefly, the victory of the proletariat over the bourgeoisie and the reorganization of society by the abolition of all class distinctions. To accomplish this, we need not only the proletariat . . . but also a bourgeoisie in whose hands the productive forces of society have developed to such a stage that they permit the final elimination of all class distinctions."[67] The founders of modern socialism might not have been right about their conclusion, but the distinction they made between societies with well-developed "productive forces" and those with precapitalist Asian economies pointed to the differences between Japan and China in terms of their developmental stages of Marxism.

Third, Hu joined the circles of left-wing intellectuals and revolutionaries in both Japan and the new Republic in his identified role as a Chinese Marxist critic. Kiyoshi Eguchi highlighted Hu's national and professional identity and how not in spite of but because of his Chineseness and critical knowledge that Hu found a relationship with the Authors' League. In Eguchi's words, "Zhang Guangren [Hu's birth name] was the *only* Chinese writer [in the Authors' League]. *Put accurately, Zhang was a theorist more than a writer.* His Japanese was excellent. Since he had also joined the Japanese branch of the Chinese League of Left-wing Writers . . . he acted discretely and tactfully as a bridge between the Authors' League and the Left-league."[68]

Last but not the least, Hu's participation in the Authors' League and literary work for Japanese Marxists brought him fame. In September 1930, one year after Hu started his studies in Japan, with the help of Aoiko, the wife of Takatsu Masamichi, the Bolshevik, he translated into Chinese the Japanese version of the Soviet novel *The American in Petrograd*. When the book appeared in Shanghai under the title *Yanggui* 洋鬼 and the penname Gu Fei, together with his preface and afterword of the translation, Hu became a known name in Chinese left-wing literary circles. Jia Zhifang recalled that he had long known the name Gu Fei because he "spent one silver dollar on *Yanggui* . . . in the Kunming Bookshop . . . in Peking in 1932."[69] Lou Shiyi also acknowledged the name Gu Fei in 1931 when he began working for the Left-league: "At that time, I read a [Chinese] translation of a popular Soviet novel entitled *Yanggui* and knew [Hu] to be the translator. It was very refreshing and interesting."[70] As *Yanggui* introduced Hu to the community of Chinese Marxist revolutionaries, it marked the beginning of Hu's productive relationship with CCP-member writers and leaders in the new Republic. After all, the translation project was first suggested and commissioned by Xiong Zimin.[71] In commissioning Hu to translate *The American in Petrograd*, Xiong not only introduced Soviet Communism to the Chinese reading public but also, on the sidelines, helped to reduce Hu's financial pressure.[72]

In many respects, the roots of Hu's affiliation with the Communist Party, his ideological commitment, and his revolutionary passion lay in his *literary* relationship with and *humanist* interpretation of Marxism as an international movement against human exploitation. A court sentence against a member of the Anti-imperialist League, an organization listed by the Japanese government as "Communist-dominated" and of which Hu was a member, showed how internationalism constituted the dominant force of Japanese left-wing radicals at the time: "The defendant is fully cognizant of the fact that the Left-league supports the Communist Party of Japan and aims principally at spreading among the Japanese people the seditious slogans, 'Down with Imperialist War!' 'Down with Intervention in China' and 'Protect the Soviet Union!'—slogans which also are being advocated by the said Party."[73] These slogans against imperial capitalism found their way into Hu's antiwar poem "The Sacrificial Rites of the Enemy," written in the aftermath of the 9/18 Incident.[74] The poem traces the "invisible hand" of Japanese nationalism—the mass support of military expansion and aggression against China—to its imperialism. To Japanese soldiers, Hu wrote:

> You will eventually come to understand:
> the power of these forces:
> airplanes, cannons, automatic machine guns, poisonous gas . . .
> belong to you not.
> These weapons are only temporarily placed in your hands,
> for you to massacre those brothers on the other side of the shore,
> to help them colonize new land, establish a new reign.
> They have succeeded—
> Those hands that should extend to secure friendship and brotherly love
> are now stained with the blood of those brothers on the other shore whose fate
> you share!
> This sin makes the commander shout:
> —Do not attack these Chinese brothers!
> Such a shout shall ring across your camps,
> shall wake you from your frenzied blood pool,
> crying out:
> —Do not attack these Chinese brothers!
> —Turn your gun back; the enemy is in your camp![75]

The poem, though skirted by slogans, manifested not only an anti-imperialist agenda but also humanist values. In the end, the poetic "I" called upon "*all* slaves in the world" to "rise" and to "struggle free from the chain around your head," to "struggle for a free and equal 'motherland' . . . whose name is 'the land.' "[76] A comparison of this poem with "To the Dead," an earlier antiwar poem Hu composed before he went to Japan, shows how Hu's involvement with the JCP helped shape his understanding of the Marxist notion of universalist humanity. That poem was a response to the 3/16 Incident in 1926, in which thousands of demonstrators demanded that the government resist Japanese aggression and put an end to the imperialist occupation.[77] Hu wrote "To the Dead" to commemorate the casualties of the demonstration: "Like fire, you lived! / Like fire, you died!" For the poet, the blood of the dead staining "the claws and teeth of the murderers" gave "loved ones cold nights" and "kind mothers a gloomy old age," but it also "moved" and aroused national resistance against imperialism. In the last stanza, not without irony, Hu appealed to populist nationalism by turning patriotism into militarism:

> We are moved,
> come, come,
> our brothers!
> We are infuriated,
> come, come,
> our enemies![78]

In aesthetic and political terms, "The Sacrificial Rites of the Enemy" is more lucid, subtle, and intellectually reflective than "To the Dead." Whereas the latter is a patchwork of broken poetic lines and images of excessive emotionalism, "The Sacrificial Rites of the Enemy" attempted to achieve some intellectual depth and reflexive subtlety in addressing the same set of problems. In the former, Hu spoke through the voice of the "infuriated" young rebel of 1926 who, *infected* by social indignation, rushed to justify militarism in a remarkably immature language.[79] He seemed to have the theoretical recourse to reflect, though only singularly within a Marxist framework, upon the nature of events and modern warfare. "Without the overt expression of anger and sentimentalism," Hu in this poem "resorted to the pathos of critical theory, which is much more powerful than imagery," wrote Kondo Tatsuya in an essay on Hu.[80] With specific reference to Hu's "The Sacrificial Rites of the Enemy," Tatsuya continued: "Written from the stance of the proletariat, the poem called strongly upon the forces of anti-imperialism and internationalism, and did not appeal to [reactive] nationalism that was the political weapon of most [Chinese] students."[81]

Considering the historical context of Japanese imperialism in the early 1930s, it was not difficult to imagine how a Chinese student concerned with the fate of China found solace in the margins of Japanese political culture, particularly in the internationalism and humanism of the Japanese left.[82] As Rodger Swearingen and Paul Langer explained in their study,

> Brotherly ties have marked the relation between the Communist movements of China and Japan since the day when the Chinese Communist Chang T'ai-lei visited Tokyo in 1921 to bring about the crystallization of the left-wing movement. The traditional Sino-Japanese antagonism has never been allowed to affect cooperation between the two parties [the CCP and the JCP]. Throughout the years, Japanese and Chinese Communists have worked together in Russia, China, and Japan.[83]

The collaboration, built on a shared ideology between two peoples at war, was best recapitulated in an official statement that first appeared in the *People's Daily*, Peking, on January 17, 1950, and reprinted by the JCP for its members. The article, titled "The Road toward the Liberation of the Japanese People," captured the content of "brotherly ties":

> Japanese and Chinese . . . are friends. The peoples of Japan and China have common enemies, that is, Japanese imperialism. . . . The people of the two countries have common friends. They are the Soviet Union and the people's democracies as well as the proletariat and oppressed peoples of the whole world who are carrying on the fight against imperialism. The Chinese people are greatly concerned with the liberation of the Japanese people.[84]

Despite the CCP's ideological ambition behind this statement—its intense interest in the development of Communism in postwar Japan—the report acknowledged the existence of a shared belief in a humanistic cause among Communists of different nationalities. For Hu, even as the Japanese people were citizens of the Great Japanese Empire, they were, like the Chinese, also victims of class oppression. They "could not but lead a life harder and [more] bitter than necessary" due to "the Japanese imperialistic desire to conquer the whole of China."[85] Ultimately, it was Marxism's moral commitment to social justice and its vision of social equality that informed and gave meaning to Hu's lifelong faith. Such faith, translated into practice, was expressed in the attempt to fuse his understanding of himself with a national and social consciousness, to construe a dialectical relationship between literature and politics, and to take on the task of stimulating, affecting, and implementing social changes.

CROSSING BORDERS

By associating with the Japanese Marxists, Hu moved closer to the orbit of revolutionary writers in China. Intellectually, as he became theoretically informed, he found a path on which to collaborate with comrades who shared a similar vision of a new China. Institutionally, Hu's JCP membership bound him up in the power structure of the CCP.[86] While in Japan, he kept in touch with the community of left-wing writers in China. Therefore, when the Japanese police deported him to Shanghai in 1933, Hu quickly emerged as a critical player in the organizational structure of the Chinese Left-league. Even before his "heroic" return from Japan on June 15, 1933, Hu had already been recommended by Feng Xuefeng for a place in the Left-league's literary division, and then for the position of officer-in-charge in the Left-league's Propaganda Department.[87] This was one reason for his trip to Shanghai at the end of 1932.[88] The short visit turned out, for Hu at least, to be a marker of Hu's lifelong intrigue with CCP members and writers. He remembered this turn of fate in his life with emotional tenderness:

> Feng and I started to correspond during my time in Tokyo. Our first meeting was like the reunion of old friends after [a] long separation. [Feng] talked warmly, rid of any bureaucratic formalities. He won my trust. . . . Yi Qun, whom I once met in Tokyo, introduced me to one of those regular meetings of the Left-league and to Ding Ling, (then secretary of the Left-league), who seemed like a long-time friend. . . . The meeting with Zhou Qiying (Zhou Yang) was also like one with someone familiar.[89]

Yet out of practical consideration of the complex personal relationships within the Left-league,[90] Hu turned down both offers: "Given the conflicts and arguments among the Left-league members, I considered myself inadequate, whether in qualification, experience, or ability, for a job in the leadership rank."[91] That Hu twice rejected Feng's invitation revealed his status in left-wing literary circles. In general, he was a welcomed addition to different left-wing literary groups based on his association with left-wing writers in Japan and his JCP membership.

The ideal situation of friendship and collegiality between Hu and members of the Left-league continued throughout the first half of the 1930s. Even Mu Mutian (1900–1971), another Left-league writer who would later spread rumors about Hu's "connection" with the Nanjing Government in 1934, was at that time also "surprisingly friendly."[92] In stressing his feelings for a productive relationship with Chinese left-wing literary figures, Hu brimmed with unconcealed delight in finding a sense of belonging among radical Chinese writers. In August 1933, within just a matter of days after Hu's return from Japan, Zhou Yang visited him twice and appointed him officer-in-charge in the Propaganda Department of the Left-league. At the time, Zhou was a leading Marxist literary critic and the CCP's representative in the Left-league. Soon after, Zhou became the veteran general of left-wing literature and art. He occupied the role of cultural commissar and policy designer for many years, which included being the leader of literature and art during the liberation era in the 1940s, the director of the cultural campaigns in the 1950s, the spokesman for Mao Zedong Thought in the 1960s, and the pioneer of thought liberation in the late 1970s and early 1980s.

Studies on Zhou's literary criticism have afforded significant insights into the formation and development of Marxist literary theory as a hegemonic discourse and, specifically, the ideological force behind the marginalization and liquidation of Hu's literary theory. In the Left-league camp of the 1930s, when Hu was officer-in-charge in the Propaganda Department, Zhou was the secretary of the Party committee.[93] Their meetings were mostly held at Hu's apartment and sometimes at Zhou's.[94] Against the background of the general purge of Communists in 1930s Shanghai, the residential addresses of Left-league members, especially those of Party members, were confidential. Hu's access to Zhou's residential address indicated his position as a trusted colleague and a valued member of the Left-league.

Hu's popularity in left-wing literary circles offered an additional example of what was happening in the history of the Chinese radical cultural movements of the 1930s, which was an autonomous window of time characterized by revolutionary enthusiasm, populist nationalism, and, above all, government ineffectiveness.[95] In this temporary space where cultural and intellectual circles came together to form critical communities *in the making*, the CCP's ideological control was not as complete as it would be after 1949. The Left-league, for example, served as an early formation of the CCP's cultural state apparatus, but it did not have a well-defined structure of power or a stable political hierarchy among its revolutionary writers and intellectuals. Specifically, as insiders of what is now called left-wing film criticism recalled some sixty years after the Republican period, Marxist film criticism by the newly established underground Communist film team headed by Xia Yan was a political narrative and imagination constructed only retrospectively.[96] In effect, the CCP could not provide the Shanghai municipal committee of the Communist Party its overarching support, either financially or institutionally.

In the wake of the Japanese invasion of Shanghai in January 1932, and in the absence of what Mikhail M. Bakhtin called an "authoritative" and "monologic" discourse that demanded "unconditional allegiance,"[97] writers and critics formed parallel lines of cultural groups based on their schools of thought within the revolutionary camp. Whether one was a Party representative of the Left-league or a sympathizer of the Communist cause, one enjoyed much freedom in the manner and degree of political positioning. The absence of pressure from one ruling ideology enabled Hu to continue working in the revolutionary camp despite internal conflicts and tensions.[98]

To summarize, Hu discovered Marxist literary criticism as a means to redefine his passion for literature in Japan. His friendship with Japanese left-wingers transformed him from a social rebel into a committed critic who would come to understand and realize his value through literature and criticism as an integral part of the Chinese Revolution. The question of praxis since the very early stage of his literary career had been how to participate in the Chinese Revolution in two different but inseparable roles—that of a writer and that of an activist. In the end, he found in Marxist criticism *the* "suitable" channel through which he played a part in the CCP's revolutionary project.[99] Given his emerging sense of sociopolitical conscience and nationalism as a budding idealist of revolutionary romanticism, Hu engaged in a contractual relationship with the Communist Party but kept a geographical and personal distance that masked an awareness of his weakness in partisan business. If that relationship was collaborative, romantic, and full of youthful idealism in the late 1920s and early 1930s, it was experimental, dynamic, and dialogical by the mid-1930s. Such a transition was well reflected in Hu's poiesis.

In the second half of the 1920s, when Hu composed his first poetry volume *Wild Flowers and Arrows* 野花与箭, he indulged in the sentiments of a young idealist. By the late 1930s, after his Japan years and during the Second Sino-Japanese War, which dragged him out of "the shadows of what a youthful life loves and treasures,"[100] Hu, "in his excitement" and "deeply immersed in the high tide of war," [101] saw the fighting spirit manifested in the people's national resistance. He celebrated the power of the pen in wartime China:

> Oh motherland
> for you
> for your brave sons and daughters
> for tomorrow
> I need to sing with passion abound:
> gratitude
>   frustration, anger
>   hot tears
>   blood that has perhaps flown onto the soil!
> Someone said: oh that useless pen,
>   good to have it thrown away.
> But, oh motherland
> even when holding a knife
>   a gun
> when camouflaging in mountains and bushes
> I still need to sing passionately:
> to listen to those brothers' true-hearted songs—
> . . .
> For you, who've given me life and nurtured me, who've taught
>   me about
>   love and hate, who've made me painfully in love and hate
>   Who's . . . still giving me hope[,] giving
>   me power
> My suffering motherland!
>   August 24, 1937
>   when I met from afar the enemy's plane bombing the city.[102]

These lines from "Sing for the Motherland 為祖國而歌," the leading poem of Hu's second volume of selected poetry under the same title, were composed to commemorate the dead and wounded in the Marco Polo Bridge Incident (1937). The open-ended rhyming scheme emulated the excitement brought about by the outbreak of war with Japan, where

Hu was first acquainted with Marxist socialism, proletarian literature, and left-wing criticism, prompting him to practice his belief in literature as an instrument of politics.

In *What Is Literature?*, Jean-Paul Sartre described the writer's moment of social engagement and political commitment in close terms with the writer's ability to synchronize opposing determinations and forces. The writer in Sartre's mind could, specifically, "mediate" between the conscious being and the "embarked" self, between the "immediate spontaneity" of the events of the time and the "reflective" writer who saw writing as "the free exceeding of a certain human and *total* situation."[103] Sartre defined commitment regarding a writer's moment of embarking on a "consciousness of being" that was "the most lucid and complete" in the sense that it "cause[d] the commitment of immediate spontaneity to advance . . . to the reflective."[104] In his words, "The writer is, *par excellence*, a *mediator* and his commitment is to mediation."[105] To be a committed writer, Hu had no regrets in neutralizing some of his previous notions of literature, including his earlier conception of romanticism that he now found had "completely lost color."[106] One cannot but be struck by the anticipation of the coming of age of a Marxist literary critic, in the confidence of a newly emerged self carrying some knowledge and experience of Marxist praxis. Hu and his generation of Marxist writers wanted not just a grand theory of progress but a praxis, although that very praxis, as the decade of the Cultural Revolution would show, eventually emerged as a hegemonic ideology that alienated the writers themselves from the political state that they had envisioned and helped establish.

III
THE PATH OF LU XUN

> Everyone is free to write and say whatever he likes, without any restrictions. . . . We are now becoming a mass Party all at once, changing abruptly to an open organization, and it is inevitable that we shall be joined by many . . . perhaps . . . even by some . . . mystics.
>
> —V. I. Lenin[1]

This chapter will trace how Lu Xun—the man himself, his critical spirit, and his writings—profoundly influenced Hu in his development into a Marxist literary critic. As a confidential conduit of the CCP, Lu Xun corresponded with Hu from 1934 to his death in 1936, during which he proved to be a model writer-critic. Despite his sponsorship of the left and staunch support for left-wing New Literature, Lu Xun's criticism of the problem of intellectual servitude did not spare Party members. He considered ideological formalism the new equivalent of Confucius's anti-intellectualism and an ally of the CCP's hegemonic cultural policies. Lu Xun's *intellectual* resoluteness in his allegiance to Communism during that period was instructive in Hu's development as a revolutionary and moralistic in his choice of position as a fellow traveler.[2] After Lu Xun died in 1936, and well into the historical threshold of 1949, Hu continued to uphold Lu Xun as a model and an example of critical synthesis, which set the standard for both his willing participation in left-wing politics and his work.

Lu Xun and Hu had developed a relationship that was more than personal influence or mentorship. Liu Xuewei (1912–98), a Party member and a Left-league writer in the 1930s, pointed out how Lu Xun's attitude toward Party members renewed and sharpened Hu's skepticism of factional conflicts, and how it acted as a force that would both make and undo Hu. "At that time, I was considered a member of the 'Hu Feng *pai* [派, "clique"].' This was a mistake. The so-called 'Hu Feng *pai*' was . . . in reality, the 'Lu Xun *pai*,'" reflected Liu.[3] What did it mean to be a member of the "Hu Feng *pai*," which was the "Lu Xun *pai*?" The Chinese character 派 "*pai*" has an ambiguous range of meanings. In the Two-Slogan Debate (1935–36), which started with a disagreement over two slogans and soon turned into a bitter factional fight that would result in far-flung consequences for both Hu and Zhou, it was a negative term employed by Hu's opponents. From Hu's and his school of writers' perspective, they were followers of Lu Xun; to describe them as "Hu Feng *pai*" was to make them a convenient target of the literary community established around a literary icon. In other words, as far as Hu was concerned, Lu Xun was the leader of their side in critical debates against Zhou, with Hu playing only a minor role in them. Considering Lu Xun's prestige, Hu told Geng Yong that he made a more natural and softer target, a scapegoat, so to speak.[4]

Hu's relationship with Lu Xun as a close associate and protégé became one of the earliest reasons for the CCP's persecution of Hu, despite Mao's call for "learning from the Lu Xun spirit."[5] Indeed, if Marxist literary criticism had begun with a somewhat naïve praise of the revolutionary spirit in literature, the left-wing writers and critics soon came to see that the doctrinal, the bureaucratic, and the recklessness had never been a separate part of it. If Lu Xun had apostrophized Marxist aesthetics as that which interposed no boundary between art and life, where art entered directly into the life of ordinary people, he became increasingly indiscreet in his contempt for the CCP's operation of ideological straitjackets late in life. Lu Xun could not tolerate the way "political commitments" enforced "thought reform" through which "class consciousness" was a product of chauvinism and jingoism. At one level, the "Lu Xun spirit" stood for the independence of mind that the CCP approved of because it constituted the revolutionary cause against Chinese feudalism. Meanwhile, this independence of mind also admitted a potential transformation into a kind of critical spirit that would not exempt the PRC from scrutiny. Long considered "a principal architect of the New Literature,"[6] Lu Xun epitomized the May Fourth spirit critical of not only the "old evils" of feudalism but also their newly mutated form—hegemonic abstractions in Marxist critical practices that became dominant in the post-1949 era.

Thus, identifying Hu as a unique exemplar of what Theodore Huters called the "critical legacy"[7] of Lu Xun not only distinguished their intellectual affinities but also their understanding of the different historical circumstances in which they operated. Without qualifying any aspects of the Lu Xun spirit in his course of following Lu Xun, Hu nevertheless demonstrated that practicing criticism consistently and regardless of one's relation to power was the only way to join and participate in the Chinese Revolution. Understanding this intellectual kinship provides an opportunity to examine Lu Xun's values beyond his conscripted role as the CCP's triumphant symbol of the Chinese Revolution; specifically, to reflect on the afterlife of Lu Xun to evaluate the critical potentialities embedded in "the inner history" of modern Chinese literary criticism. Such a history, Erich Auerbach explained, "contains the records of man's mighty, adventurous advance to a consciousness of his human condition and to the realization of his given potential."[8]

LU XUN AND THE CHINESE REVOLUTION

Following the beginning of his political engagement and increasingly over the decades of his revolutionary career, Hu constantly immersed himself in debates with his comrades-in-arms on the various paths through which the Chinese Revolution brought about intellectual enlightenment in society. He was aware that a Marxist writer could not claim to be standing outside the powerful national-historical forces that she was theorizing and seeking to oppose. Meanwhile, against Hu's hope that political consciousness and ideological achievement would appear gradually with the learning of new ideas, actuality, political slogans, and declarations dominated the direction and habit of popular thinking to a degree beyond his revolutionary experience.

Although Marxist aesthetics had taught the "cultural workers" how writing could also be a form of "fighting,"[9] they lacked Marxist praxis, allowing indoctrination to become not only the touchstone of political consciousness but also a new trend of intellectual servitude. Hannah Arendt used the word *uncontemplative* to describe this practice of intellectual recklessness, although the example she had in mind was not Chinese Marxist intellectuals under Mao but Martin Heidegger, an intellectual sponsor of Nazism.[10] Not without skepticism, Arendt commented that "Heidegger never thinks 'about' something; he thinks something."[11] What Arendt criticized as the act of "thinking something," having in common the practice of Mao's "cultural worker," was a question of the relationship between the thinker and his problematics, between thought and practice. Ultimately, for the Marxist literary critic, it was one between the critique of the social contradictions involved in capitalist modernity and the expression of that critique. Heidegger, in engaging in the act of "thinking something" in Weimar and Nazi Germany, ironically embraced ideological and political totalitarianism as a solution to the problem of capitalism's "technological totalitarianism." Put specifically, in failing to demonstrate historical sensibility, he also blinded himself to the criminal measures through which Nazism systematically destroyed Enlightenment modernity. Arendt called such a practice and expression of critique amoral, if not "appalling,"[12] because it appeared not to have been "conditioned against evil."[13]

Taking into consideration the wartime conditions under which Marxist writers worked, it was imperative that their work inhabited the era, and vice versa. Whereas, in Lu Xun's words, revolutionary writers should "share the common destiny with the revolution and feel its pulses deeply,"[14] the reality was that "countless tragedies and comedies were played out in a thought reform movement."[15] Hu described the dramas of the time as follows:

> Some people have no clue about Chinese society. They make some row with windmills for a while, mistaking them as the giant [Chinese feudalism] and consequently lose themselves as the illusion shatters. Others want to understand and comprehend Chinese society only to find themselves soon engulfed by it. . . . In both cases, these thought reformers of a sort have grasped in the abstract some "theories," which could be memorized as quickly as they could be lost. Lu Xun does not speak theoretical slogans; he internalizes new thoughts and manifests them in a critical verse style that gives Chinese feudalism no chance.[16]

Unlike some of the political opportunists of the time, whose literary commitment was abstract and whose sympathy for the oppressed class merely sentimental,[17] Hu explored the problem of literature and life from the opposite end. Experience in and by itself may not have been enough, yet an application "in the abstract" of "some theories" on life that denied its centrality was doomed to impoverishment. Knowing full well the limits and necessity of "theories," Hu embarked on a life-long preoccupation with certain basic predicaments about the relationship between literature and the writer-critic regarding Marxist aesthetics. My examination of Hu's path to the Chinese Revolution will touch on many of these predicaments. Here, I will discuss, notably, Hu's collaboration with Lu Xun in the 1930s and how this experience enabled him to transform his instinctive repulsion toward feudalist life into a critically structured and informed understanding of the realities of early twentieth-century China. Involved as he was in the waves of revolutionary activities, it remained for him a constant preoccupation to rise above immediate actions and to reflect on the way intellectual threads connected to one firmly distinct question: How was one to define the Chinese Revolution as serving the cause of progress? This question provided a basis for Hu's affinity with Lu Xun, with whom he shared the same dissatisfaction with Chinese Confucian morality and traditionalism.

From the beginning, Hu shared Lu Xun's "instinct" or common experience of Confucian China. He identified in Lu Xun's "great experience of self-struggle"[18] *the* quality that distinguished Lu Xun from his fellow May Fourth thinkers. Locating the root of Lu Xun's antifeudalism and antitraditionalism in his family history *and* his penetrative understanding of that history, Hu wrote that the deterioration in Lu Xun's family status, from well-to-do middle class to bankruptcy, opened Lu Xun's eyes to the brutalities of social reality. "'What society is like,' his hatred of feudalist power, and his individuality . . . define his perception of society," analyzed Hu.[19] In addition to his experience of Chinese traditionalism, "Lu Xun came up against such big changes as the Sino-Japanese War, the Hundred Days Reform, the Boxer Uprising, and the Treaty of 1911 in his adolescence."[20] These experiences, Hu elaborated, "sowed the seeds of anti-imperialist, self-strengthening, and nationalist thinking in the young Lu Xun and further strengthened his determination to 'save the Chinese people and to regenerate China.'"[21] Lu Xun's familiarity with the brutalities of Chinese society and Western imperialism not only prompted him to think and write but also produced critical reflections that were typical of what Raymond Williams called "the structure of feeling" in the first few decades of the twentieth century.[22] According to Williams, the formation of modern Chinese consciousness and humanism began the moment Lu Xun abandoned medical studies for literature.

Lu Xun exemplified how the literary intellectual should position the self morally in the face of her formative society. In one of his many essays commemorating his teacher, Hu accounted for Lu Xun's decision to study in Japan against the prevailing view that to abandon the Confucian classics for foreign learning was "to sell [one's] soul to foreign devils."[23] Much as it was about Lu Xun, the account was also self-referential; it documented Hu's intellectual inclinations and his assessment of the times. As Hu read Lu Xun and adjusted his readings to align with his then largely emotive response to the conditions of the early Republic, he started from one historical time into the next, traversing one set of sociocultural practices into another in the manner of the Lu Xun type of revolutionary intellectual. Many years later, Hu still recalled his excitement in reading Lu Xun for the first time: "Having just left a secluded and remote county for a big city [Wuchang], I read Lu Xun's preface to *Call to Arms* from the *Morning Post* supplementary. Although I would not be able to understand much of it, . . . I feel instinctively that Lu Xun's writing is about the very same darkness and pain that have been enveloping me. Lu Xun became the closest of all names."[24]

A particular link between the national crisis and the task of the literary intellectual surfaced for Hu in his reading of Lu Xun's preface to *Call to Arms,* which also explained the rationale behind Lu Xun's conclusion that the problem of China was cultural and psychological. In 1906, after having watched a newsreel featuring the Japanese military beheading a "Chinese spy" in front of a group of "physically strong Chinese fellows" witnessing and "enjoy[ing] the spectacle,"[25] Lu Xun concluded that "the people of a weak and backward country, however strong and healthy they might be, could only serve to be made . . . witnesses of such futile spectacles."[26] This was because Confucian education and traditional morality had implanted in the people's mind a "slave mentality" that constituted a brutal system of "cannibalistic" social practice.[27] "The most important thing, therefore, was to change their spirit," declared Lu Xun.[28] In a foreign land away from his formative society, Lu Xun subsequently changed his original plan of becoming an army doctor, concluding that technological know-how alone was inadequate to meet the needs of Chinese modernization. He asked, "What was lacking in Chinese 'national character'? What was the cause of China's 'illness'?"[29] Lu Xun's analysis of Chinese national characteristics, like all national character studies built on biological essentialism, may have been a racialist project. Meanwhile, it did not stop one from seeing Lu Xun's attempt to overcome nationalistic sentiment and his reliance on intellectual strength and sensitivity, especially in the form of cultural awakenings. In Lu Xun's diagnosis of "the problem of China," the most effective prescription appeared to lie in "literature," and hence he "decided to promote a literary movement."[30]

Following Lu Xun, Hu, too, found in the restoration of human sentiments, in "the passion of life," the solution to fixing the "men-eating-men" relationship in Chinese society. Of all the May Fourth intellectuals and thinkers, Hu identified Lu Xun as "the only one"[31] who understood the problems of Chinese society and whose call to reform the Chinese national character was the most effective prescription. He admired Lu Xun for his ability to break off from the commonplace and question the "feudal consciousness" that had "numbed" the people for "a thousand years."[32] In inventing the characters Runtu and Ah-Q—who were figures of problematic "national characters"[33] that Confucian education sought to produce—Lu Xun established a model of thinking that helped Hu concretize his resentment of feudal consciousness. This model, which Hu called "passionate thinking" and valued as the highest form of thinking, engaged with life and functioned as the basis of a moral vision that was the ideal expression of revolutionary ethics and realism. "All great works of art," Hu once advised young writers, "are created to satisfy certain demands."[34] Without the kind of humanist *passion*—"wisdom and kindness"—that Lu Xun exemplified and embodied, one could neither address the true demands of life nor bring one's art to life, and vice versa.[35] Echoing Xu Shoushang's commemoration of Lu Xun, Hu wrote:

> Where does Lu Xun's greatness lie? In my view, it lies in the thoroughness of both his calmness and his passion. To be calm is to be profound and farsighted; to be passionate is to have the love for all, to take upon oneself the responsibility for the people. These two aspects of Lu Xun's are interrelated. His calmness that permeates with passion is *zhi* [智, "wisdom"]; the passion that is imbued with calmness is real passion, and that is *ren* [仁, "kindness"]. Lu Xun is both *zhi* and *ren*. . . . Stored in his cold pen is great sympathy. His tears brim with his words.[36]

Life, theory, and passion, Hu believed, nurtured one another, and when united, they enabled the writer to transform experience into art. It was the writer's responsibility to exercise what he called the "subjective combative spirit" to turn the creative process into a procedure by which to acquire "a spiritual force" and to "battle with life."[37] Without passion, the world was like a lifeless phenomenon floating about.[38]

In associating writing with "battle" and "life," Hu linked his apprenticeship as a Lu Xun follower to the figure of the critic-warrior whose operations included the combative essay. Critics reviewing Hu's role in Marxist literary realism and its application in New Literature have used the phrase "subjective combative spirit" to sum up his contributions. Indeed,

Hu built a substantial portion of his notion of the "subjective combative spirit" on Lu Xun's humanism—an uncompromising insistence that such human qualities as passion, creativity, and critical intellect played a role in the course of the Chinese Revolution. For Hu, the subjective combative man was Lu Xun, whose combative essay in the manner of a "dagger and javelin" was a model:

> As the prolonged experience of war has come to define everyday life, cultural workers must either produce art for a living or survive so as to continue with literary work. Specifically, as the daily experience of war enriches the cultural workers' spiritual life, it also determines the material base of life. . . . Taking into account the double work of censorship and material hardship, the chance for creative imagination to be thwarted, bogged down, eroded, and incarcerated become ever higher. The end of this process finds the subjective combative spirit deteriorating, meaning that the writer's subjectivity to comprehend life . . . has withered. Under proper circumstances, writers in their different ways and abilities would find from life the raw materials to produce a variety of works, with each following its development, giving out its scent, and exhibiting its color. Together, these writers broaden and enrich the development of [Marxist] realism. On the contrary, difficult living conditions . . . would only induce laziness of the mind, which leads to different types of [thought] slackness.[39]

In setting his notion of the "subjective combative spirit" as the benchmark of Marxist realist literature, Hu was virtually likening the perils of the left-wing literary scene to the fate of the late Qing dynasty and early modern China, and, by extension, the tasks and mission of "Marxist realist" writers to those of the May Fourth intellectuals. Realist literature became a realm in which Hu was willing to proceed on faith, despite his bittersweet acknowledgment of the CCP's ascendency from a revolutionary force to dictatorial state power. His faith was not in realist literature as ideological art per se or in a formal creed, but rather it was in the creative process in which the individual writer's subjectivism served as the root and ground of all systems of thought. Hu insisted that critical consciousness provided the basis on which rested the individual writer's *continued* struggle against the self, who suffered from what the Japanese critic Kuriyagawa Hakuson called a "depression" intimated by "angst and restlessness with the era"[40] and, as such, it was a highly personal experience.

Romain Rolland used the term *oceanic* to give literary subjectivism shape. Whereas Rolland derived his oceanic sensibility from psychoanalytical theories, which Lu Xun and Hu admired but with reservations, Hu revered and personalized his romanticism as one of his models for realist literature. In Rolland's words,

> I belong to a land of rivers. . . . Therein lies primeval Force. . . . Everything belongs to this river of the Soul, flowing from the deep unplumbed reservoirs of our Being, the conscious, realized, and mastered Being . . . of the Being without beginning and End.[41]

As a raw youth finding his self-worth in the pre-1949 era, Hu had little trouble attributing to the poetic impulse a vital role in the creative process. Yet, as a later chapter on Hu's "subjective combative spirit" will show, any failure to outgrow such a belief in the concept, especially in the post-1949 PRC, would be inadmissible on both literary and ideological grounds, for the circumstances of public criticism and intellectual liberation had by then become a thing of the past.

THE "CONFIDENTIAL CONDUIT": 1934–1936

In the years between 1934 and 1936, Hu acted as the "confidential conduit" between Lu Xun and the CCP's Central Committee and learned from the former how to deal with the realpolitik of the Left-league. Whereas "the lessons of reality" prompted him to join the Left-league,[42] such an act of politicization ultimately cohered with Lu Xun's impulse to reform China's national character. Lu Xun perceived the coming into being of China's modernity as conditioned upon the emergence of a social formation free from the contradiction between feudal traditions and revolutionary goals. Thus, he worked for the nurturing of more revolutionary-minded writers who were ideologically less dependent upon feudal ethics. Thinking of himself as a platform through which the generation of young writers related to the Revolution, Lu Xun lent his support to the CCP and its cultural bureaucrats: "The point on [my being] a ladder is correct. . . . If, in the future, somebody can climb higher with this ladder, it does not matter that I am being stepped on."[43] Concerning his decision to join the Left-league, Lu

Xun said, "Since my hope for the appearance of someone great in China was not yet dead, I again accepted the young writers' invitation and joined the League."[44]

Lu Xun had been sympathetic toward the CCP and acknowledged the usefulness of the Party's social and political functions. By 1930, "the ideological tenor of [Lu Xun's] writings reached a peak."[45] If revolutionary politics were an expression of the left-wing writers' commitment to the enlightenment of the masses, then their idea of socialism resonated with Lu Xun's vision of social progress. However, because the left-wing writers were victims of Chinese traditionalism and feudalist social practices to the same degree as the right-wing nationalists were their products, Lu Xun believed that all writers in China, no matter their political stance, were easily conservatives. In a speech given to inaugurate the Left-league on March 2, 1930, Lu Xun urged the young writers to "keep in touch with actual social conflicts" to prove that they were fully committed to the revolutionary cause:

> If you simply shut yourself up behind glass windows to write or study instead of keeping in touch with actual social conflicts, it is easy for you to be extremely radical or "Left." But the moment you come up against reality all your ideas are shattered. Behind closed doors it is very easy to spout radical ideas, but equally easy to turn "Rightist." This is what's meant in the West by "Salon-socialists." A salon is a sitting-room, and it is most artistic and refined to sit discussing socialism—with no idea of bringing it into being. . . . Revolution is a bitter thing, mixed with filth and blood, not as lovely or perfect as poets think. It is eminently down-to-earth, entailing many humble, tiresome tasks, not as romantic as the poets think. Of course there is destruction in a revolution, but construction is even more necessary to it; and while destruction is straightforward, construction is troublesome. So it is easy for all who have romantic dreams about [the] revolution to become disillusioned on closer acquaintance, or when a revolution is actually carried out.[46]

Notwithstanding his rare willingness to openly stand by a political party, Lu Xun balanced ideological positions with vigilance against dogmatism and alienation. He encouraged young writers to be "fighters in the spiritual world,"[47] which meant maintaining their romantic idealism about society—a force that had first drawn them to the Revolution—without losing their sense of self even in the face of the demands of revolutionary politics. In other words, in developing class consciousness, one must anchor it to a personal understanding of the sentiments of society at large rather than take heed of the ideological order of one organization.

Lu Xun from the beginning had a marked partiality for a situation in which artists and writers accepted party politics and partisan work as a part of their duties. It was, in a sense, this partiality that led to his reservation in giving the Left-league his entire consent. It was the same partiality that stopped him from being as enthusiastically as the Marxist writers of his rank were—such as Mao Dun and Ding Ling—in embracing institutions. Not surprisingly, Lu Xun clashed with Zhou Yang and Tian Han, who steadfastly professionalized themselves as "Marxist revolutionaries." Lu Xun had few satisfactory moments in his actual dealings with the CCP's functionaries and found it hard to accommodate their goals and practices. His relationship with the Party deteriorated rapidly; by 1935, virtually nobody on the Standing Committee of the Left-league remained in communication with him. By then, Lu Xun was as much a figurehead or "signboard" to Zhou as Zhou was a political technician to Lu Xun.[48] Were it not for his position in the CCP's political organization, which was a fundamental basis of power for any active social movement. Lu Xun would not have recognized Zhou's standing in Chinese revolutionary history, except for the fact that he was the source of many divisive and even destructive conflicts. In a letter dated September 12, 1935, Lu Xun confided to Hu:

> As soon as you join the organization, you would be drawn into meaningless personal conflicts, and become colorless and voiceless. Like myself as an example: I always feel that I am tied by an iron chain. There is a foreman who beats me from the back; however hard I work, he still beats me. When I turn back and ask where the mistake is, he then says politely that I work perfectly well, that he has a high opinion of me, and that today's weather ha ha ha.[49]

Lu Xun was clear about his purpose when he decided to join the Left-league five years before; he had hoped that the association would breed "rebellious young geniuses" or Nietzschean "supermen" for the Revolution.[50] Nevertheless, the in-house fighting consumed much of the Left-league's energy. Lu Xun's account of his own experience with the organization captured the conflicting feelings that independent-minded writers like Hu shared. On the one hand, writers in the 1930s and 1940s functioning in a time of war and national crises could not afford to be ascetically aloof. On the other hand, war and revolution could not induce Lu Xun to subscribe unreservedly to realpolitik and lose any conviction in the enlightenment potential and general communicability of literature. In an essay commemorating the third anniversary of Lu Xun's death, Hu recalled Lu Xun having the best of both politics and criticism. In his terms, the committed writer, as exemplified by Lu Xun, was, on the one hand, a "bare-chested" fighter, brave and selfless, and on the other, a loner often on the verge of despair:[51]

> Lu Xun is not an introducer or explicator of theories but a real warrior who uses new thoughts as weapons against the "old evils." Since [the] May Fourth Movement, Lu Xun alone has shaken the thousand years of dark tradition. It is because he derives his critical spirit of realism from an extensive understanding of old society.[52]

Hu's epithet—"real warrior"—expressed both his admiration for Lu Xun as a writer-essayist and his acceptance that, with the atrocities of the series of wars in the first half of twentieth-century China, writing meant narrowing down literature's subjective power to political necessity. The image of a bare-chested fighter dually measured Lu Xun in his double roles: first, the writer, who was also a revolutionary and who belonged to a political organization in which he had to obey its principles and rules; and second, the bare-chested revolutionary who wore no uniform and by virtue of his bare-chestedness stood apart from the organization. Uniformed or variegated, Lu Xun's double identity sent the message that politics did not equate with literature and a soldier was not synonymous with a writer. Because while revolutionary literature could be a record of temporary day-to-day struggles, it could also turn imagination into resources for the rank and file whose business was to breed ideological slaves. From Lu Xun, Hu learned the virtues he thought peculiar to the committed writer: combative without regard to any organizations of hegemonic forces. While continuing to be close to the CCP, Hu realized that he had to carve out for himself a space separate from the collective, an area where he could carry out the work expected of an individual critic.

Just as he sought to emulate Lu Xun in how to position the self's relation to the political organization, Hu believed that Marxism as a (pre-) state ideology should not have been a political dogma. Lu Xun taught Hu that Marxism was not a partisan type of knowledge but "an intellectual weapon."[53] In an article written in Beijing in 1984 titled "Mr. Lu Xun," Hu recalled the production of Lu Xun's "Reply to a Letter from the Chinese Trotskyists,"[54] which was drafted by Feng Xuefeng. Hu's article showed the subtle complexities in the collaborative relationship between Lu Xun and the CCP under the circumstances of the 1930s:

> In the Two-slogan Debate, the literature of [the] national defence faction went on the all-out defensive. . . . At the time, Lu Xun was seriously ill and could neither sit up nor speak; it was not possible to discuss [it] with him. The foolish Trotskyists . . . thought that they might be able to benefit from the [internal conflicts of the left-wing writers], and wrote a letter hoping to "draw" Lu Xun over to their side. Lu Xun was angry when he read the letter. Feng Xuefeng drafted . . . a reply, which he intended as a rebuttal of this slander. He . . . read out the draft to Lu Xun. Lu Xun listened with his eyes closed. He said nothing but merely nodded to indicate his approval.
>
> Later on, Feng Xuefeng . . . felt that he ought to provide some theoretical basis for the slogan [Mass Literature in the National Revolutionary War]. He drafted "On Our Current Literary Movement" and again . . . read it to Lu Xun. Lu Xun was weaker than the previous evening and was even less capable of speaking. All he did was a nod to indicate his approval, but he also showed signs of slight impatience. After we left [Lu Xun's place], Xuefeng suddenly said to me, "I hadn't expected Lu Xun to be so difficult, he's not as good as Gorki. Gorki's political comments were all written by the secretary whom the Party assigned to him; all Gorki did was sign them."[55]

Lu Xun's "signs of slight impatience" were not due entirely to his illness. They registered his struggle when he felt that Feng was hurrying to a *pronounced* political stance, a struggle that many Marxist intellectuals experienced during the Yan'an rectification movement in 1942 and later during the Cultural Revolution. Hu made emphatic what Lu Xun only gestured: "Lu Xun was exceptionally serious and principled; were he made to be responsible for ideological viewpoints that he had not thought through (and at that time he was incapable of doing so), he would feel extremely uneasy."[56] For some, such resistance to political and institutional coercion would have been a matter of life and death, as it would be for Hu two decades later.

In a letter to Zhu Qixia dated July 18, 1949, merely two months before the "national liberation," Hu wrote, "What you perhaps do not understand is that I've always been only a 'fellow traveler.' In China, to engage in literary work and, especially, in criticism, is not easy at all. There are responsibilities that I must take, even if they cost my blood."[57] Hu had ethics regarding how he should "travel" with the CCP as a "fellow." He used the example of one of his literary models, Aleksey Nikolayevich Tolstoy (1883–1945), more commonly referred to as "Comrade Count," to explain the state of fellowship. Having acknowledged that his notion of "subjectivism" owed much to A. N. Tolstoy's theory of art, which "contain[ed] lessons that are worthy of repeated learning,"[58] Hu explained that A. N. Tolstoy was not critical of the ideological content of literature but that of revolutionary literature's lack of aesthetic values. Remarkably, in the same essay, he also specified the criterion that future generations should use to understand A. N. Tolstoy as a "fellow traveler." In his assessment, Leon Trotsky had turned A. N. Tolstoy into a fellow traveler of the October Revolution for the wrong reasons.[59] A. N. Tolstoy was a fellow traveler not because he left Imperial Russia for Paris as a white émigré in the wake of the Russian Revolution and the Civil War. Instead, it was by the writer's own experience of a "self-inflicted sense of moral pressure" at the moment he started writing *The Calvary Road* (1921–40) that, Hu argued, future generations should consider him a revolutionary fellow traveler.[60]

Typical of the sentiment of revolutionary romanticism of the modern Chinese intellectual, Hu's allegiance to Marxist socialism was a "choice of position" that was at once conscious and conscientious, individualistic and social. He learned from Lu Xun that the committed writer, while maintaining critical sympathy for revolutionary politics, participated in them only by degrees and stages. For both Lu Xun and Hu, though there was a deep affinity between social responsibility and ideological espousal, there was never confusion between politics as a means to higher humanistic ideals and politics as an end in itself. The unity between the *passion* and political awakening, a unity that would define the pathos of one's revolutionary activities, was one critical legacy of Lu Xun that Hu would play out during situations where he faced political pressure. This level of intimate knowledge explained in part why, starting in the mid-1940s, Hu became increasingly resistant to the "orthodox" Marxism that originated in Mao's Yan'an caves. From Hu's point of view, as the next two chapters will discuss, Mao's "Talks" were a "cultural policy" that the CCP implemented to estrange and strangle creative and critical passion with the help of a bureaucratized political structure.

IN THE STEAD OF LU XUN

Mao considered Lu Xun "the first sage of China,"[61] rendering him a role model for not only Hu but also many radical writers and intellectuals of the time. However, what made Hu a unique follower of Lu Xun was not Mao's endorsement but his unswerving insistence on carrying forward Lu Xun's critical legacy. While Lu Xun influenced many within left-wing circles, his critical analysis of Chinese national character found the most committed practitioner in Hu. Some followers of Lu Xun, such as Xu Maoyong (1911–77), called Lu Xun "a revolutionary in white gloves,"[62] while others, like Zhou, utilized and reinterpreted Lu Xun for political and ideological purposes.[63] Some of "Lu Xun's disciples and friends"—for instance, Xiao Jun, Ba Jin, and Feng Xuefeng—although faithful to Lu Xun's vision of Chinese modernity, abandoned the course after Lu Xun's death.[64] Hu was one of the very few who strived to remain committed to Lu Xun's enlightenment project of reforming the Chinese national character.

On the first anniversary of Lu Xun's death, Hu reminded readers that Lu Xun expressed best his "spirit" via his dual emphasis on "liberation" and "progress." He wrote: "[Lu Xun] had always placed the goal of 'progress' side by side with the goal of 'liberation.' For him, [political] progress was the condition of liberation."[65] Later, in 1946, at the end of the Second Sino-Japanese War, Hu warned against the danger of the CCP sinking into an apparatus of oppression and argued for the need to reinforce the enlightenment project: "It is completely wrong to consider people's selfless sacrifice in the great national liberation to be a desire to change from being a slave of a foreign nation to being a slave of the Chinese nation."[66] What Hu said was almost a paraphrase of Lu Xun's comment on the Republican government in 1925, the year he witnessed, to his distress, the Guomindang (GMD) turn into a reactionary machine trapped in the internal fights of the warlords. Lu Xun said, "The so-called Republic of China has ceased to exist. I feel that before the revolution, I was a slave, but shortly after the revolution, I have been cheated by the slaves and become their slave."[67] In the two decades between the mid-1930s and mid-1950s, Hu made much of the radical originality of this insight—critical consciousness with a high degree of political realism—and did so under conditions with much higher personal stakes than the years between the late 1920s and the early 1930s, during which Lu Xun was at close quarters with the CCP. Although the space for independent thinking and intellectual autonomy diminished after Lu Xun's death, especially after 1942, Hu maintained an ungainly but plastic relationship with the CCP, as Lu Xun had in his space and time with all institutions of power, critical and political. Hu's attitude as he displayed it several times at the invitation to join the CCP, for instance, was a case in point.

Without having officiated his relationship with the CCP, Hu defined his relationship with the Party reservedly to the point of being negative—"I would not commit to any political party or group except the Communist Party"[68]—and, in fact, twice declined the chance to go to Yan'an. On May 24, 1939, Dong Biwu visited Hu in Wuhan and passed on Zhou's message. Zhou, then in charge of the Lu Xun Academy of Literature and Arts in Yan'an, sought to appoint Hu as head of the Academy's Chinese Department. Hu hesitated over the prospect of going to Yan'an and consulted Zhou Enlai the same evening. From Hu's point of view, to keep Yan'an at a distance, as an infinite ideal, gave him the plasticity to practice the CCP's social missions. Zhou Enlai, convinced by Hu, agreed that he should stay where he was, confirming that it would be conducive to the CCP's overall work to have someone with an open identity maneuvering in the GMD-controlled areas. Dong Biwu, too, was satisfied with Hu's plan and encouraged Hu to contribute further to the CCP's work in the United Front.[69] In retrospect, Hu's decision might have seemed like one of those moments in which a person, after much deliberation, arrives at a balanced assessment of her situation and chooses the best possible prospect. Yet there are two points to note. First, despite the hatred between Hu and Zhou that dominated their relationship in Shanghai, Zhou offered Hu a position of power. Second, there was an indication that personal facts might have influenced Hu's decision to decline Zhou's offer; it would not be wide of the mark to assume that Hu's complicated relationship with Zhou might have had some influence on his decision.

Two years later in Chongqing, in February 1941, the rift between the CCP and the GMD ravaged the country again despite the popular inclination for a united front. The Wannan Incident, in which the "New Fourth Army" was almost wiped out, led to protests from the CCP and beyond. As a typical practice of the Party, organized campaigns, with very few exceptions, were carefully planned to mobilize all possible social forces.

The CCP-GMD hostility once again dominated the political scene. As a gesture of protest as well as a move to protect the left-wing intellectuals in Chongqing, Zhou Enlai suggested that Hu, along with others, evacuate the city and depart for either Hong Kong or Yan'an. With historical hindsight, Hu's choice of destination was another crucial moment in his life, both as a left-wing literary critic and as a fellow traveler on the road to Communism. Although no human insight can predict historical development, let alone alter its route, it was perhaps not preposterous to think that most left-wingers would have made Yan'an their first choice. In Hu's case, the Yan'an choice was almost natural given that his wife longed for stability and a life free from domestic confinement after having endured years of an unsettled life. Against her wishes and despite Zhou's advice, Hu chose Hong Kong, acting on a decision that would change his life course and that he would regret for a long time after. Looking back at this critical moment some thirty years later, Hu rued the day he turned down Yan'an:

> At that time, Mei Zhi was keen on Yan'an and quarreled with my decision. Had we gone to Yan'an, there would have been a different way to "solve" my problem, at least my relatives and friends and those readers whom I have not met would not have suffered so greatly an unjustified infliction![70]

By "a different way" of solving his problem, Hu meant that he would not have been categorized as a "counterrevolutionary" but as a politically faulty person whose "mistakes" would be dealt with as an internal matter. One may read this moment of Hu's life and his political and ideological explanations for his decision in a positive light or argue that historical evolution is full of coincidences and twists. In my view, however, one gets much closer to Hu's way of thinking if one were to consider the moment as evidence of Lu Xun's influence on him. Indeed, when Hu reflected on Lu Xun's reasons for refusing Yan'an, he revealed one dimension of his intellectual makeup that was also primarily a source of his tragedy. Recalling Lu Xun's reasons for turning down both the All-Writers' invitation in 1932 and the prospect of receiving medical treatment in the Soviet Union, Hu wrote:

> As soon as [Lu Xun] returned [from the Soviet Union], he would find himself in a difficult situation wherein forces [from both the left and the right] clamped down on him. Just as the

> GMD would censor all his activities, the Left-league would cuff his hands and legs. After all, as the man himself said, "How could I not become docile after being fed bread?"[71]

Lu Xun remained independent and refused to enroll in the CCP for the whole of his life, even though, during the late 1920s, he was sympathetic to the revolutionary left and formed an alliance with the CCP via his role as a loyal non-Communist. Precisely so, through the years he became increasingly assured that the task of leading and determining the Chinese Revolution's final stage belonged to the critical intellectual. Lu Xun's insistence on critical consciousness as the foundation of intellectual power was soon paralleled by Hu, who continued to live as an engagé writer-critic, with the best possible independence of mind he could defend for many more years after Lu Xun's death. Lu Xun was, for Hu, the prime model for making choices about his raison d'être as a committed writer and the extent to which he became committed. During the long revolutionary years, Hu always seemed to have more reasons for working knowingly *with* rather than *for* the CCP.[72] His political loyalty, necessary and necessarily practical as it was, had not led him to join the CCP formally.

In his study of Lu Xun, Lin Yü-sheng observed that "in a fundamental layer" of his consciousness, Lu Xun "seemed still to have taken for granted the traditional Chinese notion of politics nurtured by the dichotomy between Confucianism and Legalism."[73] Due to the lack of "a mental category that saw certain aspects of politics in terms of an ethic of responsibility," Lin argued that "Lu Xun could only see the actuality of politics as a perpetual game of chicanery played out by heartless men for selfish gains."[74] In other words, for Lu Xun, it was a moral imperative to participate in Chinese social reality, even though by nature he might have been alienated from the existing political conditions. Given what he had learned from "the lessons of reality," therefore, Lu Xun, "as a moral man in search of a path . . . would commit himself to walk that path [the left-wing path] *as a moral act*, regardless of his injunctions against politics."[75]

Like Lu Xun, Hu understood the CCP's historical role in moral terms. He began the road to revolution because, "instinctively discontented with Chinese tradition,"[76] he wanted to liberate the masses from the old regimes of control. Meanwhile, he translated his youthful revolutionary romanticism into a Lu Xun spirit of passionate thinking. Following Lu Xun, Hu developed a sense of self that related closely to the political reality of the Republic. There were elements in Lu Xun's views on the relationship between the intellectual self and the CCP that struck a sympathetic chord in Hu. As it had done for Lu Xun, the CCP existed for Hu at two levels. At one level, it was representative of the progressive forces and the embodiment of great moral values; as such, the CCP was "a great existence" with whom Hu thought he could "freely speak."[77] At another level, the CCP was a political organization conditioned by and emerging from the operations and activities that power agents such as Zhou, Lin Mohan (1913–2008), and He Qifang performed daily.

It is interesting to observe at this point how Lu Xun's understanding of the causes of political commitment found a version in Hu's often inhibitive attitude toward partisan writers. Like Lu Xun in his dealings with the Left-league during the last year of his life, Hu could take no power for granted. Insofar as he remained resolute to "travel" with the CCP, Hu could not help dividing his understanding of the Party into two types: one as a beacon of moral power and the other as an organ peopled with trivial and uncomely ideologues. Thus, he attributed the problems in the cultural arena to the sectarianism of a few Party representatives and blamed Zhou for them:

> Thought-struggle has been frequent within the Party. But one cannot ground Zhou's theory on his rank. . . . I don't believe that I can engage Zhou Yang, Ding Ling, and the like, least to say Hu Qiaomu, in criticism. *Their way of doing things does not represent the Party.*[78]

Hu might have been unsophisticated and even prickly, yet, given the circumstances of his time, one should not dismiss him the way Rolf Wiggershaus dismissed Theodor Adorno, as a "bitter" and "hyperemotional" grouch.[79]

It would be wrong to infer from Hu's criticism of Party leaders that he was politically naïve, although there was no doubt that he was less a man of pragmatics than most, and his occasional political insensitivity may well have planted a seed that developed during the post-1949 years. There is no evidence to suggest that throughout his career Hu was unaware of the need to accept the CCP as a hierarchical political organization. It is likely, however, that Hu's criticism of Party leaders had as much to do with his disagreement with Zhou as with his desire to find space for the CCP's cultural policy. For one thing, much in the CCP's cultural policy conflicted with Hu's aesthetic position. Mao's call to subordinate literature and intellectuals to politics in 1942 was something that Hu could not break from; this, however, was far from implying a surrender of the self.

Hu's resistance to political pressure became censorious as time went on, until, in his "300,000-Character Report," he told the Central Committee bluntly: "The little life accounted by New Literature and nurtured in the process of revolutionary struggle in the past thirty years [has] now been smothered."[80] It was no wonder that Mao considered Hu's criticism of the cultural leaders' sectarianism to be a "bitter and *protracted* struggle" against the Party rather than an exhibition of the "interpersonal conflict between Zhou Yang and [Hu]."[81]

Critical ambivalence was the root of Hu's and Lu Xun's common conviction in independent thinking. For Lu Xun, independent thinking was medicine for a sick national spirit; for Hu, it was a double-edged sword pointing at doctrinaire Party members who policed creative work through the Party's cultural policies. At the level of realpolitik, Hu could neither follow his comrades' stead nor collaborate with them in the operation of the state ideological apparatuses. The quest for Marxist politics in Hu's case was a quest for a fuller realization of the "subjective combative spirit." The Chinese Revolution was achieved by individuals; in the same manner, individuals realized themselves through politics. Given the historical circumstances, Hu's split view dividing the CCP into dual levels—moral on the one side and institutional-organizational on the other—enabled him to be conscientious *both* politically and critically, to be simultaneously fellow traveler and critic of the CCP's leadership in cultural matters. Although Hu seemed politically naïve in thinking that he could employ a "divide-and-rule" method to engage with the CCP, this method sufficed for him to find breathing space in the conflict between literature and politics. Meanwhile, it constituted an essential origin of his tragedy, for it averted Hu's eyes from the fact that the Party members *were* the embodiment and the manifestation of the (state-)ideology.

Whether he built literary criticism on his antagonism against the cultural leaders' political practices or on the Party's cultural policy itself, or both, evidently, Hu's strategic approach to the CCP directly impacted his assessment of the general conditions of left-wing cultural circles. Rarely did he acknowledge that most of his conflicts with Zhou developed from his aversion to the institutional demands that suppressed individual creativity and compromised intellectual integrity. Even after twenty years of imprisonment, he was still perplexed by the logic of the linkage between his inability to work with Zhou and his aversion to the Party itself. Despite Hu Qiaomu's (1912–92) reminder that he needed to "make friends with the CCP as a whole"[82] and Zhou Enlai's criticism that he engaged with the CCP in the abstract, Hu insisted that Zhou was not the Party per se. Insistently, he "couldn't possibly dream of the fact that [his '300,000-Character Report'] would place him under suspicion of subverting the Party leadership."[83] For Hu, had his dissatisfaction with some Party members meant an effort to undermine the authority of the Party's leadership or even to plot against the Party, he would not have submitted his "300,000-Character Report" to Mao. After all, this report on "socialist realism and the socialist tradition of revolutionary practice" required Hu to confront forms of falsity and injustice even among left-wing writers.[84] Party membership was one-directional, and the relationship between an individual and the political organization was not reciprocal. Hu's distorted notion of this relationship continued a tradition of passionate commitment to criticism, of which Lu Xun was a monumental model and recourse.

IV

CRITICISM AS CONTEST

Only Mao Zedong's teaching is correct concerning theoretical questions.

—Zhou Enlai[1]

A different song!
Sing a different song—
Sing about man, sing about man and man,
sing about man and man and man.

—Lu Yuan[2]

While the 1930s was a time of remarkable cultural and intellectual dynamism, left-wing writers, artists, and critics in the 1940s were achieving significant success in establishing Marxism as the ruling ideology and becoming accustomed to the practice of accommodating humanistic conscience to the end of Maoist politics. In the years following the outbreak of the Second Sino-Japanese War, the CCP not only achieved political ascendancy over the Nationalist government but also built an ideological apparatus, and through it accredited an asymmetrical distribution of power within left-wing cultural circles. The Yan'an Forum on Literature and Art in 1942, notably, gave some writers and critics the channel and credentials to enter the inner circle of the CCP's structure of power. The institutional ascendency of some individuals, meanwhile, redefined the terms of the literary debates that took place in the 1930s, from a simple difference in opinion to a budding case of intellectual dissent.

This chapter will examine this structure of power—its formation, consolidation, and operation—in the discourse of left-wing literary criticism and in the circumstances defined by broader historical, social, and political forces. It will begin with a discussion of the Two-Slogan Debate that took place in Shanghai in 1936. Rather than presenting a detailed historical account of the debate,[3] the discussion will exemplify the triangular relationship of power between radical intellectuals, Marxism as a system of belief, and the mechanism of (pre)state institutional power. The debate, with developments characteristic of Chinese literati culture, began with some differences in views on literature, only to escalate into conflicts so unresolvable that it became, in Hu's words, "the number one heavy burden" on all participants in the debate.[4] This inseparable relationship between literature and politics, and the personal and the professional, played an even more significant role after the Yan'an Forum—an event in which Zhou found in Mao's authority an edifice that bolstered and rewarded his views on literature and art.

THE TWO-SLOGAN DEBATE

Hu's eventual clash with Mao's aesthetics was not an incidental case in which he was dissatisfied with specific cultural policies. As confirmed in his "300,000-Character Report," Hu ascribed his political marginalization to Zhou's politics above all and was reluctant to admit any real difference between himself and the Party. Indeed, Hu not only lived amid the Party's politicized aesthetics; he and his group of writers had, in a sense, absorbed into their being the nature of the Marxist politics of art and criticism they advocated. From Hu's point of view, Zhou utilized the Party's struggle against him for two reasons: first, "to offset the general discontent directed at the cultural leaders"; and second, to set him up as an enemy in the process of strengthening what he called "the Zhou rule of literary subjectivism and sectarianism."[5] The root of Zhou's recourse to using Mao Zedong Thought as political discourse, Hu observed, could be traced back to the 1930s; in his words, "Zhou wanted to 'avenge' the 'insult' of the Two-Slogan Debate."[6]

On June 1, 1936, Hu published an essay titled "What Do the Masses Demand of Literature?" that introduced the slogan "Mass Literature in the National Revolutionary War 民族革命战争的大众文学."[7] This act occasioned a renewed public debate on the slogan "National Defense Literature 国防文学" that Zhou had coined in response to the impending war with Japan just when it began to find general acceptance, turning the propagation of one slogan into a public debate over two. In Zhou's eyes, Hu's slogan prioritized literature's general pedagogical function over its national identity. It therefore contradicted the CCP's United Front policy—an ad hoc policy established in reaction to the Sino-Japanese War. Assuming the role of Zhou's follower and mouthpiece,[8] Xu Maoyong wrote, in a private letter to Lu Xun, that Hu's slogan was "harmful."[9] Xu's letter would have had little historical significance had it been kept within the domain of the personal. In the 1930s Republic, however, individual acts were spontaneously effaced by collective politics. In the left-wing circle, this effacement of Xu's individuality took place following a surprising operation. Lu Xun used his student's mostly good faith in maintaining their friendship to press claims for his (and Hu's) discursive space in the left-wing literary arena. On August 15, in the absence of "the author's consent,"[10] Lu Xun published Xu's letter along with "A Letter in Reply to Xu Maoyong and on the Anti-Japanese United Front" in *Writers Monthly*. The open reply, angrily toned, considered Xu an opponent rather than a former student and friend.[11]

Lu Xun's counterblast to Xu consisted of three parts. The first part accused Xu of sectarianism and engaging in a dirty business that would split and divide the revolutionary camp. Lu Xun aired his doubts about the Association of Chinese Writers and Artists, suspecting that it had a "strong tendency to sectarianism" and "features of a guild or a gang."[12] For Lu Xun, as it was also for Hu, unanimous support for the Anti-Japanese United Front, as a political choice, should not have blocked literature's general function of communicability and spiritual liberation. The second part of the reply explained the origin and meaning of the slogan "Mass Literature in the National Revolutionary War." The new slogan, which was the result of a meeting among Feng Xuefeng, Mao Dun, Hu, and Lu Xun, was not meant to oppose Zhou's "National Defense Literature" slogan; those who understood it as such were guilty of literary sectarianism. In an interview forty years after the debate, Zhou stated that "the mistake [of the Two-Slogan Debate] [lay] in sectarianism. Because 'Mass Literature in the National Revolutionary War' was put forward by Hu, we therefore argued with him."[13] In the final part, Lu Xun defended his three friends—Hu, Huang Yuan, and Ba Jin—without failing to blame Zhou, labeling him, along with Tian Han, Xia Yan, and Yang Hansheng, the gang of "four heavies 四条汉子."

After Lu Xun's open reply, Zhou understood for the first time that the slogan "Mass Literature in National Revolutionary War" was Lu Xun's idea; this understanding was powerful enough to silence him.[14] At the same time, Xu's letter intensified Lu Xun's ill feelings about Zhou, whom he satirically hailed as "our commander-in-chief" (on other occasions, also "director" and "foreman") who "shuts himself indoors" as he "orders others about."[15] After that, Lu Xun kept alive his suspicions about the Left-league and wanted to "wait and see" what would become of it.[16] In short, the two letters exposed to the public what had been hitherto kept in the dark.

Until the publication of the letters, conflicts within the Left-league were expressed through personal animosities and in the form of literary sectarianism. Even to Guo Moruo, who was then away from Shanghai studying in Japan, the Two-Slogan Debate came to him as "a real and serious 'civil war' " within left-wing literary circles.[17] By settling the debate with fame rather than reason, Lu Xun intensified the problem and thereby changed the nature of a debate that was by itself already a complicated one. As one critic assessed, "The Two-Slogan Debate [was] itself a game of chess. . . . The most unexpected move [was] that Lu Xun, in great anger, wrote in [his] sickbed [an open reply], and after that changed the course of the event."[18] Lu Xun's letter was devastating; to oppose Lu Xun would be to opt out from the center of left-wing politics and literary influence. In fact, Lu Xun's leadership role in the May Fourth Movement aside, the fact that Lu Xun cofounded the Left-league with the Party[19] was enough to change Zhou's course of career permanently. Zhou recalled:

> After Lu Xun openly criticized me, things became complicated. My life in Shanghai depended entirely on remunerations for my writing. . . . Just at that time . . . Yan'an sent a telegram recruiting literary and art workers. Therefore, people like Ai Siqi, He Ganzhi, and me left for Yan'an.[20]

History is replete with unpredictable twists. Upon arrival at Yan'an, Zhou became the first dean of the Lu Xun Academy of Arts and Literature, and he was one of the critical interpreters and advocators of Mao Zedong Thought after the Yan'an Forum. Whatever animosities were generated and condensed in the 1930s, they spilled out in the long 1940s, especially after 1949, when the power relationship between Hu and Zhou reversed. As Jin Ding recalled, "In 1937 . . . after the Left-league's dismissal, I met with some of the comrades from both sides of the debate and discovered that the incident had created some emotional estrangement that should not have existed."[21] After the event, the Hu-Zhou relationship reached an impasse. Hu declared, "It was well-known that in Yan'an, whenever Zhou mentioned Lu Xun in a speech, he would end up with an open denunciation of me."[22]

With the CCP's political ascendancy in the 1940s, to be critical of post-Yan'an Zhou meant to be critical of the Party.

After reading Hu's "300,000-Character Report," Mao Zedong concluded that Hu wanted to "purify the ranks of the emperor's closest counselors," as he became further distanced from Zhou and thereby the inner circle of the revolutionary camp's institutional power.[23] Even if, as Lin Mohan hoped to insist, the campaign series leading to Mao's persecution of Hu was "from the beginning to end led by the Party,"[24] criticism of Hu was no less the practical consequence of "a long-term conflict between Hu and Zhou concerning their views on literature and art."[25] Although there was a noticeable political difference between Zhou and Mao in terms of the way they labeled Hu's literary group—"Hu's small sect 胡风小集团" and "Hu's counterparty and counterrevolutionary clique 胡风反党反革命集团," respectively—there was a clear line of historical continuity between the two. As such, the Hu Incident was more of a politicized intellectual event than an ideological campaign.

IDEOLOGICAL COMMITMENT AND ITS LIMITS

The Two-Slogan Debate showed how the unwonted tendencies in Hu's concept of literary subjectivism could only be understood when placed against the background of some long-standing and unremitting *literary* conflicts turned personal *within* the left-wing camp. It is important to note that unlike some of the Marxist theorists who rose to power in the postrevolutionary 1950s and 1960s, Zhou was not any less severe than Hu about his literary Marxism. Zhou joined the CCP as a Marxist writer and immersed himself in the CCP's revolutionary cause as a matter of life and death. In his Shanghai years, criticized by Lu Xun and facing the risk of imprisonment and death, Zhou summoned enormous courage, for "participation in . . . left-wing literary campaigns was a grave matter. One risked one's life participating in those campaigns. . . . And many people died!," one of whom was his youngest son in 1945 after they followed the army to Fuping.[26] A conscientious Party member dedicated to the development of art and literature, Zhou made his name through a single-minded pursuit of revolutionary work. Zhang Guangnian considered him a man of "self-imposed discipline"—an ascetic who "had given his whole life to the Party" and with whom he shared "no conversations in which they spoke like friends" because "every day, Zhou either talked about work or criticized people. . . . He would only go to meetings, give speeches, study, and attend performances."[27] In his later years, despite suffering from pain and depression in the aftermath of a mental breakdown, Zhou "exhibited a kind of energy that no one, under a similar condition, could" as soon as he heard that the CCP was going to have a *zuotanhui* (座谈会 "symposium") on literature and art. Managing to "rise temporarily above illness," he asked, " 'What symposium?' His enunciation stopped being unclear. He no longer stammered. His smiles were no longer relaxing and peaceful."[28] "At that split second," Wang Meng, contemporary Chinese writer and the Nobel Prize nominee for 2000, recalled, "Zhou restored the solemn look and showed a high degree of alertness."[29] Whereas Zhou considered himself the "propagator," "interpreter," and "practitioner" of Mao Zedong Thought on literature and art,[30] he had also, for decades, been a literary writer and critic.

It might be of interest to add here that Hu demonstrated a comparable degree of alertness the moment he started talking about literature and art. In 1973, though already drenched in a world of "madness and complete fear" and "totally nonchalant to things including his meals," Hu "opened up his eyes and flashed out a beam of light" when Mei Zhi talked with him about the books Lu Xun had given him. As soon as Mei Zhi took out those books, "the lost soul was awakened! It resurrected!"[31] Like Zhou, Hu held on to his own set of aesthetic standards and measures, despite long years of imprisonment. In "A Brief Review," written in his sickbed in the 1970s, Hu reinstated his standards and rebuked that they were "too high": "That problem with my standards being too high was presumptuous. I have only been asking for genuine feelings. One needs to have real feelings . . . and genuine subjectivity. It is a matter of honesty, not ability."[32]

Hence, if Hu's commitment to the revolutionary cause and the CCP was total, Zhou's was no less severe. Ironically, it was due to this similar degree of commitment to the Chinese Revolution that Zhou and Hu became self-righteously indignant at each other. In 1980, half a century after the Two-Slogan Debate, at the hospital where Hu was being treated for hallucinations, Zhou conceded to Hu that "on the subject of literary theory, you are most profound."[33] This acknowledgment of Hu's critical intellect and depth, though genuine, expressed just half of what Zhou meant. Nie Gannu spoke of the other half: "[Zhou] had always been with the Party, while Hu was not."[34] This explained why, in the same meeting, Zhou also said, "We are old friends of fifty years. I have great respect for you. Whereas I have no unique talents, I have always been following the Party."[35] Dissatisfied with the "trend" of political rehabilitation during the 1980s, Zhou said, "At the moment: anyone who has passed away, or been rehabilitated, was right in the past. I am afraid this is not an exactly objective method of finding the truth."[36] In Zhou's judgment, Hu's political rehabilitation did not vindicate his concept of subjective idealism. In the Party's political language, subjective idealism, as opposed to Marxist historical materialism, considered sociohistorical conditions as forces that existed independently from the mind. From Hu's perspective, the degree to which a Marxist writer pronounced his political stance was a necessary but insufficient criterion for evaluating his work. Whereas Hu generally supported Zhou's assertion that Marxist writers must always stand by revolutionary politics, he also pointed out how ideological formalism masqueraded and alienated the role of judgment in critical consciousness. In Hu's experience, he had not only strived to be a Marxist theorist and practitioner, he was also eager to save the "passion of life" from sinking into the routine of a political reality that dazzled and desolated him. This accounted for his failure to make clear his political stance in his first written response to the "Talks"—an expected response the Party awaited for a long time; instead, he dwelled on the different roles literature and politics played in the Chinese Revolution, writing, "To abandon literature and art to politics is to disarm the cultural front."[37]

Both Zhou's muted assessment of Hu's historical position in the Chinese Revolution and Hu's quickstep from "abandonment" to "disarmament," from a deviation in method to a question about the distribution of power between literature and politics as two distinct revolutionary forces, are noteworthy. Zhou's unspeakable issue with Hu was that Hu was not with the Party despite both his Marxism and his perceptive literary theory; Hu, in turn, found Zhou's Marxist literary criticism substandard, as it abandoned literature and art and therefore was an ideological fraud. Meanwhile, both of these two left-wing comrades must have been aware that literature and politics were never opposed to each other in the revolutionary cause. Indeed, if literature and politics in 1940s China were separated, one could not establish the Hu Incident as an institutional, cultural, *and* political case. Hu had already chosen his political stance and declared his ideological outlook unambiguously in his 1930s debate with the "third man."

To set Hu and Zhou on two ends of a scale was not to weigh one against the other in terms of partisan loyalty or degree of ideological commitment, because these two individuals, and the literary views that they each advocated, had never for a moment been nonpartisan. Instead, it was to point out that their opposing literary politics were explicable only with reference to historical debates and developments that were an attempt to make literary trends tenable. More importantly, my effort was to establish Hu as a stakeholder of a literary modernity in which imagination and criticism remained in place to give strategic and subjective form to life.

Although Zhou and Hu both talked about the dialectic relationship between literary subjectivity and material reality,[38] they differed most on the use and place of the creative mind in the process. Hu elaborated on the concept of the "subjective combative spirit"—that is, the *result* of an original force of mind followed by repeated efforts to intensify and endure such a force with active participation in (proletarian) life. In a letter to Xiong Zimin, Hu spoke about one of the most important elements of the discourse on Chinese Marxism: material determination—the praxis that penetrated through an entirely theoretical framework of Marxist dialectics. Hu believed that ideological devotion must be traversed by a respect for and belief in what Heidegger calls *Dasein*, that is, in the factility and presentness of life, which *is* life and requires not an ideological articulation but a literary enactment of it and by virtue of it *for* itself. Thus, insofar as the writer communicates life and in the process brings the creative subjectivity to a language that commits to the enactment of life, she shall achieve an exceptional conflation of the theoretical conception of Marxism and the political practice of literature.

Against Hu's insistence that creative subjectivity and the search for the language of enactment constituted the basis of literary practice *throughout* the process of writing, Zhou argued that a writer's sense of political commitment was always already conversant with the subjectivity within—with the raison d'être of writing. Zhou, therefore, required all creative practices to start with an appropriate acknowledgment of the Marxist political stance and to end reiterating the CCP's cultural policies of the era. In his report given at the first National Congress of Literature and Art Workers on July 21, 1949, Zhou reviewed and instructed:

> For the sake of creating more profound literature, cultural workers need first to study politics, Marxist-Leninism, Mao Zedong Thought, and the basic policies of present times. It is impossible to represent life in cities and villages without knowledge of [the CCP's] policy. . . . In the new society under the absolute rule of new democracy . . . people [are] no longer politically naïve. . . . Instead, they [have] become conscious and organized; they work with specific purposes in mind. In other

> words, policies found[ed] their behavior. . . . Therefore, in the new age, once away from the policy's framework, one would not understand the basic pattern of people's way of life. Only when a cultural worker stands on a correct policy standpoint can he write about the characters' relationship, the way of life, mind-set, and fate, can his writings reflect the different classes' relationship and struggle, their habit of life, mind-set, and fate.[39]

Zhou's equation between literary subjectivity and political consciousness substantiated what he said in the 1930s: "Literature and art are themselves a certain form of politics."[40] Considering Zhou's instructions on literature and art's relationship to politics, there was little inconsistency between his conviction and what he, in his ascended role as the Party's cultural leader and Mao's mouthpiece, said to the audience at the second National Congress of Literature and Art Workers in 1953, reiterating the Party's cultural policy: "Literature and art should, of course, express the Party's policies. . . . In observing and describing life, writers must follow the Party and government policies."[41] Under Zhou's slogan of "National Defense Literature" in the Two-Slogan Debate and his advocation of Mao's "Talks" lay a common ground, which was a political continuity sustained by his genuine belief in the absolute need to answer the calls of the Party.

Whereas Hu believed that "literature and politics [were] two different paths leading to the same destination,"[42] Zhou asserted that "a revolutionary writer would never allow his/her spontaneous [sentiments] to define the development of literature."[43] In an essay written in the 1930s, Zhou made clear how a committed intellectual should translate her commitment into a practice that did not separate aesthetic form from revolutionary politics. For Zhou, "literature itself [was] an expression of politics."[44] Where Zhou differed from Hu and was similar to Mao was that Mao provided Zhou with the opportunity to see some of his personal views on literature and art translated into a standard cultural policy for practice on a national scale. One might even go further and argue that Mao derived his "Talks" in part from Zhou's views. Xiao Jun, whose aesthetic values were closer to Lu Xun's and in conflict with Zhou's, observed that "some of the ideas in the 'Talks' [were] almost the same as Zhou's."[45] Not coincidentally, some of the ideas about literature that Zhou conceived in the 1930s found their way into Mao's cultural policies in the 1940s. Mao said, for example:

> Party work in literature and art occupies a definite and assigned position in Party revolutionary work as a whole and is *subordinated* to the revolutionary tasks set by the Party in a given revolutionary period. Opposition to this arrangement is certain to lead to dualism or pluralism.[46]

Concerning the idea of literature as an expression of politics, Mao had the following to say: "What we demand is the unity of politics and art, the unity of content and form, the unity of revolutionary political content and the highest possible perfection of artistic form."[47] The affinity between Zhou and Mao's views on the relationship between literature and politics explains why, in part, Zhou, rather than Hu, rose as the spokesman for Mao Zedong Thought on literature and art after the Yan'an Forum, until his downfall at the beginning of the Cultural Revolution. Although he might not have been fully conscious of the influence his theory would have on the development of New Literature and art, Zhou's intuition knew that artistic work had to subscribe to the needs of the Party.

TOWARD A DISCOURSE OF MARXIST LITERATURE AND CRITICISM

The specific circumstances of the CCP's rise to power in the 1940s made it even more impossible to maintain literature as a vantage point of entry into the Chinese Revolution. In his remarks about the conditions under which left-wing writers emerged as an integral part of the Chinese Revolution, John Fairbank sketched the dramatic change in Hu's relationship with the CCP cultural cadres: "In the second half of 1943, the ineffectiveness of the GMD government became widely apparent. . . . To foreign observers, the left began to seem like a viable alternative. Jiang Jieshi as the symbol and forefront of the Nationalist regime had . . . lost the confidence and allegiance of China's literate leadership."[48] The primary sources of this overall sense of pessimism and distrust in the existing government were historical and situational. Both the Marco Polo Bridge Incident and the Nanjing Massacre brought the Republic to a state of near anarchy. Hunger and death were no longer just raw materials for fiction but burning realities about the bare necessities of life. A sense of sheer horror defined the tone of Ai Qing's "Beggars" (1939): "In the North / Beggars' unyielding eyes / Stare at you / They look at whatever you eat / And the way you pick your teeth with your nails."[49] Similarly, Jin Yi's "Survival" (1941) described a scene in which a starving painter used "the last bit of his energy" to record "the hunger of the children" with his "shaky hands" and "blurry eyes":

> He sees the same pair of hungry eyes / Looking at his paper / Looking at this life / Looking at the food in this life / And at the rough outline of a bold forehead—so broad that it bulges out / The hollow cheeks that used to be full and round / Make the chin a little sharp.[50]

In short, the series of historical events between the mid-1930s and the early 1940s sped up the process in which writers and intellectuals, who were until then "free-floating," became committed and "organic." In his memoir written nearly half a century later, Jia Zhifang recalled:

> Chinese intellectuals entered a different age since the beginning of the War of Resistance in 1937. They lost their furnished and clean studies and the leisure to conduct carefully thought-out research. They lost even the glory of being admired by the masses. . . . [They] could only roll and turn in filthy mud, struggle in dirty water, and live and understand life amid smoking bullets.[51]

In facing the brutalities of the war, the May Fourth intellectuals believed that a cultural revolution could change the wholly shattered world they found themselves in—but even a frail thought of it was considered an omen of an unavoidable catastrophe. As the lived brutalities of the war destroyed any sentiments of abstract romanticism left over from the May Fourth Movement, descriptions of how one experienced a feeling of utter feebleness in wartime abounded in the left-wing literary camp. Lu Ling's wartime existence, one dominated by a looming sense of isolation, cast doubt on the meaning of life if not survival. His novel *Children of the Rich* 財主底兒女們, first published in 1945, exemplified this self-conscious adoption of a narrative art highly reflective of the literary subject's uneasy feelings about being deflected or held in place by the circumstances in which he wrote and struggled to survive. "Those who escape to the deserted wilderness are completely isolated from the world."[52] "On this horrible journey, they know neither from whence they come nor to where they will be going."[53] In Jia Zhifang's assessment, *Children of the Rich* was an "immortal epic" that accurately captured “the bitterness of the age.”[54] Jia’s novel, titled *Life*, depicted the feeling of apprehension and envisaged the future of China in desperate terms: “I have been forgotten and abandoned by the life I have lived. . . . Sometimes I genuinely don’t know whether I have ever had a past. I seem now to be living in a bizarre world, like a baby.”[55]

In his essay “From the Present to the Future,” Hu made a general but judgmental comment on the literature of the 1940s, concluding that the wartime literature “had already taken root in the flesh-and-blood of real life.”[56] This assessment revealed not just how the lived experience of war impinged on writers’ consciousness; it also took note of the way “real life” aggressively altered the knowledge of the creative subject that was an inevitable part of the world. Indeed, in the face of the populist espousal of nationalist sentiment, the “free” intellectuals of the 1920s, fearing that they would be left in “the dustbin of history,”[57] gravitated toward the CCP. After the GMD’s secret agents assassinated Wen Yiduo in 1946, Zhu Ziqing said to his wife,

> From now on, there is no middle way. We need to see clearly the road and proceed bravely onward. It is not easy. We are aging and might not walk as quickly as the young, but we must walk, and walk at a forceful pace, albeit slowly.[58]

Under the influence of popular anti-imperialist sentiment, democracy as a vision and goal of individual critical conscience lost its appeal to many. Writers in the new cultural movement began to talk about collective goals in practical terms: “It is until now that I can see that man, as a man, is bound by fate to walk along a road covered with blood.”[59] This was a cry from those who “had experienced and come out of disillusions”;[60] a reflection of the psychological path of those who ultimately chose the Chinese Revolution as a way to confront and disrupt life.

Much as the modern Chinese intellectuals were fearful of being forgotten by history, they translated their nationalism into an active hostility against foreign imperialism; their patriotism reached a new height and found a new channel of expression in 1937. He Jiaqi, in Mao Dun’s *The First Stage of a Story* (1938), had the strength to live on after the Japanese occupation of Shanghai in 1937.[61] Huang Menghua, in Li Guangtian’s *Gravitation,* was able to move on with her journey after losing her husband in the so-called freedom zone of the GMD-controlled areas.[62] Like their characters, these writers had hope. The poet Tian Jian was able to keep living under the brutal conditions because he found a place at "the heart of the motherland" where "the water [was] sweet" and "the earth fragrant."[63] Evidently, there remained a good deal of romanticism in the Yan'an pilgrims. As Wang Shiwei pointed out in "Wild Lilies," "It was . . . in the spirit of being a martyr to the revolutionary cause"[64] that many students left for "the city of their heart."[65]

Romanticism, apparent among the left-wingers in the 1940s, was a typical response to the grim realities of life and was characterized by the logic of practical reason. It was, as Zhou aptly called it, "a revolutionary romanticism."[66] Yan'an, then held as "that place," that "hope out there," and that "place of the heart," achieved a status fundamentally different from the more abstract ideals that the May Fourth intellectuals sought.[67] In the minds of the intellectuals who escaped to and found sanctuary in the capital of the Chinese Revolution, the city was a "flesh-and-blood" reality, the epitome of a "perfect society," a space of conscious action and free thinking.[68] Chen Xuezhao, for example, went to Yan'an "with passionate respect for the CCP and Chairman Mao Zedong and a strong nationalist feeling."[69] It occurred to him then that "only the CCP was determined and honest" in fighting against the Japanese, that "only the CCP could save China."[70] As he volunteered to fight in the war under the leadership of the CCP, he was "prepared to sacrifice without second thoughts."[71]

The revolutionary romanticism of these writers and critics owed much to the CCP's ideological pragmaticism, which emphasized the practicality of intellectual power and de-emphasized the grandeur of Enlightenment ideals, providing the ground on which individuals of different political orientations and literary beliefs achieved the expression of their national consciousness. It was an enabling means through which a race and culture struggling toward self-consciousness established once and for all a distinctively national identity that promised collective survival, renewal, and strength. The novelists, poets, critics, and intellectuals who went to Yan'an finally converged in the discourse of Chinese socialism, even if absoluteness and ultimacy were exempt from the scrutiny of the intellect. When asked how he completed "the arduous long and lonely journey," He Qifang typically answered, "It was for [the pursuit of] beauty, understanding, and sacrifice for love" that "I finished that . . . journey, the end of which was Yan'an."[72] Yan'an was, for He, as it was for most Chinese writers of his generation, a means of catharsis; it was a place where hopes converged, at once concrete and abstract, real and surreal. Some called Yan'an a "final destination," while others considered it a "moral standard."[73]

THE DYNAMICS OF IDEOLOGICAL POWER: THE YAN'AN FORUM

Although the historical circumstances and cultural climate in the late 1930s and early 1940s were forces peculiar to the emergence of "socialist realist art" as the threshold of political engagement, the Sino-Japanese War only facilitated the CCP's task of ideological propaganda; it alone could not have built a "cultural army." Equally as important as Mao's strategy in seizing the historical opportunity to appropriate creative and critical forces was the continuous effort of the artists, writers, and intellectuals to stand watch. In a formal sense, the general climate favored the course of aesthetic politicization, but that was naïve, as it could not have achieved an ever homogeneous and coercive "truth" of Marxist criticism, which grew out of the situation within the left-wing camp itself. The true dialogic process of the CCP's aesthetic politicization and the Yan'an intellectuals' political rendering unfolded throughout 1942. At that time, the writers who traveled to Yan'an so valued the socialist faith that they began to shift the emphasis of their social critique from the GMD to the CCP. Yan'an might have been a most romantic place, but the daily operation of it could be quite unromantic; it was scarcely a fit object for abstract emulation. The Yan'an pilgrims, such as Ding Ling and Wang Shiwei, vocalized their criticism of Yan'an in their "expository essays" "Thoughts on March Eighth" and "Wild Lilies," respectively. These essays, along with Xiao Jun's "On Comrades' 'Love' and 'Patience,'" went so far as to provide the GMD with documents to appropriate the Marxists against the Marxists.[74]

As a strategic response to the situation, Mao advocated the policy of "better troops and simpler administration" that in effect sought to reorganize structural and institutional leadership, with Kang Sheng (1898–1975), then head of the CCP's security and intelligence chief apparatus, putting into place the infamous "rectification campaign."[75] Mao made it clear that his "cultural army" would follow a guiding principle in its use of criticism, and that the time to unify the different strands of thought in Yan'an had come. Significantly, with the assistance of Hu Qiaomu, Mao sought views on literature and art from a group of writers headed by Zhou Yang—Cao Baohua, Chen Huangmei, He Qifang, Liu Baiyu, Yan Wenjing, and Zhou Libo—who preferred to write articles that celebrated "the brightness" of Yan'an over the Ding Ling type of "essays" that "expose[d] the dark."[76]

On May 2, 1942, the CCP's Central Committee conducted the Yan'an Forum on Literature and Art, in which Mao gave two speeches, with the first one setting the tone for the Forum and the second concluding the Forum on May 23. Notwithstanding his claim to be "a layman in matters of culture,"[77] Mao used his power to formulate, formalize, and implement a cultural policy; his Yan'an speeches had a direct and lasting impact on the development of Chinese Marxist literary criticism. A central issue Mao sought to address at the Forum was an old one debated between Hu and Zhou in the 1930s: the place and function of literature in the institution of revolutionary politics. Though it was theoretically uncomplicated, this was a question so politically pertinent and fundamental that Mao took it as the basis on which to unify thoughts. His position was clear: art and literature should serve the Party's overall objective, which at the time that he gave the "Talks" was to achieve ultimate military victory and to establish a socialist state that he would govern.

Mao had no qualms about bringing to the forefront the strategic aspect of the question of how writers and intellectuals could help accelerate the process of the Party's final victory. He needed a consensus about the propaganda function of art and literature and through such consensus to achieve homogeneity among different factions in the left-wing camp. He began his opening speech at the Yan'an Forum thus:

> Comrades! You have been invited to this forum today to exchange ideas and examine the relationship between work in the literary and artistic fields and revolutionary work in general. Our aim is to ensure that revolutionary literature and art follow the correct path of development and provide better help to other revolutionary work in facilitating the overthrow of our national enemy and the accomplishment of the task of national liberation.[78]

As Mao was concerned with policy matters and immediate political needs, he said little about literature and art per se. Instead, he underlined the usefulness of literature and attended to questions about how the creative and critical impetus could align with the CCP's revolutionary politics and become its instrument. Reducing New Literature to a form of national consciousness in his speech, Mao declared that New Literature "at its present stage" was "an anti-imperialist, anti-feudal culture of the popular masses under the leadership of the proletariat."[79] Concerning the artistic form, Mao argued that since "rich deposits of literature and art . . . exist in popular life itself," the "most serious and central task [of literature] in regard to the people . . . is initially the work of reaching a wider audience rather than raising [the artistic] standard."[80] Without doubt, Mao's theory was a straightforward reduction of a complex historical materialist formulation: his politics were populist, his aesthetics low-brow, and his ideology reactively nationalistic. It was shaped by, on the one side, a consciousness of the importance of a dominant peasantry population; on the other, his historical knowledge. The evaluation of the masses as the leading force of the revolution was primarily a practical matter of defining and constructing a political identity for the CCP's cultural work following the revolutionary politics of the early 1940s.

As Mao adopted a high-handed approach to individual will and independence of mind, he successfully mounted a critique of intellectual liberalism for its advocacy of a thorough Westernization of aesthetic theory and its elitist tendency to isolate intellectuals from the masses. The critical procedure was to concentrate on the distance between an abstract discussion of culture and a concrete social reality. It was to show samples of literature and art that were apathetic to the masses and to claim that the petty-bourgeois standpoint was what separated their authors from the pressure of the masses and the unique problems of China. According to Mao, some artists and poets had adopted a petty-bourgeoisie standpoint with a naïveté that they could bring about a thoroughly Westernized China, which would alienate the masses, particularly the illiterate peasantry. Given the social reality unique to China, Mao argued, it was of paramount importance that writers and artists realigned their sensitivity to the Chinese masses and surrendered their freedom to the political configuration of the Party to achieve a complete identification with the masses. To be a writer or an artist was to be popular, but in succeeding, the writer and the artist were no longer individual creators of aesthetic form. In the placement of a formularized dialectic between revolutionary literature and sympathy and revolutionary practice and life, one felt the grave portent of the relationship between the would-be CCP state and its "cultural workers."

On November 19, 1943, on the seventh anniversary of Lu Xun's death, *Liberation Daily* published the two speeches Mao gave at the Yan'an Forum a year earlier, under the title "Talks at the Yan'an Forum on Literature and Art." According to Li Xin, then the editor of the literary section of *Liberation Daily*, the "Talks" were first mentioned in the newspaper on March 13, 1943, more than six months before their appearance in print. The production of the full-text version of the "Talks" was inseparable from the efforts of Hu Qiaomu, then secretary to Mao.[81]

Ideological indoctrination is dialectical insofar as the subjects interpolated lend themselves to the ideology in question. Göran Therborn was right in arguing *against* the notion of ideology as an unconscious belief: "The operation of ideology in human life basically involves the constitution and patterning of how human beings live their lives as *conscious*, reflecting *initiators* of acts in a structured, meaningful world. Ideology operates as discourse, addressing or . . . interpolating human beings as subjects."[82] For Therborn, therefore, ideology functioned to accomplish two major tasks: the constitution and subjection of subjects. Therborn suggested that there was a curious interplay between subjects and ideology: as ideology subjects individuals to its rule, it also constructs their subjectivities. In other words, ideology functions *through* human beings as agents, and social structures are mostly a matter of a subject's choice based on a collective will.

Indeed, the Yan'an Forum's goal to establish literature as a mechanism of power did not incapacitate the intellectuals; instead, it engaged the appalling compliance of what Mark Lilla called the "reckless mind"[83]—the agent of Western totalitarianism. As the revolutionary writers gaped at Marxism as a solution to national and historical problems, they were also oiling the wheels of ideological apparatuses and institutions, activating the medium through which ideology pursued its power.[84] Mao's populist politics and his detailed instructions on how literary intellectuals could participate in the Party's political action allowed the "Talks" to stand up to any intellectual challenges. Mao managed to place writers and intellectuals under the Party's leadership not just through his authority and political power but also by working on their subjectivities and historical-national consciousness. In following their revolutionary desires and values, the literary intellectuals became victims of their own god.

While the Yan'an Forum aimed to build a cultural army, its effectiveness depended on the reciprocal action of its participants. First, Mao's "Talks" addressed some of the most prominent common concerns of the time. How would literature and art "fit . . . into the whole revolutionary machine as a component part?"; how would they "operate as powerful weapons" for "attacking and destroying the enemy?"; and how would they "help the people fight the enemy with one heart and one mind?"[85] These were questions that not only Mao asked but also left-wing and revolutionary writers asked, such as Qu Qiubai, Mao Dun, Zhou Yang, and even Hu. Mao's answer turned them into a set of "must-be-solved problems" inherent in "the problems of the class stand of the writers and artists, their attitude, their audience, their work and their study."[86] Consequently, the literary intellectuals' concerns about how they could participate in the Chinese Revolution also had to find answers in the instruction that "cultural workers" must "keep to the stand of the Party" and "serve the masses of the people."[87]

Second, whether revolutionary writers as a class could provide a prophetic vision of change depended on whether they could form a cohesive political community, which had much to do with the cultivation of a critical space in close proximity to the ideological terrain. Almost all of the intellectuals and writers at the conference went to Yan'an based on their will to live for a political ideal; they gave up individuality for a vision of China and national liberation. Therefore, Mao's mechanistic formulation of literature and art as an experience of political reality and a political transposition of humanity was more than readily accepted by the intellectuals and writers and became a crucial constitutive element in the formation of their historical place and social identity. In this sense, Mao's argument that intellectuals should reform their thoughts and learn from the masses was a nonargument. Mao's principles of self-criticism and self-abnegation were concrete steps for the revolutionary intellectuals who wanted to participate in the course of national reform to a degree no less than that of their social counterparts.

To emphasize the Marxist intellectuals' agency within Mao's discourse on literature and art was not to de-emphasize the importance of using (pre) state ideological coercion on the individual. There was no doubt that the Yan'an Forum and the "Talks" were an organized attempt to form a power establishment in the cultural sphere.[88] It would be hard to assess the "success" of the Yan'an Forum and "Talks" today without wondering what possessed the intellectuals there to dish out such political enthusiasm and support as they listened to Mao. The point of my analysis of the interaction between (pre)state ideological power and intellectual self-subjugation is that those who ruled exploited the techniques of the self for the sake of disciplining an individual thoroughly. Mao's audience might have resisted at a personal level any vulgarization of their creative and intellectual activities. Still, their nationalism and national consciousness, interpreted and militarized by Mao, was too overwhelming for them to consider any possible conflicts that might arise between their critical conscience and the Party's political adventure.

INTELLECTUALS IN POWER

The differences between Zhou and Hu in terms of their vision of modern Chinese literature acquired a political significance at a different level in the wake of 1942. At a time when the Yan'an writers were celebrating the finding of a guiding principle for the development of Marxist literary and critical practices, Hu warned against the arrival of a totalitarian constitution that would abandon the entire May Fourth intervention in Chinese modernity. Revolutionary writers and critics, Hu insisted, needed room for the strength of passion in their work.[89] And since, for him, it was the critical and subjective aspects of Marxism and the forces of the mind—imagination and empathy—that held necessary power for the Chinese Revolution, the establishment of a cultural policy that aggrandized power seemed, inevitably, to be an effort of modernization in decline. Given the conflicts between the Yan'an writers and their relative positions within the CCP's structure of power, Hu found their attitude toward Mao's "Talks" and politics more troubling than the "Talks" themselves: "The most difficult question at present is the way critics turn the 'Talks' into a 'totem.' Perhaps, what matters is not so much the 'Talks' themselves but rather the increasingly objectionable ways some stupid and malicious people do things."[90] Moreover, those "stupid and malicious people" were in a position to hamper the development of socialist realism:

> Those theorists who chant the relationship between literature and politics understand politics as some high-handed concepts or power. They attempt to cut off from life the literature that has already taken root in the flesh-and-blood of real life and to turn it into paper flowers in a reception hall, into some listless and soulless decorations on a walking corpse.[91]

Indeed, so many of the Marxist critics and writers exposed the bureaucratic corruption, capitalist exploitation, and national crisis that marked the period of the Chinese Revolution under the GMD. But we must learn to single out the authentic emancipatory impulse of Marxist politics from the inferred power interests that channeled away at least part of that impulse toward a personal quest for recognition, control, and power. In the second part of the "300,000-Character Report," Hu recalled his profound disappointment with some left-wing writers active in the 1940s, who, in Hu's judgment, subjected themselves to "different forms of formulism and abstract generalization."[92] Their writings were "removed from life":[93]

> This situation has created discontent and fear everywhere and has made all writers, without exception, feel frustrated. . . . Encouraged by the success of the Revolution, and engaged with struggles

> on different fronts, many writers manage to keep up with their efforts to different degrees. . . . However, if we consider [what has been achieved] with reference to the historical demands of the time, and comparatively with what might have been achieved . . . the whole literary front now appear[s] to be in a state of confusion and depression. In this great age of the Revolution . . . our literary front is nonetheless gloomy.[94]

By focusing his criticism on a few cultural bureaucrats who attempted to express themselves in preemptory and authoritative terms and to make the "Talks" totemic, Hu mounted a double-edged criticism against Mao's cultural policy and its advocates' self-destroying practices. Such practices Hu encountered not only in Mao's "sovereign rights" but also in those "subjects in the reciprocal relations" and in their "multiple subjugations" that functioned within the political body.[95] If Zhou's political realism was an essential factor in his rise after the Yan'an Forum, the "Talks" were the CCP's verdict on the Two-Slogan Debate in 1936. As Mao reinforced the importance of considering the question of literature and art in the light of the "actual" and "undeniable" facts, he drove home the point that literature must subscribe to politics and thus rejected Lu Xun's (and Hu's) idea that literature's historical function was mass enlightenment.

On the one side, there were writers such as Hu who chose to stay in the GMD-controlled areas, functioning as fellow travelers of the CCP at a place distanced from the gyre of power. Owing to their geographical distance from Yan'an, these writers were marginalized, even if they were then not fully conscious of the implications of their marginalization. On the other side, there were Yan'an writers like Zhou who were Party cultural leaders working within the structure of power to consolidate and appropriate institutional power. As an entourage of power-agents and power-executives, they were the bridge between literature and political authority—a role that they would continue to play, successfully or not, during China's continuous journey to state socialism.

The new power relationship between the two groups of Marxist writers would soon be made clear by the Propaganda Department in its intervention in the publication of a series of essays in Chongqing. In the period between the delivery of the "Talks" in May 1942 and its publication and circulation as a policy document on November 19 the following year, a group of writers in Chongqing, including Qiao Guanhua, Chen Jiakang, and

Li Xiang, published a series of essays. It was clear that these writers, often referred to collectively as the "scholars clique" sympathetic to Hu's literary views, were writing in support of Yan'an's call to fight against the theoretical dogmatism of Marxism-Leninism, or what Mao called the Wang Ming brand of subjectivism. Yet partly because of their geographical and temporal distance from Yan'an and partly because of their intellectual proclivities, these scholars-clique writers were unable to grasp the spirit and intended purpose of the Yan'an rectification campaign. In their response, which considered the Yan'an rectification movement a campaign against dogmatism in general, almost all rejected Mao's quest for a national identity in the course of building Chinese socialism. They wrongly used dogmatism as a point of entry into the critics' rejection of traditional Chinese culture. Like Hu, the scholars-clique writers were followers of the May Fourth antitradition spirit. Li Xiang, for example, made clear his conviction in the May Fourth spirit of antitraditionalism and his opposition to old artistic and literary forms:

> [If] what is important is not [literary] form but content, then we can say that New Literature of the last twenty years has, to a substantial extent, reflected the aspirations, emotions, and life of the Chinese people and has brought to the cultural life of the nation some novelty. . . . Meanwhile, we cannot but confess that it has at the same time inherited the bad influence of our national [cultural] heritage.[96]

These views provoked a critical response from the Propaganda Department. A telegram sent to Dong Biwu on November 22, 1943, three days after the publication of the "Talks" in *Liberation Daily*, stated, "The ideological struggle in the GMD-controlled areas should not be focused on the Party's internal self-criticism but the criticism of prominent reactionary capitalists. . . . Now *New China* and *The Masses* have not yet studied seriously 'Mao Zedong Thought' and published many erroneous things that are a result of their fantasies. . . . They should be corrected."[97] The practice of the CCP's cultural policy after the publication of Mao's "Talks" did not tolerate fantasies for it aimed to establish in the shortest time possible a cultural army that could spontaneously, without any hesitancy, respond to the Party's needs and demands. Half a century later, Shu Wu (1922–2009) explained how literary views that fell short of the Party's expectations were considered devious and thus erroneous:

> At that time there was a common understanding between Chen Jiakang's group [the "scholars clique"] and Hu. . . . As I see it, the kind of subjectivism fought against in Yan'an referred to the practice of imposing upon China the Soviet experience, of which Wang Ming was the representative. The sort of subjectivism opposed by Hu was concerned with literature, that is, with the [Marxist writers'] tendency to adhere blindly to "ideology" and "politics" and thereby forgo aesthetic principles in literary practice.[98]

Therefore, Hu and Chen Jiakang, in missing the point of the Yan'an campaign against Wang Ming, were "not acting in line with Yan'an."[99]

A crucial aspect of the Yan'an experience, as David Apter and Tony Saich observed, was the formation of an "instructional community" in which "[the 'Talks'] and their study" became "the basis of exegetical bonding."[100] After the "Talks," Hu felt the coming of an elite paternalism that put him on the defensive. He found it impossible, for example, to engage in any intellectual discussions with He Qifang on equal terms. Upon hearing He's report on the Yan'an Forum in Chongqing in 1944, Hu recognized the hierarchical relationship between the Yan'an writers and the rear-area writers immediately, as well as the political power implied in He's role as an angel descending from the Holy Land to the nonliberated areas. Hu described in his "300,000-Character Report" the general response to He's and Liu Baiyu's "sharing" of their Yan'an experience:

> Comrade He used himself as an example [of a successfully reformed writer] in his report on the thought-reform movement in Yan'an. He left people with a wrong impression that he was arrogant and simple-minded. . . . The way he carried himself made people feel that he had come out of his thought reform and was now an authentic proletarian. Right after the meeting, some said: he has finished his reform in such a short time! He has now come to reform us! Even Comrade Feng Xuefeng retorted, "Damn him! Where was he when we were in the revolution?"[101]

For Hu, Marxism, like all ideologies, was potentially both conducive and threatening to writers' subjectivity. The individual, in the process of becoming committed and acquiring his identity as a Marxist, Hu observed, "always gains and loses something at the same time. . . . What is important is the little that one can do, that one can contribute."[102] Consider the following lines that Hu wrote in 1944 in an attempt to calm Shu Wu, who responded in alarm to the Party's huge ideological machine against the "scholars clique";[103] Hu spoke of the defense of critical consciousness and the sacrifice of personal freedom or even life as two sides of the same coin:

> You are shocked only because you lack experience. These things happen regularly. . . . We cannot tolerate what others have tolerated. . . . Consequently, from a marginalized position, we might start doubting ourselves. . . . Even those radical friends [left-wing and revolutionary writers] . . . may misunderstand me. . . . If we do not want to trim the sails to the [political] wind or change course for convenience, we would be unlikely to work in favorable circumstances.[104]

Hu was conscientiousness personified. His frustration over his limitations in averting the degeneration of the Marxist critical community, from an organic community to an ideological bloc, not only deepened his perception of the importance of his own beliefs and struggles but also added to the moral weight of his life as a kind of prophet crucified for some self-imposed responsibilities. Hu's consciousness of his role and function as a Marxist intellectual compelled him to make grave moves and decisions. As discussed in chapter III, there was a delicate but irreducible difference between Marxism as a theory and Marxism as an ideological stance, the former meaning the assertion and practice of Communism as a conscious choice of position that entailed moral and personal responsibilities, and the latter meaning a dramatic performance of a world outlook. This difference produced two types of Marxists, each with different attitudes toward their functions in historical processes. For Hu, because literary practices were the mediation through which a writer engaged with Marxism, and because literature "[stood] in a place higher than life" and "ha[d] a power that pushe[d] life forward,"[105] the choice of Marxism was ultimately internalized and ethical, one in which the writer bore personal responsibilities. For Hu, to accept the instructional and political effectiveness of art and literature did not answer the question of how literature was enriched and authenticated by its political value and its impact on social movements. The Marxist literary intellectual, typically, sought communion with politics without neglecting his commitment to moral aesthetics.

In short, during the 1942 Yan'an rectification movement, ideological struggles against the intellectuals and their subjectivism threatened to extinguish the May Fourth spirit. Against this background, Hu's continuous defense of the tradition of intellectual enlightenment that Lu Xun represented[106] only quickened the coming into being of a political environment in which intellectuals sought to form a vital class but eventually failed to overcome or take full political power. The Yan'an Forum was the beginning point of the CCP's intellectual despotism. The publication of the "Talks," moreover, established both the leadership of Mao in the domain of literature and art and a manifesto that inscribed a relation of domination.

Without being too teleologically deterministic, I would argue that the publication of Mao's "Talks" in 1943 had already predetermined the Hu Incident in 1955. The Hu Incident, which spanned across two sovereign and political eras, manifested best the complex way intellectuals of the 1940s negotiated and collaborated with political power to produce Marxist literary criticism as a monochronic discourse. The Yan'an writers were more than bearers of the CCP's cultural politics and policies. The thought control in Mao's regime started with their submission to a ruling ideology of literature and art, which evolved into a systematic organization of intellectual power that wreaked great terror and havoc during the second half of the twentieth century. After the Yan'an Forum and the publication of the "Talks," the activities of and related to literature and criticism *were* the CCP's political life and the players of these activities a vital part of the Party's leadership machine.

Hu's fate became entangled in a network of power that left nobody free. The major critical campaigns against Hu's theory of literary subjectivism that took place before and after the establishment of the PRC, for example, documented the different stages in the CCP's continuing efforts to centralize its control over literature and art and portrayed Marxists as the embodiment of state ideology. As the coming chapters will show, all critics of Hu in the late 1940s and early 1950s—Zhou, He, Lin, and Shao Quanlin—came from Yan'an, and all of them occupied essential positions within the CCP's structure of power in 1955. These critics represented a model of state power and contributed to Mao's interest in Hu. In their criticism of Hu, these Yan'an writers assumed the role of Mao's spokespersons to interpolate Hu and to execute a procedure parallel to the one Mao used on them in 1942. Through thought reform, these Marxist critics transformed themselves into subjects of the CCP's ideological apparatus, occupying a position where they both submitted to and were enabled to exercise ideological power. In that sense, the Yan'an Forum conscripted a cultural army whose power emerged from the ashes of "devious" views.

V

THE PROBLEMATICS OF LITERARY SUBJECTIVISM

> What I have done is only to have said a few more words for the intellectuals.
>
> —Hu Feng[1]

> Even though ninety-nine percent of what you've said is correct, it would topple over, and be all wrong, if you're wrong on one vital point.
>
> —Zhou Yang[2]

As the previous chapter has shown, the Civil War period marked the transitional fighting ground between two camps within left-wing circles historically. One camp, represented by the Yan'an writers and artists, assumed the general principle that an extensive grasp of Maoist Marxism was a necessary qualification for building New Literature in the 1940s. Consequently, what had been an era of intellectual combativeness, tenacity, and willfulness became impoverished as the Yan'an repercussion abrogated the condition of freedom. The critical and imaginative intellectuals became absorbed within a structure of political power, and the different ways in which they adhered to the will of that power structure stigmatized their political identity. Against this background of the CCP's dominance in terms of its pragmatic view of the Civil War, this chapter will attempt to describe the problematics of Hu's revolutionary praxis via a theoretical point of departure: literary subjectivism. The chapter will discuss why, under the increasing fear of cultural and critical terror, some literary concepts that Hu held were of historical value and significance.

For one thing, to insist on the importance of moral conscience against the moment-to-moment demands of the collective that precluded human subjectivity was to risk becoming an object of Mao's persecution. Hu's literary subjectivism, in particular, his concept of "subjective combative spirit," had both practical importance at personal and social levels and theoretical ramifications, and as such, was key to understanding the Chinese socialist path. Hu singled out the concept as the one criterion to assess a poet's ability to develop a consciousness of her position when acting as an agent of socialist change. As practice, he described "subjective combative spirit" somewhat romantically as the committed writer's ability to command human imagination in lived experience, holding literary practice as the point of entry into Chinese national reform. In this sense, Hu and his associate writers found in poetry and revolution an extricable union in which the ethics of the one became the foundation of the other, while regarding such a union as self-motivated and accountable.

When Mei Zhi, after ten years of imposed separation, was finally allowed to visit the imprisoned Hu in 1965, the Party instructed her to help Hu "intensify his thought-reform" and "examine his idealist literary thought."[3] In response, Hu insisted, with suppressed anger, that the Party should not have asked Mei Zhi to intervene because his concept of aesthetic subjectivism was a "dead-knot" that he "could not untangle."[4] Over the years, despite well-meaning advice from his wife, friends, and some Party cadres, Hu feigned that he was at a loss for ways to correct his theory of literary subjectivism, suggesting that it be treated best as an imposture of an impossible "problematic." "He did not know whether the problem lies in his 'theory' or 'attitude.' Perhaps, both were problematic, but he did not know which one was more seriously wrong," recalled Lu Yuan, rationalizing Hu's resistance to understanding his problems so that he might avoid political and personal calamity.[5] Even in the heat of 1967, when the Public Security Department asked Hu to reach into his soul and expose, criticize, and accuse his literary-political enemies, Hu said,

> I must maintain my own opinion. . . . Zhou Yang has been dragged out before the masses, but I don't feel like applauding. Theories of art and literature are a grave issue. They should be under scrutiny through a free discussion and [are] irresolvable by mass repudiation.[6]

However, how that tension between literature and politics eventually became a "dead-knot" for Hu requires some explanation. Under what circumstances did Hu insist so much on literary subjectivism, which led to entangling himself in a series of irreconcilable combats with the Party's cultural representatives? There were even occasions in which Hu played the role of a political dunderhead rather than modify his literary theory. Note well that Hu was never politically naïve about literature's political function, as he understood the structure of power that defined the relationship between literature and politics; moreover, he was especially politically sensitive.[7] At times Hu was even boastful about his political foresight, claiming that he could court the Party's cultural policy. A crude way of putting this "talent" of Hu is to use his words: "I know just by the smell of the air when it's going to rain."[8] Ironically, it was Mao who perhaps understood Hu most in this respect. Among his numerous comments on the correspondences between Hu and his followers was one about a letter that Zhang Zhongxiao, "the youngest and yet the most 'counterrevolutionary' among the leading members of the Hu group,"[9] wrote to Hu on July 27, 1950. Mao wrote:

> [Zhang] has a pretty good counterrevolutionary nose and outmatches many in our revolutionary ranks, including a number of Communists, in the level of class consciousness and keenness of political sense of smell. Compared with men of the Hu clique, many of our own people are vastly inferior in these respects. . . . If there is anything positive the Hu clique can offer, it is that through the present soul-stirring struggle we shall increase our own political consciousness and sensitivity.[10]

Some virtues are better tackled as disguised weaknesses. The virtue of critical tenacity posed a problem to both Hu and the Party. The revolutionary critic was herself that problem; this was because, summoned only by critical consciousness, she infinitely but incoherently entangled herself with dominant discourses. As a critic, Hu evinced a brand of intellectuality akin to Gramsci's description of the organic intellectual—an individual *forever* maintaining the generality of the intellect despite her specific consent to a certain political agenda's appropriation of intellectuality. In this regard, Hu represented the pessimism of the critical intellect who was anxious but not fearful in the very core of the Yan'an writers' act of domination. His blindness to what the Party had identified as problematic became revealing in his innate struggle for self-realization as a critic in the Gramscian sense.

THE "SUBJECTIVE COMBATIVE SPIRIT"

Hu could not have been heedless of the need for political pragmatism,[11]and his literary theory was a branch of Mao's mythology of the intellectual's role in the socialist process. Still, he faced a classic dilemma in the Marxist history of revolutionary praxis: specifically, between Mao's rationalizations of the intellectual's ways of relating to the socialist revolution and the critical consciousness of the intellectual. The latter, by dint of the force of passionate thinking, attempted to simultaneously secure and test doctrines and often did so at the risk of losing one's foothold in the ideological apparatus to come. Perhaps Hu's views on literature and art were only a scapegoat and persona of a more fundamental and profound "problem" lodged in the man himself. Hu Sheng may have been correct in his review of the short stories of Lu Ling, who had been "profoundly influenced by Hu,"[12] saying "this writer has too much of subjectivism."[13]

When considered in the longer historical view of the Chinese Revolution, Hu's notion of the "subjective combative spirit" was a weapon of the mind in the moment of precipitate politics and generally an expression of dissatisfaction with the Yan'an critical paradigm. Perhaps, short of a better, more pragmatic act, the notion was even a placeholder standing in for his resentment at having the necessity of political power forced upon him. In this sense, the "subjective combative spirit" was a masked critical position; it worked toward the direction of performing intellectual work as human's capacity for imagination and critical courage, as an action of the human mind capable of creating new beginnings through literature and criticism and in so doing not bounded to the commands or threat of conformity. To advocate the role of the writer's subjectivity in the creative process was to strive to engage and expand the intrinsic uniqueness of human creativity through an affirmation of a future that was sustained and imagined through the Marxist worldview. For Hu, Mao's critique of feudal and semicolonial China was an agenda that must be answerable and oriented to Lu Xun's May Fourth discourse on national enlightenment and national reform. In other words, as Mao's socialism began historically as an intellectual call of action to inhabit the material reality of war-torn China for better or for worse, such an intellectual effort soon engendered fissures between itself and its habitat.

From the Party's point of view, the critical spirit of May Fourth had to metamorphose into the Marxist revolutionary ideology. Indeed, after the Japanese occupation and the Civil War, left-wing literary historiography followed the general tendency to propagate "New Literature"—a term designed to describe literature after the May Fourth cultural movement as "birthed" by the Chinese Revolution under Mao[14]—as a *military* achievement of the Left-league. The birth of the PRC was inseparable from the CCP's utilization and politicization of New Literature, which emerged from the bond between political commitment and intellectual awakenings. Put differently, New Literature, as a practical extension of Mao Zedong Thought in literature and art, had emerged to become much more than "one of the newer additions to the doctrinal storehouse of the May Fourth period."[15] As a key component of a "progressive" cultural form, New Poetry in the vernacular of *baihua* (白話, "colloquial language") envisioned not only the emerging May Fourth world of a society "liberated" by European Enlightenment ideas but also the Communist indoctrination of Chinese socialist modernity. This envelopment of "modern Chinese literature" with "New Literature" was a process parallel to the one that witnessed the CCP utilizing and constructing Mao's "Chinese road to socialism" as *the—singular and incomparable—*beginning point of the Chinese Revolution.

Though the Communists contributed to the end of Chinese feudalism, in the process of aligning artistic works with political goals, they also put an end to the May Fourth heritage that provided the conditions for the development of modern criticism. Revolution, in the most general sense, involves radical changes in human institutions and in life. In the nineteenth and early twentieth centuries, "revolution" referred to a historical eruption, which was closely associated with the idea of history as teleologically moving in a particular direction. For Marx and members of the Frankfurt School, revolution meant not only a break with existing political, social, and cultural reality but also a "cataclysmic leap" from one era to another, from one "mode of production" to another. It envisioned an irreversible change in the historical direction toward increased human freedom.[16] The concept of "cataclysmic leap" provides yet another chance into reading Hu's Marxist literary criticism beyond the basic Chinese framework that was hugely defined by Mao's military pragmatism: national survival, social revolution, regime change. Hu's concept of the "subjective combative spirit" thus highlights distinct elements of social radicalism within the Chinese Revolution, marking the period as not only a struggle against Western colonialism out of the need for national survival but also a historical "leap" from feudalism to socialism. In placing Hu along the continuum of Marx's understanding of the socialist revolution, which was in turn also the driver of Lu Xun's "national reform," we can uncover and recover a more self-reflective and self-constituted subjectivism running *co-constitutively* with other, better-known terms in the triumphant discourse of Marxist historical materialism.

Unmistakably, Hu lived in the reality of the wartime Republic. From the Two-Slogan Debate to his 1945 preface for *Hope*, he had never failed to develop his literary theory by relating it to what he called "the real conditions and demands of history."[17] Even with the "subjective combative spirit," which was full of references and allegiance to Marxist dialectics, Hu neither denied the importance of materialism nor conceived of the subjective self as a self-contained existence. Hu's notion of the "subjective combative spirit" was thus not to be confused with the aesthetic category "subjective spirit," one that referred to a self-contained subjectivity independent of reality. Instead, Hu presupposed the conditions of Chinese society at a specific time as the source of a writer's creativity. Under the circumstances of wartime China, he promoted some sort of "thought reform" through which the individual writer could transform personal feelings and desires into a kind of national consciousness and an organized collective force of resistance against imperial territorial threats.

In an essay written in the 1930s, Hu explained how the concept of the "self" and the "spirit of the age" developed in parallel and why self-realization required "unification with the times."[18] He presented the essential Marxist-Leninist argument that one could only realize one's subjectivity by becoming part of the historical process to which one belonged. Therefore, what was "subjective" was also "objective." He wrote: "It is obvious that writing is most 'free' and 'subjective' when the writer's mental activity is most intense. Yet . . . the very 'subjectivity' and 'freedom' attained in the creative process have their own 'objective' foundation and 'objective' purposes nonetheless."[19] For Hu, as for his fellow writers, the creation of socialist China was inseparable from the establishment of a dialectical relationship between the suppression of the self and the development of a collective self-identity—a communal identity of revolutionary fighters—as a basis on which individuals could fulfill the promise of life. Thus, the so-called objective reality of the Chinese Revolution was a world of meaning defined by a collective ideal that responded to and attempted to install sociohistorical change. Rather than working against Marxist historical materialism and emphasizing the function of some subjectivist idealism, as critics of Hu claimed, he coupled political strategies with his creative theory to lubricate the dryness of revolutionary politics with a kind of dialectic that was nonetheless characteristic of Marx's socialist theory.

In the aftermath of 1942, Hu was less concerned with determining the degree to which the Chinese Revolution after the "Talks" stemmed from Mao's revolutionary politics than with their practical effects on the intellect and imagination. For him, the "Talks" were inevitably part of the larger national movement. The poet, meanwhile, despite wartime experiences and aspirations, arrived at a life outlook by committing to processes of imagination and sympathy—the power of entering deeply into the people she represented, of assuming all their plights and feelings. In other words, poetry and revolution, as analogs, were connected on the grounds of parallel development, two coextensive pathways forever binding each other without ever intersecting. Hu called the agents on these pathways two incarnations of the same god: the soldier advanced the revolution by fighting for its causes while seldom calling forth imagination, whereas the poet *might* stir up a revolution when she exercised the faculty of moral imagination to perceive and project different realities. The Chinese Revolution, as a product rather than an agent of human creativity, then, was elicited by the contemplative value of poiesis, not by prepossessing political demands.

What struck the intellectuals of Hu's generation and after was the prescient nature and persistence of the "subjective combative spirit" throughout the decade of the CCP's assumption of state power, as it was raised and theorized in protest well before Hu's marginalization, persecution, and final imprisonment. In other words, Hu advocated the "subjective combative spirit" *throughout* the backdrop of the CCP's authoritarianism—from its inception to the final full-scale clampdown on all manifestations and theories of intellectual and literary subjectivism. Hu's defense of the poet and claims on poetry were already under way in the 1930s and escalated even before the decisive turning point of 1949. One can trace the perseverance of this conviction in literary subjectivism to (1) the bitter feud that developed between Feng Xuefeng/Lu Xun and Zhou Yang in 1930s Shanghai; (2) the Yan'an rectification movement, which ended in the period of terror, from intellectual self-criticism in 1942 to the execution of Party journalist Wang Shiwei in 1947; (3) Mao's promotion of a particular practice of revolutionary art and literature through study sessions on the "Talks" and, later, the Cultural Revolution; and (4) the dramatic rise in hostilities toward literary subjectivism in Marxist intellectual circles in the 1950s, including ideological criticisms and self-criticisms by Hu's former allies Qiao Guanghua, Shu Wu, and others.

In short, long before the Hu Incident in the mid-1950s, Hu had already viewed Marxist writers and intellectuals as, simultaneously, egocentric agents and unreflective foundationists of an insidious discourse. He was intellectually pessimistic and took the lead in criticizing certain habituated critical methods that were undermining their intellect. It was fitting that the concept of the "subjective combative spirit" found its way into Hu's letters, essays, and critical texts, especially those accumulated in the post-Yan'an years. The idea that Mao's conception of New Literature served as a tool for (rather than the end of) Chinese socialist liberation was even more telling after the United Front gave way to the CCP's single-party authoritarianism. Motivated by the CCP's rise in power in the 1940s, Hu felt that he could and must repeat his emphasis on the distinction between poetry as a revolutionary product and revolution as a poetic product. In a letter to Nie Gannu in 1942, Hu made clear his determination to wage war against ideological formalism—the danger of looking down on the mass of suffering individuals from a detached height of dispassionate "thought":

> In the past ten years, especially in the five years after the outbreak of the War against Japan, I (or, we) had not been engaged in real struggles. It pained my heart to see the stupidities and sins of those "cultural fighters." . . . I hated them, but they hadn't sensed my hatred. . . . I had always thought that I did not live at peace with them. . . . Had I honestly felt the seriousness of the problem? Is it the case that I had not passed my days idly and slept like a pig? No doubt, I could say that I had struggled hard to create a [literary and intellectual] trend. . . . Have I seen the world clearly? What can I do? . . . I can only . . . choose to live like a mouse in the street. But still, how should I work? Do I have the ability? I am finding my way forward as I interrogate myself. I have been confident for the past ten years, but I am now experiencing a crisis. I cannot fully articulate this, but you may believe me that this is going to be a severe test.[20]

This letter revealed Hu's state of mind in 1942, probably after he had learned about the "Talks." In Chongqing in January 1945, Hu wrote a preface titled "In the Struggle for Democracy" for the inaugural issue of *Hope*, which expounded ever more clearly on the notion of literary subjectivism and emphasized the writer's "vivifying creative power and strength of thought."[21] Hu wrote that when writers "armed with ideological weapons" begin writing, they must interact with the reality of life at all levels and turn the creative process into one in which they "reconstruct" and "reinvent" themselves.[22] He went on to describe, in a vivid and combative tone, how this two-way process involving the active engagement of the writer and real life should take place:

> In the real-life, flesh-and-blood struggle, what is examined and understood, what is required, is a sensational living existence. . . . In the process of representation, the life of the objective is embraced and brought into the writer's subjectivity and thus enables the writer to enlarge her [consciousness]. The writer uses her subjectivity to both embrace and actively . . . resist the objective world, and the objective world on the strength of its realness stimulates, transforms, and even overturns the writer's assimilation and resistance. Such a dialectic process will bring about a deep self-struggle on the part of the writer, after which the writer will be able to expand the self: she incorporates into her subjectivity the real conditions and demands of history. This is the source of artistic creativity.[23]

Differently put, the writer expanded the self to act as a catalyst for the masses to fulfill her potential as an agent of the Revolution. By "self-expansion," Hu meant the expansion of one's mind and feelings to enlarge and empower the self with a sense of historical and national responsibility, to internalize revolutionary ideals, and to own up to the task of actualizing the unfulfilled potentialities of the not-yet-conscious masses. Self-expansion was one of the key steps toward the attainment of the writer's moral conscience, or "subjective combative spirit."

The above block quotation was one of the most important passages in Hu's system of thought for two related reasons. First, critics have often used it to document how Hu's theory of literary subjectivism stood against Mao Zedong Thought. Second, it brought up a sensitive and recurrent issue in the debates among left-wing critics: the relationship between the writer's "ideological weapons" (theory), the creative process (subjectivity), and life (the Chinese Revolution). By highlighting the role that subjectivity played in the process through which the writer became committed, Hu refused to consider the relationship between Marxism as a correct worldview and one's participation in left-wing politics as a historical and political act as characteristic. Contrary to many of the Party members' contention that the Marxist worldview produced New Literature, Hu argued against the overestimation of the importance of left-wing politics at the expense of other methods of developing the Marxist subject. This is because, for Hu, one could not arrive at her worldview from without but had to discover it organically or acquire it through "a continuing process of self-expansion and self-struggle."[24] Since the creative process involved "the blood-and-flesh struggle in real life," it demanded that the writer undergo a "thought-reform" that would "transform her (Marxist) worldview into the will to live."[25]

"In the Struggle for Democracy" was a position paper; it pointed out that the "Talks" were inapplicable to the GMD areas since "different places had different duties and responsibilities." Meanwhile, Hu published the paper along with Shu Wu's "On Subjectivism," leaving the Party the impression that his notion of literary subjectivism was not an occasional thought. Lin Mohan claimed that "Shu Wu's ['On Subjectivism'] provided a theoretical foundation for Hu."[26] He Qifang said openly, "As the 'Talks' were spread to the GMD areas and became the guidelines for the revolutionary work in those areas . . . to insist upon one's thought on literature and art, as Hu did, was, in essence, to resist against Mao's directions."[27] The publication of "In the Struggle for Democracy" was, argued Zhou Yang, a well-organized literary movement against Mao.[28]

The next chapter will discuss Hu's and his associates' place in the many branches of aesthetic Marxism. This review of Hu's notion of literary subjectivism has attempted to show how specific political pragmatism demanded the continual subordination of critical intelligence and how Hu's literary work was out of sync with the CCP's rationalizations of the function of intellectual discourse. The crucial question is, who owned Chinese Marxism or who had the authority to interpret it? Hu was not in a coveted situation, but it was arguably the best possible position that a revolutionary writer-critic could assume under the circumstances: it was most cautiously and consciously that literature participated in the politics of a national-historical time. Paradoxically, Hu's theory of literature found him a place in the Chinese discourse of Marxist socialism, and then subjected him to the criticism of Mao's orthodox Marxism in 1948 and after. What was particularly dangerous to the vanguard Party members, as Kirk Denton pointed out, was not Hu's intellectualism qua intellectualism but that "his ideas were framed in a Marxist theoretical discourse that threatened to co-opt their own appropriation and reconstruction of that discourse."[29]

When asked why they started the campaign against Hu in 1948, Shao Quanlin replied, "It is because *Hu appears to be a Marxist. We think that he is not a Marxist.* Some people even misunderstand that Hu's theory represents the Party's. The [misunderstanding] must be clarified clearly."[30] Regarding Hu's place in the development of Marxist literary criticism in China, Zhi Kejian pointed out that "for a long time in China, Marxism and even more so the development of Marxism were [state] monopolized. And the sinicization of Marxism was also monopolized."[31] These remarks conclusively demonstrated the ever defensive and hence provocative and polemical nature of Hu's literary subjectivism and, by inference, the whole of his thoughts on art and literature. Even though it was Hu's critics who initially adopted the term *subjective combative spirit* in the 1950s,[32] Hu did not object to his association with the term.

"I RAN TO THE MARSH": HONG KONG CAMPAIGN IN 1948

If criticism of Hu in the wake of the "Talks" failed to persuade him to face the rise of the CCP squarely as a totalitarian state apparatus, the general expectations of the founding of the People's Republic did the task.[33] Recalling one of his private meetings with Zhou Enlai in 1945, Hu wrote, "When I visited Comrade Zhou . . . before I left [Chongqing] . . . he pointed out my ideological problem, saying that while Yan'an was fighting against subjectivism, I fought against [literary] objectivism in Chongqing."[34] With a good sense of self-assessment, Hu understood that it was "only stupid" of him to have dismissed Zhou's warning: "I didn't take his words seriously because I was single-minded in thinking that my views on literature and art had nothing to do with philosophy and politics."[35] Hu was more politically sensitive than he admitted;[36] this was verified in his measured slowness in responding to Zhou's warning about his literary theory in terms of his particularly combative practices of criticism. After meeting Zhou Enlai, Hu replaced the term *objectivism* with *subjective-formulism* in his critical essays to distinguish the kind of literary subjectivism he upheld from the Wang-Ming brand of subjectivism—a dogmatic adherence to the Soviet revolutionary experience and theory—that Mao opposed in Yan'an.

This triumph of the Yan'an experience as an orthodox Marxist critical practice, which superseded the relatively liberal atmosphere of the GMD-controlled areas and, historically, that of the 1930s, and which created a new cultural-institutional order, was expressed at its rawest by the left-wing magazine *Literature and Art for the Masses*. In 1948, the inaugural issue of the magazine released "The New Directions of Art and Literature," showcasing the CCP's ability to "carry out ideological struggle."[37] Shao, then editor-in-chief of the magazine, penned the first essay, "Views on the Current Movements in Literature and Art," delineating the boundaries of left-wing literary criticism as much as the tone of the future direction of literature and criticism. Between March 1948 and June 1949, the magazine published essays by such key Yan'an figures as Feng Naichao, Hu Sheng, Lin Mohan, Xia Yan, Guo Moruo, Mao Dun, and Ding Ling. Unsurprisingly, these writings prioritized praxis over theory, collectivity over individuality; they were also inclined to dismiss the role of human subjectivity in the socialist process. Without exception, they built their criticism on the denouncement of Hu's notion of literary subjectivism, accusing him of both putting undue emphasis on human agency and neglecting Party guidance in creative and critical writing.[38]

Literature and Art for the Masses was no ordinary outlet of popular art and literature. Targeted to "critically review the revolutionary work in literature and art" and "look ahead,"[39] it was the product of a theoretically informed political design motivated by the Party members' sense of themselves as orthodox Marxists and the CCP's cultural delegates. It was also an attempt to translate and extend the Yan'an experience of intellectual conversion by putting into place a highly centralized structure of authority that could effectively unify various literary tendencies in areas outside of the CCP's control.[40] In this process of apprehending intellectuals within Mao's framework of the Chinese Revolution, the Yan'an critics identified Hu as a negative example. Qiao recalled later in life the motivation for publishing the magazine: "For a long time . . . party members had problems with some of Hu's views. During the years of the War of Resistance in Chongqing, his thought on literature became more developed and more explicit. Given the situation, the divergence in opinion that took place in not only Hong Kong but also Shanghai and other areas led some party members to start criticizing Hu."[41] Qiao's rather bland account of the genesis of *Literature and Art for the Masses*, though informative, left some important questions unanswered. Why did Hu's views suddenly become a problem for a group of comrades? And why was the year 1948 strategically crucial to the task of critically reviewing the past and looking ahead? A widely shared concern about Hu's literary theory thus formed the basis of a political consensus. Zhou Erfu supplemented further details:

> One day, we talked about [the question of literature] in our residence. . . . We all thought there was the need for a publication devoted to literary theory. Xia Yan and Feng Naichao were very supportive. Shao Quanlin was the most enthusiastic and looked as if he had for long been having an immediate plan about the publication.[42]

The fact that Xia, Feng, Shao, and others collectively materialized "a ready plan" in the act of publishing the magazine spoke of the nature and preoccupations of the magazine. *Literature and Art for the Masses*, founded on the eve of national liberation in 1948, upheld a stable political structure. In other words, Feng and Shao, respectively secretary and deputy secretary of the Party's Culture Committee in Hong Kong, had long conceived, awaited, and demanded this prestate ideological apparatus. One could thus link the CCP's imminent ascendance to state power to the significance of the magazine and its organized criticism of Hu. Years later, Lin Mohan, in explaining the historical importance of the magazine, outlined the central issues of contention that made Hu and his associate writers distinctly deviate during the Hong Kong period: "In order to consolidate revolutionary efforts, it was so important to clarify these issues within the camp of progressive literature and art at a time of life-threatening struggles between the forces of light and darkness on the eve of new China's difficult birth, when we urgently needed all kinds of ideological weapons to help hasten that birth."[43] The Hong Kong campaign against Hu was, therefore, part of the CCP's "ideological struggle" that meant to "bring about greater ideological unity in literature and art"[44] and to accelerate and prepare for the arrival of the socialist PRC.

If the People's Republic equated its triumph of founding its establishment with the defeat of the Japanese and the GMD, then the CCP's assumption of state power should have meant that the removal of imperialist forces and political enemies was the full condition of that triumph. This rationalization of the CCP's triumph of the will unseated the intellectual discourse of transformative socialism—the continuous struggle for human emancipation—from the Chinese Revolution, reducing what should have been a complex historical event to a linear and one-way process of power struggle.[45] For Lin and many other "cultural workers" in the late 1940s, the end of the Civil War meant not only the end of capitalism as a state ideology but also that of all "problems of China"; consequently, it meant the beginning of what Marx called "a postrevolutionary transitional period" characterized by "the dictatorship of the proletariat."[46] The Chinese Revolution became an overnight success; suddenly, there was an urgent need to translate the concept of the "proletariat" in the ideological and sociological abstract into a real social presence.[47]

On the front of literature and art, writers and artists took measures to adapt to the new conditions defined by the CCP's newly found state power.

Mao's "Talks," which became a policy document after its publication five years before, articulated a vision of a socialist ambition in which workers, peasants, and soldiers would form an ideal collectivity that was distinctly opposed to the individual intellectual's critical consciousness. "Many comrades like to talk about 'a mass style.' But what does it really mean?," asked Mao in his opening speech at the Yan'an Forum; he continued with an instruction: "The thoughts and feelings of our writers and artists should be fused with those of the masses of workers, peasants, and soldiers. . . . If you want to be one with the masses, you must make up your mind to undergo a long and even painful process of tempering."[48]

Although appearing to solicit a discussion of some important policy matters, Mao was in effect laying down directions for thought reform. After that, the socialist process could no longer follow the intellectual's critical and moral judgment. During the critical Hong Kong campaign, Party writers had begun schematizing Mao's thoughts on literature and art as the CCP's cultural policy to eliminate intellectual elitism and nonconformity. It was at this critical historical point of a life-and-death struggle that Hu's literary views instantly became a symbol of everything the Party must stamp out, entering the vocabulary of left-wing literary criticism and politics as a negative watchword. Hu recalled in his memoir how he came to know about the critical campaign organized in Hong Kong: "Yao Pengzi . . . told me he heard from Liu Baimin that a literary movement against [me] had been taking place in Hong Kong.[49] Much surprised, I doubted its truthfulness. I had always been a fellow traveler of the CCP, how could a cultural movement against me be possible now?"[50] Shortly after his encounter with Yao, Hu received a letter from Feng informing him of *Literature and Art for the Masses* and "courteously inviting [his] thoughts" on it:[51]

> The day after [I received Feng's letter], the Hong Kong Life Bookstore sent me a complimentary copy of the magazine. Just by looking at the table of contents, I could see what was going on. The article "Views on the Current Movements in Literature and Art" was targeted at me, but it misunderstood and even misinterpreted the original meaning of my views in multiple ways. The most unacceptable part was Hu Sheng's criticism of Lu Ling's novel. In my opinion, it was thoroughly misguided, and thus Lu Ling naturally became a defective petit-bourgeois writer.[52]

Hu was ambivalent as to whether he should reply. In Hu's initial apprehension of the organized attack, he adopted a twofold defense. At one level, he expressed his reservations about the Party's ideological positions on intellectuals, considering the problem a result of some individuals' air of triumphalism. Meanwhile, he tried to resolve the issue of his literary subjectivism by reconstituting, if not equivocating, an ideological-political problem within his critical framework as a mere "misunderstanding." These two evasive responses enabled Hu to assert that while the Party was correct in conscripting literary and cultural forces into the Chinese Revolution, it went astray owing to some individual critics' inability to conduct criticism. As it turned out, while Hu was still rationalizing if not calculating the situation, and mainly trying to resist an open confrontation,[53] responses from without compelled him to act:

> Hong Kong criticism focused on several [literary] concepts of mine, such as the writer's "subjective combative spirit." . . . It induced a great deal of severe trepidation and countercriticism. . . . All of the writers were followers of the CCP; some of them were even party members. In the face of the development of [Marxist literary] criticism into such a state of confusion, I must think of my responsibility. I must make open to both sides my views on the problem and some essential points at issue.[54]

While Hu was vigilant about the power function of criticism and ready to work closely *with* and *within* the structure of political power, he aspired to be the conscience of the Chinese Revolution by holding on to his subjectivity and his combative spirit. It would be difficult to imagine him willingly accepting a view only because it had popularly been held to be politically correct, or to become collegial in exchange for a comfortable place among the revolutionary intellectuals. From Hu's point of view, the task of the modern Chinese intellectual was to treat the wounds of spiritual servitude that feudalism and imperialism had inflicted on the people. The kind of dogmatism, conformism, and formulism so manifest among the Marxist cultural circles in the late 1940s were, in Hu's eyes, yet more examples of the wounds of spiritual servitude. In his preface to *The Path of Realism* 論現實主義的路, Hu described "subjective-formulism and objectivism" as "two malignant tumors," or "two manifestations of . . . vicious feudalism,"[55] identifying them as the impetus to the organized campaign in

Hong Kong. One of the things that Hu found problematic and particularly disturbing was the irresponsible manner in which Qiao gave up his earlier literary beliefs for momentary success in being a legitimist of the Party's line.[56] Hu wrote:

> The second issue of the *Literature and Art for the Masses* . . . contained in it Qiao Mu's (Qiao Guanhua's) direct criticism of my writings. What I could not understand is that his criticism targeted many of my views to which he had agreed; he, however, didn't own up to his responsibility for those views.[57]

Most objectionably, Qiao's act of denial was one of compliance, if not cowardice, in the face of ideological pressure: "[Qiao] can forget about the past irresponsibly, but I need to be responsible to readers. I cannot talk nonsense and then disprove, on a daily basis, what I said the day before. I need to think carefully and seriously."[58] A manuscript that accounted for the deterioration of the friendship between Hu and Qiao revealed what exactly convinced Hu of the necessity to write his rebuttal in 1948:

> Both the nature of their theory and their way of doing things . . . testified to the fact that Qiao and those like him took themselves to be the representatives of the proletariat and the Communist Party. They claimed their writings [were] genuinely Marxist and accused their opponents of this or that, in the language of extreme leftist doctrines. They had not taken into consideration the particular historical conditions for criticism, nor had they studied carefully the pieces of criticism under attack. . . . But Qiao was different from others. Before [the Hong Kong criticism], he had been taken as a representative of subjective idealism and was a major target of [the CCP's] attack in Chongqing. Now he suddenly "discovered" Hu to be a subjective idealist, and in so doing, made himself a Marxist materialist. He used the name of Hu to "wash hands." What process had he gone through? This had been kept entirely unknown. . . . He owed the Party and history an explanation.[59]

Hu's reply not only rejected an excessive emphasis on one's political position in critical evaluation but also held firmly to the belief that a person's outlook must be a product of critical knowledge based on some concrete experience of life.[60] Hu expressed his revulsion against political opportunism in general and Qiao's betrayal and willingness to pay the price of intellectual integrity in particular. For Hu, the process Qiao should have gone through was one of struggle that informed the writer's road to Marxism; without it, Marxism as an institution of criticism only created ideologues.

Provoked by Qiao's essay, Hu felt bound to dedicate himself to the task of criticism. What appeared as a response to the Hong Kong campaign was in effect his continuous war against Chinese traditionalism and his rejection of conscription, a symptom of his fear that his comrades had become the specter of Chinese feudalism. Hu decided to write a reply and compose a rebuttal in the explosive summer of 1948, asserting his critical consciousness in a fashion comparable to what Herbert Marcuse called intolerance of repression, under which betrayal became, for some, an act of redemption.[61] Once engaged in criticism, Hu's political pragmatism started to give way. For Hu, the literary intellectual, criticism was the most appropriate and effective response to forms of political repression. To write was to testify to one's will to truth and perhaps to provide an alternative to the existing order of things. At 3:00 a.m. on September 17, 1948, Hu finished writing his reply, which took the form of a pamphlet titled *The Path of Realism*, debunking the criticisms against him in *Literature and Art for the Masses*. The pamphlet, permeated with a visible sentiment of self-sacrifice, opened with the following quotation from Dante's *Divine Comedy*: "I ran to the marsh, and the reeds and the mire so entangled me that I fell, and there I saw formed on the ground a pool from my veins."[62] Concerning his sense of martyrdom, it might be worth pointing out that Hu's "300,000-Character Report" adopted the same tone of readiness for self-sacrifice. In his letter to the Central Committee attached to the "300,000-Character Report," Hu wrote:

> I earnestly look forward to the Central Committee's examination.
> I earnestly look forward to the Central Committee's criticism.
>
> I am ready to supplement my criticism following instructions.
> I need to answer to serious responsibilities I should take.[63]

"WHAT IS THE CRUX OF THE MATTER?"

In the acclaimed book *The Structural Transformation of the Public Sphere*, a study of bourgeois coffeehouse culture in the eighteenth century, Jürgen Habermas traced historically the way political discourses entered into the public arena through "literature" as an object. Moreover, he argued that it was "without any guarantee" that "critical debate ignited by works of literature and art" would be "inconsequential" when "extended to include . . . political disputes."[64] Habermas's assertion facilitates an understanding of the archeology of Marxism literary discourse in China, for it shares with Hu an assumption about the ethics of intellectual power. For them, the literary intellectual's creative energy must grow in politics because politics was essential to the power of the mind. At the same time, the poet must hold politics to literary standards: politics must be adequate not in correspondence to realpolitik but to the situated tasks of what it meant to act as and so be a poet abiding by aesthetic principles—freedom of thought, speech, innovation, and creativity.

Intellectually, the process through which Hu decided to write a response to the Hong Kong campaign compelled him to understand his historical function in China's socialist process. Historically, during this time, Hu was made most conscious of the incompatibilities among the many demands to which he had to respond. Within the discourse of Marxist revolutionary pragmatism, Hu was resigned to the situation wherein, shrouded in a "dead-knot," an authority above him predetermined any views he might have on literature and art. Yet the situation did not preclude him from mastering his own opinion about literature's social function and value. There was an inescapable need to reflect on the assumptions about the relationship between literary intellectuals and the CCP and to rethink the validity of the notion of "contractual obligation" commonly thought to exist between them. It was one thing to valorize a Marxist intellectual like Hu, who considered revolutionary politics an instrument of freedom, and metaphorically as if it was a creative process. On the other hand, it was quite another to consider him one of the many actors in history with a role and agency defined in terms of how closely he followed Mao's revolution.

The paradox of intellectual commitment and revolutionary praxis was something to be acknowledged but was necessarily dangerous if resolved. In Hu's journey to the revolution, there was neither a sudden pronouncement of the engagé nor an unmediated compromise. The satisfaction, excitement, and confidence derived from day-to-day politics may have constituted Hu's blindness to the CCP as the ultimate authority on the revolutionary agenda, but they never turned him into a professional Party revolutionary. Hu was not unlike his comrades in Yan'an in the sense that he also believed in Mao's revolutionary praxis and was keenly aware of the need to have recourse to the Marxist theory of knowledge. Like them, he was drawn into the Chinese Revolution and had a strong aversion to the free and independent writers and artists who prioritized aesthetic values or the absolute autonomy of literature and art. Meanwhile, he also took a resolute interest in human subjectivity and individual empirical premises. For Hu, even errors or slippages in the dialectic process of practice and theory, in both subjectivism and material objectivism, had value. He believed that the ambiguities and ambivalences experienced in the poet's self-struggle (i.e., the course of developing one's "subjective combative spirit" through experience, reflection, and thinking) contributed to the development of appropriate moral and critical consciences, while indoctrinating the individual would only lead to a weakening of the ability to conduct social change.

Using Nikolai Gogol as an example, Hu explained how the institutional authority of criticism should challenge old forms of consciousness and thinking: "Gogol's *Dead Souls* is famous. It creates the central character Chichikov, a typical swindler" who traveled around a backward district of Russia buying up "dead souls."[65] After Gogol submitted the first part of the novel, the censors felt that it was an attack on the church's doctrine of the immorality of the soul. In an attempt to respond to the church's interests, Gogol thus decided to write about the redemption of Chichikov. Hu continued, "Gogol couldn't but admit that [Chichikov's] redemption is fake—an epiphany led to the eventual burning of the manuscript. Even after the burning and rewriting of the manuscript, [Chichikov] cannot enter . . . Purgatory. Eventually, Gogol cried and fasted himself to death."[66] No doubt, Gogol "must have been very sure that the arguments of the priest were right"[67] for him to overcome his emotional attachment to what he had created, and the attachment was abnormally strong in this case. The fasting that led to death shortly after the destruction of the manuscript resulted from Gogol's feeling that he could not write about the reformation of Chichikov until he too had reformed himself.[68]

Gogol's creative experience imparted to Hu a valuable lesson regarding literary practice. Unlike his colleagues in Yan'an, Hu placed his theory and practice in the gap between intellectual idealism and political pragmatism, between the moral-aesthetic and the contingent and strategic. He had a deep psychological need to engage critically with authority; he knew how important it was to dissent when he was confident that the catastrophic consequences of state ideological power on the intellect had become inevitable and irreversible. I would argue that it was a certain critical willfulness that brought about Hu's *inability* to adapt to the political demands of the time, and ultimately to the Hu Incident. Whether working in GMD areas such as Shanghai, Chongqing, and Hong Kong before 1949, or in Shanghai and Beijing after 1949, the changes in sociopolitical circumstances might have impressed on Hu the need to be more responsive to the principle of political utility and institutional demands, but they did not cause him to modify his understanding of his mode of being and his position on literature. Real physical and mental suffering could neither tame Hu's critical vigor nor open his eyes to the true nature of his "problem." As mentioned at the beginning of this chapter, Hu could not admit that he had a "problem" with his literary subjectivism, even though he was fully aware that his refusal to renounce his creative theory would lead to prolonged imprisonment and an ever-heavier debt to his writer-followers.[69]

VI

TIME HAS BEGUN

> He was incorrigible, do you know he had been composing poems in his cell? . . . He chose a beautiful name for them, "Songs in Memory of Spring."
>
> —Mei Zhi[1]

> Heroes, when they are in prison, choose to think about love. . . . The bravest of modern writers . . . [b]efore [they] died of cold, hunger, and exhaustion . . . recited . . . poems. . . . Perhaps to remain a poet in such circumstances is also to reach the heart of politics. The human feelings, human experience, the human form and face, recover their proper place—the foreground.
>
> —Saul Bellow[2]

This chapter will present Hu's claims on the political effect of the Chinese Revolution of 1927–50 on creative practices during the testing years of the 1940s and early 1950s, specifically, to the phenomenon presented by his poiesis. Hu's poiesis, which included not only his poetry but also his pedagogical and editorial work that had nurtured a group of emergent writers of his time, gave the poet-critic a chance to test his "literary subjectivism" and to put into practice his concept of "subjective combative spirit." Since conversations with those who came to be called the "*July* writers"[3] involved poetry, personal letters, and work-related correspondence, this chapter will cover only a broad selection of materials to give an account of what Hu found at stake in poetry. The discussion will focus on *Time Has Begun*, Hu's book-length elegy to the founding of the PRC.[4] Written amid his perennial conflicts with Party writers, the elegy conflated many of Hu's mixed sentiments regarding the arrival of a power regime he simultaneously revered, anticipated, and dreaded.

The Marxist poet, Hu argued, recognized the unique role literature played concomitantly with politics in the socialist process. It was only through writing and the experience of life, and not the other way around, that the poet practiced Marxist socialism. By way of an example and drawing on his own experience, Hu set out on the path of the revolutionary poet, always in and through literature, with this advice:

> For myself and [revolutionary] work . . . I begin to undertake literary work. How do I begin? I start from the basics. I get in touch with writers by way of studying them . . . with works of art by reviewing them. . . . I advance towards the pulse of social development and the direction of literary development. As to the so-called theoretical questions, I focus on only those related to literary practice.[5]

Similar advice abounds in many of Hu's letters to younger writers. For instance: the poet is "a soldier in life,"[6] "a fighter of human freedom and happiness," and "a monk who sacrifices himself for the good life of millions of people"; he is "the owner of a philanthropic soul":[7] and those who aspire to be a poet must aspire to be a real man.[8] Anyone who lived up to these standards "[could] be honored as a poet even if she ha[d] not written a single line [of poetry]."[9] These statements were some of Hu's plainest and most instructive claims on the personae and tasks of the poet, claims that lay at the heart of his writing and his editorial and pedagogical work. Each of these claims led to the image of the poet as "a soldier in life," providing a precise figure to grasp the more practical aspects of Hu's criticism. What sort of person could shape such a central place during a decade of wars that defined much of the sociopolitical reality of China and that bore the mark of China's long journey to modernity?

The terms *soldier* and *poet* bore ideologically specific connotations running concurrently with the commonly evoked wartime images deriving from the discourse of the Chinese Revolution. In wartime China, most literary intellectuals confronted the question of how to maximize their potential to contribute to the national struggle and emancipation. The poet and the soldier started from the same belief system, yet their reflexes developed differently following their modes of being in the war and as soon as the immediate presence of the war gradually became part of the revolutionary past. Whereas the soldier of Mao's army engaged in the immediate wars against Japan, the poet insisted on continuous progress, that is, on taking the war as one moment in the continuity of a much grander historical project of intellectual enlightenment. Thus, the poet-soldier, as a representative of the conjoint forces of body and spirit, of military might and effective criticism, was a historically specific notion Hu espoused.[10] By putting them together, Hu presented a vision of different temporalities and goals of the Revolution that entered the same historical moment while waiting for the day they would be in equilibrium—a balance of forces guaranteed by the condition of poiesis. Under circumstances as challenging as those in the 1940s, military stratagems, creative desires, and intellectual imaginings coexisted in uneasy suspension, sometimes in open conflict. The complicated interaction among these demands, desires, and imaginings was the recourse of Hu's poiesis.

TIME HAS BEGUN

In October 1949, Hu recorded in his diary, "a song has been churning in my mind for two months; it strikes the strongest chord and reaches the height of harmony."[11] This song, which Hu wrote to celebrate the PRC's founding, was the grand historical epic *Time Has Begun*. In this epic of heroes inciting historical events and imagery of the triumphant joy of transformations in society, Hu presented an overview of the critical moments that emerged during the new PRC's expansion into political, ideological, and social institutions and its historical role in Chinese socialist struggle. The complete epic, around 4,600 lines in length, was structured around five songs:

1. "Joyous Praise 欢乐颂" (November 11–12, 1949);
2. "Commendation of Honor 光荣赞" (November 26–28, 1949);
3. "Songs of Youth 青春曲" (December 4, 1949–1985);
4. "Requiem 安魂曲" (December 31, 1949–January 1, 1950); and
5. "The Song of Triumph 胜利颂," originally titled "Another Joyous Praise 又一个欢乐颂" (January 13–14, 1950).

The first song, "Joyous Praise," described the opening ceremony of the PRC's first People's Political Consultative Conference, reflecting the joy of Mao and memorializing the Civil War. The second, "Commendation of Honor," focused on several women, including Hu's mother. In the context of the making of socialist China, these women, in their roles as mothers and as representatives of the peasant-worker class, symbolized the "modesty" and "purity" of the people. The third, "Songs of Youth," featured such characters as "Little Grass," "Morning Light," "Snowflakes," and "Sleeping Village." These characters represented the voice of a new generation of youths born in the People's Republic as well as optimism for the future. This song stood out as the most lyrical of the five, with strong evidence of an emotional investment in lives at the "beginning of time," at the juncture of the old and new regimes. The fourth, "Requiem," likened to a continuation or extension of the second song, began with the inauguration ceremony of the "Monument to the People's Heroes" in Tiananmen Square and contained many biographical details of the revolutionary martyrs—some of them were also Hu's friends and comrades. The fifth, "The Song of Triumph," the shortest of the five songs, was an intensified version of the first song in terms of both content and sentiment. In its march of passion, and a tempo more intense than the rest of the epic, this song was a reflection of Hu's feelings of excitement on the PRC's first National Day.

Collectively, these songs embodied moments of the Chinese Revolution from related perspectives, but each one was panegyric and passionate in its own way. Each song touched on the sensitive question, driven by the historical threshold of 1949, of the relationship between the partisan and the fellow traveler, between the "heroic" and the "ordinary." Ultimately, the epic was a eulogy to Mao's triumphant rise—a subject that, notably in Hu's words, would come to "suffocate" him.[12] In the wake of Mao's rise to absolute power, fellow travelers of the CCP, like Hu and those who had worked in the GMD areas, needed to justify and defend themselves more than ever. The songs and Hu's diary entry describing their creation showed his thoughts on the problematic relationship between the individual and the collective, albeit in codified terms. Hu considered the fate of the intellectual amid the imminent arrival of a dictatorship and the reality of losing a relatively autonomous foothold in critical and creative work.

The dynamic interconnection of the "strongest" and the most "harmonic" expressed the intensely self-conscious awareness of the relative, conciliatory, and threatened reconciliation of the individualistic with the collective, as well as that of the heroic with the average and the imaginative with the political. In Hu's imagination and understanding, the fate of "the strongest" was as much a matter of artistic compromise, or the subjugation of the critical intellectual to the party-state, as it was the eventual retrocession of authorial power to the people. One recurring theme in the epic was its depiction of Mao as a great source of control, a commanding figurehead, deep in the sea of power to the point of standing frozen in time, as exemplified by the following passage from "The Song of Triumph":

Mao Zedong
He stood here
He stuck out his chest
like the commander of the surrendering poisonous dragon
  the mythical giant
He oversees the newborn motherland
He witnesses the beginning of time
He looks at the standing people
He looks on the sea that converges into itself
  laborious, combative, and creative lives.[13]

By giving "the strongest" an expression, against the background of the "harmonic," Hu's epic laid the groundwork for a three-dimensional structure. It also created a space—a reality in which absolute state power ("the strongest") became a productive basis for the collective ("the height of harmony"). Inherent in the "praise" was the idea that Mao climbed to the highest point of power by being expansive and inclusive; inclusiveness compelled the "strongest" to remain stable:

Mao Zedong
He stands firmly at the top
As if he is announcing to himself
which also means to the world:
  Let what surges up from the deepest part of the earth
    come here.
  Let what springs down from the top of the mountain
    come here.
  Let what struggles out from the cleavages of rocks
    come here.
  Let what smells of flowers and trees
    come here.

Let what streams through the sun and moon and iridescent clouds
come here.
Let thousands and ten thousands of virtuous scholars in dance and songs
come here.
Meanwhile
Let also those who arrive in dust and sand
come here.
Let those who are stained with dirt and blood
come here.
Let those who are redolent of dead bodies
come here.
Let the hundreds and thousands of sinful scholars, humbly and timidly,
come here.[14]

In the context of modern China, Hu imagined the essentials of a revolutionary leader and figurehead. The previous excerpt, from the song "Joyous Praise," expressed Hu's expectations for Mao and his instructions on the responsibilities of statesmanship. Nowhere else had Hu written as openly and extensively about Mao; only when imagining Mao "announcing to himself" and "the world" that he was living up to the task of an "accommodating" and "boundless" leader did Hu express himself as eloquently:

I am the sea.
I need to be capacious
Capacious as to
embrace the world
as to
expand beyond time.
I am the sea.
I need to encompass all who seek accommodation,
purify all who seek clarification.
I—this clear crystal waters and boundless blue
forever
and ever
will use its pure, buoyant, and shimmering waves
to shed light on the center of the universe.[15]

For Hu, the revolutionary leader of modern China was not only a source of absolute power but also the cause of a centripetal process that brought ordinary people together. He depicted Mao as appealing to the "we" and "they":

We
from the axis of the motherland
from the beginning of history
in joy
in songs
in dance
in pride
  spread out.
Like ocean waves
Like space currents
in front of Mao Zedong
  [we] spread out.

Those from the Jinggang Mountains[16]
who chopped woods with peasants
in front of Mao Zedong
  [they] spread out.

Those from the Long March
who fired with the Red Army
in front of Mao Zedong
  [they] spread out. . . .

Those from the farmers' caves in Yan'an
. . .
who, with the battle-scarred workers,
  talked long and dear
In front of Mao Zedong
  [they] spread out.[17]

The heroic and the strongest were scattered, while, in a state of passionate action and movement, synchronic in its intention and direction, the harmoniously forged connections and collectivity formed the grounds for the nurturing of their strength and consciousness. The last few stanzas of

"The Song of Triumph," which concluded Hu's historical epic, powerfully represented the collective's ever-growing strength, which could be summoned, perhaps justifiably at this point, by a stupendous effort of will as surely as Mao remained at a standstill:

Mao Zedong
His eyes glare
His cheeks flush
His heart ponders
He is looking at you
He is listening to you
He is calling out to you
For the motherland
For the future
For the species
Mao Zedong
  A newborn
  A maiden in her first love
  A wronged man seeking justice
  The pioneer of a wasteland
Out of his heart to give happiness
Out of his genuine compassion
Out of his undefeatable will
is the passionate voice
that calls out to the hard-working people
that calls out to the brave people
that calls out to the innocent people
that calls out to the wise people
    —Long Live Comrades!
    —Long Live Comrades!
    —Long Live Comrades!

The heart of the whole nation's working force
The heart of the whole nation's combative force
The heart of the whole nation's creative force
hears him
feels his heart
feels his passion
gains from his sensibility
benefits from his will

and echoes back joyously
    "Long Live our Success!"

The heart of the whole world's working force
The heart of the whole world's combative force
The heart of the whole world's creative force
hears him
feels his heart
feels his passion
gains from his sensibility
profits from his will
and echoes back joyously
    "Long Live our Success!"

The stars echo back joyously
    "Long Live our Success!"

The universe echoes back joyously:
    "Long Live our Success!"[18]

These last moments of the historical epic show that Hu found confidence in synchronizing divided ideals: the individuality and authoritarianism of the singular, the intensity and desire of the collective, and, ultimately and ideally, the organic flow between the individual and the organization. The image of Mao reaching the pinnacle of power might have been imposing, but it immediately descended into a subterranean space and surrendered to a swarm of "echoes," which were not visually translatable impressions but sounds that blurred and continuously interrupted the center.

"SONGS OF YOUTH"

Hu's panegyric on Mao and the CCP's leadership, urged on in part by his political sensitivity, drew attacks from his opponents. Only the first song enjoyed immediate success upon its publication: the *People's Daily* printed the song immediately after receiving it, and it was also translated into Russian in *Oktyabr*, a monthly literary magazine based in Moscow. Its success, however, was short-lived. By 1948 and 1949, the Yan'an writers had singled out Hu as the head of a "deviant" literary trend in the first official assessment of the pre-1949 literary field in GMD areas.[19] Historically, it was a profound intellectual phenomenon. On the one hand, writers and critics involved in debates about ways to militarize "a new direction in literature and the arts" had to find a position in that new direction.[20] On the other hand, such a context, which witnessed criticism serving power and saw only the negative in all attempts of literary subjectivism, induced Hu to ground his poetry in a style at odds with the didactic style of propagandist writing normalized in the 1950s. Notwithstanding the manifest passion of *Time Has Begun* in celebrating Mao and the CCP, the Party called for an end to all publication plans and attempts, including destroying newly printed copies of the epic at Xinhua Bookstore. Hu did not have an opportunity to publish the epic in its entirety until after rehabilitation in the 1980s.[21] Hu was not surprised by the censorship and even expected that his poetry would provoke negative critical responses. In his letter to Lu Yuan dated January 18, 1950, he admitted:

> The publication of #1 has shocked all (I hear that the poet-novelist Zang Kejia[22] too has commended it), despite dismissal by some of those "core writers." That is fine. About #2, except those who are in the vicinity, no critical reviews have reached [Beijing]. In Tianjin, though, it has made a hit. (Even so, be careful not to be too optimistic. Just yesterday, there were these writers-in-power[23] who, despite affirming the song, criticized my characters for their spiritual elitism. . . . Such kind of criticism I have long anticipated.) #4 is provocative.[24]

Although *Time Has Begun* began and ended with an apotheosis of Mao, Hu anticipated two reasons for the Party's dismissive reception of the work. One was his "literary subjectivism," as reflected in the epic's structure, writing timeline, and imagery. The writing schedule of the poem showed that, once Hu had paid tribute to Mao and the newborn PRC, Hu returned to the third song, a quintet. Yet, whether by pure mischance or other circumstantial reasons such as sickness, traveling, or censorship,[25] Hu took two years to gradually add to "Songs of Youth" what he called his "most beloved songs":[26] "Little Grass Says to the Sun 小草对阳光这样说"; "Morning Light 晨光曲"; "Snowflakes Say to the Land 雪花对土地这样说"; "The Moon 月光曲"; and "Thus Speak the Sleeping Village 睡了的村庄这样说."

Hu wrote the quintet in two months, issuing the first, second, and fifth songs first. In a letter to Niu Han, Hu outlined the emotional stages involved in the creative process: "At the time of writing, the whole of history and universe emerged into a galloping *sea* (song #1), a galloping *river* (songs #2 and #4), and a silvery *sea* (song #5). These songs echoed in my heart."[27] Hu's description of his emotions stored up in the shape of a "sea" and a "river" suggested a further correspondence between the "strongest" and the "most harmonic" discussed above:

> The sea
> seething
> It is swirling around a peak
> Mao Zedong
> He perches solidly on that peak . . .
> as if he is looking down at all those forthcoming
> rivers, big and small[28]

Hu's account of his flow of emotions in the creative process formed two concentric shapes, with a space of possibility in the middle, awaiting the right inhabitants:

#1	#2	#3	#4	#5
GALLOPING SEA				SILVERY SEA
	GALLOPING RIVER		GALLOPING RIVER	
			"Requiem":	"The Song of Triumph," aka "Another Joyous Praise":
"Joyous Praise":	"Commendation of Honor":	"Songs of Youth":	Yang Tianzhen	
		Little Grass,	Fu Guaquan	
	Li Xiuzhen	Morning Light,	Wan Xiyan	
Mao Zedong	Rong Guanxiu	Snowflakes,	Wu Tiehan	Mao Zedong
	Hu's mother	The Moon,	Qiu Dongping	
	Li Fenglian	Sleeping Village	Takiji Kobayashi	
			Lu Xun	
	GALLOPING RIVER		GALLOPING RIVER	
GALLOPING SEA				SILVERY SEA

Hu's creative mind seemed to be a vast repository for a *hierarchy* of tropes, such as the sea as related to the river, before he matched this set of carefully selected images to the characters represented in the poem. In Hu's analogy, the "sea" in the first and fifth songs was to Mao's engulfing "greatness" what the "river" was to the combative spirit of the individual revolutionaries and comrades-in-arms whom the poem commemorated in the second and fourth songs. While recovering from an illness and after returning to Shanghai, Hu decided on the remarkably poetic characters to be featured in the third song, which also incorporated his best lyrics about life in transit. The first of these characters, "Little Grass," is a romantic, allegorical, and biographical figure:[29]

Winter has arrived
ice has come
snow has come
how pleasant
a stretch of light and white
The ice freezes me
the snow envelops me
I cannot see you
or hear you

Never mind
My heart gives out heat
I am blessed
The ice protects me
The snow carries me
I am falling asleep
soundly
sweetly
I will pass all that warmth of yours
onto my roots
I will sleep in warmth
and dream soundly.

Next year
I will bring Spring
When it is time
I will open my eyes

raise my head
straighten my waist
I will smile the purest of the pure smiles
I will use the greenest of the green leaves
I will use the reddest of the red flowers
to greet you, love you

The lyrical ballad continues at some length, repeatedly conjuring the impression of the poetic I's abstraction from the historical context and the general epical quality of an otherwise intensely politicized eulogy. As the political background, like the "sea" looming large at the beginning and end of *Time Has Begun*, it gives space to the song of "Little Grass" and the poetic I's authentic voice sings eloquently:

When you see them
your heart is drunk with happiness
    it knows well how I watch you hear you love you
My nanny who nurses me
My beloved who loves me
I who can feel my pulses
Bless me
your blessings are huge
I have to receive them gratefully
Accept too my blessings
    they are inadequate
    but you will still kindly accept them[30]

In this set of lines that Hu wrote on December 4, 1949, "at night, seeing first snow, in Beijing,"[31] "Little Grass" addresses the Sun in a clear effort to redeem those who, in the first song, were "humbly and timidly" gathering around Mao.

In terms of structure, the third song, occupying the heart of *Time Has Begun*, created an effect of poetic subjectivity, which the first two songs anticipated and from which the last two proceeded. The protagonists of "Songs of Youth" embodied the rosy romanticism of lives surrounded by the excitement of change. Except for song #3.3, "The Moon," all the songs adopted the voice of a first-person narrator: "Little Grass," "Morning Light," "Snowflakes," and "Sleeping Village" were neither merely poetic objects nor materials but characters and actors. As "Little Grass" tells the Sun that "when it is time / I will open my eyes / . . . / to greet you, love you,"[32] "Morning Light" speaks directly about personhood and selfhood:

> I am a person
> I have a heart
> a flesh-and-blood life
> burning in youth[33]

These "youthful" voices constituted a practical complement to Hu's creative theory and exemplified his "literary subjectivism" at work. They were remarkable not only because of the lyrical quality guaranteed by the form of the modern free verse but also for their counterpoint to the idealized image of Mao in the first and fifth songs. Often in the "Songs of Youth," the characters emphasized subjective, individualistic feelings based on no specific ideological power politics. If, as a whole, some of *Time Has Begun*'s least romantic moments portrayed the ascendance of power, so too did some of its most lyrical moments, even if it had to be power of a different worth and class. Similarly, while the least poetic moments (like those portraying Mao's rise to power) frequently contained indigestible images ("the heart of the whole nation"), the most lyrical moments that permeated the "Songs of Youth" did not.

Indeed, reflecting on the title of the epic, following whose sense of temporality had time begun? According to Heraclitus, real time, as it passes, is like a *river*. Sailing down this river, readers encountered such characters as "Little Grass," "Snowflakes," and "Sleeping Village" and views such as the "morning light" and "the moon" on the banks of the river in a sequence of past, present, and future. Meanwhile, the man who stood "firmly at the top," perched on a crag in the "Jinggang Mountains," saw this sequence as all one vision, outside time. In their position in the middle of *Time Has Begun*, these five poems presented five lyrical accounts of the revolutionary struggles of various *individuals* within the context of Marxist ideology as personified by the timelessness of Mao's "greatness."

Given his emphasis on the poet's "literary subjectivism" in both revolutionary and creative processes, Hu expanded on the third song, and well into his postprison years in the 1980s, insisted that the entire five-song version of his epic appear in one complete edition, as he had always imagined it to be. In a letter to Lu Yuan dated September 9, 1984, having made the point that "*Time Has Begun* never appeared as a single whole" even as the PRC was celebrating its 35th anniversary,[34] Hu continued, "I probably couldn't write another long piece. My feelings for the people and the motherland are all contained in those songs. I wish against wish that they could come out as a whole."[35]

FREE VERSE, A STYLISTIC INCONGRUITY

The second historical reason for the Party's antipathy toward *Time Has Begun* was Hu's use of modern free verse. Poetic free verse, as opposed to popular "national forms," was one critical weapon that Hu employed to fight against the tendency toward what he called "formulism" in revolutionary literature. (I will explain momentarily the genealogy of "national forms" and how "core writers" and "core writings" of the period[36] came to appropriate and revive traditional cultural forms in revolutionary China. Hu's problem with "formulism" constituted perhaps the most extended episode in his critical war with Party writers and intellectuals.) The word *formulism* emerged first in Hu's critique of Zhou in the Two-Slogan Debate, and then recurrently, notably, in *The Path to Realism,* written in response to the Hong Kong campaign, and in a major speech that attacked the *Literary Gazette* in 1954.[37] Shu Wu, the perceived "traitor" of the Hu group and author of the controversial essay "On Subjectivism," understood well this genealogy. In 1955, Shu Wu published a set of conclusive "editorial comments" on the tug-of-war between Hu and the Party intellectuals, along with the "Collection of Materials on the Hu Counterrevolutionary Clique." In those "comments," he traced the trajectory of Hu's continuous discontent with the Party's literary and cultural policies from the late 1920s through the whole of the 1930s and 1940s to the early 1950s. Preparing his comments at the height of the Party's all-out ideological purge of Hu, Shu Wu wrote most carefully:

> Hu has been consciously, consistently, and increasingly rebuttable and surreptitious in his work and his critical war with party-ideologues and party-leaders. He calls the ideological-leaders "the authoritarian force of mechanical formulism 机械论的统治势力," against whom he conscripts members of his literary group to "make an effort" to "root out." In a letter from 1948, Hu defines the literary scene of the past two decades as one under the reign of formulism. Included in those "two-decade reign of mechanical formulism" are such events as the founding of "revolutionary literature" in 1928, the Left-league's propagation

> of "proletariat revolutionary literature" [in the 1930s], and the publication of Mao's "Yan'an Talks on Literature and Art" in 1942; all of which Hu seeks to oppose and attack.[38]

"Subjective-formulism," or simply "formulism," as Marston Anderson defined it, was "the term by which critics referred to fiction that advanced its ideological message in an overly mechanical or schematic fashion."[39] Indeed, as early as the mid-1930s, Hu was already concerned about two manifestations of "vulgar Marxism" in the literary trend and wrote an essay to warn against them in terms that were anticipatory of what he would eventually lay out on the brink of 1949:

> There are writers whose passion has receded. . . . They have become contented and adopted a passive attitude toward life, taking writing as a professional task that they perform dispassionately. . . . This is called objectivism, an evident tendency in the literary circle at present. If . . . [these writers] . . . cannot forget the general [sociopolitical circumstances of our time] and write [about the war] . . . with some preconceived concepts, then they have replaced objectivism with subjective-formulism.[40]

In his pamphlet *Realism Today*, written in the mid-1940s, Hu again used the term *subjective-formulism* in his critique of some writers' perfunctory applications of Marxist views and their reductionist representation of life following formulaic literary designs. Literary works produced under the influence of "subjective-formulism" were "self-indulgent," "self-delusive," and "devoid of historical content," Hu argued.[41] Meanwhile, "literary objectivism" looked at life with the sort of cool-headedness commonly found in natural science. It considered reality an empirical object, as "a phenomenal form," paying no attention to Marx's call for the need to "penetrate" the "illusory" surface of social relations and to discover the underlying structures and forces that generate fundamental historical tendencies or changes.[42] Though seemingly two opposite tendencies in creative practice, both subjective-formulism and objectivism blocked the "path of realism"; the former was "a feeble deduction of political phenomena" and the latter an "illustrative inventory" of political concepts.[43] Both tendencies were marked by the use of abstract generalization to replace actual thinking as a necessary agency for the production of literature about society and life.

For Hu, therefore, neither subjective-formulism nor objectivism met the revolutionary expectations or maximized the potentialities of New Literature. He referred to "New Literature" as "*May Fourth* New Literature," in the hope that it voiced humanist demands and recorded "living phenomena brought into existence by . . . man."[44] In his words, because May Fourth New Literature developed from the decisive historical *and* humanistic processes that instilled those "demands" and "phenomena," it contained "materials taken from the street" and a "sincere heart" capable of "extracting" something "lively and living" from existences such as "Little Grass" and "Snowflakes."[45] The catalyst of this complete union of life (materials) and a life invested with meaning (an ideological outlook) was the poet's "subjective combative spirit" through which literary practice established an analogous connection with revolutionary life, ensuring that any political stance gained in the creative process was a position born from lived experience.

In his letters to writers and editorial notes, Hu documented and gave birth to his theory of the creative process. He also sought to rehabilitate "free verse" as a critical heritage of the May Fourth Movement, against the CCP's calls for the use of "national forms" to popularize revolutionary literature and art. By "free verse," Hu meant "the crystal and ripple formed in the process through which concrete life events strike on the poet's sea of emotions."[46] For Hu, Tian Jian's early poetry was a case of New Poetry approaching the conditions of "crystal" and "ripple." In the preface to *Chinese Shepard's Song*, Hu praised this "drummer of the era" for his intensely "simple and straightforward" style and for his "most courageous" attempt to search for form.[47] According to Hu, Tian Jian remained untouched by the "two different streams" of "vulgar Marxism"—"formulism" and "objectivism"[48]—because of the originality of his poetry's form. Hu particularly commended the following lines from "How Do I Write Poetry?":

> I,
> grew up in a southern village,
> the city, I spent yet another decade wandering.
> I have neither wept in her arms,
> nor dropped a tear!
> In this world,
> in China,
> I rear my small self![49]

He also praised the following excerpt from "I Am a Part of the Sea 我是海的一个":

I,
am hearty,
am healthy,
am a little fighting fella.[50]

Tian Jian's short and self-contained verses not only created silences and space for thought but also, and importantly for Hu, effectively produced an image series that was a replica of the poet's immediate response to the lived "feelings," "images," and "events."[51] Remarkably, notwithstanding his best hope for the potential in Tian Jian's free verse and the images in the lines—he likened the latter to "a pool of sequins mixed together"[52]—Hu also warned of the limits of those imagistic lines. Concerned, as always, with the poet's strength of mind and imagination, with the ability of the "subjective combative spirit" to unite form and content, Hu feared that Tian Jian's free verse could not give readers "a replete and perspicuous" overall picture if it remained at the level of "immediate response."[53] In a reply letter written some years after his 1936 preface to *Chinese Shepard's Song*, Hu conceded that despite Tian Jian's "instinctive" closeness to poetic "feelings" and "emotions," the poet had "regressed" because his free verse now failed to "completely merge with life":[54]

> Tian Jian has not completed his self-making as a poet. (How many of us have achieved this making of the self as a poet?) He is one who knows least his shortcoming[s]. If he failed to acquire that strength necessary to go deep into the realities of life, that strength capable of finding the meaning of life [ideological outlook] and embracing emotions, he would then be fragmented and lost in his feelings. . . . You said Tian Jian's poetic form is "rigid and inflexible" rather than "natural." I disagree. Rather than form, his is a problem of content. [Tian Jian's] poetic form is not only the least "rigid" but also excessively "flexible." This is because his feelings and emotions [of life] remain cursory; they flit on the surface of his subjects. . . . Rather than "boxing up his flood of emotions and songs" into a "small wooden box," he is only using a form that is appropriate to [the size of] his content. His emotions have not yet emerged into a "flood."[55]

In effect, even a poetic form as such, however original and unformulaic, was not Hu's concern: "Form alone is not enough for determining the value of poetry";[56] critics and writers should "pay attention to content, assessing the degree to which such content feeds upon the writer's 'subjective combative spirit,' which must, of course, be sincere and adherent to the literary object."[57]

Hu's creative theory differed from the work of some core writers of his time in its argument that the revolutionary mind and poetry did not entirely exist, or at least lacked maturity, until they emerged from "a continuing process of self-expansion and self-struggle."[58] By using the metaphors "crystal" and "ripple"—the result of a continuing process—to describe his standard of New Poetry, Hu was concerned with the creative process as a whole rather than aspects of poetry serving different ends in isolation from one another. Ultimately, Hu's attempt to define, demonstrate, and defend poetic lyricism in wartime China, or what David Der-wei Wang called "the lyrical in epic time,"[59] was a treacherous task. Hu recognized the impossibility of distinguishing May Fourth New Literature from revolutionary politics, and the possibility of radicalism among the revolutionaries of his time. Wang aptly described this process in Hu's poetic practice in his examination of the relationship between lyricism and subjectivity in an epic time:

> Hu Feng was different from Guo Moruo, who equated lyricism with a romantic, populist call to arms, and from Ai Qing, who sought to create a voice between self-indulgence and propaganda. The lyrical mode Hu Feng aimed at neither serves any direct political function nor finds any subtle balance between selfhood and the collective cause. Preferably, it is a process through which the poet comes to a tantalizing point where utopian personhood was in formation, and yet its realization is put on hold. The lyrical is, therefore, a mode "in the making," instantiating the poet's continued struggle, in language as in lived experience, to render the desire and frustration of his time. To that effect, Hu Feng lends a new dimension to his mentor Lu Xun's Mara poet, who does not promise anything but to "pluck one's heart."[60]

Throughout his poetry and editorial work, Hu tried to sing the songs of youth. He sang about his sentiments at the beginning of time, before the revolutionary mind was corrupted and distracted by vulgar politics. His "songs of youth" were never simply outbursts of political fervor or aesthetic indulgence but tests of the potency of the mind in the postrevolutionary

PRC—tests that were necessary in a time of fervent thought reform and ideological reconstruction. They were a recourse to the Lu Xun style of "combative criticism." Recalling Lu Xun and celebrating new blood, Hu embraced the warrior figure in his characterization of the poet as "a little fighting fella" and "a soldier in life."[61]

JULY POETRY: A MODERNISM LOST IN "NATIONAL FORMS"

Wartime China produced national literature and art more extensively than Hu had ever conceived. Where Hu regarded national forms as the opposite of free verse in the historical development of May Fourth New Literature, Mao defined "national forms" as the "fresh lively Chinese style and *spirit* the common people of China love."[62] In 1940 Chongqing, in the wake of Mao's resolution to answer the national question and to develop Marxism-Leninism "with specific national characteristics,"[63] Hu published the two-part pamphlet *On the Question of National Forms* to reiterate his (and Lu Xun's) position in the Two-Slogan Debate.[64] In the pamphlet, notwithstanding the CCP's policy of massification of revolutionary art,[65] Hu argued against Zhou Yang, Ai Siqi, and Chen Boda (and, along with them, principal promoters of "national forms" such as Xiang Linbing and "core writers" like Mao Dun and Guo Moruo), insisting that "national forms" were Confucian relics and as such unfit for revolutionary causes. In Hu's critical genealogy, May Fourth New Literature, which served to anticipate and facilitate social changes, should have been ahead of its time, and therefore should continue with the critical heritage of purging the people of their "intellectual servitude." In Hu's account,

> evidently, in the several thousand years of Chinese cultural history, some elements reflect the dreams of the working classes and contain democratic thoughts. Because of the strong pressure from feudal power and the absence of a foundation whereupon democratic elements could be built, democracy is either destroyed or trapped in a primitive state: it exists as a dream, without being able to be developed into a system of thought or pattern of life. . . . Therefore . . . because there is neither a democratic system nor desire informed by democratic ideas, people's sense of injustice, vexation, bitter pain, sadness, skepticism, resistance,

> demand, and dream . . . would only be rushing and swerving disorderly within their feudal *consciousness*. Like flies searching for light, they hit aimlessly against a glass window.[66]

For Hu, any type of formulism, in general, and traditional and popular cultural forms derived from a Confucian "ruling-class" ethic, specifically, had no prerogative claim on New Poetry. The proposal to mobilize the collective and to promote the practice of pouring "new wine into old bottles" was thus an extreme political pragmatism.

Against their uncompromising assumptions about the vice of nationalist discourse and politics, Hu and his associate writers, the *July* poets, made paradigmatic distinctions between new and old, free verse and national forms, and, by extension, poetry-driven revolutions (i.e., the enlightenment of the masses 化大众) and poetry for the Revolution (i.e., mass entertainment 大众化). Hu's protégé Lu Ling went so far as to describe the "prisons" of Confucian China and "palaces" of the People's Republic in interchangeable terms. He warned his readers that "prisons surrounding us are impermanent" and "lurking in secrecy."[67] Significantly, the distinctive working of sociopolitical oppression and its prevalence in one "secretive" form or another found an afterlife in post-1949 modern Chinese writers' degeneration into the practice of "vulgar Marxism." As "human life is a process of struggle," continued Lu Ling,

> palaces are not only impermanent but also, needless to say, pasted with paper. . . . Young people dare to despise, unsettle, and destroy them and this contempt and attack amount to creativity. . . . However, if the young people, after a few trials, hope to save themselves from the trouble [of struggling] and start doting on the paper-pasted palaces and the dark prisons [and become revisionists], new writers, in the name of life, will supersede them, no matter what tears or smiles they put on.[68]

Despite the historical turning point of 1949, Hu and his close associates never wavered in their belief that ideological achievement and commitment could only come after a sustained process of negating the "intellectual servitude" that characterized and plagued "old China." Hu explained that writers in the GMD's Republic had lost an arena for their own experience of feelings and exercise of sympathy. Often, they threw themselves into the Chinese Revolution by a force of schematized will. For Hu, the gradual perceptions of the proletarian ideals that took place over time were the ones that would have a lasting impact on the collective outlook and aspirations of the time. These transformations could take place with guidance—from Party writers and intellectuals, for example—but they must have been developed deep inside each for them to be genuine over time. Although revolutionary literature was an immediate response to radical politics at the beginning, eventually it had to emerge from the enthusiasm of daily struggles intact. By encompassing life—and along with it the sociopolitical reality of the time—in art, it formed with the experience of life a single organic touchstone, groundwork, if not also a beacon of the Revolution. In Hu's words, "Great knowledge [ideology] must result from a persistent effort in sublimating and synthesizing important experience[s] of life. It should never become the shackle of life or be like roaming clouds."[69]

This debate between Hu and Party leaders on the modalities of representation had implications that far exceeded the technical aspect of literary production, as it touched on foundational questions: What constituted the basic needs, functions, and objectives of literature and art in the Chinese Revolution? Should poetry respond to the strategic need to entertain the masses or should it attempt to improve and raise their "consciousness" of the specific set of historical conditions created by the Chinese Revolution? Specifically, the debate on "national forms" was also one about two traditions of Chinese literary modernism. One contained professional revolutionaries and writers who were at home with national politics and whose creative works were used for enlisting writers to become Mao's *biganzi* (笔杆子, "effective writers"). The other consisted of marginalized writers (i.e., formerly GMD-controlled-area writers) who, oriented toward the May Fourth discourse of national *reform*, were not entirely satisfied with the confines of "national characteristics" or "the national question."

In the history of Chinese literature and literary thinking, the transition from traditional to modern was so abrupt that it was a paradigm shift, linguistically, formalistically, stylistically, and, above all, historically and nationally.[70] This shift was akin to a revolution or a war, an abruptness that Hu considered fundamental to the May Fourth enlightenment project. In this respect, it was no surprise that some *July* poems read like palimpsests of what Carolyn FitzGerald called "fragmenting modernisms."[71] These poems demonstrated that Chinese socialist realism added to "Western" modernism as much as it remade the genre, overcoming or liberating the "limits of realism" that Marston Anderson identified in Chinese revolutionary and postrevolutionary literature.[72] The close affinity between the *July* writers' poetic works and their Western counterparts created the opportunity to use Hu's theory of "literary subjectivism" as an *Ansatzpunkt* (starting point) of finding a "non-Maoist" tradition of "aesthetic Marxism" in socialist China and beyond.[73] Formerly marginalized works such as *Time Has Begun* may have been further points of entry into the study of *Weltliteratur* (world literature) in the Auerbachian sense of the word. In his essay "Philology and *Weltliteratur*," Erich Auerbach acknowledged the irrefutable power of a "leveling process" taking place despite the existence of ever "stronger and louder" national wills.[74] He thus conceptualized postwar, post-Holocaust *Weltliteratur* away from Goethe's Eurocentric approach and urged scholars of his time to go beyond old methodologies and mentalities "so that an inner history of mankind—which thereby created a conception of man unified in his multiplicity—could be written."[75]

Even with his distance from socialist China, Auerbach's advice established in every sense the underlying economy of reading Hu's poiesis, especially in terms of how it connected Chinese socialist realism—via the critical spirit of the May Fourth Movement—as something in the world. That advice helped challenge nationalist assumptions that "Chinese New Literature" was something "formal," an artifice construed for certain political and ideological imports. Ah-long's "White Flower," for instance, exemplified how another *July* school poem achieved a sense of universal humanism by standing on the shoulders of Christian martyrdom rhetoric:

> Do not tread on the dewdrops—
> for a passer-by had whimpered in the night. . . .
>
> Oh, my people, I remember quite well,
> Having read you the Song of Songs in the candlelight.
>
> Don't pray for me in this manner, don't!
> I am innocent, and shall go to God with this bare body of
> yours. . . .
>
> Don't count the space between one star and another.
> Don't count by light-years, but by gravitation, by contrasting
> lights.
>
> Do blossom into a white flower—
> For in this manner, I proclaim ourselves sinless, only to wither
> and fall.[76]

The innocence and the whiteness of the flower in this poem were neither "national characteristics" nor biblical references for the poet-soldier, but rather "living phenomena brought into existence by . . . man,"[77] the poetic I's realities of life—revolutionary sacrifice and resurrection—given proper, direct expression, as when soldiers died, entombed in a snowy battlefield.[78] Any insurgent attempt to reinforce "national characteristics" or biblical messages would only rupture understanding, as though short-circuiting a whole universe of meanings. This instance of a "non-Maoist," nonnationalist experiment of aesthetic Marxism is an example of *Weltliteratur*'s strong confidence in the virtue of fruitful multiplicities, the power of sympathetic imagination and synthesis, the potential of "sequins mixed together," and poiesis.

VII

THE HU FENG INCIDENT REVISITED

> We don't execute people like Hu. . . . not because their crimes don't deserve capital punishment but because such executions would yield no advantage. . . . Counterrevolutionaries are trash, they are vermin, but once in your hands, you can make them perform some kind of service for the people.
>
> —Mao Zedong (1956)[1]

> Power is exercised only over free subjects, only insofar as they are free. . . . When the determining factors saturate the whole there is no relationship of power; slavery is not a relationship.
>
> —Michel Foucault (1982)[2]

The preceding chapters have discussed Hu's involvement in the politics and practices of Marxist literary criticism—his revolutionary romanticism, his intellectual genealogy, his literary subjectivism and "subjective combative spirit," and his poiesis. Within the broader context of discussing literary criticism's "service" in the political reality of Communist China, this chapter will focus on the development of Marxist criticism in the post-1949 era. In this larger context, the fact that Hu was the first intellectual purged in the PRC and in the wake of the CCP's one-party rule denoted another fact: criticism and power. Concretely, criticism in the PRC worked as a hegemonic discourse of "truth" through individuals as agents of power, through what Foucault called "the bodies that are constituted as subjects by power-effects."[3] In other words, much as Hu's dialogic relation with the CCP's ideology characterized his adaptability to changing political circumstances, the CCP's establishment of state power depended on the reification and appropriation of intellectual power.

The close connection between these two phenomena—the substitution of discourse for criticism and criticism for power—was directly illustrated by the pernicious character of critical practices in the PRC. While it is true that the CCP had dictated literary practices to accommodate its political agenda, in actual history it had never arrived at a consistently practiced ideological principle that could serve, independent of human will, as a standard of judgment. On the contrary, as shown by the Hu Incident and throughout the history of socialist China, the CCP's practice of cultural policy was characteristically inconsistent. What was politically correct or wrong, revolutionary or counterrevolutionary, progressive or reactionary, was never fixed or frozen. A standard political position held at one point might, at any subsequent moments, be abrogated and wielded into its political other.[4] Under the circumstances, from the mid-1950s to the end of the 1970s, the literary scene repeatedly placed Hu in close association with the major literary figures purged after him, even though some of them were his political or professional foes. For three decades, the name Hu served as a symbol of political criminality: whoever connected with it had at least the potential of being categorized as "counterrevolutionary."

The relationship between Hu and Zhou is a principal case in point. In a position of power before his arrest at the beginning of the Cultural Revolution, Zhou made every effort to exclude Hu from the CCP's mainstream cultural life.[5] Given his leading role in the series of campaigns against Hu, it might have seemed logical to expect Hu's rehabilitation to come after Zhou's persecution in 1966. Yet, in the late 1970s, just as Hu had learned about the fall of Zhou and awaited the end of his fourteen-year sentence, the CCP demanded an investigation of "Hu's double-sidedness" and recategorized him as a supporter of Zhou, his former persecutor and by then the Party's ideological enemy and political prisoner. In this light, any logic achieved from history was but another testimony to human will.

In 1969, without regard to the earlier standard for literary criticism, of which Zhou was its representative and against which the Party imprisoned Hu,[6] the Party enforced a corrupt ideological union between them. It redefined Hu as a member of the Zhou "clique." By reversing the critical conventions in the 1950s that ratified Zhou as a figure of power in his role as a Party representative, Yao Wenyuan added yet another layer of irony to the Hu Incident. In his infamous 1967 critical essay on Zhou, he demonstrated the impossibility of a critic escaping from discursive Marxism at a time when critics were systematically refuting critical power to define just what "Marxist ideology and Mao Zedong Thought" meant:

> Zhou, like Hu, has repeatedly advocated the idea that "the highest principle of art is truth" (1952) and opposed Marxist ideology and Mao Zedong Thought. Like Hu, he is against the principle that literature and art should serve the workers, peasants, and soldiers . . . arguing that [the writer] should have "total freedom" in [her] "choice of subject matter." . . . Zhou, under better disguise, shares all of Hu's reactionary views on literature and art.[7]

Here, not attempting to follow a consistent use of cultural policy—or the absence of such a policy—Yao evaded the apparent difference between Hu and Zhou in terms of their literary theories and charged them both with the same crime. Framed by critics like Yao, who chose to use literary criticism by his political calculations, Hu was simultaneously a friend of his enemy and a friend of his enemy's enemy. In Yao's critical schemata, Hu and Zhou were class enemies alike, who stood against Mao and Mao's position on art and literature: "Zhou takes advantage of himself being Hu's target and presents himself as a spokesman of Mao's cultural line. . . . He is a counterrevolutionary in the guise of a revolutionary."[8] The fact that Hu or Zhou could be at once on the "right" and "wrong" sides of the same law made explicit how incoherent and self-serving the CCP was in its employment of ideological doctrines. Equally important, it revealed how cultural production and practices in socialist China were central to a "revolutionary" discourse, which the critics themselves had helped build to intervene into left-wing politics as the Party established and dictated them.[9]

LITERARY CRITICISM AS A DISCURSIVE PRACTICE

The instrumental discursive nature of Marxist literary criticism in socialist China played out most dramatically in the long years of the Cultural Revolution, which the Hu Incident had prefigured a decade earlier. At the turn of the twenty-first century, many scholars began to investigate the function and agency of the modern Chinese intellectual. Why did a plethora of writers and critics, who were the source of intellectual and language power, become at once authors and subjects of Mao's revolutionary ideology? In most cases, studies of the modern Chinese intellectual solved the mystery of the seeming "irrationality"[10] in the left-wing intellectual's critical positions by specifying the trajectory through which "Marxist literary criticism" developed as a sphere of intellectual power and a source of political agency. The 1955 national campaign against Hu was an excellent starting point.

The Hu Incident inaugurated the beginning of a new epoch in the PRC's intellectual history. It announced no less than the beginning of what Wan Tonglin referred to as "the age of a big critical discourse" that "smothered Chinese society."[11] In other words, the process of China's transformation from a half-feudal and half-colonized country into a sovereign nation was simultaneously a process through which literary intellectuals added and empowered discourse as a method of criticism into the forces of historical transformation. Yi-tsi Feuerwerker observed that the literary intellectual's "tremendous power of language" had "important consequences in . . . the turbulent relations between the writer/intellectual and the party-state."[12] Speaking of the Chinese Communists' "overriding obsession" with language, Feuerwerker also noted the CCP's extraordinary ability to attract intellectuals, writers, and critics. He argued that their discursive and narrative power to shape the identity and history of modern China had contributed significantly to the CCP's political ascendency: "When we consider the astonishing evolution of the Chinese Communists in Yan'an from a band of stragglers . . . into a political party that would take control of all China within a short dozen years, Mao Zedong's narrative reconstruction of reality and its capacity to engage the broad participation of the intellectuals and writers was singularly effective."[13]

The CCP constructed knowledge around a self-enemy paradigm. Specifically, it engaged in an effort of political mapping onto the social classes so that intellectuals would not have a proper place unless they were willing to deny their subjectivity, agency, and freedom and give up their traditional sense of superiority over the masses. Such an effort of class segregation began with two questions—"Who are our enemies?" and "Who are our friends?"—that Mao asked in his 1926 essay "Analysis of the Classes in Chinese Society."[14] Following these questions, Mao classified Chinese society into five groups—the landlord class and the comprador class, the middle bourgeoisie, the petty bourgeoisie, the semiproletariat, and the proletariat. According to Mao's classification, writers and artists belonged to the petty bourgeoisie class, while "the proletariat" was "the leading force" in the Chinese

Revolution. Mao's social class stratification created a belief system wherein two categories of signification—"the proletariat" and "the bourgeoisie"—were defined against each other.[15] Given the circumstances of wartime, it engaged writers and intellectuals who were preoccupied with the question of national survival to join with the CCP in its effort to ostracize the "capitalists" and in the process tightened their bonds with the Party. The idea of capitalists as representatives of "the evil of imperialist domination," as Zhang Guotao called them,[16] was deeply entrenched in popular understanding, largely because they were the *conditio sine qua non* of global capitalist expansion, which entered China at the beginning of the twentieth century. To participate in the Party's political action, one had to accept Mao's identification of "the masses of workers, peasants, and soldiers" as the progressive social force.[17] Specifically, "cultural workers" had to admit their inadequacy as the agency of Chinese modernization and acknowledge their ignorance about the language and thinking of the masses, although the "masses" were also a political construction and a product of arbitrary authority.[18]

Mao's "Analysis of the Classes in Chinese Society" had far-reaching implications for literary intellectuals in terms of their worldview, which defined their self-worth and critical methodology. First, as Mao unseated writers and intellectuals from the back of the masses, he exiled them to the margins of the Chinese Revolution and instilled in them deep anxiety about their historical value and relevance. Because of the Sino-Japanese War, the CCP's attempt to establish, control, and manipulate its narrative about modern Chinese history[19] not only did not drive writers and intellectuals away, it even heightened their sense of commitment to radical politics, producing in them an apprehension that called into question literature's use value in the processes of Chinese modernization and nation-building. Second, the constitution of this group of committed writers and intellectuals marked the beginning of a long-standing, interdependent tie between literature and politics. It offered literary intellectuals some form of resolution to the question of their place in the new social order. Defined by a political discourse that simultaneously denied their subjectivity and made meaningful their potential social function and historical place, literary intellectuals dedicated their creative and critical energy to Mao's revolutionary politics. Li Yang offered a perceptive reading of their perplexity:

> Why is it necessary and possible for intellectuals to undergo self-reform? . . . [Modern Chinese] intellectuals need such "others" as "the proletariat" and "the peasant." . . . When intellectuals

> create social constructs such as "the proletariat" and "the peasant," they are in effect implanting some essential qualities into the workers and peasants. From then on, "workers" and "peasants" have some ontological qualities. Precisely because of those qualities, intellectuals can prove their existence and transform themselves into the masses of workers. They do so in order to find their essence. This is the true meaning of self-reform and self-transformation.[20]

I will not go into detail about the extent to which the CCP abused the category of "masses of the workers, peasants, and soldiers." Instead, I will only point out how Mao's analysis of Chinese society gave birth to a conceptual framework in which critics and intellectuals used Marxism crudely as a political instrument and transmuted criticism into an opportunistic form of political engagement. The way to participate in effective administration was to "go among the masses"; this crucial suggestion would become a life-and-death instruction sixteen years later. In the Yan'an Forum on Literature and Art held in 1942, Mao, then the highest commander of the CCP, gave two talks. In the opening speech on May 2, Mao said, "China's revolutionary writers and artists . . . of promise must go among the masses; they must for a long period unreservedly and whole-heartedly go among the masses."[21]

To ask literature and art "to serve the masses of workers, peasants, and soldiers" was, as chapter IV has discussed, to define literature and art as part of the CCP's social and political practice. The stakes were high, for Mao was asking writers and artists to give themselves up to the Party's imaginings of the intellectual's role and function in post-1949 socialist China. Positioned against the "masses," which in Mao's certain political judgment had always been demonstrably transient, the Party offered the intellectuals no stable subject position or criterion of evaluation. In other words, what originated as a military strategy that sought to find a place for literary intellectuals to participate in the Chinese Revolution created constant internal pressures for writers and critics to change, transform, and reinvent themselves following the need to refute and reform themselves! Writers and critics had a narrow field on which to fight for their political interests by proving their determination to undergo thought reform. As for the measure—and the issue of its consistency or inconsistency, logic or illogic—Mao's model of categorical critical judgments allowed those who were in the position of power to define who the "masses" were and to subject any individuals of *differential* relations to the "masses" so described. It all depended on the self-interests and sensibilities of the critical intellectual. Hu was a victim of such power because he was self-alienated from the standard of that abstract notion of the "masses."

DISCOURSE AND POWER

In the summer of 1971, Hu suffered from hallucinations and depression. There was no place for him in this world; intractable figures were everywhere, perpetually poised to deploy fatal attacks against him. One day, he picked up a brick and struck his head; this suicide attempt was as much a protest against the Party's treatment of him as it was a sign of his total despair. After this brief moment of despair, Hu renewed his confidence in the CCP as a new point of origin in China's literary Marxism. The CCP, he concluded, was the ultimate embodiment of logic, the institutional expression of *the* moral truth he had long believed in; it was the source of his life and meaning of life. Reflecting on how he felt about the Party's decision to sentence him to fourteen years of imprisonment, Hu wrote: "I accepted the sentence, but the verdict didn't convince me."[22] The same sentiment prevailed despite yet another ten years of imprisonment. In 1977, reflecting on his state of mind after receiving the CCP's final verdict on his case from the court, Hu wrote:

> The officers in the detention center asked for my opinion [about the sentence] one day after the sentence. They were reluctant to pass a verdict that seemed right but was wrong. I replied: I dare not judge [the verdict]. Though unconvinced, I accept it; for it's only natural for the government to make decisions profitable for its future and the people. . . . And yet, the punishment is severe. It considers my debates with the cultural leaders and my "Report" to the Central Committee to be counterrevolutionary. From the Party's perspective (not from that of the legal system), my activities and views have undermined the prestige of the cultural leaders if not that of the Party. Such is a principally mistaken view. I have not intended to cause political trouble and have never been against the Party (or the Central Committee); on the contrary, my activities and views aim at supporting and protecting the Party.[23]

Considering Hu's belief in the CCP as an embodiment of a certain kind of "moral truth" in politics, his suicide attempt was, I think, a consequence of both the experienced cruelty of life and a tragic epiphany. Given the corrupt and massive use of Marxist literary criticism as political capital and a discursive weapon, Hu, for a moment, lost faith in the CCP's ability to provide a credible frame of reference in critical practice. Many years later, Hu explained that he was not entirely hopeless during his long imprisonment but wished to end his life the moment he read about criticism's marriage to power for power: "In August 1971, I saw the power over my life and death laid in the hands of . . . Yao Wenyuan and Zhang Chunqiao. . . . I attempted to liberate myself by breaking my head with a brick."[24] What Yao and Zhang (1917–2005) as a joint force meant to Hu hinted at certain qualities in intellectual power that Hu did not fully perceive during his persecution in the 1950s, but that he now understood in prison, once he knew better and had lost his "foolishness."

The year 1971 was one in which the CCP shrank into a state of nonpresence and acted like a clueless puppet for a group of "intellectuals for power" and "intellectuals in power." The fact that Hu had remained optimistic about his future for sixteen years but broke down in 1971 provides a unique perspective from which to account for the historical "leaps" and fate of Mao's intellectuals. While Hu's pessimism was largely vestigial, the fear about certain problematic tendencies in the literary circle that he had detected was real: literature's total submission to politics, which created the right conditions for the practice of cultural adventurism and opportunism. This problem reminded Hu of the role his comrades played, at their initiative and often unreservedly, in the events that precipitated his persecution. In the same letter to Xiong Zimin, Hu wrote:

> The problem of Lin Biao and the Gang of Four is the most severe one in the history of the Chinese Revolution. . . . One needs to find out its historical roots and ideological origin in order to fight against it and to prevent it from happening again. *In China, the problem begins in literature and art, from within the Party.* The same old problem cause[d] the "rectification movement" in Yan'an, the campaign against Hu's counterrevolutionary clique after the liberation, and the seizure of power by Lin Biao and the Gang of Four during the Cultural Revolution.[25]

The collaboration of literature and politics, as a foundational ideology of the CCP, was contemplated in the 1920s, formalized in the 1940s, and was entirely played out during the Cultural Revolution. Goldman described the intellectuals who emerged in the early 1960s as "academically trained" radical intellectuals who played "a conspicuous role in condemning the views of the older, established intellectuals" from whom they "differed" given their "more Marxist-oriented education" and "lower" position "in the academic hierarchy." Thus, "their opposition to the senior intellectuals was generational, personal, and opportunistic, as well as ideological."[26] Although Zhou and Yao were men in power within the political establishment, there was a qualitative difference between them in terms of their politics of literary criticism. Zhou's embodied something that Hu found controversial, but Yao and his critical practice invoked in Hu nothing but horror, anger, and despair.

Yao's political fortune began with his teenage dream of becoming a creative writer. Contrary to popular belief, Yao did not first become famous as the "gold cudgel" that Jiang Qing used to beat political enemies. He built fame and success first as a "Marxist literary critic" of Hu.[27] Yao knew about Hu through his father Yao Fengzi, whose engagement with left-wing literary activities in the 1930s and 1940s provided him with the opportunity to read extensively and with admiration Hu's literary theory.[28] Certainly, he would not have been able to churn out thirteen pieces of criticism of Hu's literary thought within a matter of months, with half of them published in *Liberation Daily*, had he not spent years studying Hu. According to Ye Yonglie's biography of Yao, as the Party was instigating a large-scale public campaign against Hu, Yao was busy writing his second book, *On Hu Feng's Literary Thought* 论胡风文艺思想,[29] to *commend* and *compliment* Hu's literary theory. Yao, attempting to fulfill his dream of becoming a writer, sought to follow Hu's path by making a career out of writing criticism.[30] He was at that time twenty years old and working as a correspondent in the Propaganda Department of the Luwan District in Shanghai.

It was in vain to expect that history would follow a rational course. Just as Yao was preparing to send off his monograph on Hu's literary theory, Zhou gave a speech titled "We Must Fight," which the *People's Daily* subsequently published on December 10, 1954. This speech announced the call for a critical campaign against Hu and made public for the first time what had been until then an internal conflict in the Party's cultural arena.[31] At midnight on December 16, Yao, revoking the views expressed in *On Hu Feng's Literary Thought*, wrote, with no reference to his earlier admiration for Hu, "Isn't it clear that Hu has taken a stance directly opposed to Marxism and the Party?"[32] A swift change indeed—and a reaction not just against Hu but against the very set of "literary thought" that Hu had used to guide the practice of Marxist criticism. To say that

Hu opposed Marxism and the Party in 1955 was nearly saying that Hu was a counterrevolutionary.

With his uncanny sensitivity about the direction of the political winds, Yao swiftly reinvented himself and made possible his membership in the central-power caucuses: "Having read Comrade Zhou's 'We Must Fight' . . . I feel that there is the absolute need to draw a boundary between Mr. Hu's views and mine."[33] Soon after the publication of Zhou's article, Yao gave the longest speech at a meeting held in Shanghai, redefining the tone of the meeting's criticism of Hu.[34] This speech, published in *Literature and Art Monthly*,[35] caught the attention of Zhang Chunqiao, then head of Shanghai's Propaganda Department and editor of *Liberation Daily*, and helped established an alliance between Yao and Zhang. The Yao-Zhang alliance that constituted at least half of the "glory" of the Gang of Four began with a shared understanding of the kinds of ideological uses members of the Gang of Four made of Marxist literary criticism during the Cultural Revolution. Yao's and Zhang's readiness to utilize the bureaucratic machine for power and their sense that the institutional power inherent in Marxism as the new ideological state apparatus was invaluable to them revealed precisely that shared understanding.

"Literature and art are subordinate to politics. Literary and art critics must first be politicians and pay attention to the changing climate of politics. I have inside information," Zhang instructed and informed Yao during their first private meeting.[36] This "inside information" led to the publication on March 15 of Yao's essay, "Marxism or anti-Marxism? Review of a Few Points in Hu's 'Report on Literary and Artistic Practice since Liberation' to the Central Committee," which filled a full page in *Liberation Daily*.[37] That evening, Yao paid another visit to Zhang and solicited more inside information: the CCP would elevate its struggle against Hu to another level.[38] Since not many people in Shanghai dared to confront Hu, especially directly, Zhang suggested that Yao should write some more for *Liberation Daily*.[39] Whether out of a sense of gratitude or personal ambition or a mixture of both, Yao became even more receptive to Zhang's calls. On March 28, the *Wenhui Post*, the other major newspaper in Shanghai, published Yao's "The Reactionary Nature of Hu's Literary Thought."[40]

In the week before *Liberation Daily* published Hu's "300,000-Character Report" and, along with it, Mao's "Editor's Comments," Yao published three essays in the newspaper to condemn Hu's "subjective historicism."[41] Notably, *Liberation Daily* published not only Yao's critical essays every other day consecutively for six days but also Hu's "300,000-Character Report" and Mao's

"Editor's Comments" on May 13, *barely* two days after the publication of Yao's last essay in the series. There was no mistake that Yao's pieces appeared to prepare for the final launch of a national campaign against Hu. Zhang's private information enabled Yao to reinvent himself—from a loser lost in his teenage dream to a "prophet" and "hero"—first in the politics of literary criticism and later in mainstream politics. After the Party formally launched a public campaign against Hu, the print media continued to publish Yao's anti-Hu polemics.[42]

There is little need to go into detail about these critical essays on Hu as the titles alone show that Yao's critical language and logic were at once imprisoned and empowered by Mao's analytical framework of China's social classification, which followed a self-contained circular envelopment. Yao's "proletarian" stand was firmly displayed vis-à-vis his antagonism toward Hu's "bourgeois" or "petit-bourgeois" stand. Once again, political categories were employed to usurp and homogenize thinking into system-serving ideas. This series of essays recorded the working of a mind that appeared to be uncannily sensitive and anticipatory of major upcoming political shifts and turns. After "reading Shu Wu's 'Materials on Hu's Counterrevolutionary Clique,' " published in the *People's Daily* on May 13, Yao said that he was greatly angered: "We can see that these materials reflect an extremely shameless soul, a soul that is nurtured by fanatical subjectivism and the lowest kind of tactics of a politician."[43] Yao's language was almost the same as that used by the Party in denouncing Hu.

Within the cultural domain, there would be no force more devastating than writers and literary intellectuals co-opted by and with political power. The Yao-Zhang alliance emptied Hu of all hope because it set a precedent for and anticipated the worst kind of literary politics. Indeed, with the continual rise and centralization of state-ideological power in the post-1949 years, increasingly more individuals joined the ranks of the "radical intellectuals" and became detached from critical and literary practices. With an eagerness to pose as Marxist ideologues, they beefed up cultural and political rectification movements, including the one against Hu.

THE "YAO WENYUAN PHENOMENON" AND THE HU INCIDENT

Although no other modern Chinese writers demonstrated Yao's abilities to use criticism for political ends and personal advantage to the same extent, his life and career typified a generation of Marxist writers and critics who understood the force of literature in the service of party politics. In *The Martyrs*, Wan pointed out that Yao was a "phenomenon" in that his use of literary criticism, even if unprecedented in its excessively political way, was not unique: "Yao represented a group of literary men, a Yao type of people, and a Yao phenomenon. These men were . . . tools for political struggle and political fights."[44] Yao shared with the "radical intellectuals" a set of commonalities, especially in terms of their position on Hu. Like Yao at the beginning of the Cultural Revolution, these individuals were in the inner circle of political power and among the most active in the Party's several campaigns against Hu.

One must examine the specific ways the CCP's political structure empowered this "group of literary men" to understand their ideological use of Marxist literary criticism in post-1949 China. By the 1950s, Marxist literary criticism had ceased to be a public discourse. It became a closed system intolerant of marginalized writers and critics who, like Hu, were "individualistic" and therefore inconsistent with the Party's cultural policy of ideological homogeneity among writers and critics. Cultural leaders like Zhou were more than merely the practitioners of revolutionary literature, art, and criticism they were before the founding of the PRC. As they grew with the power of the CCP, they embodied state authority and ideological law and order. For all their appeal for and to power, their criticism of Hu developed from a dispute about literary and art theory and became a nation-wide political movement. On May 13, 1955, three days before the arrest of Hu, the *People's Daily* published the first batch of Hu's letters under the title "Collection of Materials on the Hu Counterrevolutionary Clique 关于胡风反革命集团的材料" (hereafter "Collection of Materials"). It consisted of Hu's article "My Self-Criticism"; a collection of thirty-four private letters between Hu and Shu Wu written in the years between 1944 and 1950, which Shu Wu excerpted, compiled, and grouped;[45] and an "Editorial," which, as is now understood, Mao penned. Mao's words were severe:

> The reason for our publishing only now Hu's "My Self-Criticism," which he first wrote in January, revised in February, and to which he added an "afterword" in March, along with Shu Wu's "Materials on the Hu Counterrevolutionary Clique," is to prevent Hu from making use of our newspapers to continue to deceive the readers. From the materials brought to light in Shu Wu's article, the readers can see how early Hu and the anti-Party,

> anti-people, counterrevolutionary clique he led showed their hostility, enmity, and hatred for the Communist and non-Communist progressive writers. . . . It is possible that there are still more members in the Hu counterrevolutionary clique who, like Shu Wu, have been deceived and decide now to stop running along with Hu. They should hand over to the government still more materials exposing Hu. Concealment cannot last long; the day will inevitably come when the truth is exposed. Even the strategy of shifting from attack to retreat (i.e., self-criticism) cannot deceive people. Self-criticism must be like that of Shu Wu; phony self-criticism won't do. . . . Everyone who was mixed up with Hu and who has received secret letters from him should hand them over. . . . Hu should undertake the task of peeling off his mask and not make deceitful self-criticism.[46]

Upon these words, the campaign against Hu that had been going on since January changed in nature, taking all involved by surprise. In less than a month, the *People's Daily* published the second and third batch of "Collection of Materials" on May 24 and June 10, respectively; they consisted mainly of excerpts from a total of 130 letters between Hu and his friends and followers, including new writers who approached Hu for advice on writing. On June 10, following the appearance of the last batch of "Collection of Materials," the Central Committee redefined the "Hu small clique" from an "anti-Party clique" to "a counterrevolutionary clique." In June, the three batches of "Collection of Materials," together with Mao's "Editorials," were collected and published in a monograph.[47] Within a month, the book was reprinted seven times and sold over one million copies.

There was no doubt that it was Mao who finally decided to change the definition of the "Hu clique" from one of "anti-Party" to one of "counterrevolutionary," and thus to change radically the nature of what was originally and primarily a difference in views on literature. Lin Mohan, director of the Art and Literature Section in the CCP's Propaganda Department in 1955, claimed that this was a development "no one could have anticipated" at the time, and he could not fully explain what had happened.[48] There was no good reason to dispute Lin. He might not have wanted to see Hu arrested and was not fully conscious of his role in the arrest of Hu. Still, Mao could not have made this decision had many others not conceived the idea of Hu as a political dissident. More critical, thus, is to understand how the structure of state power interacted with the institution of literature and criticism; one must first recognize the continuity between the cultural leaders' discursive position and Mao's ultimate verdict on Hu and follow from that realization the turn of events that was to come. January 15, 1955 was historically *the* day that the Hu Incident changed in nature. On that day, Zhou sent a letter to Lu Dingyi, the minister of the Central Committee Propaganda Department. He reported on his discussion with Hu, which included Hu's erroneous views on literature and art, and asked for guidelines for response to Hu's plea to hold his "300,000-Character Report" off from publication, or, if it must, that it appear along with a statement by Hu. Zhou wrote:

> Last night Hu . . . admitted that he made mistakes, that he had adopted a bourgeois point of view instead of a proletarian one, that his ideological methods were one-sided and contained in them individualistic heroism, and that his thinking had developed to the point where he opposed the Party's leadership in literature and art. . . . I said that his self-critical attitude toward his erroneous thinking was good; however, realizing and criticizing one's own mistakes is by no means easy. *One has to go through a painful process. He should expect more criticism from others.* . . . Finally, he expressed the hope that the Central Committee would not publish his "[300,000-Character] Report." Even if it did, he hoped to make some revisions. He said some of the contents were not factual. *I said that its publication and some public discussion of it would be beneficial.* . . . He said that if this was the case, he hoped to add a statement[49] to preface the Report.[50]

Zhou forwarded this letter to Mao; he would not have known that such an ordinary act, which must have been a regular part of his bureaucratic existence, was to become one of the most defining moments in the literary history of Communist China. Although there are few published documents about Mao's initial interest in the matter, after Zhou forwarded the letter, things took a sharp turn and started to develop in a direction that no one claimed to have anticipated. What role did Zhou, a writer and critic himself, play in the campaign against Hu? What did it reveal about the historical relationship between literary critical freedom and political realities within a one-party system? Like many of his colleagues in the Propaganda Department, Zhou started as a committed writer but ended up as a constitutive element of the state ideological apparatus. He had no sympathy toward those who were losing the debate. He advised against allowing Hu to make a statement about his "Report":

> Hu's purpose in publishing this statement is to create a wrong impression before the people that he has already admitted his mistakes . . . and to resist criticism. Its publication would harm us. I am therefore opposed to its publication.[51]

Aspects of this letter recommended that it be treated historically as well as ideologically instructive. Paramount throughout was the presence of Zhou's lead recommendations, which entirely preempted Hu from having a voice in the center of state ideological power. On the very same day, Mao made the following comments on Zhou's letter: "first, such a 'statement' cannot be published; second, Hu's bourgeois idealism and his anti-Party and anti-masses views on literature and art must be thoroughly criticized. Do not let him ensconce himself in a mere admission of his 'bourgeois point of view.'"[52] On January 20, 1955, the Propaganda Department sent the Central Committee a report on the launching of a critical campaign against Hu. "At that time," according to Li Xin, "the Central Committee usually approved documents that were drafted by the Propaganda Department."[53] The report began by noting that the inherent errors in Hu's views on literature and art were as follows:

> [Hu] has systematically and continuously propagandized his *bourgeois* idealism and his anti-Party and *anti-masses* thinking on literature and art. Under a "Marxist" cover, he denies the role of literature as serving the Party in the name of "realism," ignores Marxism's role in literature and art, denies the importance for writers to live among the masses and to study Marxist-Leninist theory, and denies the national literary heritage and national forms in literature and art. . . . He . . . vilifies the current leaders in literature and art as "insane" and "factional."[54]

Note here in this passage, as in many of its other documents on art and literature, how the CCP's language of literary criticism adapted itself to suit a language of political authority empowered by and empowering the state's ideological apparatus. Six days later, on January 26, the Central

Committee approved the report and promulgated it to the whole Party. In the circular that went with the report, identifying Hu as an "anti-Party element," the Central Committee decreed:

> Under the guise of "Marxism," [Hu] has been waging war against the Party and the masses for a long time. . . . The CCP committees at all levels must pay attention to this ideological struggle and treat it as a major struggle between the working class and the bourgeoisie, and as a strategic opportunity to promote materialism and oppose idealism both inside and outside the Party.[55]

This Propaganda Department report and the circular from the Central Committee that followed marked a turning point, but not only in the case of Hu. Much of this cross-referencing between the two documents indicated a significant change in the Marxist literary critic's role in revolutionary politics and sense of self as a critical intellectual. The CCP's assumption of state power in 1949 did more than upset the still reasonably balanced relationship between ideological power and intellectual power in the early 1940s; it created a climate and opportunity for rampant careerism and political opportunism. The workings of the CCP's ideological state apparatus rested not only on the censoring of all individualistic and "capitalistic" kinds of thought and expression but also on the effective elimination of any independent intellectual attempt. By 1949, criticism had become a career avenue; it was a form of proactive, participatory advancement. In their new roles of power, using criticism to defend and announce their political and revolutionary identity, Mao's "cultural workers" no longer addressed, as they attempted to in the 1930s, the ethical question of how literature and criticism relate to social development and moral life.

At this point, Hu had no possibility of escape. Although, as Lin claimed, "no one could have anticipated" the way the Hu Incident developed, the very idea that there was a "Hu clique" came from the political invention of a few opportunistic individuals. The way the Hu clique became an object of public censure was both fortuitous and predetermined. In fact, before the *People's Daily* published the first batch of "Collection of Materials," the *Literary Gazette*, following the Central Committee's and Mao's instruction on January 12, 1955, was already preparing to publish the materials with an editorial from its editor-in-chief, Kang Zhuo.[56] Yet, at the moment Zhou and Lin were to send the proofs to Kang Zhuo, Zhou "suddenly" felt that they "should let Chairman Mao take a look at the materials" because "they were rather important."[57] On May 9, Zhou sent Mao Hu's "My Self-Criticism" along with Shu Wu's "Materials on the Hu Small Clique" and Kang Zhuo's editorial.

There have been different and sometimes conflicting accounts of how these letters between Hu and his friends were selected, edited, and sorted, and of how Central Committee members, including Mao, were given the chance to access and approach them.[58] As far as Hu and other victims of the Hu Incident were concerned, however, it made no real difference whether Shu Wu's initiative or Lin Mohan's suggestion brought their letters to the attention of the highest level of political authority. *No one* involved in the process demonstrated the slightest degree of intellectual honesty or moral conscience. Lin claimed in his account of the "Hu counterrevolutionary case" that they had taken extra caution to ensure the accuracy of the materials they put together in the process of collating the private letters.[59] This was not true. When the letters arrived on Mao's desk, they had been edited, truncated, and annotated so extensively that they provoked authoritarian hostility.[60] Though replaced by Mao's in the end, Kang Zhuo's editorial, which had "incorporated Zhou's and Lin's views,"[61] played a major role in defining the nature of this critical campaign against Hu. The editorial is worth quoting at some length:

> The nationwide criticism of Hu's bourgeois idealist thought on literature and art has been going on for five months. Hu has now written "My Self-Criticism," which we have gained special permission to print. Although Hu has admitted to some of his mistakes, he claims that the root of his mistakes lies in his "confusion between bourgeois standpoint and proletarian standpoint." He emphasizes that his mistakes originated in the fact that "he understood things only in terms of concrete practice rather than under the political principles." . . . Here he evades the fundamental problem: his thinking characterizes bourgeois idealism. It is precisely this conservative outlook that constitutes the foundation of Hu's anti-Party, anti-people, and anti-socialist theory and the practice of his small clique. Therefore, Hu's self-criticism is not acceptable.[62]

It might be true that Kang's editorial was, as Lin said, "much more moderate in tone and content" than Mao's;[63] however, it was surely not the case that Kang attempted to define "the Hu problem" as one "with his views on literature and art and his ideology," that is, a problem that was "still an internal problem within the masses."[64] Cultural leaders like Zhou, Lin, and Kang played a crucial role in the development of the Hu Incident, despite their insistence that they had not anticipated and thus had not prepared for the elevation of the case from "a difference in opinion over literature and art" to "a political problem" and a class conflict.[65]

Historically, Shu Wu was one of the first to frame Hu's problems in literature and criticism in political and even criminal terms. His act of submitting Hu's private letters to the Party altered the historical course of the Hu Incident. Mao was not the first one to use the term *anti-Party* to define the nature of Hu's critical writing and practice; Shu Wu was. As early as 1954, Shu Wu used the term in his essay "Hu's Anti-Marxist Thought on Literature and Art,"[66] which led the way for the publication of another one, entitled "Hu's Anti-Party and Anti-People Thought on Literature and Art," in the *People's Daily* on April 13, 1955.[67] For Shu Wu at least, that Hu was finally charged as a "counterrevolutionary," as he had implied him to be, could not have come as a surprise.[68] Much of the language he used in denouncing Hu reappeared in and fed the CCP's official verdict on the critic. Shu Wu's primary purpose in providing the materials was, as Lin said, "to help us all further understand the nature of Hu's mistaken *ideology* as reflected in his views on literature and art."[69] However, in his criticism of Hu, Shu Wu consistently invoked Mao's theory of the social classes in China and attempted, as Lin emphasized, to direct attention to Hu's diction in his rejection of materialism. He highlighted how, for example, Hu used "philistine" as an epithet for "materialism"—a term that not only persuasively demonstrated Hu's "revulsion" toward materialism but also might have infuriated Mao.[70]

In Communist China, revolutionary writers, critics, and other literary intellectuals were victims of the regime not only because every one of them had experienced persecution. From the first day of the Chinese Revolution, they entered into a lifelong collaboration with the CCP, embracing orthodox Marxism as *the* guiding principle for the revolutionary cause and subsuming their subjectivity within an extraordinary form of subjectivity—that of the collective revolutionary ideal. As the very goal of their practice, the collective revolutionary ideal had two political and historical functions. First, insofar as their life was inseparable from the Chinese Revolution, it served as the foundation of these literary intellectuals' will to live and motivated them into action. Second, it provided a framework and language with which to think, to express, to judge, to calculate, and to act. However, this collective revolutionary ideal did not remain static. In response to the conditions of the Chinese Revolution, literary intellectuals compelled themselves to behold different criteria for "truth" during different rectification movements and to perceptually and perpetually utilize that "truth," insofar as various political ends illuminated their perception. Therefore, any ideal was more presupposed than real: its existence permeated the literary debates and campaigns through which the politically correct and the politically deviant took turns creating categories to constitute reality.

In 1986, a year after the death of Hu, Ba Jin wrote the essay "Remembering Hu Feng." What Ba Jin wanted contemporary intellectuals to learn from Hu and his case was what Hu had emphasized throughout: the intellectual pessimism and consciousness required to resist the temptation of ideological opportuneness. Profoundly apologetic to Hu, Ba Jin criticized the writers' and intellectuals' impotence in their public role and responsibility to speak the truth to power. He asked whether they too should be responsible for Hu's tragedy: "Nobody would stand up to admit to their mistakes and accept their responsibilities, but should those who added fuel to the fire bear no responsibility? History cannot be made up in whatever way one pleases; silence would not stop the truth coming to light in due course."[71] Ba Jin also wrote against Hu in 1955; however, three decades later, he felt the need to apologize and, more significantly, to reflect upon the role that the intellectuals and their literary discourse had played in the making of the Hu Incident.

EPILOGUE

> Commitment, if it means anything, is surely conscious, active, and open: a choice of position. . . . The key question, in the matter of alignment and commitment, is the nature of the transition from historical analysis.
>
> —Raymond Williams[1]

At his birthday party hosted by Princeton University in February 2004, Liu Binyan, known outside of the PRC as "the conscience of China,"[2] reminded his guests of Hu. Referring to the bronze statue erected in his honor, Liu said, "In the cultural circle, Hu should have been the first to deserve this honor. . . . In the future, I believe there shall be erected in the PRC more than one statue of Hu."[3] Liu's acclaim, offered on such an occasion, showed the wealth of respect and posterity Hu had produced among intellectuals of his own and subsequent generations. Liu did not provide the exact pattern of the lives or examples of individuals who fit his general qualifications for intellectuals worthy of public honor. However, time and again, what defends one's continuing interest in honorable intellectuals is their struggles to search for or help create the values and codes of ethics their societies both call for and eradicate. Recalling the career of Hu, and, moreover, remembering and reading the *July* poets, one also learns to pay attention to the more anonymous, to those who belong to cultures of resistance and revolution, who make efforts in those insurrections.

The Hu Incident has provided the present time grist for historical humanists to mill. In the first place, the Incident turned out to be a moment in the history of modern criticism; it foreshadowed a series of nationwide intellectual events, from the Anti-Rightist Movement in 1957 to the Cultural Revolution between 1966 and 1976. Furthermore, in his day-to-day engagement with revolutionary politics, Hu exemplified a degree of critical tenacity and rigor that continued into the late 1930s and beyond the threshold of 1949, bringing consequences to bear on his fate as an ideological prisoner of the CCP. Significantly, Hu's dissidence resulted directly from his unfailing engagement, even more than from his "dissidence." In his role as a critic and poet-warrior, Hu stood his ground and established a historical place as a Marxist critic representative of an engagé writer—intellectually truthful, politically engaging, and literarily combative. This last characteristic contributed to a structure of interpretation and judgment of Hu's critical style later enacted by the so-called members of the Hu Feng clique—a group of largely younger, ideologically committed Marxist writers and critics. In that structure, certain individuals took Hu's writings and critical acts as permission to understand and contend that literature was the principal revolutionary characteristic because it was at work at the beginning of the Chinese Revolution. In its struggle for authority to rebel against feudalist conservatism, political violence, and ideological terror, literature grounded critical consciousness in the act of poiesis (indeed, for Hu and his followers, poiesis was the sine qua non of insurgency); and it was part and parcel of the severe criticism by Lu Xun and the May Fourth Movement he led, and of the task of building historical and historically consequential movements that might come to assist and assure the building of a national modernity rid of "intellectual servitude."

As one of the most significant *intellectual* events in the CCP's long history of ideological homogenization and control, the Hu Incident was an adjuvant of a "besetting sin" of criticism. On the fiftieth anniversary of the Hu case, Judge Wang Wenzheng, one of the fifty-odd interrogators who took part in the prosecution, attempted to underline Hu's importance in the development of modern Chinese literature and contemporary China and to identify elements in Hu's work that should assert place and importance in the history of criticism. These elements were without exception all literary concepts, meaning that, ultimately, they showed little regard for the forces that claimed power and authority for political position and sensitivity, especially the kind that sought to act in the service of ideological correctness, the collective good, and the Chinese Revolution in general. Wang wrote:

> Half a century has passed. How many still remember the name of Hu? How many young writers today can explain such concepts as "subjective combative spirit" and "the wounds of spiritual servitude," which led to the crisis on the literary scene of the

> young Republic? . . . The whole nation should not forget the pain brought along with the Hu Incident. . . . To commemorate Hu is to remember our national history, a crisis, and a tragedy.[4]

Elsewhere, in her review of Mei Zhi's memoir, *F: Hu Feng's Prison Years*, Sheila Melvin reaffirmed the morals of Hu's critical consciousness and its relevance to the future of criticism:

> Hu Feng still matters, and his case is well worth our study. Artistic and literary expression still sometimes get writers and artists detained and jailed—in the worst cases, innocent spouses suffer too, just like Mei Zhi. *Hu's ideas also remain critically important.* Debates between those who advocate the May Fourth Spirit and those who prefer something closer to Mao's Yan'an vision remain very much alive—*and Yan'an, in recent years, is gaining ground.* . . . History has proven that Hu was correct—real innovation and creativity can happen only when artists and innovators have space and the freedom to test ideas, express creativity, and make mistakes without fear of punishment. We should all continue to support Mei Zhi's quest, and learn from Hu Feng.[5]

Following Wang and Melvin, in this book, I have intended to commemorate and make prominent Hu's experience as a Marxist literary intellectual in socialist China by holding him as a marker in the genealogy of our thinking about contemporary engaged writers' possibilities and tasks in the face of power. Throughout, this book represents Hu as belonging to a historically specific time, the era of Chinese modernity and modern authoritarianism in the making. As such, Hu was not only a prescient warning of the PRC's still continuous history of intellectual persecution but also a testament to the qualities of literature in critical work: authority, creativity, imagination, freedom, engagement, passion, judgment. Hu's struggle evidenced that these qualities could have a valuable and relevant frame even when confined within cultural and critical orthodoxy and when dictated by the commonplaces of Chinese one-party rule.

Perhaps for us today, the potentially most useful way to think about Hu's career and fate is as an example of the futility of Marxist praxis, at least in and despite the PRC as a Communist state, if not globally. Concerning impossibility, the point I want to make is this: the necessity of basing a political act on literary criticism's pessimism, consciousness, and the principle of humility to battle against both the willful and the temptation to claim too much power for the self. The Marxist intellectual was not only a soldier as the circumstances of the Chinese Revolution dictated but also someone who was not so in a meaningful way: "the critic's job of work," as R. P. Blackmur coined the term in his 1938 essay,[6] tied political acts not to efficacy or state power but to the mind relying on the creative process from the outside to engage itself with the inside of collective politics. This demanded that revolutionary work be adequate to the situated tasks of what it meant to function as and so be an intellectual, that is, the "amateur"[7] who knows the truth so that the mind can speak, or act, in the face of power without succumbing to its temptations or to the tendency to become dogmatic, bigoted, and fundamentalist. This "critic's job of work" was both unavoidable and impossible since the revolutionary obliged to perform from and through the aesthetic realm was, by definition, private and distanced from what Edward W. Said called "the norms of power"[8] and hence forever inadequate and disinclined to the demands of power.

In "The Concept of the Left" by the Polish philosopher Leszek Kolakowski, about the political life of the left in 1960s Poland, he observed that "the division into a Party Left and Right did not exist . . . [when] the Party was deprived of any real political life, its ideology did not grow out of its own historical experience but was to a large degree imposed upon it regardless of experience."[9] What Kolakowski said about the Polish Communist Party might well have applied to the CCP in the late 1940s, in that the critique of Hu evolved from small group discussions to organized nationwide campaigns. The PRC in the mid-twentieth century, as one will recall, began to feel pressure to achieve a "new high tide of production."[10] Consequently, the mind in the service of statist rule appeared everywhere, leaving the indoctrination and militarization of Maoist socialism "entirely uninhibited."[11] Creative practices residing in doctrine or power served the state and its institutions. The fashioning of Hu first as an unorthodox individualist and then as a "counterrevolutionary" reflected and testified to an institutional aggressiveness, while at the same time showed how the CCP understood the necessity of power consolidation, of drawing toward itself the grip of thought control and homogeneity. This development of Marxist literary criticism into an invariant set of convictions designed to ensure conformity through discipline was inseparable from the Yan'an writers' fascination with power. Zhou, who lost Lu Xun to Hu in the Two-Slogan Debate, found compensation in the office, which he built in Yan'an in his role as Mao's cultural advisor and representative. His views on literature and art supplied the Yan'an Forum with major doctrinal components of Mao Zedong Thought. Since 1942, Zhou had helped Mao formulate and articulate the CCP's principles of cultural work, while Hu, who had twice declined the Party's invitation to go to Yan'an, stayed in Chongqing. Hu's self-distancing from the center of power resulted in the rewriting of his personal history and that of many others in the 1950s.

One crucial question follows suit: Why did members of the *July* School stay so close to one another despite Hu's difficult but necessary refusal to move to Yan'an? For Lu Yuan, this issue had not received any serious scholarly attention, and his full answer rested on his personal experience: "As a poet and a critic, and as a distinguished organizer in the history of Chinese New Literature, Hu had his unique cachet."[12] Whereas Lu Yuan fully appreciated the basis of Hu's work and literary politics, Mao persecuted Hu precisely for the same reason. Mao recognized that Hu sought from *within* left-wing politics a "literary subjectivism" that, in substance, was indistinguishable from a developmental extension of May Fourth enlightenment and intellectual liberation—the spiritual foundation of the Chinese Revolution. The CCP persecuted Hu for two reasons: first, the "bourgeois" nature of his poetics; and second, his literary criticism and acts, which existed in the form of an organized faction. Mao's "Editor's Comments to the Second Collection of Materials on the Hu Counterrevolutionary Clique" explained why the Party had to deal with Hu and his followers ideologically and intellectually, not only politically:

> A faction—called "coterie"[13] by our forefathers and "ring" or "outfit" [stalls[14]] by people today—is something quite familiar to us. To attain their political ends people who pursue factional activities often accuse others of being factional, and being factional, they say, is not upright; for themselves, they claim to be upright, and upright people just don't have anything to do with factions. Those who followed Hu's lead were said to be "young writers" and "revolutionary writers" "hated" and "persecuted" by the Party, the faction that fostered "bourgeois theories" and "formed an independent kingdom"; therefore, Hu and his company wanted revenge. . . . The question of the *Literary Gazette*[15] was "merely a breach that has been seized upon" and was "by no means an isolated one," it was most necessary to "extend and generalize" it and "show that the question was one

> of factionalist rule," and "factionalist and warlord rule" at that. The matter was so serious that they "fired off" a lot of ammunition to mop us up. In so doing Hu and company attracted attention. After careful investigation of many of these persons, this clique was found to be of some size. Previously they were known as "a small group." No, that's not so, [there] are quite a few of them. Previously they were known simply as a group of men of letters. No, that's not so, they have wormed their way into political, military, economic, cultural and educational departments. Previously, they seemed to be a group of revolutionaries operating in broad daylight. No, that's not so, most of them have a very shady background.[16]

Yet, "was there a Hu clique?," He Manzi, allegedly "a core member of the Hu clique," retorted.[17] Geng Yong, a dedicated follower of Hu and a younger member of the circle, doubted the presumed existence of a "Hu clique" and was eager to find out more about the formation of this group. He thus asked Hu whether there was indeed such a thing as a "Hu group" and recalled Hu saying that the close association of his name with a literary group had an ominous origin: the term "Hu Feng *pai*" was first employed as a negative term by the Zhou-led critics in the Two-Slogan Debate, which started in 1935 and soon turned into a characteristically bitter fight among members of the Left-league.[18] Hu's response, though ambivalent, was remarkably revealing. Pejorative as the term was, Hu had never denied the existence of a "Hu Feng *pai*," even though he hastened to assert that it was all very natural to have different schools of literature and criticism. For him, different *pai* in the literary domain were primarily *literary* schools, rather than small salon-type societies that were intellectually distinguished, ideologically distinguishable, and socially exclusive. Under the circumstances, literary factionalism took place in the form of a blind fight for and defense of an esprit de corps that constituted a fundamental basis of an individual literary group.[19]

Essentially, all kinds of beliefs, whether intellectual, literary, or political, were factional. Although there was considerable overlap between "the *July* School" and "the Hu clique," it is important to consider the former a literary association and the latter a political formation, belonging to two historical points. Lu Yuan, in his extended commemorative essay "Hu Feng and Me," distinguished between the two. Given his role as a *July* poet and one participant in Hu's "300,000-Character Report," Lu was active in both historical points and with insights from lived experience and asked that one distinguish the forces that formed the *July* School in the 1940s from those that named and smashed the "Hu clique" in the mid-1950s. For Lu, the former was concerned with the formation of an ideological allegiance that took the form of a literary association, and the latter with the suspicious collaboration between state operation and intellectual power.

Hu believed in literature and *differences*, which were the foundations for the effective working of "a republic of criticism," a mode of progress toward a "better" future and a path to the truth committed to knowledge and practice, not the automatism of state ideology.[20] Vast as the differences of opinion between Hu and his comrades were, one sentiment ran fiercely throughout, which Hu summed up in the phrases "literary subjectivism" and "subjective combative spirit"! In an ideal world, a good Marxist should and *could* be a "poet-soldier," that is, an individualist in a collective whole. This was what Hu learned from the very beginning: in Japan, where he first encountered many Communist writers,[21] and in Lu Xun's image of a "bare-chested soldier."[22] Underlying Hu's continued engagement in revolutionary politics was his sense of responsibility for the collective *and* his acute awareness of his role as a poet-critic among the Marxists. Half a century after his persecution, Hu explained, with sympathy in his voice, the nature of his comradeship with Zhou and other Party functionaries:

> I have reflected on myself. What has *redeemed* my friendship with Zhou are our shared position on the people (and the revolution) and our intellectual exchange on cultural work. Naturally, I have my views. However, my achievement in creative writing is insignificant. The suggestions I submitted to the Central Committee stemmed from my knowledge about the lived and creative experience of Western writers and their literary theory.[23]

For Hu, the setbacks in his literary and political career might have resulted from personal conflicts with some isolated Party members, which could have been just a *technical* problem on the way to achieving a shared vision of China in the broadest sense possible. In effect, his vision of China, even if Zhou sympathized with it, was neither compatible with Zhou's pragmatics nor in dialogue with Mao's blueprint of the People's Republic. His was of a national modernity empowered and delivered by critical imagination rather than by populist nationalism, shifting political needs, and statist ideologies. His criticism and ideological commitment embodied and urged a psychological and polemical reaction to the "dark sociopolitical forces" found in the self and the social formations that created them. Like various contemporary Western intellectuals, Hu's theory of the "subjective combative spirit" embraced the critical and liberatory elements of Marxism, but it also sought to overcome, or surpass, its tendency to institutionalize socialist realism. Even if still confined within the political thought of the CCP, such a version of "Chinese modernity" contained within it a self-reflexive mechanism that was not afraid of pointing out moments at which oppressive power hardened imagination into ideology and subjected criticism to power discourse.

The CCP and its intellectuals had one of the most tortuous and ironic interrelationships. The tension between literature, one custodian of humanistic truth, and Party politics, the generator of a vitally essential but distinctly lesser order of truth, was *not* a genuine paradox for Hu. The idea of integrity and total engagement was at the heart of Hu's understanding of the relationship between the intellectual and her society, as well as the function of subjectivism and critical passion for life. Hu's "dissidence" was not ideological but practical, characterized by a persistent refusal of authoritarian operations, a refusal that cost him an entitled place in the PRC's "elite" community and caused him to build an alternative version of that community. At a time of frustration and atrocity, the question for Hu was not how to free the self from politics, but how to *engage* with it *more* effectually. As a revolutionary, he took on the task to combat and, if possible, overcome the conditions of "isolation." Rather than the problem of what was wrong with politics, Hu tackled the real issue of how to create a literary style and a critical language in and with which to defend Marxism and its ethics.

"Commitment," as Jean-Paul Sartre argued in his attempt to link the word with the values of resistance and socialist democracy in the wake of the Second World War, is theoretically a humanist involvement in the production of *literary* texts that "reverberate at every level of man and society."[24] The humanist tradition of resistance and the literary subjectivist quality that Sartre identified in the term *commitment* are particularly appropriate in my study of Hu. Living and writing in the prevailing climate of war and Chinese Marxism, Hu aspired to be a "first-order poet"—"a fighter committed to the cause of human happiness and emancipation."[25] His work shed light on readers' engagement with literature and criticism as an element of their existence, or what Hu called "the poet of life."[26] The poem "Leaving the Country 去国," written in the mid-1940s by Ah-long, a *July* poet and one of Hu's closest students and friends, compelled readers to examine Hu and his associate writers' propositions about what it meant to be a committed writer in their time:

> I am guilt-free; does this make me guilty?—
> Are flowers guilty of their color and scent
> Is the Yangtze River guilty of its current and thunderstorm?
> Is Jesus Christ guilty of universal love
> Is Archimedes guilty of having the brain for geometry?
>
> Take away my corolla, take it away; take away my sword, take it away.
> Leave my head uncovered completely; let the white rose wither for you in your coronation ceremony.
> Let my two arms hang down quietly; let your flashing sword strengthen you the moment you hold it.
> . . . .
> Flowers are blossoming;
> A thunderstorm is brewing.
> Children awakened from their dreams are calling their fathers home;
> The grass sheds its dewdrops in the graveyard of loved ones;
> The army marches through the city.
> Since there are no candies, there is no hesitation.
> I am not guilty; yet I carry the guilt[27] as if it were my shaggy shiralee
> I have robbed my country, bare-chested and solemn, in the journey.[28]

Ah-long's poem externalized the emotional state of a committed writer who was ready to forgo the traditional scholar's sense of elitism and who offered the self to both the nation and the masses. The ringing lines above, reminiscent of Plato's *Apology of Socrates*, about how Socrates had been "guiltless of wrong-doing" all his life, contain the self-mockery and confession of the CCP's fellow traveler. Ah-long appealed to both realpolitik and personal courage when he attempted to assuage personal danger with a moral conscience. Ah-long's certainty about the necessity of the Chinese Revolution, which Hu shared, was based on a near-impossible combination of critical passion, revolutionary idealism, and a practical understanding of reality. Perhaps, in the end, what is worth remembering about these individuals is neither their patriotism nor their doomed fate, but the moral strength of their nay-saying, their courage to act with the single-mindedness of a guiltless outlaw, and their "bare-chestedness" and "solemnity." These sentiments provoked them to mount criticism indiscriminately against those in power.

In his 1999 presidential address to the Modern Language Association, Edward Said defined humanism in relation to the role of the critical intellectual in modern society: "The humanistic service . . . always entails a heroic unwillingness to rest in the consolidation of . . . existing attitudes."[29] Why was this kind of unwillingness characteristic of a humanist a "heroic" one? Appraising Sigmund Freud's and Giambattista Vico's attempts to "venture beyond," to "disclos[e]," and to "recover" from the known, the accepted, and the given, Said explained,[30] "It is heroic because the critical intellectual is often stretched and stretched thin by the chasm that separates the established and the possible. As long as the thinking does not break off, it remains 'true to intellectual coherence and . . . humanistic dignity.' "[31] With his literature and criticism, Hu demonstrated the modus operandi of the Saidian "heroic ideal in humanism": how resistance to consolidate "what is already known" and the combativeness of the mind against "the powers that be" need each other.[32] If the poet-warrior felt the presence of his combative spirit in the "flesh-and-blood struggle" of life, he did not invent it; he was the instance and embodiment of that spirit. Although ideological entrapment and political demands could grind critical consciousness and imagination to a halt, real intellect could not be thoroughly enslaved, and human agency could not be eradicated. In that same 1999 speech, Said pointed out the importance of following the tradition of Baruch Spinoza, Karl Marx, and Heinrich Heine, which was that of a "non-Jewish Jew," or a "nonhumanistic humanist" who saw in an "unafraid and unapologetic critique the path to human freedom."[33]

In Hu's case, the inherent paradox of the intellectual tradition could be expanded to include the non-Marxist Marxist in socialist China. It was in response to increasing tension in thought control that Hu emphasized the importance of human agency in history, even if with humility and only minimally. The difference between Hu and his comrades lay in their different points of departure and arrival in life and intellectual work. In response to the pressures of the situation wherein historical causes and national projects more fundamental to criticism conjoined to alienate criticism from its tasks, Hu believed that the Marxist intellectual should bring the poiesis of criticism up against the limit of negation and demarcate a boundary beyond which critical work could not recoil were it to persist at all.

CHRONOLOGY OF HU FENG'S LIFE 1902–1985

1902 Born to the Zhang family in **Hubei** on November 1, the third of five children. His given name is Zhang Guangren.

1912–1918 Pursues his education in various Confucius-style primary schools and under private tutoring.

1919–1920 Goes to Zhanchun County School. Begins reading May Fourth New Literature and Lu Xun 魯迅 (1881–1936).

1921 Enters Qiwang Middle School in **Wuchang**. Becomes editor of *New Zhanchun* 新蘄春, a twelve- to sixteen-page magazine.

1922 Winter: Marries Hong Cuie 洪翠娥 in a prearranged marriage. December: Publishes his first essay, "On Educational Reform in Hubei 改進湖北教育的討論," under his given name, Zhang Guangren, in the *Morning Post Supplementary*.

1923 Goes to **Nanjing** and studies at the same secondary school as Ba Jin. Receives revolutionary education from such fellow students and Party members as Yuan Xiyan 宛希儼, Yang Chao 楊超 (1904–27), and Fu Guoquan 扶國權 (1903–30). March: Writes his first story, "Two Members on a Labor-Union Sub-committee," and publishes it under the name Zhang Guangren in *Awakenings*, a supplementary to the *National Daily*, a newspaper in Shanghai. Winter: Yuan Xiyan recommends him for membership in the Socialist Youth League.

1925 Writes "The Dead Sun," an elegy commemorating the death of Sun Yat-sen 孫中山 (1866–1925). Participates in the 5/30 revolutionary activities. Leaves Nanjing for **Peking** with Yang Chao and Zhu Qixia 朱企霞 (1904–84) and enrolls in Peking University's Preparatory School. Audits one of the lectures in the course "History of the Chinese Novel" by Lu Xun.

1926 Leaves Peking University and enrolls in the English studies program at Tsinghua University. Hong Cuie dies in childbirth. During the Northern Expedition, leaves Tsinghua for his native town of **Zhanchun**, Hubei, to participate in GMD-CCP-led revolutionary propaganda work. Meets Dong Biwu 董必武 (1886–1975), a CCP member and native of Hubei.

1927 August–October: Invited by Deng Chumin 鄧初民 (1889–1981) to work in the propaganda section of the GMD's Hubei Provincial Party Headquarters, which is under the control of Kong Geng 孔庚 (1871–1950), Li Hanjun 李汉俊 (1890–1927), Deng Chumin 邓初民 (1889–1981), and Zhan Dabei 詹大悲 (1887–1927). Asked by Deng to help edit and proofread *Wuhan Review*, the house publication of the GMD's Hubei headquarters.

1929 Goes to **Tokyo** with Zhu Qixia. Studies Japanese for three months at the East Asia Japanese Language School. Reads proletarian literature for the first time.

1930 Translates into Chinese the Soviet novel *The American in Petrograd*, using the pseudonym Gu Fei 谷非 to publish the translation under the title *Foreign Devil* 洋鬼. Befriends such proletarian writers as Hirokichi Otake 大竹博吉 (1890–1958), Kiyoshi Eguchi 江口渙 (1887–1975), Ujaku Akita 秋田雨雀 (1883–1962), and Takiji Kobayashi 小林多喜二 (1903–33).

1931 Accepted by Keio University to read for the degree of bachelor of arts in English. Makes a trip to Shanghai in the summer and stays with Han Qi 韓起. Meets with Zhang Tianyi 張天翼 (1906–85). Returns to Tokyo and meets with Guo Moruo 郭沫若 (1892–1978). Enrolls in Keio University; becomes a member of the Association for Art Studies of the Proletarian Science Center, a unit under the Japan Proletarian Culture Federation established by Koreto Kurahara. Begins publishing articles about Chinese left-wing cultural movements under the pseudonyms Mamoru Nakamura 中村護 and Gu Fei. Writes the antiwar poem "The Sacrificial Rites of the Enemy" in commemoration of the 9/18 Incident. Forms within the Japanese Anti-Imperialist League a Chinese group consisting of himself, Fang Han 方翰, and Wang Chengzhi 王承志. The Chinese group is also a reading group. Joins the Japanese Communist Party and the Japanese branch of the Chinese League of Left-wing Writers.

1932 Publishes two essays, "Whitewashing and Distorting Hard Facts 粉饰, 歪曲, 铁一般的事实" and "On Thematic Progressiveness and Third-Category Men's Criticism 論主題積極性和第三種人的批評等," respectively, in *Literature Monthly* 文學月報 and *Synthesis* 綜合 under the pseudonym Gu Fei. Goes to Shanghai in the winter, reports to the "Left-wing Cultural Coalition" on the "Rally against War in the Far East," a meeting organized by the Japanese Anti-War League. Meets Feng Xuefeng 冯雪峰 (1903–76), Ding Ling 丁玲 (1904–86), and Zhou Yang 周扬 (1908–89) for the first time. Returns to **Tokyo** on the same ship as Lou Shiyi 楼适夷, who was to serve as the Chinese representative at the "Rally against War in the Far East."

1933 Takiji Kobayashi is arrested and tortured to death by the police in Tokyo. On behalf of the Chinese Left-wing Cultural Coalition, Hu writes a condolence and protests against the Japanese government. Publishes the condolence in the March issue of *Proletarian Culture*. Arrested by the Tokyo police for propagating anti-Japanese sentiments. Deported to China after serving a three-month detention. **Shanghai** in mid-June: Lu Xun, accompanied by Zhou Yang, meets with Hu. Appointed by Zhou Yang to be the officer-in-charge in the Propaganda Department of the Chinese League of Left-wing Writers. Organizes meetings with Left-league members. Contributes to and helps edit *Literature and Life*, a Left-league literary journal aimed at young readers. Recommended by Yang Xinzhi 楊辛之, friend of Han Qi, to do translation work for *Guide to Current Affairs* 時事類編, a periodical published by the Zhongshan Cultural and Educational Institute. Marries Mei Zhi 梅志 (1914–2004).

1934 Appointed by Wu Xiru 吴奚如 (1906–85) as "a confidential conduit" between Lu Xun and the CCP Central Committee in Shanghai. Mu Mutian (1900–1971) spreads rumors about Hu being a Nationalist spy and exposes Hu's connection with the Left-league. Resigns from both the Zhongshan Cultural and Educational Institute and the Left-league. Becomes a professional writer using the pseudonym Hu. Relationship with Lu Xun deepens. Publishes his first long critical work, "On Lin Yutang 林語堂論," in volume 4.1 of *Literature Monthly*.

1935 Meets with Xiao Jun 蕭軍 (1907–88) and Xiao Hong 萧红 (1911–42) through Lu Xun. Writes "On Zhang Tianyi 張天翼論" and publishes a large number of reviews, including those of Duanmu Hongliang 端木蕻良 [Cao Hanwen 曹汉文] (1912–96), Wu Xiru, Ouyang Shan 歐陽山 (1908–2000), and Ai Wu 艾蕪 (1904–92). Edits and contributes to the underground literary magazine *Sawdust Prose Series* 木屑文叢, which publishes Qu Qiubai's translations of Engels's letters on literature, Soviet short stories, and theories of socialist realism. The magazine is short-lived but influential. According to Hu, Mao Zedong read one of the issues.

1936 Edits *Seagulls* 海燕, a literary journal closely associated with Lu Xun. Contributors to *Seagulls* include Xiao Hong, Xiao Jun, Duanmu Honglian, and Tian Jian 田间 (1916–85). April: Publishes *Notes on Literature and Art* 文藝筆談, a collection of his critical articles written between 1934 and 1935. The Left-league dissolves in the spring and the Association of Chinese Writers and Artists 中國文藝家學會 is formed on June 7. Ignores the invitation from Zhou Yang to join the new association; signs the "Declaration of Chinese Literary Workers," which Lu Xun also supports. June: Zhou Yang makes a public statement on behalf of "National Defense Literature," a term adopted in response to the CCP's declaration of a national united front against Japan. Proposes, with the approval of Lu Xun, the formulation of "Mass Literature in the National Revolutionary War" in the essay "What Do the Masses Demand of Literature 人民大众向文学要求甚么," which is published in *Literary Series* 文学丛报. The Two-Slogan Debate is launched. October 19: Lu Xun dies. Writes "Painful Departure 悲痛的告别" in memory of Lu Xun.

1937 January: Publishes *Wild Flowers and Arrows* 野花与箭, a volume of his early poetry. Spring: publishes *Work and Study* 工作與學習 (4 vols.), a literary journal that was established by Feng Xuefeng to carry on the spirit of Lu Xun. July 7: The Marco Polo Bridge Incident breaks out. Writes anti-Japanese poems: "Singing for the Fatherland 为祖国而歌" and "The Pledge of Blood 血誓." September: Launches *July* 七月, a literary journal he considered to be "a lone voice in a cultural wasteland," and publishes three pieces (numbers 1 through 3) weekly with the Shanghai Magazine Company 上海雜誌公司. September 25: Leaves Shanghai for Wuhan. October 1: Arrives in **Wuhan** and meets with Zhou Enlai 周恩来 (1898–1976) for the first time. October 16: *July* becomes a bimonthly journal distributed by Life Bookstore 生活書

店 in Hankou (vols. 1.1–6). Contributors to *July* include such Yan'an writers as Ding Ling, Ai Qing 艾青 (1910–96), Qiu Dongping 丘东平 (1910–41), Tian Jian, Xiao Jun, Xiao Hong, Huang Ji 黃既, and Luchuan Yingzi 綠川英子 (1912–47). December: Appointed editor of *Literature Weekly* 星期文藝, the literary supplement of *New China Daily* 新華日報, a CCP-controlled paper.

1938 January: Publishes *July* (2.1–6, 3.1–6), again with the Shanghai Magazine Company. *July*, though "a literary journal," publishes mainly war reportage and poetry. Leading writers include Ah-long 阿垅 (1907–67) and Qiu Dongping in reportage and Ai Qing and Tian Jian in poetry. *July* (no. 10, March 1) publishes Mao Zedong's "On Lu Xun," a speech given at the meeting commemorating the first anniversary of Lu Xun's death held at the North Shensi Public School on October 19, 1937. March 27: Appointed board member of the All-China National Cultural Organization for Literary Resistance 中華全國文藝界抗敵協會 (hereafter Literary Resistance Organization). April 24: Organizes *July* talks in preparation for the publication of *July Series*, a book series consisting of *July Prose Series* 七月文叢 and *July Poetry Series* 七月詩叢. August: Haiyan Bookstore 海燕書店 publishes *Notes Taken in Hard Times* 密雲期風習小紀, a collection of critical essays written between 1935 and 1938, in Wuhan. September: End of *July*'s contract with the Shanghai Magazine Company. September 28: Leaves Wuhan for **Yidou**. October 27: Appointed lecturer at Chongqing Fudan University. December 2: Arrives in **Chongqing**.

1939 January 10: Gives a report on wartime poetry at a Literary Resistance Organization meeting on poetry. April 9: Literary Resistance Organization youth group reads Hu's "Telegram to Worldwide Writers Fighting in the Anti-Fascist War 致全世界反法西斯侵略戰爭的作家電." Begins seeking financial support for *July* from Dong Biwu, with the support of Xiong Zimin. Wu Xiru, then Zhou Enlai's political secretary, oversees *July*. May 24: Turns down Zhou Yang's offer of appointment as Head of the Chinese Department at the Lu Xun Academy of Arts and Literature in Yan'an and remains in Chongqing. July: Publication of *July* resumes; *July* becomes a monthly and publishes four volumes (vols. 4.1–4, 5.1–4, 6.1–4, 7.1/2) with the Huazhong Book Company 華中圖書公司 in Chongqing. The *July* circle expands from Yan'an writers to young and less established writers like Lu Ling 路翎 (1923–94). October: Hu's father dies.

1940 October 13: Finishes writing the long critical essay "On the Question of National Forms 論民族形式問題," which would be published in Chongqing by Life Bookstore in December.

1941 January: The Wannan/New Fourth Army Incident breaks out, signifying the end of the first United Front between the GMD and the CCP. Pressure from the GMD against left-wing writers and artists increases. March: *July* is forced to stop printing, with 7.1/2 (combined issue) being the last volume. March 17: At a meeting with Zhou Enlai, Hu is offered the option of going to Yan'an but decides, against the wishes of Mei Zhi, to go to Hong Kong instead of Yan'an. May 7: Flees Chongqing for **Hong Kong**. Attempts to resurrect *July* in Hong Kong but in vain. December 8: Japan invades Hong Kong. December 25: Hong Kong falls, and the Japanese occupation begins.

1942 March 6: Arrives in **Guilin**. May 2–23: The Yan'an Forum on Literature and Art 延安文藝座談會 takes place. June: Establishes Nantian Association 南天社, a one-man publishing house. Edits *July Poetry Series* and *July Prose Series*. Writers and editors involved in the series are perceived as core members of the Hu group after 1949, including Fang Ran 方然 (editor of *Breath* 呼吸), Zhu Guhuai 朱谷懷 (1922–92) (editor of *Mud* 泥土), and such contributors as Shu Wu 舒芜 (1922–2009), Ah-long, Lu Ling, and Ji Fang 冀汸 (1920–?). Included in the series is a collection of Hu's critical essays titled "The National War and the Nature of Literature 文族戰爭與文藝性格." Edits Lu Ling's *Hungry Guo Su'e* 飢餓的郭素娥 and *Blessings of Youth* 青春的祝福. June 12: Mao's "Talks" first reported in Chongqing by Xiao Jun in *New China Daily*.

1943 Continues with propaganda work for the Literary Resistance Organization. The CCP cultural leaders in Yan'an begin to identify Hu's literary theory as having ideological problems. The Central Committee sees reports on Hu's response to Mao's "Talks." March 14: Leaves Guilin for Chongqing. March 24: Arrives in **Chongqing**. April–October: Attends various meetings of the Literary Workers Committee and gives a few talks defending his concept of "subjective combative spirit" in literature: "On a Few Trends in the Understanding of Literature and Art 論對於文藝的二、三流行見解" (July 29), "A Few Fundamental Concepts in Literature and Art 文藝上的幾個基本觀念" (August 10), and "On the Creative Process 論創作底過程" (August 14). November 19: Publication of Mao's "Talks at the Yan'an Forum on Literature and Art" in *Liberation Daily* in Yan'an.

1944 April 16: Submits, in the capacity as director of the Literary Resistance Organization, a draft report titled "The Development of Work in Literature and Art and the Direction of Our Efforts 文艺工作底发展及其努力方向," to the board of directors for the sixth annual meeting of the Association of Chinese Writers and Artists. May: Moves the Nantian Commune from Guilin to Chongqing. Continues editing *July Poetry Series*; reprints books printed in Guilin; copyedits Lu Ling's *Children of the Rich* 財主底兒女們. Conceives the publication of *Hope* 希望, a successor of *July*. November: Receives from Zhou Enlai 30,000 French francs as guaranteed money needed for registering *Hope* with the GMD authorities.

1945 January: Publication of the first issue of *Hope*, which reflects Hu's dissatisfaction with the CCP's rectification campaign in Chongqing and its attempt to impose upon writers the "Talks" as a "totem." The inaugural issue contains, among other things, a leading article by Hu and "On Subjectivism 論主觀" by Shu Wu. January 25: Beginning of the first Party-led criticism against Hu. A discussion group chaired by Feng Naichao 冯乃超 (1901–83), then an officer in charge of the Party Culture Committee, and convened by the Literary Work Committee under Guo Moruo's leadership, discusses *Hope*. Attends a meeting chaired by Zhou Enlai at Zhou's residence in Zengjiayan, which examined Hu's thinking on literature and art. April: Writers Bookstore 作家書屋 publishes *In State of Confusion* 在混亂裡面, a volume of critical essays written between 1941 and 1943. April 29: Huang Yaomian 黄药眠 (1903–87) publishes "On Joseph's Coat" in Chengdu and classifies Shu Wu's philosophy of subjectivism as typical of capitalist idealism. August: Victory in the War of Resistance against Japan. November 10–11: Hu Qiaomu 胡乔木 (1912–92), then accompanying Mao to Chongqing to talk with the GMD, talks with Hu and Shu Wu.

1946 February 25: Back to **Shanghai**. October: Publishes the second and last volume of *Hope*. Publishes the second volume of Lu Ling's *Children of the Rich* and his *Days of Running against the Current* 逆流的日子, a volume of critical essays written between 1944 and 1946.

1947 January: Learns the news of the death of his elder brother Zhang Mingshan 张明山, who was killed in a clan dispute.

1948 January: Publishes *Collected Essays of Hu Feng* 胡風文集, one volume, with the Shanghai Chunming Bookstore 上海春明書店. March: The second Party-led critical campaign and first public forum against Hu is launched in Hong Kong. Shao Quanlin 邵荃麟 (1906–71) criticizes Hu in his article "Views on the Current Literature and Art Movement," which is published in the first volume of *Literature and Art for the Masses* 大众文艺丛刊, a series edited by the Culture Committee, with Feng Naichao in charge. September 17: Finishes writing *The Path of Realism* 論現實主義的路, a long theoretical pamphlet in response to the Hong Kong criticism. December 9–14: Travels to **Hong Kong** together with Guo Moruo, Mao Dun 茅盾 (1896–1981), and others by arrangement of the Party.

1949 January–March: Goes to **Beijing** via Shenyang 瀋陽, Andong 安東, and Benxi 本溪. July 2–19: In the capacity as a presidium member, gives a speech titled "United, Make Further Progress 團結起來, 更前進" in celebration of the opening of the first National Congress of Literature and Art Workers 中华全国文学艺术工作者代表大会. Appointed Standing Committee member of the China Federation of Literary and Art Circles 中国文学艺术界联合会 (hereafter CFLAC) in Congress. Mao Dun makes a report titled "Struggle of Revolutionary Literature under Reactionary Opposition 在反动派压逼下斗争的革命文艺," in which he singled out Hu's literary theories on criticism, though without mentioning his name. This is the third Party-led criticism of Hu and the first after the founding of the People's Republic. August 4: Returns to **Shanghai**. September 8: Goes to **Beijing** to participate in the first National Committee of the Chinese People's Political Consultative Conference 中國人民政治協商會議 (hereafter CPPCC) on September 21. October 1: Attends the PRC Founding Ceremony at Tiananmen Square. October: Writes the epic poem *Time Has Begun* 時間開始了 to celebrate the founding of the PRC.

1950 January: Haiyan Bookstore publishes the first two parts of *Time Has Begun*. February 12: Returns to **Shanghai**. March: Tianxia Book Company 天下图书公司 publishes #4 and #5 of *Time Has Begun*. April: Appointed committee member of the Huadong Cultural and Educational Standing Committee at the Shanghai Municipal People's Congress. August: Writers Bookstore publishes *For Tomorrow* 為了明天, a collection of Hu's critical essays written between 1946 and 1948. September: Mud Commune 泥土社 publishes Hu's collected prose titled *Two Chronicles from Human Link* 人環二記. September 22: Goes to **Beijing** at the invitation of the People's Press. Writes the report titled

"Together with New Characters 和新人物在一起" to commemorate the trip. November: Writes the long poem "For North Korea, for Mankind 為了朝鮮, 為了人類" to commemorate the People's Liberation Army's participation in the Korean War.

1951 February: Returns to **Shanghai**. April 22: Goes to **Beijing**. May 20: An editorial in the *People's Daily* condemns the film *The Life of Wu Xun*. November: The CFLAC decides to conduct a rectification movement, setting off the fourth (and final) Party-led open criticism of Hu. December 3: Meets with Zhou Enlai, who suggests that Hu critically reflect on his literary factionalism and that he discuss with Ding Ling and Zhou the arrangements for his job. Zhou also suggests that Hu write to the Central Committee about his literary thought.

1952 January 13: Returns to **Shanghai**. April: Letters proposing a critical campaign against Hu appear in the "Internal Correspondence" in issue no. 15 of the *Literary Gazette*. Reprimanded by Zhou, who meets with Hu in Shanghai on the recommendation of Peng Boshan 彭柏山 (1910–68), then the deputy director of the Shanghai Municipal CCP Committee's Cultural Department, for "regarding the Party abstractly." May 4: Writes a letter to Mao and Zhou Enlai, complaining about his marginalized position in the PRC literary scene, especially his dissatisfaction with the *Literary Gazette*. Writes also the "Study for Practice 學習, 為了實踐" to commemorate the tenth anniversary of the publication of the "Talks." The essay is not accepted for publication. May 25: The Wuhan *Changjiang Daily* publishes Shu Wu's article titled "Study Anew 'The Talks at the Yan'an Forum on Literature and Art' 從頭學習《在延安文藝座談會上的講話》." June 8: The *People's Daily* reprints Shu Wu's article under the instruction of Hu Qiaomu, who calls Hu and his associates "a small literary and art clique headed by Hu." June–July: Shanghai's *Xinwenyi* 上海新文藝出版社 publishes Hu's collected essays titled *From Source to Flood* 從源頭到洪流 and his report titled "Together with New Characters." July 19: Goes to **Beijing** at the request of Zhou to discuss the "problem" of his literary theory. July 23: Zhou writes a letter to Zhou Enlai discussing the "problem of Hu's literary theory." July 27: Zhou Enlai replies to Zhou's letter, asking Zhou to "diligently help Hu to expose and criticize" problems so that Hu "can and must conclude his restless ideological life of the past twenty years." September: Attends four discussion meetings organized by the CCP Propaganda Department under the instruction of Zhou Enlai at Ding Ling's home in Dongzongbu Hutong. The *Literary Gazette* (no. 18) publishes Shu Wu's "An Open Letter to Lu Ling 致路翎的公開信." November: Sends an article titled "A Period of Time, Some Reflections 一段時間, 幾點回憶" to the Central Committee.

1953 January 31: The *People's Daily* reprints Lin Mohan's article "The Anti-Marxist Literary and Artistic Ideology of Hu Feng 胡風的反馬克思主義的文藝思想," which was first published in the *Literary Gazette* (no. 2). February 15: The *Literary Gazette* (no. 3) publishes He Qifang's critical essay "The Path of Realism, or the Path against Realism? 現實主義的路, 還是反現實主義的路?," criticizing Hu and marking the end of the fourth open criticism against Hu. July 19: Returns to **Shanghai**. End of July: Closes down Hope Commune. August 2: Hu and his family move to **Beijing**. September 23–October 6: Appointed executive director of the Writers Union at the second National Congress of Literature and Art Workers.

1954 July 22: Submits to Xi Zhongxun 习仲勋 (1913–2002), the deputy chairman of the Government Administration Council's Culture and Education Commission, "Report on Literary and Artistic Practice since Liberation: A Letter to the Central Committee 关于解放以来的文艺实践情况的报告: 给党中央的信" (i.e., the "300,000-Character Report"). August: Sichuan Province elects Hu as a delegate to the National People's Congress (hereafter NPC). September 15–28: Attends the first plenary session of the first NPC. October: Mao Zedong criticizes bourgeois tendencies in the studies of *The Dream of the Red Chamber*. October 28: The *People's Daily* publishes Yuan Shuipai's article "Questions to the Editor of the *Literary Gazette*." Misinterprets the criticism as an opportunity to launch a counterattack on Zhou Yang. October 31–December 8: Gives two speeches at the enlarged meeting of the eighth presidium jointly held by the presidium of the CFLAC and the presidium of the Writers Union, directing criticism against Party cultural leaders, particularly Zhou Yang. December 8: Zhou Yang gives a speech titled "We Must Fight 我们必须战斗" at the conclusion of the enlarged meeting held jointly by the presidiums of the CFLAC and the Writers Union, the third part of which pointed out a "fundamental disagreement [the cultural leaders] have with Hu." December 10: The *People's Daily* publishes "We Must Fight 我們必須戰鬥"; Hu writes "My Self-Criticism 我的自我批評."

1955 January: The *Literary Gazette* publishes the second and fourth parts of Hu's "300,000-Character Report." January 19: Submits to the Central Committee "My Self-Criticism." May 13: The *People's Daily* publishes the "First Collection of Materials about the Hu Anti-Party Clique." May 17: Arrested and detained by the Ministry of Security. May 24: The *People's Daily* publishes the "Second Collection of Materials on the Hu Anti-Party Clique." May 26: Expelled from the Writers' Union and deprived of all his posts at an enlarged meeting held jointly by the presidiums of the CFLAC and the Writers Union. June 10: The *People's Daily* publishes the "Third Collection of Materials on the Hu Counterrevolutionary Clique." June 15: The *People's Daily* publishes a small handbook of the Hu materials. The handbook, with a preface by Mao, redefined "Hu Anti-Party Group" as "Hu Counterrevolutionary Group." July: The first NPC decides to cancel Hu's status as a delegate to the NPC.

1955 May–1965 May: Imprisoned in a single ward in **Qincheng Prison** in **Beijing**.

1965 June: Visited by Mei Zhi for the first time since 1955. November 10: Shanghai's *Wenhui bao* publishes Yao Wenyuan's attack on *The Dismissal of Hai Rui* by Wu Han; beginning of the Cultural Revolution. November 26: Tried and sentenced to fourteen-year imprisonment; stripped of political rights for six years. December 30: Begins to serve sentence under house arrest.

1966 January: Ordered by the Ministry of Public Security to move to Chengdu, Sichuan Province. Writes to Zhou Enlai and requests to stay in Beijing; letter to Zhou receives no reply. February: Jiang Qing convenes a forum on literature and art in the army, commending such Peking operas as *The Red Lantern* and *Shajiabang* as "pioneer efforts which will exert a profound and far-reaching influence on the socialist cultural revolution." February 17: Arrives in **Chengdu**. September 8: Sent to the **Miaoxi Tea Farm** 苗溪茶場, a political rehabilitation site under the Lushan County Correction Department.

1967 November 7: Separated from Mei Zhi; kept in a single ward at a detention center.

1969 May: End of the fourteen-year sentence. No reply to inquiry about release date.

1970 January: Sent to **No. 3 Prison** in **Dazhu County** for solitary confinement. Sentenced to life imprisonment without appeal.

1971 August: Attempts to commit suicide but in vain. Begins to suffer from hallucinations in prison.

1972 Begins sharing a ward with four or five prisoners. Mental illness worsens.

1973 January: Mei Zhi moves to No. 3 Prison to take care of Hu.

1974 March: Released from No. 3 Prison with Mei Zhi and put under house arrest.

1976 September: Writes "Reflections on Days of Living a Hard Life 在極沈重的日子裡的一些感受" to commemorate the death of Mao, who passed away on September 9. December: Transferred together with Mei Zhi to **Chengdu**.

1977 March 20: Sent with Mei Zhi to **No. 3 Prison** in **Dazhu County**. Resumes writing diary.

1979 January 14: Released from prison and sent to **Chengdu** under the order of the Ministry of Public Security. February 10: Sichuan Province Public Security Department revokes the sentence of life imprisonment. June: Appointed committee member of the Sichuan Province Political Consultative Conference.

1980 March 30: Returns to **Beijing** by arrangement of the Central Committee. March–July: Admitted to a psychiatric ward. July 10: Appointed advisor to the Culture and Art Research Department of the Ministry of Culture. September 22: Partially rehabilitated. The Central Committee issues its reversal of the anti-Hu campaign in official internal document no. 76, which insisted that Hu's literary thought was problematic, and that Hu had engaged in "factional activities."

1981 March 13: Hospitalized for mental illness. May 23: Goes to **Shanghai** and is admitted to the Shanghai Psychiatric Hospital. October 15: Returns to **Beijing**. December 14: Appointed Standing Committee member of the CPPCC. December 23: Appointed advisor to the Writers Union.

1982 June 25: Appointed committee member of the Writers Union. November 24–December 11: Attends the fifth meeting of the fifth CPPCC.

1983 June 4–17: Attends the first meeting of the sixth CPPCC. August 24: Visits the Lu Xun Museum.

1984 May 12–26: Attends the second meeting of the CPPCC. December 29: Listed as a presidium member of the fourth Writers Union meeting.

1985 March 25–April 8: Attends the third meeting of the sixth CPPCC. March 26: Attends the opening ceremony of the National Museum of Modern Chinese Literature. Meets Ba Jin. March 29: Attends the second meeting of the presidium of the Writers Union. April 11: Hospitalized for cancer. June 8: Passes away at the age of 83 in **Beijing**. The CCP reasserts its assessment of the incorrectness of the 1955 campaign and the charges against Hu.

1986 January 15: Memorial ceremony at the Babaoshan Revolutionary Cemetery.

1988 July 22: Final rehabilitation of Hu. The *People's Daily* publishes this sentence: "The Central Committee has released more documents to further make a complete rehabilitation of Hu Feng."

LIST OF CHINESE NAMES AND TERMS

abstract generalization 概念化
Ai Qing 艾青
Ai Siqi 艾思奇
Association of Chinese Writers and Artists 中国文艺家协会
Ba Jin 巴金
Ba Ren 巴人
Bai Lang 白郎
Bi Lei 毕磊
Cao Baohua 曹保华
Chen Duxiu 陈独秀
Chen Huangmei 陈荒煤
Chen Jiakang 陈家康
Chen Shoumei 陈守梅; pseudonym Ah-long 阿垅
Chen Xuezhao 陈学昭
Chen Zhuyin 陈竹隐
Cheng Fangwu 成仿吾
Chinese League of Left-wing Writers 中国左翼作家联盟
China Youth 中国青年
Creation Monthly 创造月刊
Dagong bao 大公报
Dong Biwu 董必武
Fan Zhongyan 范仲淹
Fang Han 方瀚; pseudonym He Dinghua 何定华
Fang Juehui 方觉慧
Feng Naichao 冯乃超

Feng Xuefeng 冯雪峰
Fu Guoquan 扶國權
Fuping 阜平
Geng Yong 耿庸
Guidance 向导
Guo Moruo 郭沫若
Guomingdang 国民党
He Ganzhi 何干之
He Manzi 何满子
He Qifang 何其方
Hong Cuie 洪翠娥
Hong Lingfei 洪灵菲
Hu Feng 胡风
Hu Jiansan 胡缄三
Hu Qiaomu 胡乔木
Hu Sheng 胡绳
Hu Zhimin 胡志民
Huang Yaomian 黄药眠
Huang Yuan 黄源
Hurricane Society 狂飙社
Jia Zhifang 贾植芳
Jiang Chunzhu 蒋纯祖
Jiang Guangci 蒋光慈
Jiang Jieshi 蒋介石
Jiang Qing 江青
Jin Yi 靳以
Kang Sheng 康生
Kang Zhuo 康濯
Les Contemporains 现代
Li Fenglian 李鳳蓮
Li Guangtian 李广田
Li Liewen 黎烈文
Li Lisan 李立三
Li Weihan 李維漢
Li Xiang 黎項
Li Xin 黎辛
Li Xiuzhen 李秀真
Lin Biao 林彪
Lin Mohan 林默涵

Lin Yutang 林语堂
Literary Gazette 文艺报
Literature and Art for the Masses 大众文艺丛刊
Literature and Art Monthly 文艺月报
Literature Monthly 文学月报
Literature Review 文學評論
Liu Baimin 刘百闵
Liu Baiyu 刘白羽
Liu Binyan 刘宾雁
Liu Qing 柳青
Liu Shaoqi 刘少奇
Liu Xuewei 刘雪苇
Liu Zaifu 刘再复
Lou Shiyi 楼适夷
Lu Dingyi 陆定一
Lu Ling 路翎
Lu Xin 路莘
Lu Xun 鲁迅
Lu Yuan 绿原
Luo Feng 罗烽
Mao Dun 茅盾
Mao Zedong 毛泽东
Mei Zhi 梅志
Morning Flower Society 朝花社
Morning Post 晨报
Nameless Society 未明社
National Daily: Awakenings 国民日报: 觉悟
New China 新华
New Life 新生
New Youth 新青年
New Zhanchun 新蕲春
News Daily 新闻日报
Nie Gannu 聂绀弩
Niu Han 牛汉
objectivism 客观主义
pai 派
Pan Hannian 潘汉年
Peng Yanjiao 彭燕郊
Qian Mu 钱穆

Qian Shibo 钱石波
Qian Xingcun 钱杏村
Qian Yanbin 钱雁宾
Qiao Guanhua 乔冠华; pseudonym Qiao Mu 乔木, Yu Chao 于潮
Qin Zhaoyang 秦兆阳
Qiu Dongping 丘東平
Qu Qiubai 瞿秋白
Qu Yuan 屈原
Restoration Society 光复会
Rising Point 起点
Rong Guanxiu 戎冠秀
Sha Ting 沙汀
Shao Quanlin 邵荃麟
Shu Qun 舒群
Shu Wu 舒芜
subjective combative spirit 主观战斗精神
subjective-formulism 主观公式主义
Tang Tao 唐弢
The Mainland 中原
The Masses 群众
Tian Han 田汉
Tian Jian 田间
Tian Jiaying 田家英
Wan Xiyan 宛希俨
Wang Chengzhi 王承志
Wang Ming 王明
Wang Ruowang 王若望
Wang Shiwei 王实味
Wang Wenzheng 王文正
Wen Yiduo 闻一多
Wenhui Post 文汇报
Writers Monthly 作家月刊
Wu Tiehan 吴鐵漢
Wu Xiru 吴奚如
Wuchang 武昌
Xi Zhongxun 习仲勋
Xia Yan 夏衍
Xiang Linbing 向林冰
Xiao Feng 晓风

Xiao Jun 肖军
Xiaoshan 晓山
Xiong Zimin 熊子民
Xu Bingzhi 徐冰之
Xu Fuguan 徐复观
Xu Maoyong 徐懋庸
Xu Shaochang 许寿裳
Yan Wenjing 严文井
Yan'an 延安
Yang Chao 楊超
Yang Hansheng 阳翰笙
Yang Mo 杨沫
Yang Tianzhen 杨天真
Yao Pengzi 姚蓬子
Yao Wenyuan 姚文元
Ye Yiqun 叶以群
Yi Ding 一丁; pseudonym Lou Zichun 楼子春
Youth Post 青年报
Yu Dafu 郁达夫
Yuan Xiyan 宛希严
Zang Kejia 藏克家碧野
Zhang Chunqiao 张春桥
Zhang Guangnian 张光年
Zhang Guangren 张光人; pseudonym Hu Feng 胡风, Yan Ao 宴敖
Zhang Guotao 张国焘
Zhang Mingshan 张明山
Zhang Pijie 张丕介
Zhang Tianyi 张天翼
Zhang Zhongxiao 张中晓
Zhao Shuli 赵树理
Zheng Boqi 郑伯奇
Zhou Enlai 周恩来
Zhou Erfu 周而复
Zhou Libo 周立波
Zhou Yang 周扬
Zhou Zouren 周作人
Zhu Qixia 朱企霞
Zhu Yifu 朱以茀
Zhu Ziqing 朱自清

NOTES

CHAPTER 1

1. Maxim Gorky, "Anton Chekhov: Fragments of Recollections (1899)," in *Reminiscences of Anton Chekhov, Maxim Gorky, Alexander Kuprin, and I. A. Bunin*, trans. S. S. Koteliansky and Leonard Woolf (New York: B. W. Huebsch, 1921), http://www.eldritchpress.org/ac/gorky.htm. These two quotations appeared in Hu's long introductory essay on Chekhov written in August 1944. Hu used part of the second quotation—"Work with love and with faith"—as the epigraph of his essay. See Hu Feng, "Reminiscences of Anton Chekhov A. P. 契诃夫断片," in vol. 3 of the *Complete Works of Hu Feng* 胡风全集 (*HFQJ* hereafter throughout the book), 10 vols. (Wuhan: Hubei People's Publishing House, 1999), 221.

2. Mao Zedong, "The Chinese Revolution and the Chinese Communist Party," in vol. 2 of *Selected Works of Mao Tse-tung* 毛泽东选集 (Peking: Foreign Languages Press, 1965), 322.

3. Amitendranath Tagore, *Literary Debates in Modern China: 1918–1937* (Tokyo: Centre for East Asian Cultural Studies, 1967), 9–10.

4. T. A. Hsia, *The Gate of Darkness: Studies on the Leftist Literary Movement in China* (Seattle: University of Washington Press, 1968), 176.

5. Qu Qiubai, "Political Movement and the Learned Class 政治运动与知识阶级," *Guide Weekly* 向导周报, no. 18 (1923), 47–49.

6. With specific reference to the context of modern revolutionary China, Richard Solomon's psychological analysis of the function of Communist ideology—how it transformed ideas into an emotional crutch for individuals looking for a new sense of external authority during the Chinese Revolution—is one of the earliest and typical ones. Richard H. Solomon, "From Commitment to Cant: The Evolving Functions of Ideology in the Revolutionary Process," in *Ideology and Politics in Contemporary China*, ed. Chalmers Johnson (Seattle: University of Washington Press, 1973), 60.

7. Mao Zedong, "Analysis of the Classes in Chinese Society 中国社会各阶级的分析," in vol. 1 of *Selected Works of Mao Tse-tung* (Peking: Foreign Languages Press, 1965), 15.

8. Mao, "Analysis of the Classes in Chinese Society," 15–16. For a discussion of the interdependent relationship between the CCP and its "cultural workers" in wartime, see James Cotton, "The Intellectuals as a Group in the Chinese Political Process," in *Groups and Politics in the People's Republic of China*, ed. David S. G. Goodman (Cardiff: University College Cardiff Press, 1984); Merle Goldman, *China's Intellectuals: Advise and Dissent* (Cambridge, MA: Harvard University Press, 1981); Ma Shuyun, "Clientelism: Foreign Attention, and Chinese Intellectual Autonomy," *Modern China* 24, no. 4 (1998): 445–471; and Jin Yaoji, *Politics and Culture in China* 中国政治与文化 (Hong Kong: Oxford University Press, 1997).

9. Zhou Yang, "Defend Mao Thought on Literature and Art, Rebuke 'Totalitarian Talks about the Literary and Artistic Black Line' 捍卫毛泽东文艺思想, 驳斥〈文艺黑线专政论〉," in *People's Literature* 人民文学, a speech given at the editorial meeting of the *People's Literature* on December 30, 1977.

10. Zhou, "Defend Mao Thought on Literature and Art."

11. See Innes Herdan, *The Pen and the Sword: Literature and Revolution in Modern China* (London: Zed Books, 1992), 105.

12. See Mei Zhi, *F: Hu Feng's Prison Years*, ed. and trans. Gregor Benton (London: Verso, 2013), 14; also see Mei Zhi, *Past as Smoke: Hu Feng's Prison Years* 往事如煙: 胡风沉冤录 (Beijing: Kexue chubanshe, 1989), 31–32.

13. Mei, *F*, 30.

14. Mei, *F*, *30.*

15. Mei, *F*, 132.

16. For a discussion of the lack of agreement over this issue, see Shiping Hua, "One Servant, Two Masters: The Dilemma of Chinese Establishment Intellectuals," *Modern China* 20, no. 1 (January 1944): 92–121, esp. 94–96.

17. David Kelly, "The Emergence of Humanism: Wang Ruoshui and the Critique of Socialist Alienation," in *China's Intellectuals and the State: In Search of a New Relationship*, ed. Merle Goldman, Timothy Cheek, and Carol Lee Hamrin (Cambridge, MA: Council on East Asian Studies, Harvard University, 1987), 163.

18. Between the mid-1950s and the end of the Cultural Revolution in 1976, the CCP persecuted a great number of Chinese intellectuals, and Hu was the first. Among the early works that show a particular interest in the life and case of Hu, see Yang I-fan, *The Case of Hu Feng* (Hong Kong: Union Research Institute, 1956); Merle Goldman, "Hu Feng's Conflict with the Communist Literary Authorities," *Harvard Papers on China* 11 (1957): 149–191, reprinted in the *China Quarterly* 12 (1962): 102–138; and Peter Benenson, *Persecution 1961* (Harmondsworth, UK: Penguin, 1961), 135–150. Separately, see Andrew Endrey, "Hu Feng—Return of a Counter-revolutionary," *Australian Journal of Chinese Affairs* 5 (1981): 73–90, which was among the few studies on the Hu Incident in English-language schol-

arship that appeared before Hu's rehabilitation in the late 1980s. For a discussion of the brutality against intellectuals considered politically dissenting or ideologically deviant in those years, see Rudolf G. Wagner, "The Sufan Campaign, the Orthodox Personality, and the Political Climate," in *Inside a Service Trade* (Cambridge, MA: Council on East Asian Studies, Harvard University, 1992), 27–70; also see Donald A. Gibbs, ed., "Dissonant Voices in Chinese Literature: Hu Feng," *Chinese Studies in Literature* 1, no. 1 (1979–80): 3–89.

19. In the PRC, the Hu Incident has attracted scholarly attention since the late 1970s, when the CCP started to rehabilitate many veteran writers persecuted in different rectification movements. In the twenty-first century, a substantial number of critical studies on Hu and his literary theory have appeared. Examples include Fan Jiyan and Qian Wenliang, *Hu Feng: His Views on Culture and Literature* 胡风论: 对胡风文化与文学阐释 (Wuhan: Hubei People's Publishing House, 1999); Zhi Kejian, *On Hu Feng* 胡风论 (Nanning: Guangxi jiaoyu chubanshe, 2000); and Wang Lili, *Between Literature and Ideology: A Study of Hu Feng* 在文艺与意识形态之间: 胡风研究 (Beijing: Zhongguo renmindaxue chubanshe, 2003). Shortly after his rehabilitation, the People's Press published a three-volume collection in 1984 titled *Collected Criticism of Hu Feng* 胡风评论集, 3 vols. (Beijing: Renmin wenxue chubanshe, 1984–85). Hu's other writings—poems, prose work, letters, and personal memoirs—have been collected, edited, and published in quick succession. They include *Collected Translations of Hu Feng* 胡风译文集 (Beijing: Renmin wenxue chubanshe, 1986); *Selected Works of Hu Feng in His Late Years* 胡风晚年作品选 (Guilin: Lijiang chubanshe, 1987); *Collected Essays of Hu Feng* 风杂文集 (Beijing: Shenghuo, dushu, xinzhi sanlianshudian, 1987); *Hu Feng's Poetry* 胡风的诗, ed. Xiao Feng (Beijing: Zhongguo wenlian chubangongsi, 1987); *Hu Feng on Poetry* 胡风论诗 (Guangzhou: Huacheng chubanshe, 1988); *Collected Letters of Hu Feng* 胡风书信集, ed. Xiao Feng (Tianjin: Baihua wenyi, 1989); *Collected Essays on Hu Feng* 胡风论集, ed. Wen Zhenting and Fan Jiyan (Beijing: Zhongguo shehuikexue, 1991); *Complete Poems of Hu Feng* 胡风诗全编, ed. Niuhan and Lu Yuan (Hangzhou: Zhejiang wenyi chubanshe, 1992); *Hu Feng and Lu Ling's Literary Correspondence* 胡风路翎文学书简, ed. Xiao Feng (Hefei: Anhui wenyi chubanshe, 1994); *Selected Works of Hu Feng* 胡风选集, 2 vols., sel. and ed. Xiao Feng (Chengdu: Sichuan People's Publishing House, 1996); *Posthumous Works of Hu Feng* 胡风遗稿 (Jinan: Shandong youyi chubanshe, 1998); and *Selected Letters of Hu Feng* 胡风书话, sel. Xiao Feng and ed. Jiang Deming (Beijing: Beijing chubanshe, 1998). The *Complete Works of Hu Feng* 胡风全集 (*HFQJ*), ten volumes in total, appeared in 1999. Shortly after Hu's rehabilitation, a long list of such critical biographies as the following appeared: Mei Zhi, *An Account of Keeping a Prisoner Company* 伴囚记 (Beijing: Gongren chubanshe, 1988); Ma Tiji, *A Biography of Hu Feng* 胡风传 (Chengdu: Sichuan People's Publishing House, 1989); Mei Zhi, *Past as Smoke: A Memoir of Hu Feng's Prison Years* 往事如煙: 胡风沉冤录 (Beijing: Ke xue chubanshe, 1989); Dai Guangzhong, *A Biography of Hu Feng* 胡风传 (Yinchuan: Linxia People's

Publishing House, 1994); Xiao Feng, *Forever Unregretful: A Biography of Hu Feng* 九死未悔: 胡风传 (Taipei: Yeqiang, 1996); and Mei Zhi, *A Biography of Hu Feng* 胡风传 (Beijing: Beijing shiyue wenyi chubanshe, 1998). Hu also wrote extensively about his past experiences, and his autobiographical writings appeared in a single volume, *A Memoir of Hu Feng* 胡风回忆录 (Beijing: Renmin wenxue chubanshe, 1993).

20. Over the past three decades, scholars have paid increasing attention to instances of intellectual persecution in the PRC. A widely accepted view is that literary intellectuals in modern China are targets of political abuse because they are dissenting. See, for example, Jerome B. Grieder, *Intellectuals and the State in Modern China: A Narrative History* (New York: Free Press, 1981), 278–279.

21. "Victims of the Powers That Be," *Times Literary Supplement*, no. 3123 (January 5, 1962), 7.

22. "Victims of the Powers That Be"; my emphasis.

23. Raymond Williams, *Marxism and Literature* (Oxford: Oxford University Press, 1977), 200.

24. In his discussion of Hu, Kirk Denton took the problematic of self as a point of departure and considered it to be a product of the uniquely Chinese sociopolitical context in the period between the 1930s and the 1940s. Kirk A. Denton, *The Problematic of Self in Modern Chinese Literature: Hu Feng and Lu Ling* (Stanford, CA: Stanford University Press, 1998), 258.

25. Whether or how this thesis about the representation of the self in modern Chinese literature will withstand criticism remains an open question, as Michel Hockx indicated in his book review, adding that it should be the responsibility of future research. See Michel Hockx, "Review of *The Problematic of Self in Modern Chinese Literature* by Kirk A. Denton," *China Quarterly* 160 (December 1999): 1088. For other reviews of the book, see Wendy Larson, *China Journal*, no. 45 (January 2001): 218–220; and Q. S. Tong, *Journal of Asian Studies* 58, no. 2 (May 1999): 484–486.

26. See Kirk A. Denton, "The Hu Feng Group: Genealogy of a Literary School," in *Literary Societies of Republican China*, ed. Kirk A. Denton and Michel Hockx (Lanham, MD: Lexington Books, 2008), 413–473. For a similar study on Hu-related literary groups in Chinese, see Zhou Yanfen, *Chance Encounter: July School, Hope School, and Related Literary Schools* 因缘际会: 七月社、希望社及相关现代文学社团研究 (Wuhan shi: Wuhan chubanshe, 2011).

27. Denton, "The Hu Feng Group," 422.

28. It anticipated and enabled, for example, Shu Yunzhong's monograph on the *July* poets, *Buglers on the Home Front: The Wartime Practice of the Qiyue School* (New York: State University of New York Press, 2000), which is a fundamental study of the political representations and intellectual genealogy of the school of writers associated with Hu.

29. For one of the few attempts in this effort, see Liu Kang and Xiaobing Tang, eds., *Politics, Ideology, and Literary Discourse in Modern China: Theoretical*

Interventions and Cultural Critique (Durham, NC: Duke University Press, 1993), 11–16. For an attempt to show how some Western academic trends have "theoretically informed" Chinese intellectuals in the 1980s and allowed them to "achieve a historical breakthrough," see Wang Jing, *High Culture Fever: Politics, Aesthetics, and Ideology in Deng's China* (Berkeley: University of California Press, 1996), 1–7. Aside from these more general accounts of the Chinese experience of modern criticism against the background of intellectual globalization and contemporary theories, see also D. K. Fokkema, *Literary Doctrine in China and Soviet Influence 1956–1960* (The Hague: Mouton, 1965); Hsia, *The Gate of Darkness*; and Theodore D. Huters, "Hu Feng and the Critical Legacy of Lu Xun," in *Lu Xun and His Legacy*, ed. Leo Ou-fan Lee (Berkeley: University of California Press, 1985), 129–152.

30. See Fredric Jameson, "Third-World Literature in the Era of Multinational Capitalism," *Social Text*, no. 15 (Autumn 1986): 65–88.

31. There was a consensus in the 1950s that Hu pointed out that "formalism" and "objectivism" could and should be criticized. See Zhou Yang, "Fight for the Creation of More and Better Literature and Art 为创造更多的优秀的文学艺术作品而奋斗,"*Literary Gazette*, no. 19 (September 1953): 77–78. Other critical articulations about the same problems in literary and artistic practices of the time include Qin Zhaoyang's *On Formulism, Abstract Generalization* 论公式化, 概念化 (1953) and Ba Ren's *Treatise on Literary Theory* 文学论稿 (1954). For a short biography of Qin Zhaoyang, see Vibeke Børdahl, *Along the Broad Road of Realism: Qin Zhaoyang's World of Fiction* (London: Curzon Press, 1990), 1–9.

32. Hu Feng, "Afterword to the Third Typesetting of 'Notes on Literature and Art' 文艺笔谈: 第三次排字后记," in vol. 2 of *HFQJ*, 275. This monograph was typeset twice without being published due to wartime conditions in the 1930s.

33. Jürgen Habermas, *The Structural Transformation of the Public Sphere: An Enquiry into a Category of Bourgeois Society*, trans. Thomas Burger (Cambridge, MA: MIT Press, 1989), 163. For a discussion of the public sphere in China, see Leo Ou-fan Lee's *Shanghai Modern: The Flowering of a New Urban Culture in China, 1930–1945* (Cambridge, MA: Harvard University Press, 1999).

34. See Jürgen Habermas, *The Theory of Communicative Action: Reason and Rationalization of Society*, trans. Thomas McCarthy (Boston: Beacon Press, 1984), 177.

35. Speaking about the bureaucratic characteristics of the Italian Socialist Party in the 1920s, Antonio Gramsci wrote in his *Prison Notebooks*: "The error of the intellectual consists in believing that it is possible to *know* without understanding and even more without feeling and being impassioned." Antonio Gramsci, *Selections from the Prison Notebooks of Antonio Gramsci*, ed. and trans. Quintin Hoare and Geoffrey Nowell Smith (London: Lawrence and Wishart, 1971), 418.

36. See Cao Qinghua, *Historical Accounts of Chinese Leftwing Literature: 1921–1936* 中国左翼文学史稿: *1921–1936* (Beijing: Zhongguo shehui kexue chubanshe, 2008), 276–287.

37. Zhi, *On Hu Feng*, 7.

38. The full title of the "300,000-Character Report" is "A Report concerning the Situation in Literary and Artistic Practice since Liberation: A Letter to the Central Committee of the Communist Party 关于解放以来的文艺实践情况的报告: 给党中央的信." Hu wrote the "Report" between March and July of 1954 and submitted it as a "suggestion letter" to Xi Zhongxun, then chief secretary of the State Council, together with a cover letter addressed to members of the Central Committee on July 22, 1954. Of the four sections of the "300,000-Character Report," the second one has five parts, with each focusing on a problem in literary practices in the 1950s that Hu identified. Hu referred to these problems figuratively as "the five knives lodged in the head of the writer and the reader." In January 1955, much against Hu's wishes, the *Literary Gazette* published the second and fourth parts of the "Report" in a booklet under the title "Hu Feng's Opinions on Literary Issues 胡风对文艺问题的意见." After Hu's rehabilitation, *Historical Data of New Literature* reprinted the first, second, and fourth parts of the "Report" in 1988. For a complete version of the "Report," see vol. 6 of *HFQJ*, 93–458.

39. Lu Yuan, "Hu Feng and Me 胡风和我," in vol. 2 of *Hu Feng in My Eyes: Thirty-Seven Reminiscences of the Hu-Feng Incident* 我与胡风: 胡风事件三十七人回忆, ed. Xiao Feng, 2 vols. (Yinchuan: Ningxia People's Publishing House, 1993), 623.

40. Wu Xiru, "The Hu Feng I Knew 我所认识的胡风," in vol. 1 of *Hu Feng in My Eyes*, ed. Xiao Feng, 30.

41. Jürgen Habermas, "Political Culture in Germany since 1968: An Interview with Dr. Rainer Erd for *Frankfurter Rundschau*," in *The New Conservatism: Cultural Criticism and the Historians' Debate*, ed. and trans. Shierry Weber Nicholsen (Cambridge, MA: MIT Press, 1990), 187.

42. Mao Zedong, "Editor's Comments to the Third Collection of Materials on the Hu Counterrevolutionary Clique," first published in the *People's Daily*, June 10, 1955; collected in vol. 1 of *The Writings of Mao Zedong 1949–1976: September 1949–1955*, 2 vols. (Armonk, NY: M. E. Sharpe, 1986), 576.

43. Michel Foucault, "Truth and Power, an Interview," in vol. 3 of *Essential Works of Foucault, 1954–1984: Power*, ed. James D. Faubion and trans. Robert Hurley et al. (New York: New Press, 2000), 131.

CHAPTER II

1. Hu Feng, "Requiem 英雄谱," *Time Has Begun* 时间开始了, in vol. 1 of *HFQJ*, 245, 248.

2. Hu Feng, "My Self-Criticism" 我的自我批评, in vol. 6 of *HFQJ*, 475.

3. Mao Zedong, "Editor's Comments (to the First Collection of Materials on the Hu Counterrevolutionary Clique)," first published in the *People's Daily*, May 13, 1955; reprinted in vol. 1 of *The Writings of Mao Zedong 1949–1976*, 563–564.

4. Hu Feng, Letter to Qiao Guanhua, February 14, 1966, in vol. 9 of *HFQJ*, 467.

5. See Karl Marx, *Economic and Philosophical Manuscripts of 1844*, trans. Martin Milligan (New York: International Publishers, 1964), 113.

6. Hu's trope was one expression of his romantic idealism, which many young intellectuals shared at the time. He was indeed idealistic. In the summer of 1926, because his "idealism could not be satisfied," Hu left Peking University Preparatory School for Qinghua, where he stayed for only a couple of months before returning to Hubei to take part in the revolution there. Twice in his autobiography, Hu called himself an idealist. In the article "Whitewashing and Distorting Hard Facts 粉饰, 歪曲, 铁一般的事实," written in Japan in May 1932, he pronounced the need to deal with his own "crippled idealism"—to unify literature with the revolution by unifying literature with life. Hu's most explicit self-reference to his idealism came from his reading of Romain Rolland's (1866–1944) *Jean-Christophe*, a splendid example of idealism. See Hu Feng, Letter to Lu Ling, October 26, 1943, in vol. 9 of *HFQJ*, 218.

7. For a survey of the history and development of revolutionary literature in the 1920s and 1930s in the Republic, see *The History of the Development of Chinese New Literature* 中国新文学发展史, ed. Feng Guanglian and Liu Zengren (Beijing: Renmin wenxue chubanshe, 1998), 27–61, 270–293. For a discussion of the topic in English, see Marián Gálik, *Mao Tun and Modern Chinese Literary Criticism* (Wiesbaden: Franz Steiner Verlag Gmbh, 1969), 56–58, 83–85, 98.

8. Published in *New Youth* 新青年 2, no. 6 (February 1, 1917), 1–4; reprinted in vol. 2 of *New Youth*, 14 vols. (Tokyo: Daian, 1962), 487–490.

9. These essays include Cheng Fangwu's "From a Literary Revolution to a Revolutionary Literature 从文学革命到革命文学" (February), Jiang Guangci's "The October Revolution and Russian Literature 十月革命与俄罗斯文学" (April), and Guo Moruo's "Revolution and Literature 革命与文学" (May).

10. Bonnie S. McDougall, "The Impact of Western Literary Trends," in *Modern Chinese Literature in the May Fourth Era*, ed. Merle Goldman (Cambridge, MA: Harvard University Press, 1977), 49.

11. See Hu Feng, "An Idealist's Memories of the Epoch—Written for Literature and Me, an Anniversary Issue of Literature 理想主义者时代底回忆," in vol. 2 of *HFQJ*, 267. In this memoirist account of his years before studying in Japan, Hu recalled his attraction to such Marxist publications as *Vanguard* 先驱, the precursor of the magazine *China Youth* 中国青年 (published by the League of Chinese Communist Youth between October 1923 and October 1927 in Shanghai, and later moved to Guangzhou and Hankou). *Vanguard* had a column devoted to the promotion of "revolutionary literature" as a tangible manifestation and pointer of the era's literary taste. *China Youth* granted revolutionary politics historical importance, impelling writers to be "committed," so to speak. Its exemplary publications included Qiu Shi's

"To the Young Students Studying Literature 告文学的青年," Dai Ying's "Literature and Revolution 文学与革命," Ze Min's "The Youth and Literary Movements 青年与文学运动," and Zhang Renguang's "The Writers China Needs 中国所要的文学家." In 1927, the 144th issue of *China Youth* published a translation of Lenin's "Party Organization and Party Literature" (1905). This essay summarily declared the defense of revolutionary and political aesthetics in the history of modern Chinese literature.

12. Hu, "Requiem," 197–199.

13. See Hu, "Requiem," 189–190.

14. Wu, "The Hu Feng I Knew," 15.

15. See Qian Yanbin, "Anecdotes of Hu's Adolescent Life 胡风的青少年时期生活琐记," *Hubei Writers* 湖北作家论丛 3 (1989).

16. Lu Xun, "Thoughts on the League of Left-wing Writers, a Speech Given at the Inaugural Meeting of the League of Left-wing Writers on March 2, 1930," trans. Yang Hsien-yi and Gladys Yang, in vol. 3 of *Selected Works of Lu Hsun*, 4 vols. (Beijing: Foreign Press, 1956–60), 104.

17. Hu's "The Dead Sun" appeared in a school magazine and at a public performance. For comments on the elegy, see Wan Jiaji and Zhao Jinzhong, *A Critical Biography of Hu Feng* 胡风评传 (Chongqing: Chongqing chubanshe, 2001), 24, and Wang Ginshan, "Two or Three Things about Ba Jin the Senior 巴金老学长二三事," in people.com 人民网, 2003 (March 2005). http://www.people.com.cn/GB/14738/14759/21864/2227809.html.

18. Ba Jin, "Remembering Hu Feng 怀念胡风," in *Free Thoughts* 随想录 (Beijing: Renmin wenxue chubanshe, 2000), 735. See also Wan and Zhao, *A Critical Biography of Hu*, 25–26.

19. Ba, "Remembering Hu Feng," 735.

20. Hu was first tried and sentenced to fourteen years of imprisonment on November 26, 1965, and to life imprisonment at the height of the Cultural Revolution in 1970. He finished twenty-four years of prison on January 14, 1979. When the Hu case finally went to trial after the CCP had detained Hu for a decade, the court decided to imprison Hu for fourteen years and required him to serve the last four as a "controlled element" in Sichuan. From 1965 to the end of 1967, Hu and Mei Zhi lived in Chengdu under house arrest before he was arrested again by the Cultural Revolution committee. In January 1968, Hu received a life sentence without trial.

21. Wan and Zhao, *A Critical Biography of Hu*, 449.

22. Wan and Zhao, *A Critical Biography of Hu*, 449.

23. Wan and Zhao, *A Critical Biography of Hu*, 449.

24. For an insightful discussion of Arishima's influence on Lu Xun and a comparative study of their humanism and belief in "universal love," see Christopher T. Keaveney, *Beyond Brushtalk: Sino-Japanese Literary Exchange in the Interwar Period* (Hong Kong: Hong Kong University Press, 2008), 76–83.

25. Wan and Zhao, *A Critical Biography of Hu*, 451.

26. In his early revolutionary years, Hu was critical of theories in support of aestheticism and such notions as literary genius and "naturalism" in literature. Hu held these theories and notions responsible for the production of "hollow" and "formalistic" literature. See Hu Feng, "On Hollowed Literature 关于抽骨留皮的文学论," in vol. 3 of *HFQJ*, 20–28.

27. See, for example, Zhao Shuli, *Young Blacky Gets Married* 小二黑结婚 (1943)," in *The Complete Novels of Zhao Shuli* 赵树理小说全集 (Changchun: Shidai wenyi chubanshe, 1997), and the controversial and popular historical novel *The Song of Youth* 青春之歌 (1958) by Yang Mo 杨沫 (1914–95). The latter is especially of interest here because it is a story about modern Chinese intellectuals' road to revolution. The protagonist, Lin Daojing, though a woman and sharing the fate of modern Chinese women, shares some similar features with Hu in terms of her road to the Chinese Revolution.

28. Hu, "Requiem," 197–199.

29. Records of Hu's literary and political activities in Japan abound in autobiographies and biographies. See, for example, Sakai Hiroshi, "The Hu as Found in Oda Takeo's Memoir *Bungaku seishun gunzo*," *Studies of Lu Xun Monthly* 鲁迅研究月刊, no. 1 (2003); and Kondo Tatsuya, "Notes on Hu [1] 胡风研究札记1," in vol. 1 of *Collected Articles on Writers of Hubei* 湖北作家论丛, 3 vols. (Wuhan daxue chubanshe, 1987), 55–84.

30. Cheng Ching-mao, "The Impact of Japanese Literary Trends on Modern Chinese Writers," in *Modern Chinese Literature in the May Fourth Era*, ed. Merle Goldman (Cambridge, MA: Harvard University Press, 1977), 72.

31. Bertrand Russell, vol. 2 of *Autobiography* (London: Allen and Unwin, 1968), 133.

32. The reception for the lecture took place on the morning of July 26. Quoted, with notes in brackets, by William Snell, "Bertrand Russell at Keio University, July 1921," *Kindai Nihon Kenkyu (Modern Japan Study)* 14 (1997): 175.

33. *Kaizo*, no. 10 (September 1921): 98.

34. Snell, "Bertrand Russell at Keio University," July 1921, 192.

35. For details on Hu's literary activities that facilitated cross-border exchanges among left-wing writers, see Hu Feng, "My Work Related to the Cultural Exchange between China and Japan 我做的一些中日文化交流工作," in vol. 7 of *HFQJ*, 220–226.

36. The Japan Proletarian Culture Federation (Nihon Purorateraria Bunka Renmei) aimed at unifying the proletarian cultural front, including the artists' federations and the Proletarian Science Center (Puroretaria Kagaku Kenkyujo). It was also known as the KOPF, from its Esperanto name Federacio de Proletaj Kultur-organizoj Japanaj. The KOPF became increasingly radical, resulting in the arrest of many of its members until the federation's disbandment in 1934. For details, see Rodger Swearingen and Paul Langer, *Red Flag in Japan: International Communism in Action, 1919–1951* (Cambridge, MA: Harvard University Press, 1952), 53–55.

37. Hu Feng, "A Memoir胡风回忆录" (Beijing: Renmin wenxue chubanshe, 1993), in vol. 7 of *HFQJ*, 276.

38. Hu Feng, "A Memoir."

39. Hu met with Kiyoshi Eguchi (1887–1975) through the introduction of Oya Soichi, the translator of Maxim Gorky's (1868–1936) *Zhizn klima samgina* (*The Bystander*). In 1930, J. Cape and H. Smith (New York) published an English version of the tale, translated from the Russian by Bernard Guilbert Guerney, and Hu wanted to translate it into Chinese. He therefore wrote Oya Soichi to inquire about the availability of an English translation of the novel only to find that *The Bystander* was "too big" for him. Even so, Hu established a friendship with Oya and, via Oya's introduction, also with Eguchi. See Hu, "A Memoir," 278–279; and Wan and Zhao, *A Critical Biography of Hu Feng*, 50–51.

40. An organization of radicals, the Japanese Proletarian Authors' League was an affiliate of the KOPF.

41. Takiji Kobayashi (1903–33), author of *Kanikosen* (The Cannery Boat), was a member of the Japanese Communist Party since 1931, as well as a member of the KOPF. According to Swearingen and Langer, Kobayashi was "an outstanding representative of the many proletarian writers who refused to heed the government's warnings, continued to write as they saw fit, and as a result not infrequently landed in jail" (Swearingen and Langer, *Red Flag in Japan*, 53). In February 1932, the Japanese police arrested and tortured Kobayashi to death under the guise of investigating his "subversive activities." On behalf of the Chinese Left-wing Cultural Coalition, Hu wrote a condolence letter in protest against the Japanese government. For narratives about Kobayashi's political career and persecution, see people.com 人民网, April 20, 2004 (2006), http://www.people.com.cn/GB/tupian/1097/2349809.html; and Tadashi Imai's 1974 biodrama *Takiji Kobayashi: The Life of a Communist Writer*, 1 hr. 59 min. (Japan: Takiji, 1974).

42. Hu Feng, "My Impression of Ujaku Akita 秋田雨雀印象记," in vol. 2 of *HFQJ*, 256–260 (my emphasis).

43. Hu, "My Impression of Ujaku Akita."

44. See Hu, "My Impression of Ujaku Akita," 258–259. Using Kiyoshi Eguchi as a model, Hu explained in his essay how Japanese popular writers were real Marxists. Hu also talked about his admiration for Eguchi's genuine concern for the well-being of the Chinese masses: from a historical perspective, there were practical reasons, both strategic and personal, for the Japanese Communists to be internationalists in the purest Marxist terms; see Robert A. Scalapino, *The Japanese Communist Movement: 1920–1966* (Berkeley: University of California Press, 1967), 44–47.

45. Mei, *Biography of Hu Feng*, 212.

46. Mei, *Biography of Hu Feng*, 212.

47. Guo Moruo, exiled in Japan in the spring of 1931, was against the naturalist idea of mimesis and considered the artist to be an active agent in the

creative process. He lent support to left-wing artists who were preoccupied with the sociopolitical potential of art and with the question of the relevance of art to the proletarian revolution. Guo's oft-cited essay "The Heroic Tree 英雄树" (first published under the pseudonym Mo Keang in the first issue of *Creation Monthly* in 1927) demanded that young writers and critics "fight against individualism" and "overcome bourgeois ideology" to "propagate, intensify, and strengthen" the proletarian spirit of the times. This essay is collected in vol. 10 of *Literary Works of Guo Moruo* 沫若文集, 17 vols. (Beijing: Renmin wenxue chubanshe, 1959).

48. Ma, *A Biography of Hu Feng*, 46.

49. Hu Feng, Letter to Zhu Qixia, October 4, 1932, in vol. 9 of *HFQJ*, 690.

50. See Hu Feng, "Whitewashing and Distorting Hard Facts," in vol. 5 of *HFQJ*, 129.

51. Karl Marx, "The English Middle Class," first published in the *New York Tribune*, August 1, 1854; reprinted and collected in *Marx and Engels on Literature and Art*, ed. Lee Baxandall and Stefan Morawski (New York: International General, 1973), 106.

52. See Conor Cruise O'Brien, introduction to *Power and Consciousness*, ed. Conor Cruise O'Brien and William Dean Vanech (London: University of London Press), 7 (emphasis in original).

53. Albert Camus, *L'Homme révolté* (Paris: Gallimard, 1951), 30.

54. Hu Feng, preface to "Notes on Literature and Art 文艺笔谈," in vol. 2 of *HFQJ*, 3.

55. Hu, preface to "Notes on Literature and Art," 3.

56. Hu, preface to "Notes on Literature and Art," 3–4.

57. R. P. Blackmur, "The Critic's Job of Work," in *Language as Gesture: Essay in Poetry* (New York: Columbia University Press, 1981), 372.

58. Hu, Letter to Zhu Qixia, October 4, 1932, in vol. 9 of *HFQJ*, 691.

59. It is not my intention to explore, as a topic, the romantic roots of Marxism. Critical studies and extensive discussions of the topic are numerous; for example, see Paul Breines, "Marxism, Romanticism, and the Case of Georg Lukács: Notes on Some Recent Sources and Situations," *Studies in Romanticism* 16, no. 4 (Fall 1977).

60. Hu, "An Idealist's Memories of the Epoch," 273.

61. Hu, "Requiem," 223.

62. Hu, "Requiem," 240–241.

63. See He Dinghua [Fang Han], "Hu in His Adolescence," *Hubei Writers*, no. 1 (1987): 47.

64. *Sekki*, first distributed on February 1, 1928, was an underground proletarian literature magazine distributed among potential Communist Party members in the form of a mimeographed news sheet bearing the title *Red Flag*. See Swearingen and Langer, *Red Flag in Japan*, 30n5.

65. See Hu, "A Memoir," 283, 291.

66. Hu, "A Memoir," 279.

67. Friedrich Engels, "Russia and the Social Revolution," in *From Karl Marx and Friedrich Engels, the Russian Menace to Europe*, ed. Karl P. W. Blackstock and B. F. Hoselitz (Glencoe, IL: Free Press, 1952), 205.

68. Quoted in Tatsuya, "Notes on Hu [1]," 59 (italics mine).

69. Jia Zhifang, "Fragments of Memory 片断的回忆," *Historical Data of New Literature*, no. 4 (1987): 70–71.

70. Lou Shiyi, "Reminiscences of Hu 回忆胡风," *Historical Data of New Literature*, no. 4 (1987): 59.

71. Xiong Zimin was a CCP member who worked in the Wuhan office of the Eighth Route Army in 1939.

72. See Hu, Letter to Zhu Qixia, October 4, 1932, in vol. 9 of *HFQJ*, 689.

73. Teikoku Zaigogunjinkai Hombu (Headquarters of the Imperial Association of Reservists), *Seikai imbo to Nippon kyosanto* (*World Plots and the Japanese Communist Party*) (Tokyo, 1933); quoted in Swearingen and Langer, *Red Flag in Japan*, 50.

74. The poem, first published in October 1931 in the first issue of the first volume of *Spreading Fire* 流火, was later reprinted in the first issue of the second volume of *Big Dipper* 北斗, a left-wing literary magazine edited by Ding Ling.

75. Hu Feng, "The Sacrificial Rites of the Enemy 仇敌的祭礼," in vol. 1 of *HFQJ*, 51–52. Whether in terms or logic, what Hu said here resonated with what Sanzo Nozaka (also known by his Moscow pseudonym Susumu Okano) would say two years later. In his "Speech before the Executive Committee of the Communist International, Moscow" given in 1933, Okano urged Japanese soldiers "to revolt against their commander . . . and . . . transform their units into a Red Army which will turn its weapons against the Mikado." See Okano Susumu, "The Revolutionary Struggle of the Toiling Masses of Japan, the Thirteenth Plenum of the Executive Committee of the Communist International in Moscow, December 1933" (New York: Workers Library Publishers, 1934), 28.

76. Hu, "The Sacrificial Rites of the Enemy," 53–54.

77. After an assembly in Tiananmen Square, the protestors, headed by Duan Qirui, demonstrated in front of the State Department. Forty people were killed and about 200 were wounded. See Ho Kan-chih, *A History of the Modern Chinese Revolution* 中国现代革命史, trans. the English Faculty of the Western Languages Department of Peking University (New York: AMS Press, [1959] 1979).

78. Hu Feng, "To the Dead 致死者," in vol. 1 of *HFQJ*, 12–13.

79. As Hu stated in his preface to *Wild Flowers and Arrows* 野花与箭, a collection of Hu's early poems, including "The Sacrificial Rites of the Enemy," recorded in those poems were "the traces of an adolescent" who attempted to "search for a road in the wilderness" (vol. 1 of *HFQJ*, 3).

80. Kondo, "Notes on Hu [1]," 64.

81. Kondo, "Notes on Hu [1]," 64.

82. Scalapino observed that "in this period [the prewar 1920s] the Japanese Marxist movement itself was an overseas movement to a substantial extent. Its

main adherents were overseas students or refugees" (Scalapino, *Japanese Communist Movement*, 6). It is highly possible, moreover, that Hu was attracted to the JCP as an intellectual force, both radical and marginal, in opposition to the mainstream Japanese intellectual discourse, which at the time was defined by Japanese nationalism and imperialism. When the JCP was officially established on July 15, 1922, it was "merely a group of some forty radically inclined intellectuals" (Swearingen and Langer, *Red Flag in Japan*, 15), "a tiny band of men who had little or no connection with the main intellectual stream in Japan" (Swearingen and Langer, *Red Flag in Japan*, 5).

83. Swearingen and Langer, *Red Flag in Japan*, 235.

84. Reports and resolutions of the Eighteenth Enlarged Plenum of the Central Committee of the Japanese Communist Party, quoted in Swearingen and Langer, *Red Flag in Japan*, 236.

85. Hu, "An Idealist's Memories of the Epoch," 273.

86. See Mei, *Biography of Hu Feng*, 226.

87. Hu, "A Memoir," 286.

88. At the request of the Japanese Anti-War League to find a Chinese representative to participate in the Rally against War in the Far East, Hu went back to Shanghai with Lou Shiyi of Tokyo at the end of 1932. Hu, "A Memoir," 287. See also Lou Shiyi, "About the Rally against War in the Far East 关于远东反战大会," *Historical Data of New Literature*, no. 2 (1984): 45.

89. Hu Feng, "Remembering the Time [I] Joined the Left-league," in vol. 7 of *HFQJ*, 98.

90. In November 1932, Hu visited Shanghai to seek Chinese representatives to attend the Rally against War in the Far East to be held in Tokyo. In Shanghai, he found Zhou and Feng drawn into the Left-league's debate on the "third-category men" 第三种人 and the "free men" 自由人. The debate with the "enemies" from the other ideological camp soon turned into an argument between comrades on the same side. The incident began with the publication, in *Literature Monthly* 文学月报 (1, no. 4 [1932]), of a poem by Qiu Jiuru titled "The Testimony of a Traitor 汉奸的供词" under the pseudonym Yunsheng. The poem, though politically in line with the leftists, was "vulgar" and "trivial" because it attacked people at a personal level. Feng found it "completely against the policy of the Party" and held Zhou, then editor of *Literature Monthly*, accountable for the mistake. In his role as secretary of the Arts Committee, Feng requested that Zhou make a public correction in the subsequent issue of *Literature Monthly*. During his debate with the "third-category men," Zhou also wrote an essay titled "Who Has Given Up Truth and Literature? 到底是谁不要真理, 不要文艺么?" As he was also personal in his attack on Su Wen, a former member of the Left-league, calling Su "a dog" of the capitalist class, Lu Xun reprimanded him. According to Hu, Feng and Zhou, acting in self-defense, gave him various accounts of the debate (Hu, "A Memoir," 286). See also Feng Xiaxiong, ed., "Feng Xuefeng Talks about the Left-league 冯雪峰谈左联," *Historical Data of New Literature*, no. 1

(1980): 10; Lu Xun, "Humiliation and Intimidation Are Not Fighting 辱骂和恐吓决不是战斗," first published in *Literature Monthly*, nos. 5–6 (1932), 247–248; collected in vol. 2 of *Materials on the History of Modern Chinese Literature* 中国现代文学史资料 (Tokyo: Daan, 1968), 517–518. For details on the background of Hu Qiuyuan and the respective roles taken by Zhou and Feng in the debate, see Wong Wang-chi, *Politics and Literature in Shanghai: The Chinese League of Leftwing Writers, 1930–36* (Manchester: Manchester University Press, 1991), 128–129, 129–132.

91. Apart from the one between Zhou and Feng, the conflicts and arguments within the Left-league referred to those between Mu Mutian on the one side and Lu Xun and Feng on the other. In his preface to *Three Leisure* 三闲记 written in April 1932, Lu Xun included a satirical critique of the Creation Society in the summary of his debates with revolutionary writers between 1928 and 1929. For Lu Xun's satire, see preface to *Three Leisure*, in vol. 3 of *Lu Xun Selected Works*, trans. Yang Xianyi and Gladys Yang, 4 vols. (Beijing: Foreign Press, 1957), 172–173.

92. Hu, "Remembering the Time [I] Joined the Left-league," 99. The spring of 1934 was a turning point in Hu's relationship with the Left-league. In October of that year, Mu Mutian, whom the Guomingdang police had freed from a three-month detention, spread a rumor that Hu was a spy for the Nanjing government. With the rumor spreading within the Left-league, it was difficult, if not impossible, for Hu to continue working as an administrative secretary for the Left-league. Hu, hearing the rumor, resigned from the Left-league and complained to Zhou but to no avail. By removing Hu from his circle of power, Zhou succeeded in distancing himself from Hu and, by extension, Feng Xuefeng and Lu Xun. Notably, Hu first went to Zhou to appeal for justice, believing that Zhou, then the person in charge of the CCP's cultural organization in Shanghai, had both an institutional responsibility and the power to rectify his name among the members of the Left-league; it never occurred to Hu that internal conflicts within these left-wing circles would be politically consequential. A more objective account of the incident lies in Wu Xiru's reminiscent essay "The Hu Feng I Knew 我所认识的胡风": "Hu had sought, in advance, permission from the Party Committee before he worked as editor and translator for the Institute for Culture Studies" (Wu Xiru, *Hu Feng in My Eyes*, ed. Xiao Feng, 19–20). For a secondary account of the rumor about Hu's relationship with the Guomindang, see Xia Yan, *Old Dreams Recollected at Leisure* 懒寻旧梦录 (Beijing: Henghuo, dushu, xinzhi sanlianshudian, 2000), 178–179.

93. For details on the actual work involved, see Hu Feng, "Some Recollections of the Relation between the 'Left-league' and Lu Xun 关於左联于鲁迅关系的若干回忆," in vol. 7 of *HFQJ*, 11.

94. Hu, "Remembering the Time [I] Joined the Left-league," 115. The friendly relationship between Hu and Zhou at that time extended beyond professional terms. There were a few occasions, for example, in which Zhou borrowed money from Hu. For details, see Mei, *Biography of Hu Feng*, 258–259, 280–281.

95. The crisis at that time not only produced chaos and anxiety but also nurtured a sense of excitement and a general feeling that the present would change.

Meanwhile, as the Sino-Japanese War and the internal ideological struggles brought the young Republic a prolonged period of social and political radicalism, rendering this part of Chinese history thoroughly war-torn and close to a state of anarchy, these events also enabled intellectual strife and liberation. In *Anarchism in the Chinese Revolution,* Arif Dirlik provided a critical survey of Communism's historical development in China and argued that anarchism played an essential role in bringing about the Chinese Communist revolution. See also Feng Guanglian and Liu Zengren, eds., *The History of the Development of Chinese New Literature* 中国新文学发展史 (Beijing: Renmin wenxue chubanshe, [1991] 1994), 517.

96. See Lu Si, *Film Criticism in Recollection* 影评忆旧 (Beijing: Zhongguo dianying chubanshe, 1962); and Chen Bo, ed., *The Leftist Film Movement in China* 中国左翼电影运动 (Beijing: Zhongguo dianying chubanshe, 1993), 60–225.

97. "Authoritative discourse permits no play with the context framing it, no play with its borders, no gradual and flexible transitions . . . one must either totally affirm it, or totally reject it." Mikhail M. Bakhtin, *The Dialogic Imagination*, ed. Michael Holquist and trans. Caryl Emerson and Michael Holquist (Austin: University of Texas Press, 1981), 343.

98. After Hu resigned from his post in the Left-league in 1934, he kept in touch with Sha Ting, betting on the fact that he was a close friend of Zhou and as such would pass on his views to the Left-league. As Mei Zhi recollected, "Hu thought that since he could not see Zhou face to face, any suggestions he had for the Left-league would need to be passed on to Zhou through Sha Ting. Included in the suggestions were, of course, some critical comments that Sha Ting, as a good friend of Zhou, would not love to hear. . . . For Hu, to cease contacts with Sha Ting meant to break away from the Left-league." Mei, *Biography of Hu Feng*, 298.

99. As recalled by Wu, "The Hu Feng I Knew," 20.

100. Hu, "A Memoir," 310.

101. Hu, "A Memoir," 351–352.

102. Hu Feng, "Sing for the Motherland 为祖国而歌," in vol. 1 of *HFQJ*, 76–77.

103. Jean-Paul Sartre, *What Is Literature?*, trans. Bernard Frechtman (London: Routledge, 1993), 56–57 (emphasis in original).

104. Sartre, *What Is Literature?*, 57 (my emphasis).

105. Sartre, *What Is Literature?*, 57.

106. Mei, *Biography of Hu Feng*, 227.

CHAPTER III

1. V. I. Lenin, "Party Organization and Party Literature," in vol. 10 of *Lenin Collected Works* (Moscow: Progress Publishers, 1965), 48. This decree, first published in Russian in Moscow in 1905, was translated into Chinese and appeared in the 144th issue of *China Youth* in 1927.

2. Lu Xun began his conversion to Communism in 1927, after which he engaged in a decade-long alignment with left-wing writers until his death in 1936. This period of alliance is better understood when divided into three stages: (1) his transition to communism between 1927 and 1930; (2) his productive collaboration with Party members, such as Qu Qiubai and Feng Xuefeng (1930–33); and (3) his suspicion of partisan politics and factionalism, particularly Zhou Yang's sectarianism (1934–36).

3. Liu Xuewei, "Details of My Relation with Hu Feng 我和胡风关系的始末," in vol. 1 of *Hu Feng in My Eyes*, ed. Xiao Feng, 69.

4. Geng Yong, "Memories Bristling with Profusions and Complications 枝蔓丛丛的回忆," in vol. 2 of *Hu Feng in My Eyes*, ed. Xiao Feng, 642.

5. In a speech given during a memorial at North Shaanxi Public School on the first anniversary of Lu Xun's death on October 19, 1937, Mao urged Party members to "learn from the Lu Xun spirit." Mao Zedong, "On Lu Xun 论鲁迅," in vol. 4 of *Mao's Road to Power: Revolutionary Writings, 1912–1949*, ed. Stuart R. Schram (Armonk, NY: M. E. Sharpe, 2004), 96–98.

6. Jerome B. Grieder, *Intellectuals and the State in Modern China: A Narrative History* (New York: Free Press, 1981), 270.

7. Theodore D. Huters, "Hu Feng and the Critical Legacy of Lu Xun," in *Lu Xun and His Legacy*, ed. Leo Ou-fan Lee (Berkeley: University of California Press, 1985), 129–152.

8. Erich Auerbach, "Philology and Weltliteratur," trans. Maire and Edward Said, *Centennial Review* 13, no. 1 (Winter 1969): 5.

9. For Hu, a true poet was a true fighter. It should be noted, however, that although left-wing politics considered literature a form of fighting, a left-wing writer did not need to define her sense of self in institutional terms. The case of Yu Dafu might be of interest here. At the time the Left-league was being established, Yu Dafu's name did not appear on the list of its founders. Lu Xun asked Xia Yan and Feng Naichao why Yu Dafu was absent from the list of founders. Feng replied, "Yu Dafu has recently been quite moody and has stayed mostly out of touch with old friends." Lu Xun said, "I think he is a very good writer, and is also patriotic and progressive. He should be accepted by [the Left-league]." Although Lu Xun's intervention allowed Yu Dafu to become one of its founders, Yu was expelled from the organization on November 6, 1930, at its fourth general meeting. Years later, Zheng Boqi, Standing Committee member of the Left-league and chairman of the general meeting on that day, recalled the process with deep regret: "In the meeting, somebody came up with the following suggestion: Yu said to Xu Zhimo of the Crescent Moon Society, 'I am a writer, not a fighter.' To make such an open remark in front of our [ideological] enemy would disqualify him as one of us; we should ask him to leave. At once the group became excited, and all members supported [the motion]. . . . I regret this incident . . . deeply. Time has proven that Yu Dafu remained revolutionary until the end and kept in contact with the Party."

(See Zheng Boqi, "Random Memories of the Left-league 左联回忆散记," *Historical Data of New Literature*, no. 1 [1982]: 16.) However, even before the meeting, Yu had already written to the officer-in-charge of the Left-league Party committee: "My character is not suitable for these tasks [assembly, and so forth.]. I know myself very well, and am determined to stop carrying an empty title." This was probably the first case of open withdrawal from the Left-league. Like Yu, Hu would soon distance himself from the Left-league as an organization.

10. Hannah Arendt, "Martin Heidegger at Eighty," in *Heidegger and Modern Philosophy*, ed. Michael Murray (New Haven, CT: Yale University Press, 1978), 295–298.

11. Hannah Arendt made this observation in response to Karl Jaspers's critique of Heidegger's philosophy as one "without love" and "in an unlovable style." Arendt, "Martin Heidegger at Eighty," 295–298.

12. Elizabeth Kamarck Minnich, "Arendt, Heidegger, Eichmann: Thinking in and for the World," *Soundings: An Interdisciplinary Journal* 86, nos. 1–2 (Spring/Summer 2003): 103.

13. Hannah Arendt, vol. 1 of *The Life of the Mind*, 2 vols. (New York: Harcourt, 1981), 5.

14. Lu Xun, "A Quick Glance at Shanghai Literature and Art 上海文艺之一瞥," in vol. 4 of *Complete Works of Lu Xun* 鲁迅全集, 16 vols. (Beijing: Renmin wenxue chubanshe, 1981–), 300.

15. Hu Feng, *Collected Essays of Hu Feng*, vol. 2, 9.

16. Hu, *Collected Essays*, vol. 2, 9–10.

17. See Hu Feng, "The Development and Direction of Our Work on Literature and Art 文艺工作底发展及其努力方向," in vol. 3 of *HFQJ*, 178–179.

18. See Hu Feng, "A. S. Pushkin and China 普式庚与中国," in vol. 3 of *HFQJ*, 397.

19. Hu Feng, "It Grew from 'a Particle of Heat and a Particle of Light' 从〈有一分热,发一分光〉生长起来的," in vol. 3 of *HFQJ*, 45.

20. Hu, "It Grew," 47.

21. Hu, "It Grew," 47.

22. See Raymond Williams, "Structures of Feeling," in *Marxism and Literature* (Oxford: Oxford University Press, 1977), 128–135.

23. See Hu Feng, "If He Were Still Alive 如果他还活着," in vol. 2 of *HFQJ*, 675–676; see also Lu Xun, preface to *Call to Arms* 呐喊, in vol. 1 of *Selected Works of Lu Xun*, trans. Yang Hsien-yi and Gladys Yang (Beijing: Foreign Languages Press, 1956–60), 34.

24. Hu, "If He Were Still Alive," 675–676.

25. Lu, preface to *Call to Arms*, 34–35. See also Xu Shoushang 许寿裳, *The Lu Xun I Knew* 我所认识的鲁迅 (Beijing: Renmin wenxue chubanshe, 1978), 7.

26. Lu, preface to *Call to Arms*, 34–35.

27. Lu, preface to *Call to Arms*, 34–35.

28. Lu, preface to *Call to Arms*, 34–35.

29. Lu, preface to *Call to Arms*, 34–35.

30. Lu, preface to *Call to Arms*, 34–35.

31. Hu, "It Grew," 55.

32. Hu, "It Grew," 49.

33. Hu, "It Grew," 49.

34. Hu Feng, "For New Writers on Writing 为初笔者的创作谈," in vol. 2 of *HFQJ*, 240.

35. Hu, "It Grew," 57. The word *passion* was Hu's original term to describe the writer and his characters' sense of martyrdom in the revolutionary process, referencing his reading of both Hakuson Kuriyagawa's *Symbols of Anguish*, trans. Lu Xun (Beijing: Renmin wenxue, 1988), and Lu Ling's *Children of the Rich* 财主底儿女们, 2 vols. (Beijing: Renminwenxue chubanshe, 2004). See Hu Feng, "A Brief Discussion of Literature from Nowhere 略谈文学无门," in vol. 2 of *HFQJ*, 427–430; and Lu Ling, "Youthful Poetry 青春的诗," in Hu Feng, preface to *Children of the Rich*, in vol. 2 of *HFQJ*, 265.

36. Hu, "It Grew," 57.

37. Hu, preface to *Children of the Rich*, 268.

38. See Hu Feng, "Thoughts on the Creative Process 关于创作发展的二三感想," in vol. 3 of *HFQJ*, 10–11.

39. Hu, *Collected Essays of Hu Feng*, vol. 3, 10.

40. See Kuriyagawa Hakuson, *Symbol of Depression* 苦闷的象征, trans. Lu Xun (Beijing: Renmin wenxue chubanshe, 1973).

41. Romain Rolland, *The Life of Ramakrishna*, quoted in David James Fisher, *Romain Rolland and the Politics of Intellectual Engagement* (Berkeley: University of California Press, 1988), 12.

42. The most important "lessons" were the 4/12 coup d'état in 1927 and the murder of five left-wing writers in 1931 (see Lu Xun, preface to *Two Minds* 二心集, in *Complete Works of Lu Xun*, vol. 4, 191). In the first event, the GMD persecuted a young Communist, Bi Lei. In the second, the GMD launched a murderous attack against the Communists. These two events struck a blow against Lu Xun's "hope" for China's future under the GMD. Hu wrote: "Previously I always had a certain optimism. I was under the impression that it was generally the old who oppressed and slaughtered the young; and as these old people gradually died off, China would become relatively vitalized. Now I know that this was an illusion: generally speaking it seems to be the young who slaughter the young" (Hu Feng, "A Reply to Mr. Youheng 答有恒先生," September 4, 1927, in *Selected Works of Lu Hsun*, trans. Yang Hsien-yi and Gladys Yang, vol. 2, 346–347). See also Hu Feng's understanding of Lu Xun's "conversion" to Marxism in "Views on Lu Xun's 'Conversion' 关于鲁迅〈转变〉论的一点意见," in *Hu Feng on Lu Xun* 胡风论鲁迅 (Zhengzhou: Huanghe wenyi chubanshe, 1985), 135–141.

43. Lu Xun, Letter to Zhang Tingqian, March 27, 1930, in vol. 12 of *Complete Works of Lu Xun*, 8.

44. Hu, "It Grew," 8.

45. Leo Ou-fan Lee, *Voices from the Iron House: A Study of Lu Xun* (Bloomington: Indiana University Press, 1987), 144. In 1930, Lu Xun concluded that "the revolutionary literary movement of the proletariat is, in fact, the *only* literary movement" (Lu, "Two Minds," 285). For a discussion of how Lu Xun's attitude toward politics went through several stages of change and how he eventually arrived at the ideological position of the left, see Lee, *Voices from the Iron House*, 133–150.

46. Lu Xun, "Thoughts on the League of Left-Wing Writers, a Speech Given at the Inaugural Meeting on March 2, 1930," in *Selected Works of Lu Hsun*, trans. Yang Hsien-yi and Gladys Yang, vol. 3 (Beijing: Foreign Press, 1956–60), 103–104.

47. Lu Xun, "This and That 这个与那个," in *Complete Works of Lu Xun*, vol. 3, 140.

48. As Mao Dun recollected, "After Hu stepped down as Secretary of the Left-league in the second half of 1934, nobody had succeeded in establishing a close relationship [between the Left-league and Lu Xun]. Gradually, Lu Xun's role as the Left-league's Secretary of the Standing Committee became in effect a signboard; he would receive invitations for events the Party considered him useful and otherwise left aside." Mao Dun, *The Path I Walked Past* 我走过道路, vol. 2 (Hong Kong: Sanlian shudian, 1984), 281. Not surprisingly, Lu Xun said to Feng Xuefeng upon his return to Shanghai from Shanbei in April 1936: "For two years I had been manipulated by them!" See Feng Xuefeng, "Concerning the 1936 Activities of Zhou Yang and Others and the 'Mass Literature in the National Revolutionary War' Slogan Put Forth by Lu Xun 有关一九三六年周扬等人的行动以及鲁迅提出〈民族革命战争大众文学〉口号的经过," *Historical Data of New Literature*, no. 2 (1979): 248.

49. Lu Xun, Letter to Hu Feng, September 12, 1935, in *Complete Works of Lu Xun*, vol. 13, 211.

50. For a treatment of Lu Xun's intellectual kinship with Friedrich Nietzsche, and in particular with the Nietzschean idea of the "superman" in relation to his "A Madman's Diary," see Cheung Chiu-yee, *Lu Xun: The Chinese "Gentle" Nietzsche* (Frankfurt: Peter Lang, 2001), esp. 101–105.

51. See Hu Feng, "Annotations of 'Passenger' 〈过客〉小译," in vol. 2 of *HFQJ*, 591.

52. Hu Feng, "Two or Three Fundamental Points about the Spirit of Lu Xun 关于鲁迅精神的二三基点," in vol. 2 of *HFQJ*, 500–501.

53. Hu, "Two or Three Fundamental Points about the Spirit of Lu Xun." On the first anniversary of the death of Lu Xun, Hu responded to the criticism of Lu Xun having failed to create a complete system of thought: "Lu Xun did not need to create an integral system of thought. . . . He had never fought in the name of Darwinism or historical materialism. He only assimilated his knowledge of different theories into his thinking, and continuously fought against feudal elements."

54. See Feng Xuefeng, "Reply to a Letter from the Trotskyists 答托洛斯基派的信, June 3, 1936," in *Complete Works of Lu Xun*, vol. 6, 586–589.

55. This article did not come out until eight years after Hu's death. Gregor Benton translated parts of it into English; see Gregor Benton, *China's Urban Revolutionaries: Explorations in the History of Chinese Trotskyism, 1921–1952* (Atlantic Highlands, NJ: Humanities Press, 1996), 102–103 (my emphasis). There were two responses to its publication: Lou Guohua (Yi Ding)'s "A Historical Case Unsettled for Half a Century 长达半世纪的一件历史公案" in September 1993; and Zheng Chaolin's "A Response to Hu Feng's 'Mr. Lu Xun' 读胡风《鲁迅先生》长文有感" in August 1993 in *Studies of Lu Xun Monthly* 鲁迅研究月刊, no. 10 (1993): 48–50. See Hu Feng, "Mr. Lu Xun 鲁迅先生," first published in *Historical Data of New Literature*, no. 1 (1993).

56. For a detailed account of the incident in English, see Benton, *China's Urban Revolutionaries*, 101–104.

57. Hu Feng, Letter to Zhu Qixia, July 18, 1949, in vol. 9 of *HFQJ*, 696.

58. See Hu Feng, "Humanism and the Path of Realism 人道主义与现实主义的道路," in vol. 3 of *HFQJ*, 236–237; and "A Brief Account of Foreign Literature and I 略谈我与外国文学," in vol. 7 of *HFQJ*, 252.

59. Trotsky first used the term *fellow travelers* (*poputchiki*) to refer to a group of young Russian writers in the 1920s who accepted the ideals of the 1917 Revolution without becoming Communist writers, and who produced some of the most innovative and original works of the period. See Leon Trotsky, *Literature and Revolution* (Ann Arbor: University of Michigan Press, 1966), 56–58.

60. Hu, "Humanism and the Path of Realism," 236–237.

61. Mao, "On Lu Xun," 96.

62. See Yi Ding (Lou Zichun), "Lu Xun and the Chinese Communist Party 鲁迅与中国共产党," *Open Magazine* 开放 (1995).

63. See Merle Goldman, "The Political Use of Hu Feng in the Cultural Revolution and After," in *Lu Xun and His Legacy*, ed. Leo Ou-fan Lee, 180–196.

64. See Hu Feng, "Out of Context 断章," in vol. 2 of *HFQJ*, 588.

65. Hu, "Two or Three Fundamental Points," 502.

66. Hu Feng, "In the Days of Rising Passion 热情升华的日子," in vol. 3 of *HFQJ*, 374.

67. Lu Xun, "Sudden Thoughts 豁然想到," in *Complete Works of Lu Xun*, vol. 3, 16.

68. Hu, "A Memoir," 292.

69. Ma, *A Biography of Hu Feng*, 125–126.

70. Ma, *A Biography of Hu Feng*, 126.

71. Hu Feng, "Mr. Lu Xun 鲁迅先生," in vol. 7 of *HFQJ*, 109.

72. Concerning his Party membership, Hu recalled how he repeatedly failed to apply for it: "When I was in the Left-league, I mentioned to Yang Hansheng or Zhou Yang the question [of my Party membership]. They asked me to fill in an application form; I hesitated. My concern was that once the connection was resumed, it would be difficult to situate myself in the conflict between Feng Xuefeng

(including Lu Xun) and Zhou Yang. When Feng Xuefeng went to the soviet region, I thought the conflict could be overcome and mentioned once again the question. This time, however, Yang and Zhou did not make any suggestions; and I had to stop mentioning the question again." Hu, "A Memoir," 292.

73. Lin Yü-sheng, "The Morality of Mind and Immorality of Politics: Reflections on Lu Xun, the Intellectual," in *Lu Xun and His Legacy*, ed. Leo Ou-fan Lee, 125.

74. Lin, "The Morality of Mind," 125.

75. Lin, "The Morality of Mind," 126.

76. See Hu, "An Idealist's Memories of the Epoch," 268.

77. See Hu Feng, "300,000-Character Report," in vol. 6 of *HFQJ*, 153, 383, 381.

78. Hu Feng, "A Brief Review 简述收获," in *Memories Bristling with Profusions and Complications* 枝蔓丛丛的回忆, ed. Ji Xianlin, Niu Han, and Deng Jiuping (Beijing: Beijing shiyue wenyi chubanshe, 2001), 53; also collected in part in vol. 6 of *HFQJ*, 656 (my emphasis).

79. Rolf Wiggershaus, *The Frankfurt School: Its History, Theories, and Political Significance*, trans. Michael Robertson (Cambridge, MA: Harvard University Press, 1994), 245, 246, 254, 458, 510.

80. Hu, "300,000-Character Report," 300.

81. Mao, "Editor's Comments to the Third Collection of Materials on the Hu Counterrevolutionary Clique," 576 (my emphasis).

82. Hu, "300,000-Character Report," 114.

83. Hu, "A Brief Review," 71.

84. Hu, "A Brief Review," 69.

CHAPTER IV

1. Zhou Enlai said this to Hu in a private meeting that took place in January 1945. Hu, "A Memoir," 624.

2. Lu Yuan, "A Different Song 另一只歌," in *A Different Song, Poets Series* 诗人丛书, no. 4 (Chengdu: Sichuan wenyi chubanshe, 1985), 74.

3. There has been an extensive critical literature on the Two-Slogan Debate. For analytical accounts of the debate, see Hsia Tsi-an, "Lu Hsün and the Dissolution of the League of Leftist Writers," in *The Gate of Darkness*, ed. T. A. Hsia, 101–145; Leo Ou-fan Lee, "Literary Trends: The Road to Revolution 1927–1949," in vol. 13 of *The Cambridge History of China: Republican China, 1912–1949*, ed. John K. Fairbank (Cambridge: Cambridge University Press, 1986), esp. 440–445. Hsia's account of the debate contains several errors and oversights due to inadequate documentation at the time of its writing. For a fuller picture of the debate, see Feng, "Concerning the 1936 Activities of Zhou Yang and Others in 1936," 251–256; Hu, "A Memoir," 331–341; Mao, *The Path I Walked Past*, 285–290,

293–306, 307–309; Zhao Haosheng, "Zhou Talks about Historical Achievements and Mistakes 周扬笑谈历史功过," *Historical Data of New Literature*, no. 2 (1979): 232–235; and Xu Maoyong, *Memoirs of Xu Maoyong* 徐懋庸回忆录 (Beijing: Renminwenxue chubanshe, 1982), 90–92.

4. See Hu Feng, Letters to Lou Shiyi, September 13 and October 8, 1970, in vol. 9 of *HFQJ*, 170–171. The debate over the two slogans began between Zhou on the one side and Feng (and Hu) on the other, with Mao Dun in between. At Feng Xuefeng's request, Hu wrote nothing following his first short article responding to Zhou's slogan "National Defense Literature," not because he had nothing to say in his counterattack, but because Lu Xun was the real target. See Lu, "Hu Feng and Me," 596.

5. Hu, "300,000-Character Report," 138, 309.

6. Hu, "300,000-Character Report," 383.

7. Hu Feng, "What Do the Masses Demand of Literature? 人民大众向文学要求甚?," first published in *Literary Series* 文学丛报 2 (1936). See *Modern Chinese Literary Thought: Writings on Literature, 1893–1945*, ed. Kirk A. Denton (Stanford, CA: Stanford University Press, 1996), 415–417, for Richard King's English translation of the text.

8. Regarding the origin of the letter, Xu recalled: "After Lu Xun's open reply, Zhou and Xia Yan . . . conducted a meeting to criticize my 'individualist act,' considering it as 'harmful' to their 'unity with Lu Xun.' I rebutted and said to Zhou, 'I wrote what you've been indoctrinating me. The letter might be an 'individualist act,' it, however, articulated [your thoughts] on your behalf.' " Xu, *Reminiscences*, 90–91.

9. On August 1, 1936, six months after the dissolution of the Left-league and two months since the publication of Hu's essay "What Do the Masses Demand of Literature?," Xu wrote a private and measuredly toned letter to Lu Xun for two purposes: to win Lu Xun over to Zhou's side; and to change Lu Xun's mind about the establishment of the Association of Chinese Writers and Artists (hereafter the Association) to replace the Left-league in the wake of the new "United Front policy." See Xu Maoyong, Letter to Lu Xun, August 1, 1936. An English translation of the letter is available in Hsia, *The Gate of Darkness*, 135–136.

10. It is hard to pin down Lu Xun's reasons for publishing a private letter. Perhaps Lu Xun thought that Xu expected him to publish the letter (see Lu Xun, "Open Reply," in *The Gate of Darkness*, ed. T. A. Hsia, 139), or that the matter discussed in the letter was not private. In a letter to Yang Jiyun, Lu Xun said, "Although Xu alone wrote the letter, [his writing] represents a certain group of people" (Lu Xun, Letter to Yang Jiyun, August 28, 1936, collected in *The Letters of Lu Xun* 鲁迅书简, ed. Xu Guangpijng [Shanghai: Lu Xun quanji chubanshe, 1948], 710). The two letters are collected in *Complete Works of Lu Xun*, vol. 6.

11. For a close reading of the tone and language of the "Open Reply," see Hsia, *The Gate of Darkness*, 136–143. Feng Xuefeng witnessed Lu Xun's anger after

receiving Xu's letter, who said, "They indeed come at me, knowing well that I am sick! It is a provocation." See Feng, "A Report on the Activities of Zhou Yang and His Likes in 1936," 255.

12. Lu, "Open Reply," 139.

13. Zhao, "Zhou Talks about Historical Achievements and Mistakes," 234.

14. See Mao, *The Path I Walked Past*, 300, 302.

15. See Lu Xun, Letter to Hu Feng, June 28, 1935, in *Complete Works of Lu Xun* 鲁迅全集, vol. 13, 160.

16. Mao, *The Path I Walked Past*, 278.

17. Guo Moruo, "An Inspection of the Military Exercise 搜苗的检阅," first published in *Literary World* 文学界 1, no. 4 (September 10, 1936).

18. Wang, *Between Literature and Ideology*, 102.

19. At the time of its establishment, the Left-league had around fifty members, most of whom were from one of three literary groups: the Creative Society, the Sun Society, and students and friends of Lu Xun. A few days after the inauguration ceremony on March 2, 1930, a Standing Committee of seven people—Xia Yan, Feng Naichao, Qian Xingcun, Lu Xun, Tian Han, Zheng Boqi, and Hong Lingfei—was formed. The CCP controlled the Standing Committee through a Party Committee of three to five Party members who were under the orders of the CCP Literary Committee, which, in turn, was under the direction of the Propaganda Department in Shanghai. The Literary Committee passed on the CCP's directions and decisions to the Party Committee for implementation. When the CCP had important matters to discuss with Lu Xun, it would do so through Feng Xuefeng in his role as its *tepaiyuan* (特派员 "special representative"). The relationship between Lu Xun and the CCP was, accordingly, a special one. As Feng Xuefeng recalled, "One could say that the Party, in general, led Lu Xun; but it is not true to say that the Party Committee of the Left-league led Lu Xun." See Feng Xuefeng, "Talks about the League of Leftwing Writers 冯雪峰谈左联," *Historical Data of New Literature*, no. 1 (1980): esp. 5–6.

20. Zhao, "Zhou Talks about Historical Achievements and Mistakes" 236.

21. Jin Ding, "Memories of the Left-league 有关左联的一些回忆," in *The Past and the Man of Culture* 往事与文化人 (Beijing: Zhongguo renmin daxue chubanshe, 1988), 19.

22. Hu, "300,000-Character Report," 107.

23. The original Chinese "清君侧" describes Hu's intention to launch "a bitter and protracted struggle" against the CCP and its members: "Ever since Liu Bi, Prince Wu in the Han dynasty, discovered the famous strategy of requesting the execution of Chao Cuo (the principal adviser of Emperor Jingdi of the Han dynasty) to 'purify the ranks of the emperor's closest counselors,' many ambitious careerists have held this up as an extremely valuable [stratagem]. The Hu clique was an heir to this bag of tricks. In the '300,000-character Report,' they attacked several people, such as Comrades Lin Mohan, He Qifang, and Zhou. They said

that these people were 'messing everything up.'" Mao, "Editor's Comments to the Third Collection of Materials on the Hu Counterrevolutionary Clique," a section in "Preface and Editor's Notes to Material on the Hu Feng Counterrevolutionary Clique (May-June, 1955)," first published in the *People's Daily*, June 10, 1955; in vol. 1 of *The Writings of Mao Zedong, 1949–1976*, ed. Michael Y. M. Kau and John K. Leung (New York; London: M. E. Sharpe, 1986), 576.

24. "Throughout the process of criticizing Hu, Comrade Zhou had asked for instructions and received them from the Central Bureau Committee." Lin Mohan, "The Ins and Outs of the Hu Incident 胡风事件的前前后后," *Historical Data of New Literature*, no. 3 (1989): 14.

25. Lin, "The Ins and Outs of the Hu Incident," 14.

26. See Zhou Yang, "Respecting History and Evaluating Historical Figures Fairly 尊重历史, 给历史人物以应有评价," first published in the *People's Daily*, August 30, 1983; in *Recent Work of Zhou Yang* 周揚近作 (Beijing: Zuojia chubanshe, 1985), 264; see also Yu Guangyuan, *Zhou Yang and Me* 周扬和我 (Xianggang: Shidai guoji chuban youxiangongsi, 2005), 7.

27. Zhang Guangnian, "Remembering Zhou Yang 回忆周扬," in *Reminiscences of Zhou Yang* 忆周杨, ed. Wang Meng and Yuan Ying (Huhehaote: Nei Menggu People's Publishing House, 1998), 4–6.

28. See Wang Meng, "Zhou Yang's Eyes 周扬的目光," in *Reminiscences of Zhou Yang*, ed. Wang Meng and Yuan Ying, 407–408.

29. Wang, "Zhou Yang's Eyes," 407–408.

30. See Zhou Yang, "First, Insistence; Second, Development 一要坚持, 二要发展," in vol. 5 of *Collected Essays of Zhou Yang* 周扬文集 (Beijing: Renmin wenxue chubanshe, 1985), 405; see also Miao Junjie, "Zhou Yang and the Chinese Style of Literary Criticism 周杨与中国式的文艺批评," in *Reminiscences of Zhou Yang*, ed. Wang Meng and Yuan Ying, 316.

31. Mei Zhi, "The Lasting Influence of Scholarship 书香余韵," in *Wild Peppers Turn Red* 花椒红了 (Beijing: Zhongguo huaqiao chubanshe, 1995), 173.

32. Hu, "A Brief Review," 650.

33. Xiaogu, "Indelible Memories 没有忘却的记忆," in *My Father Hu Feng* 我的父亲胡风 (Shenyang: Chunfeng wenyi chubanshe, 2001), 219.

34. Xiao Shan, "Fragments of Memory 片段的回忆," in *My Father Hu Feng* (Shenyang: Chunfeng wenyi chubanshe, 2001),174.

35. Xiao Shan, "Fragments of Memory," 174.

36. Xiao Shan, "Fragments of Memory," 174.

37. Hu Feng, "Study in Order to Practice 学习, 为了实践," in vol. 6 of *HFQJ*, 46. Hu was in Chongqing when the Yan'an Forum took place, but he should have been able to read about it in June 1943, when Xiao Jun reported on the "Talks" in Chongqing in *New China Daily*. In October, articles criticizing Wang Shiwei, too, began to appear in *New China Daily*. Moreover, in the nine years between June 1943 and the writing of "Study in Order to Practice," an essay written in

May 1952 to commemorate the tenth anniversary of the Yan'an "Talks," Hu had attended several roundtable talks organized by Party cultural leaders in which he showed support for the Yan'an "Talks." The few meetings in January 1945, in particular, were necessary, as they took place under the chairmanship of Feng Naichao, officer-in-charge of the Party's Culture Committee, and Guo Moruo's leadership via the Literary Work Committee. The last significant meeting took place in November 1945. During that time, Hu Qiaomu, then accompanying Mao to Chongqing to negotiate a peace deal with the GMD, talked with Hu and Shu Wu.

38. As Zhi Kejian observed, there were moments when Zhou's and Hu's views on the creative method become so close that they were almost indistinguishable. See Zhi Kejian, *On Zhou Yang* 周扬论 (Kaifeng: Henan daxue chubanshe, 2004), 174.

39. Zhou Yang, "The New Literature and Art of the People 新的人民的文艺," in *Collected Essays of Zhou Yang*, vol. 1, 530–531. For a historical account of the first National Congress of Literature and Art Workers, see Cyril Birch, "Literature under Communism," in *The Cambridge History of China: The People's Republic, Part 2: Revolutions within the Chinese Revolution 1966–1982*, ed. Roderick MacFarquhar, John K. Fairbank, and Denis Twitchett, vol. 15, chap. 11 (Cambridge: Cambridge University Press, 1991), esp. 743–745. For a report on Hu at the first National Congress of Literature and Art Workers, see Wu Yongping, "The First National Congress of Literature and Art Workers and Hu," in *News of the Communist Party of China*, people.com.cn 人民網 November 12, 2006. Accessed March 20, 2009. http://cpc.people.com.cn/BIG5/64162/64172/64915/5028110.html.

40. Zhou Yang, "A Critical Review of the Free-Men's Literary Theory 自由人文学理论检讨," in *Collected Essays of Zhou Yang*, vol. 1, 49.

41. Zhou Yang, "Fight for the Creation of More and Better Literature and Art 为创造更多的优秀的文学艺术作品而奋斗," a speech given at the second National Congress of Literature and Art Workers in September 1953, in *Literary Gazette* 文艺报, no. 19 (September 1953); translated into English in *China's New Literature and Art: Essays and Addresses* (Beijing: Foreign Languages Press, 1954).

42. Hu Feng, "Lu Xun on Gorky 关于鲁迅论高尔基," in vol. 4 of *HFQJ*, 230. In an essay published in 1940, Hu argued that left-wing writers should be concerned with "the relationship between creative practice and lived experience" rather than with the issue of "the relationship between literature and politics." For Hu, the political function of literature could only emerge from the writer's lived experience of reality, and "poetry must be poetry first" before it is politics. See Hu Feng, "What Is the Central Question of Today? 今天, 我们的中心问题是甚么?," in vol. 2 of *HFQJ*, 609.

43. Zhou Yang, "My Expectations of *Battlefield* 我所希望于〈战地〉的," in *Collected Essays of Zhou Yang*, vol. 1, 232. In the same volume, see also Zhou Yang's "New Realities and Literature's New Responsibility 新的现实与文学上的新的任务," 256.

44. Zhou Yang, "The Realness Nature of Literature 文学的真实性," in *Collected Essays of Zhou Yang*, vol. 1, 67.

45. Xiao Jun's comments on the Yan'an "Talks" are collected in Wang Chuanyong, "Events before and after *Wild Lilies* 〈野百合花〉 的前前后后," *Historical Data of New Literature*, no. 3 (2000): 44. The conflict between Xiao Jun and Zhou was most manifest in their debate on whether literature in the 1940s should be like May Fourth literature and continue to "expose [the] darkness in society." As mentioned briefly in note 78 of this chapter, Xiao Jun belonged to Ding Ling's group, and he held that the revolution aimed to enlighten the masses. He, therefore, found it difficult to accept Zhou's view that essays that were critical of the dark forces in society were no longer desirable in revolutionary base areas, especially in Yan'an, the capital of the Revolution. See Zhou Yang, "Random Notes on *Literature and Life* 文学与生活漫谈," first published in the July 17, 18, and 19, 1941 issues of *Liberation Daily*, and Xiao Jun's response to Zhou's "Random Notes" in "A Collection of Random Notes on 'Random Notes on *Literature and Life*' and Discussions with Comrade Zhou 〈文学与生活漫谈〉 读后漫谈集录并商榷于周扬同志" *Literature Monthly*, no. 8 (1941). For Zhou's position in and recollection of the debate, see Zhao, "Zhou Yang Talks about Historical Achievements and Mistakes," 232–235.

46. Mao Zedong, "Talks at the Yan'an Forum on Literature and Art 在延安文艺座谈会上的讲话" (May 2 and 23, 1942), in vol. 3 of *Selected Works of Mao Tse-tung* (Peking: Foreign Languages Press, 1965), 86 (my emphasis).

47. Mao, "Talks at the Yan'an Forum on Literature and Art," 90.

48. John King Fairbank, *Chinabound: A Fifty-Year Memoir* (New York: Harper and Row, 1982), 244, 264. For some Chinese liberal intellectuals, the year 1943 was especially significant; during that year, many of them became disappointed with Jiang Jieshi and his GMD and started to turn left. Also in that year, Jiang Jieshi published his "China's Destiny 中国之命运." Jiang's article, which advocated the protection of the national cultural heritage, was considered highly conservative and insulting to the May Fourth Movement. In response to it, Zhu Ziqing (1898–1948), who had been for much of his life a "free" intellectual, poet, essayist, and university professor (of Chinese literature at Qinghua University from 1925 to his death), wrote in his diary, "[Jiang] has no vision at all. The publication tarnished his reputation. This complete betrayal of his beliefs would be met with opposition sooner or later." See Jiang Jian and Wu Weigong, *A Chronicle of Zhu Ziqing* 朱自清年谱 (Hefei: Anhui jiaoyu chubanshe, 1996), 271. Wen Yiduo (1899–1946), poet, scholar, and member of the Crescent Society since 1928, recalled: "The publication of 'China's Destiny' was a turning point for me. I was totally shocked by the spirit of the Boxers in it. Could it be true that our astute leader thought that way? . . . No matter what, I find it unacceptable." Wen Yiduo, "Memories of and Reflections on the Eight Years 八年的回忆与感想," manuscript written by Ji Kan, in *Eight Years in the United Universities* 联大八年 (Chengdou: Xinan lianda xuesheng chubanshe, 1946), 4.

49. Ai Qing (1910–96), "Beggar 乞丐," in *Selected Works of Ai Qing* 艾青选集 (Beijing: Kaiming shudian, 1952), 85.

50. Jin Yi (1909–59), "Life: To My Young Friends 生存—献给忘年的朋友," in vol. 4 of *Selected Works of Jin Yi* 靳以选集 (Chengdu: Sichuan People's Publishing House, 1983–84), 689–690.

51. Jin, "Life: To My Young Friends," 689–690.

52. Lu Ling, vol. 2 of *Children of the Rich* 财主底儿女们 (Beijing: Renmin wenxue chubanshe, 2004), 698.

53. Lu, vol. 2 of *Children of the Rich*, 678.

54. Jia Zhifang, "In This Complex World—a Memoir 在这个复杂的世界里—生活回忆录," *Historical Data of New Literature*, no. 1 (1992): 43.

55. Jia Zhifang, "Life 人生赋," in *Collected Works of Jia Zhifang: Creative Writing* 贾植芳文集: 創作卷 (Shanghai: Shanghai shehui kexueyuan chubanshe, 2004), 48, 49.

56. Hu Feng, "From the Present to the Future 由现在到将来," in vol. 3 of *HFQJ*, 34.

57. "The dustbin of history" was a phrase used by Leon Trotsky (1879–1940) in a speech on October 25, 1917 in St. Petersburg to describe the destiny of those center and right-wingers from within the revolutionary socialist camp. They, along with the Mensheviks, believed that Lenin and the Bolsheviks were conspirators who seized power illegally. As they were about to leave the October Revolution, the second phase of the Russian Revolution in 1917, Trotsky called them "pitiful isolated individuals" and "miserable bankrupts": "Your role is played out. Go where you belong from now on—into the dustbin of history!" In response to this description, Martov, Lenin's old comrade, shouted "in a moment of rage which he must have agonized over for the rest of his life: 'Then we'll leave!' and walked in silence towards the exit without looking back—into the political wilderness." Leon Trotsky, "The Dustbin of History," excerpted in *The Penguin Book of Twentieth-Century Speeches*, ed. Brian MacArthur (London: Penguin Books, 1999), 65–66. See also Orlando Figes, *A People's Tragedy: The Russian Revolution: 1891–1924* (London: Jonathan Cape, 1996).

58. Chen Xiaoquan, *A Biography of Zhu Ziqing* 朱自清传 (Beijing: Beijing shiyue wenyi chubanshe, 1991), 277. The seeds of Zhu's political consciousness germinated during the 5/30 Massacre in 1925. Having experienced the event first-hand and seen the bloodshed and lives taken, Zhu asked himself this question: "So many people have died. What can we do?" Zhu Ziqing, "The Government Head's Massacre 执政府屠杀记," in vol. 3 of *Complete Prose of Zhu Ziqing* 朱自清散文全集, ed. Zhu Qiaosen (Nanjing: Jiangsu jiaoyu chubanshe, 1996), 189.

59. Lu, *Children of the Rich*, vol. 2, 632.

60. Lu, *Children of the Rich*, vol. 2, 691; see also 723.

61. The novel *The First Stage of a Story* 第一阶段的故事, set against the 8/13 Incident (which marked the beginning of the all-out war between China and Japan)

in 1938, was first published under the title *To Where Can You Run?* 你往那里跑? in vol. 12 of *Literary Battlefield* 文艺阵地 in October 1938.

62. Li Guangtian (1906–68) began working on *Gravitation* 引力 in July 1941, only to find it "extremely difficult" to carry on writing under the conditions of the war against Japan. He finished the novel in July 1945.

63. Quoted in Ai Keyen, "The Historical Record of the Yan'an Literary Rectification Campaign 延安文艺运动纪实," *Historical Data of New Literature*, no. 3 (1992): 194. Tian Jian (1916–85), the poet whom Wen Yiduo called "the drummer of the era," joined the northwest revolutionary service group of the Eighth Route Army as a journalist and poet in 1938 and went to Yan'an in the same year. In his ten years of military life, Tian Jian wrote a large number of poems and reports about the Chinese Revolution, many of which he sent to Hu (see afterword to *For the Fighters* 给战斗者后记, in vol. 3 of *HFQJ*, 162). Many of Tian Jian's representative works, such as "Children's Day 儿童节," "The Honored Warrior 荣誉战士," "Burn Old Ones, Build New Ones 烧掉旧的, 盖新的," and the narrative poem "She Too Will Kill 她也要杀人" appeared first in Hu's *July Series*, which was considered a window into the liberated areas during the Chinese Revolution. See Hu Feng, "Tian Jian's Poetry: Preface to *Chinese Shepherd's Song* 田间的诗－《中国牧歌》序," in vol. 2 of *HFQJ*, 442–446; see also vol. 3 of *A Selective Guide to Chinese Literature, 1900–1949: The Poem*, ed. Lloyd Haft (Leiden: E. J. Brill, 1989), 203–210, for several annotated bibliographic entries on Tian Jian's major poetry volumes.

64. Wang Shiwei et al., *Wild Lilies* 野百合花, ed. Shen Mo (Guangzhou: Huacheng chubanshe, 1992), 5. Wang Shiwei (1906–47), essayist, journalist, and literary critic, was known most famously for his expository essay series "Wild Lilies" and "Politicians, Artists 政治家、艺术家." *Wild Lilies*, satiric prose, was approved by Ding Ling for publication in *Liberation Daily* in two parts on March 13 and 23, 1942, respectively. Under the complex political conditions at the time, it was considered a "Trotskyist" piece of work and was criticized for "exaggerating the problems in Yan'an and for presenting the revolutionary base areas as places of complete darkness." As a result, Wang Shiwei was arrested and secretly executed on July 1, 1947 at the age of forty-one. Critical writings about *Wild Lilies* are numerous; two representative examples are Chen Baida's "After Wang Shiwei's 'A Short Discussion of National Forms' 写在王实味同志〈文艺的民族形式短论〉之后," *Liberation Daily*, July 3 and 4, 1942, and Zhou's "Wang Shiwei's Views on Literature and Our Views on Literature 王实味的文艺观与我们的文艺观," *Liberation Daily*, July 28 and 29, 1942. For studies on Wang Shiwei in English, see Timothy Cheek, "The Fading of Wild Lilies: Wang Shiwei and Mao's Yan'an Talks in the First CPC Rectification Movement," *Australian Journal of Chinese Affairs*, no. 11 (January 1984): 27–28, 34–35; and Dai Qing, *Wang Shiwei and Wild Lilies: Rectification and Purges in the Chinese Communist Party, 1942–1944*, ed. David E. Apter and Timothy Cheek and trans. Nancy Liu and Lawrence R. Sullivan (Armonk, NY: M. E. Sharpe, 1994).

65. A phrase Tian Jian used to describe Yan'an. See Ai, "Historical Record of the Yan'an Literary Rectification Campaign," 194.

66. Zhou coined the term *revolutionary romanticism* as early as 1933 in "On 'Socialist Realism' and Revolutionary Romanticism 关于〈社会现实主义〉与革命的浪漫主义."

67. For a historical account and critical analysis of how Chinese intellectuals shifted their attention from generalized notions of democracy to new forms of political activities, including labor organization and anti-imperialist agitation, see Lawrence Sullivan and Richard H. Solomon, "The Formation of Chinese Communist Ideology in the May Fourth Era: A Content Analysis of *Hsin ch'ing nien*," in *Ideology and Politics in Contemporary China*, ed. Chalmers Johnson (Seattle: University of Washington Press, 1973), 117–160.

68. For a brief analysis of Yan'an as the collective ideal of the intellectuals, see Wang Yunsheng, "Why Did the Intellectuals of the 1930s Go to Yan'an? 20世纪30年代知识分子为何走向延安?," *Beijing Daily* 北京日报, September 25, 2006. Accessed June 2007. http://epaper.bjd.com.cn/rb/20061107/200609/t20060925_93489.htm. See also chapter 5 of David Apter and Tony Saich, *Revolutionary Discourse in Mao's Republic* (Cambridge, MA: Harvard University Press, 1994), 141–183.

69. Chen Xuezhao, "Accounts of My Two Trips to Yan'an [continued] 两次去延安的前后[续]." *Historical Data of New Literature*, no. 2 (1980): 54. Chen Xuezhao (1906–91), a PhD student in the arts at the Universite de Clermont, went to Yan'an in 1940. As the only arts PhD in Yan'an during that time, Chen served as editor of *Liberation Daily* and as a staff member of the Communist Party School in Yan'an. She joined the CCP in July 1945.

70. Chen, "Accounts of My Two Trips to Yan'an [continued]," 54.

71. Chen, "Accounts of My Two Trips to Yan'an [continued]," 54.

72. He Qifang, "An Ordinary Story 一个平常的故事," in vol. 2 of *The Collected Works of He Qifang* 何其芳文集 (Beijing: Renmin wenxue chubanshe, 1982), 215.

73. See Ai, "The Historical Record of the Yan'an Literary Rectification Campaign," 193–222.

74. These essays can be found in Wang Shiwei et al., *Wild Lilies*. For discussions and historical accounts of the Yan'an rectification campaign in English, see Gregor Benton, "The Yenan Literary Opposition," *New Left Review* 92 (July–August 1975): 93–96; Hsia, *The Gate of Darkness*, 251–252; and Merle Goldman, *Literary Dissent in Communist China* (Cambridge, MA: Harvard University Press, 1967), 23–30. For discussions in Chinese, see Huang Changyong, "Events before and after *Wild Lilies* 〈野百合花〉的前前后后" (2000), collected in *The Literary Events I Experienced* 我亲历的文坛往事 (Beijing: Renmin wenxue chubanshe, 2004), 195–223. For some firsthand recollections of the campaign, see Li Xin, "The 'Yan'an Forum on Literature and Art,' the Writing and Publication of the 'Talks' and Forum Participants 关于〈延安文艺座谈会〉的召开、〈讲话〉的写作、发表和参加会议的人," *Historical Data of New Literature*, no. 2 (1995): 203–210; and Zhao, "Zhou Talks about Historical

Achievements and Mistakes." For a systematic and critical account of the rectification campaign, see Gao Hua, *The Rise of the Red Sun: The Cause and Effect of the Rectification Movement in Yan'an* 红太阳是怎样升起的: 延安整风运动的来龙去脉 (Xianggang: Zhongwen daxue chubanshe, 2000). Wang Shengyun, "The Yan'an Rectification Movement's Contribution to the Establishment of Mao Thought 论延安整风对毛泽东思想确立的促进作用," published in no. 6 of *Research on Mao Thought* 毛泽东思想研究 20 (November 2003): 14–16, offers some insights into the relationship between the rectification movement and the Yan'an Forum on Literature and Art. For precise accounts of the Yan'an Forum and the "Talks" in English, see David Holm, "The Literary Rectification in Yan'an," in *Essays in Modern Chinese Literature and Literary Criticism: Papers of the Berlin Conference 1978* (Bochum [West Germany]: Studienverlag N. Brockmeyer, 1982), 272–308; see also Kirk A. Denton, "Literature and Politics: Mao Zedong's 'Talks at the Yan'an Forum on Art and Literature,'" in *The Columbia Companion to Modern East Asia Literature*, ed. Joshua S. Mostow (New York: Columbia University Press, 2003), 463–469. For a discussion of the "three waves" of studies on Mao's "Talks" in Western scholarship from the 1990s to the present, see Qilin Fu, "The Reception of Mao's 'Talks at the Yan'an Forum on Literature and Art' in English-Language Scholarship," *CLCWeb: Comparative Literature and Culture* 17, no. 1 (2015). http://dx.doi.org/10.7771/1481-4374.2567.

75. The rectification movement, which aimed to fight against bureaucratism in Yan'an, began with Mao's two reports titled "Rectify the Party's Style of Work 整顿党的作风" and "Oppose Stereotyped Party Writing 反对党八股," given on February 1 and February 8, 1942, respectively.

76. In Yan'an, left-wing and revolutionary writers were generally divided into two groups. One group, headed by Zhou Yang, preferred to write about "the bright side of society" and about the achievements of the Party. The other group, headed by Ding Ling, believed that writers were responsible for revealing social problems. The question of whether literature and art should "celebrate the bright" or "expose the dark" soon divided the revolutionary camp. At the Yan'an Forum, Mao criticized such writers as Xiao Jun who preferred *zawen* ("essay") for having "petty-bourgeois reformist idealism." See Ai, "The Historical Record of the Yan'an Literary Rectification Campaign," 193–211; Huang, "Events before and after *Wild Lilies*," 195–223.

77. See Mao Zedong, "On New Democracy (January 1940)," in *Selected Works of Mao Tse-tung*, vol. 2, 339. By the early 1940s, Mao had already published his three important essays—"Introducing *The Communist*," "The Chinese Revolution and the Chinese Communist Party," and "On New Democracy" in October 1939, December 1939, and January 1940, respectively. These essays helped consolidate Mao's authority over such important matters as military strategy and the nature of the Chinese Revolution. What was yet to be dealt with by Mao was the issue of culture.

78. Mao, "Talks at the Yan'an Forum on Literature and Art," 69.

79. Mao, "Talks at the Yan'an Forum on Literature and Art," 64–65.

80. Mao, "Talks at the Yan'an Forum on Literature and Art," 69, 71.

81. The third version of the "Talks" appeared in the third volume of *Selected Works of Mao Tse-tung* published in May 1953. In the years between 1953 and 1960, the CCP reprinted the "Talks" several times, producing minor differences among these different versions. In August 1962, with Mao's approval, Tian Jiaying, along with a few experts from the Central Committee Archives, corrected the 1953 version of the "Talks." They removed all the footnotes and added a preface titled "The Guidance of the Proletariat Cultural Revolution 无产阶级文化大革命的指南针." This revision became the fifth edition of the "Talks." During the Cultural Revolution, *Red Flag* 红旗 reprinted the fifth version of the "Talks" in one volume, which remains the standard version. The text of the "Talks" has gone through many changes and stages, with each suggesting and representing a new sociohistorical moment. For a historical account, see Cao Guofei, "The First Edition of the 'Talks' and Yi Da 在延安文艺座谈会上的讲话〉第一个版本与尹达," *Publication Archives* 出版史料, no. 1 (2004): 42–43; Guo Yushi, "Revision of the 'Talks': From the First Edition to the Present Edition 谈〈在延安文艺座谈会上的讲话〉从原本到今本的增删修改," *Theoretical Studies in Literature and Art* 文艺理论研究, no. 4 (1992): 77–80; Jin Hongyu, "Editions and Revisions of the 'Yan'an Talks on Literature and Art' 〈在延安文艺座谈会上的讲话〉的版本与修改," *Modern Chinese Literature Studies* 中国现代文学研究丛刊, no. 6 (2005): 76–84; and Sun Guolin, "Editions of the 'Yan'an Talks on Literature and Art' 在延安文艺座谈会上的讲话的版本," *China Reading Weekly* 中华读书报, May 15, 2002. Bonnie S. McDougall discussed the differences between the 1943 version and the 1953 version of the "Talks" in *Mao's "Talks at the Yan'an Conference on Literature and Art": A Translation of the 1943 Text with Commentary* (Ann Arbor: Center for Chinese Studies, University of Michigan, 1980), 7–8, 87–104.

82. Göran Therborn, *The Ideology of Power and the Power of Ideology* (London: Verso, 1980), 15.

83. Mark Lilla, *The Reckless Mind: Intellectuals in Politics* (New York: New York Review Books, 2001).

84. Examples are many. In literary and intellectual circles in modern China, one of the best-known examples was Xu Maoyong's motivation for writing his "private" letter to Lu Xun in 1936: "[When I wrote the letter,] I had only one thought in mind: when it came to policy, the Party member would always understand it better. Lu Xun was not a Party member, but Zhou was. In order to follow the Party, I should follow Zhou. . . . Hence at this critical juncture, after careful consideration, I took sides with Zhou Yang, even though I was not entirely satisfied with the way Zhou dealt with matters" (Xu, *Memoirs of Xu Maoyong*, 90). At the end of the Two-Slogan Debate, feeling betrayed, Xu decided to find justice from the Party: "The main reason for me to go to Yan'an was to clarify the Two-Slogan Debate in 1936 Shanghai. Only the Party could give me clear instructions on the matter." In March 1938, Xu arrived in Yan'an.

85. Mao, "Talks at the Yan'an Forum on Literature and Art," 70.

86. Mao, "Talks at the Yan'an Forum on Literature and Art," 70.

87. Mao, "Talks at the Yan'an Forum on Literature and Art," 76.

88. After the publication of the Yan'an Talks in *Liberation Daily*, on October 20, 1943, the Central Studies Committee published an instruction on the use of the "Talks." The notice defined the "Talks" as "one of the most important documents in the CCP's development in the areas of culture and ideology, a *textbook* of Marxism and Leninism written in an accessible style by Comrade Mao," and "a compulsory reading that must be thoroughly and seriously learned and studied by cadres and Party members." See "CCCCP Central Studies Committee's Instruction on Studies of Mao's 'Talks at the Yan'an Forum on Literature and Art' 中央总学委关于学习毛泽东〈在延安文艺座谈会上的讲话〉的通知," published in *Liberation Daily* on October 22, 1943. On November 7, the Propaganda Department issued its "Decision on the Implementation of the Party's Cultural Policy." The document made clear that the "Talks," meaning more than "to solve literary and cultural problems," sought to "bring about one's outlook on life and one's way of life." See CCP's Central Committee Propaganda Department, "Decision on the Implementation of the Party's Cultural Policy 关于执行党的文艺政策的决定," published in *Liberation Daily* on November 8, 1943. See also Qian Liqun, Wen Rumin, and Wu Fuhui, *Modern Chinese Literature in Thirty Years* 中国现代文学三十年 (Beijing: Beijing daxue chubanshe, 1998), 458.

89. See Kondo Tatsuya, "The Transmission of the *Yenan Talks* to Chungking and Hu Feng: Caught between the Struggle for Democracy in the Great Rear Area and Maoism," *Acta Asiatica* 72 (1997): 81–105.

90. Hu, Letter to Zhang Zhongxiao, March 1951, quoted in Wang Wenzheng, *The Hu Incident as I Experienced It: An Oral History of Judge Wang Wenzheng* 我所亲历的胡风案: 法官王文正口述 (Beijing: Zhongguo dangshi chubanshe, 2007), 150–151.

91. Hu Feng, "From the Present to the Future," in vol. 3 of *HFQJ*, 34.

92. Hu, "300,000-Character Report," 300.

93. Hu, "300,000-Character Report."

94. Hu, "300,000-Character Report."

95. See Foucault, *Society Must Be Defended: Lectures at the Collège de France, 1975–1976*, ed. Mauro Bertani and Alessandro Fontana and trans. David Macey (New York: Picador, 2003), 47–48.

96. See Li Xiang, "On the Attitude toward Art and Life 论艺术态度和生活态度," in vol. 1 of *Literature in the Rear Areas during the Years of War against Japan* 中国抗日战争时期大后方文学书系, ed. Lin Mohan et al. (Chongqing: Chongqing chubanshe, 1989), 697–698.

97. CCP's Central Committee Propaganda Department, "Telegram to Dong Biwu 致董必武电," November 22, 1943; quoted in Wan Tonglin, *Martyrs: Hu and*

His Fellow Travelers 殉道者: 胡风及其同仁们 (Jinan: Shandong huabao chubanshe, 1998), 87 (my emphasis).

98. Shu Wu, "Postscript to *Return to May Fourth* 回归五四: 后序" (Shenyang: Liaoning jiaoyu chubanshe, 1999), 593–594.

99. Shu, "Postscript to *Return to May Fourth*," 595–596.

100. Apter and Saich, *Revolutionary Discourse in Mao's Republic*, 18.

101. Hu, "300,000-Character Report," 312.

102. Lu, "Hu Feng and Me," 565.

103. In 1943, the CCP launched an attack on left-wing writers and critics in the GMD-controlled areas who expressed support for the Yan'an rectification movement against subjectivism in a way that was unexpected by the Party. On November 22, the CCP's Propaganda Department sent a telegram to Dong Biwu, criticizing Chen Jiakang and Qiao Guanhua for their lack of understanding of Mao Zedong Thought and their publication of essays that were "a result of their fantasy" (quoted in Wan, *Martyrs: Hu and His Fellow Travelers*, 87).

104. Hu Feng, Letter to Shu Wu, March 21, 1944, in vol. 9 of *HFQJ*, 477.

105. Hu Feng, "Literature and Life 文学与生活," in vol. 2 of *HFQJ*, 318.

106. In the essays "A Brief Explanation of 'The Passerby' " and "If He Were Still Alive," written respectively in 1939 and 1941, Hu championed Lu Xun's unswerving combative spirit and pronounced that the war did not undermine his determination to continue following Lu Xun.

CHAPTER V

1. Hu to Lu Yuan in 1951, referring to the aim of his long theoretical essay "The Path of Realism," written in response to the Hong Kong campaign in 1948. See Lu, "Hu Feng and Me," 583.

2. Zhou to Hu in 1952, when Party leaders attempted to "eradicate the effects of [bourgeois] ideology on Hu and those like Hu." See the "Report on the Criticism of Hu's Thought on Literature and Art" that the Propaganda Department submitted to Zhou Enlai and the Central Committee dated February 15, 1953. From the Party representatives' point of view, "Hu made only self-examination of his . . . relations with the Party, but he has never admitted any ideological errors in his thought on literature and art. He has devoted great efforts to defending himself and showing that he is right all along." See Lin, "The Ins and Outs of the Hu Incident," 14–15.

3. Mei, *A Biography of Hu Feng*, 654.

4. Hu exclaimed, "You had best not ask about that. . . . If I'm wrong about literary thought, that's a question of understanding, not of politics." Mei, *A Biography of Hu Feng*, 654. See also Mei, *F*, 15.

5. Lu, "Hu Feng and Me," 583.

6. Mei, *F*, 125. See also Shi Yun, ed., A Historical Account of Zhang Chunqiao Yao Wenyuan 张春桥姚文元实传 (Xianggang: Sanlian shudian [Xianggang] youxian gongsi, 2012), 223, for a similar account of Hu's response to the publication of Yao Wenyuan's article "Zhou Yang's Counterrevolutionary Dealings and Double-Sidedness 评反革命两面派周扬" in the first issue of *Red Flag* (1967).

7. In his letters to Lu Yuan during the early 1950s, Hu highlighted the sociopolitical changes that were taking place and what those changes might mean to writers like him and his friends in practical terms: "Before the liberation, we each fought in the way we liked. After the liberation, we all work under [the Party's] leadership." Hu Feng, Letter to Lu Yuan, May 30, 1952, in vol. 9 of *HFQJ*, 376.

8. Hu Feng, Letter to Lu Yuan, April 16, 1950, in vol. 9 of *HFQJ*, 370.

9. See Wang, *The Hu Incident as I Experienced It*, 147.

10. Mao's comments on the letters between Hu and his followers, including this one by Zhang Zhongxiao, first appeared in the *People's Daily* on June 10, 1955 under the title "Editor's Comments to the Third Collection of Materials on the Hu Counterrevolutionary Clique." The English translation of the text can be found in vol. 5 of *Selected Works of Mao Tse-tung*, 182.

11. Hu believed in the inseparability of literature and politics. For example, in responding to Feng Xuefeng's desire to be an established writer first, and then a respected revolutionary, Hu had his reservations. He criticized, "After the war with Japan, Feng, wanting to be recognized as a writer, insisted upon working on literature and art. In his words, there would be no place for him in the Party unless his place in the literary circle was recognized. What was the situation? If there was no place in the Party, then the place in the literary circle was only in name and could very easily be taken away." See Xiao Shan, "Fragments of Memory," in *My Father Hu Feng*, 173–174.

12. Lin, "The Ins and Outs of the Hu Incident," 8.

13. Hu Sheng, "A Critique of Lu Ling's Short Stories," in vol. 1 of *A Compilation of Critical Essays on Hu Feng's Literary Thought* 胡风文艺思想批判论文汇集 (Beijing: Zuojia, 1955), 106.

14. On "New Literature," see Hong Zicheng, *History of Contemporary Chinese Literature* 中国当代文学史 (Beijing: Beijing daxue chubanshe, 1999), trans. Michael M. Day (Leiden; Boston: Brill, 2009), xiv, and chapter 1, "The 'Transition' in Literature," 3–17.

15. Benjamin I. Schwartz, "Themes in Intellectual History: May Fourth and After," in *An Intellectual History of Modern China*, ed. Merle Goldman and Leo Ou-Fan Lee (Cambridge: Cambridge University Press, 2002), 121.

16. For an analysis of "revolution," see Karl Marx, *The 18th Brumaire of Louis Bonaparte* (London: Electric Book Co., 2001), and Friedrich Engels, "The Role of Force in History" (written in 1887, first published in 1895; collected in vol. 26 of *Marx and Engels Collected Works* [Charlottesville, VA: InteLex Corp., 2001–], 453). For a discussion of the modern and Marxist concept of "revolution," see Raymond

Geuss, "Dialectics and the Revolutionary Impulse," in *The Cambridge Companion to Critical Theory*, ed. Fred Rush (Cambridge: Cambridge University Press, 2004), 103–138.

17. Geuss, "Dialectics and the Revolutionary Impulse," 189.

18. Hu Feng, "Prior to Catching the Monk 抓住和尚之前," in vol. 2 of *HFQJ*, 97–98.

19. Hu, "For New Writers on Writing 为初执笔者的创作谈," in vol. 1 of *Collected Criticism of Hu Feng* (Beijing: Renmin wenxue chubanshe, 1984–85), 240.

20. Hu Feng, Letter to Nie Gannu, [month unknown] 31, 1942, in vol. 9 of *HFQJ*, 427–428.

21. Hu Feng, "In the Struggle for Democracy 置身在为民主斗争裹面," in vol. 3 of *HFQJ*, 187. In the same issue of *Hope*, Hu also published Shu Wu's "On Subjectivism 论主观," an essay that Shu Wu would later criticize and disassociate himself from in 1952.

22. Hu, "In the Struggle for Democracy," 186–187.

23. See Hu, "In the Struggle for Democracy," 188–189. For a brief discussion of Hu's concept of "self-expansion," see Denton, *The Problematic of Self in Modern Chinese Literature*, 97–103.

24. Hu, "In the Struggle for Democracy," 188–189.

25. Hu, "In the Struggle for Democracy," 186–187.

26. Lin, "The Ins and Outs of the Hu Incident," 5.

27. He Qifang, "Preface to *Realism* 〈关于现实主义〉的序," in vol. 2 of *A Compilation of Critical Essays on Hu Feng's Literary Thought*, 27–28.

28. In a letter to Shu Wu, Hu said, "I have written a short essay to fight against literary objectivism. In retrospect, it looks as if I have acted in cooperation with you." Hu Feng, Letter to Shu Wu, October 9, 1944, in vol. 9 of *HFQJ*, 487.

29. Denton, *Problematic of Self in Modern Chinese Literature*, 78.

30. See Pang Yanjiao, "Quanlin: A Communist Saint 荃麟-共产主义的圣徒," *Historical Data of New Literature*, no. 2 (1997): 83–95, on 92 (my emphasis).

31. Zhi, *On Hu Feng*, 139.

32. Although some aspects of Hu's notion of literary subjectivism found expression in the mid-1930s, it did not appear in the form of a systematic theory until the publication of "On the Problem of National Forms," which Hu finished writing on October 13, 1940. Little noted at the time of its publication, the essay became a major piece of evidence against Hu's anti-Marxist literary subjectivism and subjective idealism. See Hu, "For New Writers on Writing," 236–248, in vol. 1 of *Collected Criticism of Hu Feng*.

33. By 1948 and 1949, many intellectuals felt that the sooner the GMD was replaced, the better. See Derk Bodde, *Peking Diary: A Year of Revolution* (New York: Henry Schuman, 1950), 24.

34. Zhou, as Hu recollected, said in the meeting in January 1945 that "concerning theoretical matters only Mao's instructions are correct" and that Hu had "better change his attitude towards the party ideology." See Hu, "A Memoir," 624.

35. Hu, "A Memoir," 641.

36. Numerous accounts of Hu by his friends and scholars described him as "politically insensitive," considering his political insensitivity a major cause of his tragedy. This generally accepted view of Hu as politically insensitive, pedantic, and inflexible might be attributable to Lu Xun's comments on Hu's personality in "A Letter in Reply to Xu Maoyong and on the Anti-Japanese United Front 答徐懋庸并关于抗日统一战线问题" (1936). According to Lu Xun, in the "Letter" Hu was someone with "a blunt honesty," "a nervous temperament," and "excessive regard for detail." (See *Complete Works of Lu Xun*, vol. 6, 555). See also C. T. Hsia, *A History of Modern Chinese Fiction* (New York: Columbia University Press, 1971), 299; and Merle Goldman, *Literary Dissent in Communist China* (New York: Atheneum, 1971), 55–57.

37. Shao Quanlin, "Views on the Current Movements in Literature and Art 对于当前文艺运动的意见," *Literature and Art for the Masses* 大众文艺丛刊, no. 1 (March 1948): 4.

38. The critical essays in *Literature and Art for the Masses* included Shao Quanlin's "Views on the Current Movements in Literature and Art" and "The Question of Subjectivism 论主观问题"; Qiao Mu's [Qiao Guanhua] "Literary and Artistic Creation and Subjectivity 文艺创作与主观"; and Hu Sheng's "On Lu Ling's Short Stories 评路翎的短篇小说" and "Development of Lu Xun's Thought 鲁迅思想发展的道路." At around the same time, Lin Mohan, in an essay titled "Individual Emancipation and Collectivism 个性解放与集体主义" and published in the *Wenhui Post* 文汇报, labeled Hu as a "scholar" with "petit-bourgeois sentiments."

39. Shao, "Views on the Current Movements in Literature and Art," 4.

40. See Hong Zicheng, *History of Contemporary Chinese Literature* 中国当代文学史 (Beijing: Beijing daxue chubanshe, 1999) for an outline and detailed discussion of the historical process through which modern Chinese literature became increasingly institutionalized after the end of the May Fourth new cultural movement.

41. See Qiao Guanhua, *Those Gone-with-the-Wind Years* 那随风飘去的岁月 (Shanghai: Xuelin chubanshe, 1997), 182. Qiao Guanhua (1913–83) was the director of the New China News Agency in Hong Kong when the 1948 criticism against Hu took place. After the liberation in 1949, Qiao successively held the positions of deputy director-general of the Foreign Policy Committee of the Ministry of Foreign Affairs, assistant foreign minister, and vice foreign minister (1964–74). In November 1971, upon the restoration of China's seat in the United Nations, Qiao led the Chinese delegation at the 26th Session of the UN General Assembly. In his speech at the General Assembly, Qiao made a comprehensive exposition of China's foreign policies. From then on up to 1976, Qiao attended each session of the UN General Assembly as head of the Chinese delegation. In May 1973, he accompanied Deng Xiaoping on his visit to France. In October 1976, Qiao paid a second visit to France as the foreign minister. After 1976, he held the position of advisor to the Chinese People's Association for Friendship with Foreign Countries.

42. Zhou Erfu, "Remembering Comrade Shao Quanlin 回忆荃麟同志," in vol. 1 of *Collected Essays of Zhou Erfu* 周而复散文集 (Beijing: Huaxia chubanshe, 1999), 284.

43. Lin, "The Ins and Outs of the Hu Incident," 7, 9.

44. Shao, "Views on the Current Movements in Literature and Art," 4.

45. The thesis that the end of liberal capitalism was only *potentially* emancipatory was one held by such Frankfurt School critics as Friedrich Pollock and Max Horkheimer. Central to their argument was the view that modern social life was made up of different but intrinsically related elements—political, legal, economic, and cultural—and that the economic development of the forces of production alone (i.e., freedom from the constraints of the market and private property) might only increase the *possibility* of human emancipation. A truly liberated society, they argued, could only come into being if all elements of the liberal capitalist society of the past were transformed. See *Studies in Philosophy and Social Science* (New York: Institute of Social Research, 1940), especially Friedrich Pollock, "Technological Trends and National Policy," 483–489, and Max Horkheimer, "The Authoritarian State," in *The Essential Frankfurt School Reader*, ed. A. Arato and E. Gebhardt (New York: Continuum, [1977] 1987), 95–117.

46. Marx defined the concept of "dictatorship of the proletariat" as a "necessary intermediate point on the path towards the abolition of class differences in general." In his letter to J. Wedemeyer (March 5, 1852), Marx considered "the dictatorship of the proletariat" a "necessary" conclusion of class struggles and the "constitut[ion] of the transition to the abolition of all classes and to a classless society." A representative example of this "dictatorship" in practice was the Paris Commune in 1871, which Marx called "the positive form of [a] republic" that was "not only to supersede the monarchical form of class rule, but class rule itself." Karl Marx, "The Paris Commune," in *The Civil War in France, Marx and Engels Collected Works*, vol. 22, chap. 3 (Charlottesville, VA: InteLex Corp., 2001), 328–342.

47. For a discussion of the peasant as a subject of literary imagination and political culture in twentieth-century China, see Helen F. Siu, "Introduction," in *Furrows: Peasants, Intellectuals, and the State, Stories and Histories from Modern China* (Stanford, CA: Stanford University Press, 1990), 1–28.

48. Mao, "Talks at the Yan'an Forum on Literature and Art," 72–73.

49. Liu Baimin (1898–1969) was the director of the Center of Chinese Cultural Services (中国文化服务总社) under the Nationalist government. In April 1949, Liu, together with Qian Mu and Zhang Pijie, set up the New Asia College in Hong Kong, which would become one of the three colleges of the Chinese University of Hong Kong established in 1963. Liu died in Hong Kong in 1969.

50. Hu, "A Memoir," 700.

51. Hu, "A Memoir," 700.

52. Hu, "A Memoir," 701.

53. "I received numerous letters from old and new friends, who all mentioned the Hong Kong essays and asked my opinion about them. Most of [these friends] sympathized with me and thought that it would be irresponsible of me not to write a critical response. . . . I thought that those writers [of *Literature and Art for the Masses*] naturally had their purpose in writing, so I resisted writing any response for a long time." Hu, "A Memoir," 704.

54. Hu Feng, "Afterword to *Collected Criticism of Hu Feng* by Hu," in vol. 3 of *HFQJ*, 615.

55. Hu Feng, "Preface to the First Edition of *The Path of Realism* 〈论现实主义的路〉初版附记," in vol. 3 of *HFQJ*, 575–576.

56. Qiao Guanhua was a friend with whom Hu felt that at one stage they could "express views to each other" (Hu Feng, "Three Manuscripts 文稿三篇," *Historical Data of New Literature*, no. 2 [1995]: 188, 122). Qiao's article "When Fangsheng Lay Dying 方生未死之间," published in *The Mainland* in March 1944, was criticized by the Party for its subjective idealist tendency, even though Qiao wrote the piece intending to support the Yan'an rectification movement against Wang-Ming-style dogmatism. See Qiao [Yu Chao], "When Fangsheng Lay Dying," in vol. 1 of *Literature in the Rear Areas during the Period of War of Resistance against Japan*, ed. Lin Mohan et al., for all quotations in this note. Hu was in line with Qiao. According to Hu, when the CCP criticized Qiao in 1944, Ye Yiqun, probably by order of Xu Bingzhi, "wanted me to voice my opinion," but Hu did not. "At that time I thought that it was inappropriate to talk about philosophical questions in party publications, as this would confuse readers . . . but there might be advantages to discuss them in popular magazines. . . . My intention to publish [Shu Wu's] 'On Subjectivism' in *Hope* followed this logic" (Hu, "Three Manuscripts," 190). Perhaps because of the Party writers' criticism of Qiao and his "idealist subjectivism," Hu felt all the more strongly the danger of formulism in the development of New Literature and therefore supported Qiao. In his 1945 preface to the inaugural issue of *Hope*, Hu was supportive of Qiao's point that "there is life everywhere": "One can find life that is made of real sword and spear, filled with traces of blood and tears . . . even in the most ordinary everyday life incident or in the most unenlightened corner of life" (in vol. 3 of *HFQJ*, 188). Such a view was to be expanded and more forcefully advocated four years later, in 1948: "Where there are people there is history. Where there is life, there is a struggle. Where there is the struggle for life, there is the possibility for poetry." It was in the same year, however, that Qiao accused Hu of advocating petit-bourgeois subjectivism. See Hu Feng, "To Those Singers Who Sing for the People 给为人民而歌的歌手们," in vol. 3 of *HFQJ*, 438–440.

57. Hu, "A Memoir," 702.

58. Hu, "A Memoir," 702.

59. Hu, "Three Manuscripts," 196 (my emphasis).

60. In Hu's critical writing, references to Dante appear more than once. In one issue of *July*, Hu stressed the importance of lived experience or *tiyan* (体验 "experience")—the ability to place the self in another's situation—in the creative process. He wrote, "I feel that heaven is fine, but it still has to be built on the ruins of hell, or at least its construction must coincide with the annihilation of hell. If we had the greatness of Dante to lead us out of hell and up to heaven, we would, of course, be most grateful; otherwise it would be best to let someone who has traveled to hell sing out his cursing songs" (Hu Feng, "Afterword," *July*, no. 4 [December 1939], in vol. 2 of *HFQJ*, 686). Speaking about Hu's literary realism in relation to *tiyan*, Yan Jiayan commented: "Among all the theorists of realism, nobody had emphasized as much the function of the writer's subjectivity as Hu had. Such an important literary thought of Hu and the *July* poets had eventually helped realize a new form of realist literature—'a literature of experienced realism'—in the history of the Chinese novel." Yan Jiayan, "A Lesson: There Should Be 'Fair Play' in the Academic Arena 教训: 学术领域应该' 费厄泼赖," a section within the article "Reconsidering Hu's Thought on Literature and Art 关于胡风文艺思想的反思," *Literature Review*, no. 5 (1988): 12.

61. See Herbert Marcuse, *An Essay on Liberation* (Boston: Beacon Press, 1969), 23–48.

62. Dante Alighieri, *The Divine Comedy: Purgatorio*, trans. Charles S. Singleton (Princeton, NJ: Princeton University Press, 1989–91), 51. This quote is from Jacopo del Cassero, one of the souls of the Late Repentant who was slain by violence but managed to repent in his final moment, talking to Dante.

63. Hu Feng, Letter to the CCP's Central Committee, July 7, 1954, in vol. 6 of *HFQJ*, 103.

64. Habermas, *The Structural Transformation of the Public Sphere*, 33.

65. Nikolai Gogol, *Dead Souls*, trans. Richard Pevear (New York: Random House, 1996).

66. Hu Feng, "A Brief Discussion of Foreign Literature and I 略谈我与外国文学," in vol. 7 of *HFQJ*, 243.

67. Hu, "A Brief Discussion of Foreign Literature and I."

68. See the review of *Dead Souls* by Nikolai Gogol, trans. David Magarshack, May 3, 2002. http://www.geocities.com/athens/academy/6422/rev1081.html.

69. Mei Zhi's *A Biography of Hu Feng* described Hu's psychological turmoil when he saw his followers in court: "It was excruciating for me to see those friends who suffered because of their relationship with me. . . . The experience of seeing their grayish yellow complexion was more torturing than the pain of being beaten up. How would I know that this would take ten years? I have squandered their future for nothing. I am sinful! These are all talented men" (Mei, *A Biography of Hu Feng*, 659; see also 742). See Niu Han, "Reunion 重逢," in vol. 2 of *Hu Feng in My Eyes*, ed. Xiao Feng, 822–823, for a description of the trial in 1965, and Lu, "Hu Feng and Me," for his response to Hu's afterthoughts on the prosecution.

CHAPTER VI

1. Mei, *F*, 19. In prison, Hu recited poems to himself. Some of the poems were about his family, others about his friends. The one about Mei Zhi was called "In Praise of Long-Lasting Love." See Hu Feng, "In Praise of Long-Lasting Love 长情赞," in *Songs in Memory of Spring* (Lullaby Collection) 怀春曲 (摇篮曲集), in vol. 1 of *HFQJ*, 538–541.

2. Saul Bellow, *To Jerusalem and Back: A Personal Account* (New York: Penguin, [1976] 1998), 22.

3. These *July* writers, whom Hu called "warriors" for modern China and "soldiers" of the Chinese Revolution, were a community at once in formation, open, and disorganized. As a whole, they were inventors and explorers who had accompanied Hu in his search for his own "strand" of modern Chinese "New Literature." They included such established writers as Xiao Hong 萧红, Xiao Jun 萧军, and Duanmu Hongliang 端木蕻良. Meanwhile, Hu, in his role as a literary editor, also worked hard to publish and promote these lesser-known writers. These emerging writers, including Ah-long 阿垅, Fang Ran 方然, Ji Fang 冀汸, Lu Li 鲁藜, Lu Ling 路翎, and Lu Yuan 绿原, formed a core group of the *July* writers. See Kirk A. Denton, "The Hu Feng Group: Genealogy of a Literary School," in *Literary Societies of Republican China*, ed. Kirk A. Denton and Michel Hockx (Lanham, MD: Lexington Books, 2008), 413–466.

4. Hu Feng, *Time Has Begun*, in vol. 1 of *HFQJ*, 101–281. The English title of the elegy, mentioned in Michael M. Day's translation of Hong Zicheng's account of Chinese literary history, is *Time Begun*. See Hong, *A History of Chinese Literature*, 74.

5. Hong, *A History of Chinese Literature*, 74.

6. Hu Feng, "A Brief Discussion of Literature from Nowhere," 427–430.

7. Hu Feng, "A Brief Discussion of Literature from Nowhere," 427–430.

8. Hu Feng, "Man and Poet: The Poet in the Second Sense 关于人与诗: 关于第二义的诗人," in vol. 3 of *HFQJ*, 74.

9. Hu, "Man and Poet," 74.

10. In an article written after his rehabilitation in the mid-1980s, Hu restated the focus of his critical writings and reminded his readers that they were the product of active engagement with major literary and intellectual issues at the time: "Since I began writing criticism, I have been searching for the principles and methods in advancing realism (socialist realism). I soon came to understand that [literary] realism should fight against two forces: subjective-formulism, with sloganeering being its primitive form, and objectivism, with naturalism being its primitive form. . . . In my understanding, [socialist realist literature] must be developed against these two dangerous forces." Afterword to *Collected Critical Essays by Hu Feng* 胡风评论集后记, in vol. 3 of *HFQJ*, 586.

11. Mei Zhi, *A Biography of Hu Feng* 胡风传 (Beijing: Shiyue wenyi chubanshe, 1998), 569.

12. See Hu, "A Memoir," 569.

13. Hu Feng, "The Song of Triumph" (original name, "Another Joyous Praise"), *Time Has Begun*, in vol. 1 of *HFQJ*, 264.

14. Hu Feng, "Joyous Praise," in *Time Has Begun*, in vol. 1 of *HFQJ*, 103–104.

15. Hu, "Joyous Praise," 104–105.

16. The Jinggang Mountains is known as the birthplace of the Chinese Red Army (predecessor of the People's Liberation Army) and the "cradle of the Chinese Revolution." After the GMD turned against the Communist Party during the April 12 Incident, the Communists either went underground or fled to the countryside. Following the unsuccessful Autumn Harvest Uprising in Changsha, Mao led his 1,000 remaining men here, setting up his first peasant soviet.

17. Hu, "The Song of Triumph," 274–276.

18. Hu, "The Song of Triumph," 279–281.

19. See Mao, "Struggle of Revolutionary Literature under Reactionary Opposition在反动派压逼下斗争的革命文艺," in vol. 2 of *A Compilation of Critical Essays on Hu Feng's Literary Thought* 胡风文艺思想批判论文汇集, 6 vols. (Beijing: Zuojia, 1955–), 1–21.

20. At the closing ceremony of the second meeting of the 1950 session of the Chinese People's Political Consultative Conference, held on June 23, Mao pointed out the task of intellectual thought reform, paving the way for a series of national campaigns against literary and cultural works and setting the tone for the intellectual atmosphere of the 1950s. The years 1950 and 1951 witnessed Mao's attack on the film *The Life of Wu Xun* (dir. Sun Yu), which was the first ideological-political campaign of the CCP regime. For a quick reference to "criticism of the film *The Life of Wu Xun*," see Henry He, *Dictionary of the Political Thought of the People's Republic of China* (Armonk, NY: M. E. Sharpe, 2001), 297.

21. After various attempts to print the complete epic had failed, Hu was eventually able to issue the songs in two installments: Haiyan Bookstore published the first two in January 1950, and Tianxia Book Company published the last two in March 1950.

22. Zang Kejia 藏克家碧野 (1905–2004), coeditor of *Selected Poems of Chairman Mao* after the PRC's founding.

23. Apropos another letter written on the same date to Lu Ling, the "powerful writer" might be referring to Hu Qiaomu, Mao's main secretary from 1942 to 1966. Hu met with Hu Qiaomu for forty minutes in which the latter called him an "aristocratic revolutionary." Hu Feng, Letter to Lu Ling, January 18, 1950, in vol. 9 of *HFQJ*, 274.

24. Hu Feng, Letter to Lu Yuan, January 18, 1950, in vol. 9 of *HFQJ*, 367–368.

25. See Charles J. Alber's study of Ding Ling's revolutionary work, *Embracing the Lie: Ding Ling and the Politics of Literature in the People's Republic of China* (Westport, CT: Praeger, 2004), particularly chapter 4, "Spies and Secret Agents," for a brief account of the publication of a series of articles criticizing *Time Has*

Begun, especially song #4 "Requiem," in *Guangming Daily* (May 5, 1950) and the *Literary Gazette* (1, no. 12, and 2, no. 4 of 1950).

26. Only the first quintet of song #3 appeared in 1950, in the first issue of *Rising Point*, a postrevolutionary magazine edited by Mei Zhi and "a few young friends" of Hu. He published the other four poems separately in 1981, after which editors assembled the songs into a quintet and compiled the complete version of *Time Has Begun*.

27. Hu Feng, Letter to Niu Han, January 16, 1951, in vol. 9 of *HFQJ*, 440 (my emphasis).

28. Hu, "Joyous Praise," 103.

29. In her biography of Hu, Mei Zhi recalled the two-month period in which Hu composed *Time Has Begun*: "One early morning, [Hu] woke up to find that the place had overnight blanketed in snow. . . . Looking at the crystal-clear snow, he finished 'Little Grass Says to the Sun' in half an hour, comparing himself to 'little grass,' and the CCP and Mao Zedong's thought to 'the sun.' Mei, *Biography of Hu Feng, 569.*

30. Hu Feng, "Songs of Youth: Little Grass Says to the Sun," in *Time Has Begun*, in vol. 1 of *HFQJ*, 157–159.

31. Hu, "Songs of Youth," 160.

32. Hu, "Songs of Youth," 158.

33. Hu Feng, "Songs of Youth: Morning Light," in *Time Has Begun*, in vol. 1 of *HFQJ*, 160.

34. Hu Feng, Letter to Lu Yuan, September 9, 1984, in vol. 9 of *HFQJ*, 394.

35. Hu, Letter to Lu Yuan, September 9, 1984, in vol. 9 of HFQJ, 394.

36. For a list of "core writers" who were "more fitted to, more reflective of the mainstream in literature," and for an account of how these writers began to occupy central positions of power in literary circles in the early 1950s and beyond, see Hong, *History of Contemporary Chinese Literature*, 36–40.

37. In November 1954, under the self-delusion that the CCP Central Committee had favorably received his "300,000-Character Report" on "certain problems of literature and ideology," and believing that the Party would study the "problems" he presented, Hu gave two speeches in response to the Party's call to criticize the editorial collective of the *Literary Gazette*. In these speeches, he charged the "core writers" representative of the Party's cultural leadership with such offenses as "crude sociology," "literary formulism," and "Scholastic Marxism." See Lin, "The Ins and Outs of the Hu Incident," 4–28; see also Merle Goldman, "Hu Feng's Conflict with the Communist Literary Authorities," *China Quarterly* 12 (December 1962): 127.

38. See footnote 1 of Hu Feng, Letter to Shu Wu, October 26, 1948, in vol. 9 of *HFQJ*, 532.

39. Marston Anderson, *The Limits of Realism: Chinese Fiction in the Revolutionary Period* (Berkeley: University of California Press, 1990), 62.

40. Hu Feng, "Some Thoughts about Literary Developments 关于创作发展的二三感想," in vol. 3 of *HFQJ*, 10–11.

41. Hu, *The Path of Realism*, 500–502.

42. See Marx's discussion of "scientific realism" in Karl Marx, "The Fetishism of Commodities," in vol. 1 of *Capital: A Critique of Political Economy*, ed. Frederick Engels and trans. Samuel Moore and Edward Aveling (Moscow: Progress Publishers, 1999).

43. Hu, *The Path of Realism*, 502.

44. Hu Feng, "Realism Today 现实主义在今天," in vol. 3 of *HFQJ*, 38.

45. Hu, "Realism Today," 38.

46. Hu Feng, "Tian Jian's Poetry 田间的诗," in vol. 2 of *HFQJ*, 444.

47. Hu, "Tian Jian's Poetry," 444.

48. Quoted in Hu, "Tian Jian's Poetry," 444.

49. Tian Jian, "How Do I Write Poetry? 我怎样写诗的?," quoted in Hu, "Tian Jian's Poetry," 443.

50. Tian Jian, "I Am a Part of the Sea 我是海的一个," quoted in Hu, "Tian Jian's Poetry," 443.

51. Hu, "Tian Jian's Poetry," 444.

52. Hu, "Tian Jian's Poetry," 445.

53. Hu, "Tian Jian's Poetry," 445.

54. Hu Feng, "On Poetry and Tian Jian's Poetry 关于诗和田间的诗," in vol. 2 of *HFQJ*, 600.

55. Hu, "On Poetry and Tian Jian's Poetry," 601.

56. Hu, "For New Writers on Writing," 228, 229.

57. Hu, "For New Writers on Writing," 228, 229.

58. Hu, "For New Writers on Writing," 88–189.

59. David Der-wei Wang, *The Lyrical in Epic Time: Modern Chinese Intellectuals and Artists through the 1949 Crisis* (New York: Columbia University Press, 2015).

60. Wang, *The Lyrical in Epic Time*, 66 (my emphasis).

61. Hu, "A Brief Discussion of Literature from Nowhere," 427.

62. Mao Zedong, "The Role of the Chinese Communist Party in the National War 中国共产党在民族战争的地位," in vol. 2 of *Selected Works of Mao Tse-tung*, 209 (my emphasis).

63. Even before Mao adopted the phrase "Sinification of Marxism" as his own in his 1938 speech "The Role of the Chinese Communist Party in the National War," he had already warmed himself to the idea of appropriating and utilizing the legacy of "feudalistic" China by appealing to Chinese national identity. Writing "On Practice" in 1937, for example, Mao brought forth "practice" as the criterion of examining the completeness and validity of theoretical Marxism: "Knowledge begins with practice, and theoretical knowledge is acquired through practice and must then return to practice." By "practice," Mao referred to the greatness of China's "thousands of years of . . . glorious revolutionary tradition and . . . splendid historical heritage."

One year later, in 1938, Mao articulated his concept of "national forms" even more clearly: "national forms" should represent the "fresh lively Chinese style and spirit the common people of China love." Mao, "The Role of the Chinese Communist Party in the National War," 209. For a discussion of how "Chinese socialism" under Mao intervened in the historical development of Marxism-Leninism, see Arif Dirlik, "Mao Zedong and Chinese Marxism," in *Marxism beyond Marxism*, ed. Saree Makdisi, Cesare Casarino, and Rebecca E. Karl (New York: Routledge, 1996), 119–148.

64. Hu Feng, "On the Question of National Forms 论民族形式问题," in vol. 2 of *HFQJ*, 722.

65. In response to Mao's call to appeal to "put Marxism into practice" by "integrat[ing]" theoretical knowledge with "the specific characteristics of [China]" and "acquir[ing] a definite national form," Party writers such as Mao Dun and Guo Moruo directed writers and artists to popularize revolutionary literature and art by mobilizing regional folk cultures and experimenting with traditional popular forms (e.g., handscrolls, regional/local dramas, oral ballads, and folk operas). See Mao Zedong, "On Practice 实战论," lecture given at the Anti-Japanese Military and Political College in Yan'an in July 1937, in vol. 1 of *Selected Works of Mao Tse-tung*, 304; Mao Dun, "Literature and Art for the Masses and the Use of Traditional Forms 大众化与利用旧形式," in *Modern Chinese Literary Thought: Writings on Literature, 1893–1945*, ed. Kirk A. Denton, 433–435; and Guo Moruo, "Discussing the Problem of 'National Forms' 〈民族形式〉商兑," in vol. 19 of *Complete Works of Guo Moruo* (Beijing: Renmin wenxue chubanshe, 1982–92), 31–47. See also Arif Dirlik, "Revolutionary Hegemony and the Language of the Revolution: Chinese Socialism between Present and Future," in *Marxism and the Chinese Experience*, ed. Arif Dirlik and Maurice Meisner (Armonk, NY: M. E. Sharpe, 1989), 27–39, for a critical analysis of the "languages" ("language of vision" vs. "language of economism") that Mao and the Party intellectuals employed and utilized in the process of describing Chinese socialism in the post-1949 years.

66. Hu Feng, "On the Problem of National Forms 论民族形式问题," in vol. 2 of *HFQJ*, 750 (my emphasis). This view found support in a contemporary assessment of the development of modernism in Communist China. Marston Anderson, for example, argued that the fostering of "national forms" brought modernists to dismiss some of the key imperatives of May Fourth literature and culture. See Anderson, *Limits of Realism*, 70.

67. Lu Ling, preface to *Children of the Rich* (Beijing: Renmin wenxue chubanshe, 2000), 2.

68. Lu, preface to *Children of the Rich*, 2–3.

69. Hu, *The Path of Realism*, 40.

70. See Q. S. Tong 童庆生, "Towards a Common Literature 走向共同的文学," in *The Meaning of the Chinese Language: Philology, World Literature, and the Western Idea of the Chinese Language* 汉语的意义：语言学、世界文学和西方汉语观 (Beijing: Shenghuo, dushu, xinzhi sanlianshudian, 2018), 313–346.

71. Carolyn FitzGerald, *Fragmenting Modernisms: Chinese Wartime Literature, Art, and Film, 1937–49* (Leiden: Brill, 2013).

72. From the standpoint of literary history, as Michelle Yeh demonstrated, modern Chinese poetry was not only fundamentally distinct from its classical form but also inherited much from English Romantic and Modernist poetry: Michelle Yeh, *Modern Chinese Poetry: Theory and Practice since 1917* (New Haven, CT: Yale University Press, 1991). See also Anderson, "Mao Dun, Zhang Tianyi, and the Social Impediments to Realism," chapter 4 in *Limits of Realism*, 119–179.

73. Liu Kang, for example, attempted to give a historical account of "aesthetic Marxism in China" by beginning with Hu's theory of the "subjective combative spirit." He wrote that "there has also persisted a non-Maoist tradition of 'aesthetic Marxism' ever since Hu Feng's theory of the 'subjective combative spirit' emerged in the 1940s to contend that subjective experience was one appropriate site of revolution and resistance." Liu Kang, "Aesthetics and Chinese Marxism," in *New Asian Marxisms*, ed. Tani E. Barlow (Durham, NC: Duke University Press, 2002), 173.

74. Auerbach, "Philology and Weltliteratur," 2.

75. Auerbach, "Philology and Weltliteratur," 4.

76. Ah-long, "White Flower" (first published without a title), September 9, 1944, in *White Flower* 白色花, ed. Lu Yuan and Niu Han (Beijing: Renmin wenxue chubanshe, 1981), 21.

77. Hu, "Realism Today," 38.

78. The theme of revolutionary soldiers being buried in snow was common among new poetry in wartime China. Ai Qing's "Snow Falls on the Land of China 雪落在中国的土地上" and Lu Li's 鲁藜 "Red Snow 红的雪花" are well-known examples of the time.

CHAPTER VII

1. Mao Zedong, "On the Ten Major Relationships (April 25, 1956)," in vol. 5 of *Selected Works of Mao Tse-tung*, 299–300. Mao gave this speech at a meeting of the CCP's Political Bureau held on April 25, 1956. Drawing on the problems in the Soviet Union, Mao presented a synoptic overview of the historical experience of the Chinese Revolution, analyzed what he called "ten major relationships" in the socialist revolution, and set forth his methods for building a socialist China.

2. Michel Foucault, "The Subject and Power," *Critical Inquiry* 8, no. 4 (Summer 1982): 790.

3. Foucault, *Society Must Be Defended*, 29.

4. See Jiang Zuquan for a list of literary intellectuals who wrote critical essays to persecute Hu in the 1955 national campaign, only to become victims of the same revolutionary discourse during the Cultural Revolution ten years later. Jiang Zuquan, "Analysing the Cultural Revolution through the Hu Case 透过胡风事件剖析

文革," in *Red Disaster: A Collection of Academic Papers on the 50th Anniversary of the Cultural Revolution* 红祸: 文革五十周年 *(1966–2016)* 论文集," ed. Wu Chengmou (Taipei: World Chinese Publishing, 2016), 131–141.

5. Lu Dingyi recalled his experience of the Hu Incident thus: "At the time the Central Committee was determining the nature of the Hu Incident, Mao discussed with Lu Dingyi, Zhou, and Hu Qiaomu. Mao pointed out that Hu was a counterrevolutionary and was inclined to persecute him. Both Zhou and Lu supported Mao's idea. Hu Qiaomu was in disagreement. In the end, they followed Mao's decision and decided that Hu was counterrevolutionary." Chen Qingquan and Song Guangwei, *A Biography of Lu Dingyi* 陆定一传 (Beijing: Zhonggong dangshi chubanshe, 1999), 399. Wang Kang's account of the incident confirmed Lu's memory. See also Wang Kang, "My Participation in the Investigation of the Hu Incident 我参加审查胡风案的经历," *Hundred Year Tide* 百年潮, no. 12 (1999): 44, 41.

6. Zhou was an ardent supporter and practitioner of Mao's directives on literature and art, while Hu was perceived to be "an anti-Party element" who was "dismissive" of the "Talks." In the late years of his life, Hu confessed that in addition to personal and communication problems, his attitude toward the "Talks" was also attributed to the cultural leaders' feeling that he was opposed to the "Talks." In his memoir, Hu wrote: "The study group of the 'Talks' held in Chongqing aimed to see how people understand and respond to [the 'Talks']. My attitude was relatively bad. . . . In retrospect, even though I thought that some of the suggestions [proposed in the 'Talks'] did not apply to the GMD areas, I should have shown at least [a more cooperative] attitude toward the Party. I didn't do so. I stayed on the road of independent thinking characteristic of the older generation of intellectuals. As a result, I was regarded formally as an enemy of the 'Talks' after the Liberation." Hu, "A Memoir," 595–596.

7. Yao Wenyuan, "Zhou's Counterrevolutionary Dealings and Double-Sidedness 评反革命两面派周扬," in *The Swaying Swing: Zhou's Rights and Wrongs* 摇荡的秋千: 是是非非说周扬, ed. Li Hui (Shenzhen: Haitian chubanshe, 1998), 301–302.

8. Yao, "Zhou's Counterrevolutionary Dealings and Double-Sidedness," 302.

9. As *generally* observed, a close partnership between Chinese political power and literary practice existed. Bertrand Russell, for example, argued that "the Chinese polity is a cultural phenomenon" (quoted in Helen F. Siu, ed., introduction to *Furrows*, 7). In the essay where she reflected on the Tiananmen Incident in June 1989, Rey Chow discussed Chinese intellectuals' past and present relation to the discursive power of language and explained how Chinese intellectuals transformed their literacy into political power. See "Pedagogy, Trust, Chinese Intellectuals in the 1990s—Fragments of a Post-Catastrophic Discourse," *Dialectical Anthropology* 16 (1991): 191–207. See also Yi-tsi Feuerwerker, *Ideology, Power, Text: Self-Representation and the Peasant "Other" in Modern Chinese Literature* (Stanford, CA: Stanford Uni-

versity Press, 1998), esp. 9–11, 36–52; and Wendy Larson, *Literary Authority and the Modern Chinese Writer: Ambivalence and Autobiography* (Durham, NC: Duke University Press, 1991).

10. It was a well-received notion, especially in the popular press and media, that the Cultural Revolution was "devoid of meaning"; it was a period of "ten years of (national) madness" (Chloé Froissart, "Xu Youyu, or How to Write the History of the Cultural Revolution so as to Set China on the Right Future Path?," *China Perspectives*, no. 42 [July–August 2002]). For a discussion of the irrationality of the event, see, for example, Jehangir S. Pocha, "Ex-Red Guards Come to Grips with Maoist Tumult: Revisiting China's Cultural Revolution," *Boston Globe*, August 31, 2006; and Feng Chi-tsai, *Ten Years of Madness: Oral Histories of China's Cultural Revolution* (San Francisco: China Books, 1996).

11. There is a need for some focused studies on Chinese critical discourse in the second half of the twentieth century. The thinking and psychological traits characteristic of some intellectuals in the PRC were so popular that they became a cultural phenomenon. See Wan Tonglin, *Martyrs: Hu and His Fellow Travelers* 殉道者: 胡风及其同仁们 (Jinan: Shandong huabao chubanshe, 1998), 258.

12. Feuerwerker, *Ideology, Power, Text*, 16.

13. Feuerwerker, *Ideology, Power, Text*, 41.

14. See Mao, "Analysis of the Classes in Chinese Society," 13.

15. Having defined "the lower levels of the intellectual—students, primary and middle school teachers, lower government functionaries, office clerks, and small lawyers" as "the petty bourgeoisie," Mao concluded at the end of the essay: "The leading force in our revolution is the industrial proletariat. Our closest friends are the entire semiproletariat and petty bourgeoisie. As for the vacillating middle bourgeoisie, their right wing may become our enemy and their left wing may become our friend but we must be constantly on our guard and not let them create confusion within our ranks." Mao, "Analysis of the Classes in Chinese Society," 19.

16. Zhang Guotao, "Is China Now Safe from International Aggression? 中国已脱离了国际侵略的危险吗?," *Pioneer Weekly* 先导周报, no. 6 (October 18, 1922): 45.

17. See Mao, "Talks at the Yan'an Forum on Literature and Art," 72.

18. Mao, "Talks at the Yan'an Forum on Literature and Art," 72.

19. For a discussion of the important role language played in Mao's attempt to create a "master narrative about the Chinese Revolution," see Apter and Saich, *Revolutionary Discourse in Mao's Republic*, esp. 294, 263.

20. Li Yang, *The Predestination of Resistance: Research on Socialist Realism 1942–1976* 抗争宿命之路: 社会主义现实主义 *1942–1976* 研究 (Changchun: Shidai wenyi chubanshe, 1993), 57–58.

21. Mao, "Talks at the Yan'an Forum on Literature and Art," 81.

22. Hu Feng, Letter to Qiao Guanhua, February 14, 1966, in vol. 9 of *HFQJ*, 467.

23. Hu, "A Brief Review," 680.

24. Hu recalled the hardship of his long imprisonment thus: "In November in the second year of the (Cultural) Revolution [November 1967] . . . Jiang Qing's closest followers put me back into the solitary cell and fed me to mosquitoes and worms. They ignored the fact that my fourteen-year sentence had come to its end. In January 1970, they sent me . . . to No. 3 Prison in Dazhu County. After a simple talk, I was sentenced to life imprisonment and sent to a labor reform camp. I was not allowed to appeal. I looked at them with a smile and declared that I would not appeal even if invited." Hu Feng, Letter to Xiong Zimin (then delegate to the fifth National Congress of Literature and Art Workers), July 11–12, 1979, in vol. 9 of *HFQJ*, 597.

25. Hu, Letter to Xiong Zimin, 597 (my emphasis).

26. For a discussion of Zhang's and Yao's alliance with Jiang Qing and their road to the CCP's political center, see Merle Goldman, "The Party and the Intellectuals: Phase Two," in *An Intellectual History of Modern China*, ed. Merle Goldman and Leo Ou-fan Lee (Cambridge: Cambridge University Press, 2002), 372.

27. Yao was well known as the author of the article "Notes on the New Historical Drama *Hai Rui Dismissed from Office*," which was first published in the *Literary Gazette* and, after much resistance, reprinted in the *People's Daily*. Commissioned by Jiang Qing and published in the *People's Daily* on November 10, 1965, the article marked the beginning of the Cultural Revolution. The play *Hai Rui Dismissed from Office*, written by Wu Han, a historian and vice-mayor of Beijing, was interpreted as an allegorical defense of the former defense minister Peng Dehuai, who had been dismissed from office in 1959 for his criticism of the Great Leap Forward.

28. Yao Pengzi, Yao's father, was the owner of the Writers Bookstore 作家書屋 in Shanghai before 1949 and was associated with a group of left-wing writers that included Lu Xun and Hu and Party members Feng Xuefeng and Pan Hannian. He had been a CCP member for six years but left the Party after he was arrested in 1933. His "confession" appeared in the *Central Daily News* 中央日报 on April 18, 1934. Despite his betrayal, Yao managed to maintain relationships with a few left-wing writers. His Writers Bookstore, for example, published many left-wing books. Because of his father's connection with left-wing literary circles, Yao had known Hu since his teenage years. See Ye Yonglie, *A Biography of Yao Wenyuan* 姚文元传 (Changchun: Shidai wenyi chubanshe, 1993), 119.

29. Yang Shangkun recalled that the CCP first wanted to label Hu's literary theory "petit-bourgeois" and "bourgeois" as early as January 1955. See *Diary of Yang Shangkun* 杨尚昆日记 (Beijing: Zhongyang wenxian chubanshe, 2001), 141–143, 205–210.

30. Yao's serious interest in Hu's literary theory began with the failure to publish his novel *Tempered a Hundred Times to Become Steel* 百炼成钢, which was inspired by the Soviet writer Nikolai Alexeevich's novel *How the Steel Was Tempered*.

The failure to be a novelist led Yao to think about becoming a literary critic, with Hu as his model. See Ye, *A Biography of Yao*, 117–118, 119–120.

31. The third part of Zhou's speech focused on the Party's criticism of Hu. It read as follows: "Crude sociology does exist. . . . Yes, we had not sufficiently criticized such crude sociology in the past; we had even incorporated crude sociological views into many articles that sought to publicize Marxist theory of literature and art. The mistake, though ours, . . . is not the issue. The current issue is that Mr. Hu has been criticizing and calling many truly Marxist views on literature examples of crude sociology." Notably, even in such a critical speech, Zhou emphasized the need to recognize his conflict with Hu as an internal problem within the masses. He continued: "We have a fundamental disagreement with Mr. Hu and others on literary and art theory, but this is not to deny the literary and artistic work and achievement of Mr. Hu, Mr. Ah-long and Mr. Lu Ling. Some of the views that Hu and Lu Ling expressed at the meeting are good and deserve attention." See Zhou Yang, "We Must Fight 我们必须战斗," in vol. 2 of *Collected Essays of Zhou Yang* 周扬文集 (Beijing: Renmin wenxue chubanshe, 1985), 326.

32. This speech by Yao Wenyuan later appeared in the May 1954 issue of the *Literary Gazette* under the title "Distinguish Right and Wrong, Mark Out the Boundary! 分清是非，划清界限!" See vol. 3 of *A Compilation of Critical Essays on Hu Feng's Literary Thought*, 59.

33. See Yao, "Distinguish Right and Wrong," 54.

34. See Ye, *A Biography of Yao*, 122–126, 129–131.

35. See Yao Wenyuan, "Hu's Three Ways to Distort Marxism 胡风歪曲马克思主义的三套手段," *Literature and Art Monthly* 文艺月报, no. 3 (March 1955). *Literature and Art Monthly*, edited by Ba Jin, Tang Tao, and Wang Ruowang, was one of the more vocal left-wing literary journals based in Shanghai after liberation. Its inaugural issue came out in April 1953 and its last issue was published in July 1959.

36. Ye, *A Biography of Yao*, 129.

37. See Yao Wenyuan, "Marxism or Anti-Marxism? Review of a Few Points in Hu's 'Report on Literary and Artistic Practice since the Liberation' to the Central Committee 马克思主义还是反马克思主义?—评胡风给当中央报告中关于文艺问题的几个主要观点," *Liberation Daily*, March 15, 1955.

38. Ye, *A Biography of Yao*, 129.

39. Ye, *A Biography of Yao*, 129.

40. Yao Wenyuan, "The Reactionary Nature of Hu's Literary Thought 胡风文艺思想的反动本质," *Wenhui Post*, March 28, 1955.

41. They were all aptly titled: "Hu Denies the Objective Rules of Historical Development—A Critique of Hu's Subjective Historicism (1) 胡风否认历史发展的客观规律性—批判胡风唯心主义历史观之一" (May 7); "Hu's Reactionary Views That Belittle the Working Masses—A Critique of Hu's Subjective Historicism (2) 胡风污蔑劳动人民的反动观点—批判胡风唯心主义历史观之二" (May 9); and "Hu Opposes

Organized Class Struggles—a Critique of Hu's Subjective Historicism (3) 胡风反对有组织有领导的阶级斗争—批判胡风唯心主义历史观之三" (May 11). See *Liberation Daily*, May 7, 9, and 11, 1955.

42. See Yao Wenyuan, "To Counterattack Decisively Hu's Double-Dealing Tactics 给胡风的两面派手腕以十倍还击," *Liberation Daily*, May 17, 1955; "Crush the Hu Counterrevolutionary Clique with the Strongest Determination 用最大的决心粉碎胡风反党集团案," *News Daily*, May 27, 1955; "Identify the Enemy and Destroy Hu's Anti-Party and Counterrevolutionary Basis 认清敌人, 把胡风反党反革命的毒巢彻底捣毁," *Wenhui Post*, May 29, 1955; "Hu's Double-Dealing Counterrevolutionary Clique Is the Diehard Enemy of the Revolution 胡风的反革命两面派是革命的死敌," *People's Daily*, June 1, 1955 (reprinted in *Liberation Daily*, June 3, 1955); "Clear Out the Hidden Double-Dealing Counterrevolutionary Elements 彻底清除隐藏的两面派反革命分子," *Youth Post*, June 14, 1955; and "We Need a Hardened Heart to Combat the Enemy 要用铁的心肠消灭敌人," *News Daily*, June 18, 1955.

43. Yao, "To Counterattack Decisively Hu's Double-Dealing Tactics," *Liberation Daily*, May 17, 1955.

44. Wan, *Martyrs: Hu and His Fellow Travelers*, 293.

45. These letters were collected under the title "Materials on the Hu Small Clique 关于胡风小集团的一些材料," which was later changed by Mao to "Materials on the Hu Anti-Party Group 关于胡风反党集团的一些材料."

46. Mao Zedong, Editorial [on the first collection of materials on the Hu counterrevolutionary clique], first published in the *People's Daily*, May 13, 1955, in vol. 1 of *The Writings of Mao Zedong 1949–1976*, 563–564.

47. See, Editorial Board of the *People's Daily*, ed., *Collection of Materials on the Hu Counterrevolutionary Clique* 关于胡风反革命集团的材料 (Beijing: Renmin chubanshe, 1955).

48. Lin, "The Ins and Outs of the Hu Incident," 23.

49. After Hu learned that the *Literary Gazette* would publish his "Report," he requested that it be published together with a piece of self-criticism. Zhou, however, rejected his request by saying that the "Report" had been printed and there would not be enough time to wait for Hu to turn in his criticism. Given the situation, Hu requested that the "Report" be published together with a preface, titled "My Statement," which read as follows: "After the launching of the current critical movement against bourgeois ideology, I received many lessons and am examining this 'Report.' With the publication of this 'Report,' I have two points to make: 1. I have already realized that the attitude expressed in this 'Report' toward the Party and toward literature is mistaken and harmful; 2. the judgments made in this material on today's literature and art movement contain a considerable amount of subjective opinion. Some of the specific circumstances and examples I spoke about are not well founded and at variance with reality, but now that the 'Report' has been printed, it is too late to make revisions. I take responsibility for everything I

have said in it and hope that comrades will offer their criticism." Quoted in Lin Mohan, "The Ins and Outs of the Hu Feng Incident," 21.

50. Quoted in Li Xin, "On the Case of the 'Hu Counterrevolutionary Clique' 关于〈胡风反革命集团〉案件," *Historical Data of New Literature*, no. 2 (2001): 91–92 (my emphasis).

51. Li, "On the Case of the 'Hu Counterrevolutionary Clique,'" 92 (my emphasis).

52. Quoted in Lin, "The Ins and Outs of the Hu Incident," 21–22.

53. Li, "On the Case of 'Hu Counterrevolutionary Clique,'" 92.

54. Archive Research Office, "CCP's Central Committee 中共中央文献研究室," in vol. 6 of *Selected Important Documents of the PRC* 建国以来重要文献选编 (Beijing: Zhongyang wenxian chubanshe, 1993), 28 (my emphasis).

55. Lin, "The Ins and Outs of the Hu Incident," 22.

56. This was the Central Committee's and Mao's instruction on January 12, 1955.

57. Lin, "The Ins and Outs of the Hu Incident," 24.

58. See Kang Zhuo, "The *Literary Gazette* and the Wrongful Case of Hu 文艺报》与胡风冤案," in *Memories Bristling with Profusions and Complications*, ed. Ji Xianlin, Niu Han, and Deng Jiuping (Beijing: Beijing shiyue wenyi chubanshe, 2001), 515–516. See also Xi Chun, "The Publication of the First Collection of Materials on Hu Feng 第一批胡风材料发表前后," an interview with Shu Wu and Ye Yao, "Remembering 'The First Materials' Related to the Unjust Case of Hu 我所记得的有关胡风冤案〈第一批材料〉及其它," respectively, in vol. 1 of *Celebrities and Unjust Cases: True Accounts of Literary Circles in China* 名人与冤案—中国文坛档案实录, 3 vols. (Beijing: Qunzhong chubanshe, 1998), 264–287, 253–263.

59. Lin, "The Ins and Outs of the Hu Incident," 25.

60. For a discussion of how some of the letters were distorted and appropriated, see Lu Xin, *Thirty Years [for] Three-Hundred Thousand Words: A Side Account of the "Hu-Feng Case" 1955–1985* 三十万言30年: *1955–1985*〈胡风案〉侧记 (Yinchuan: Ningxia renmin chubanshe, 2007), 13–17. Many of the letters collected in the "Collection of Materials on the Hu Counterrevolutionary Clique" were truncated and distorted, but these letters have been collected and published in their full form in vol. 9 of the *Complete Works of Hu Feng*. For letters written to Hu by Hu's students and followers such as Lu Ling and Zhang Zhongxiao, see *Hu Feng and Lu Ling Literary Correspondences*, ed. Zhang Xiao Feng; and Zhang Zhongxiao, *Complete Set of the Dreamless Tower* 无梦楼全集, ed. Lu Xin (Wuhan Shi: Wuhan chubanshe, 2006).

61. Kang, "The *Literary Gazette* and the Wrongful Case of Hu," 516.

62. The original editorial Kang wrote was published in full in Xu Qingquan, "Kang Zhuo's Editor's Comment on Hu's 'My Self-Criticism' Newly Discovered 新发现的康濯为胡风〈我的自我批评〉起草的按语," *China Reading Weekly* 中华读书报, August 13, 2003.

63. Lin, "The Ins and Outs of the Hu Incident," 25.

64. Kang, "The *Literary Gazette* and the Wrongful Case of Hu Feng," 516.

65. In 1962, six years after Hu's arrest, Lu Yuan had the chance to talk with Shu Wu again. According to Lu Yuan, Shu Wu repeated many times the sentence: "[I] wouldn't have thought that the [campaign] would become this serious, neither would Zhou and his friends." Lu, "Hu Feng and Me," 604. Lin Mohan wrote in 1989, "Mao's Editorial, which defined the Hu faction as a counterparty, counterrevolutionary, and counterpeople literary clique, is out of some other comrades' and my expectations." Lin, "The Ins and Outs of the Hu Incident," 23, 25.

66. See Shu Wu, "Hu's Anti-Marxist Thought on Literature and Art 反马克思主义的胡风文艺思想," first published in *China Youth* 中国青年, April 1954, in vol. 3 of *A Compilation of Critical Essays on Hu Feng's Literary Thought*, 147.

67. See Shu Wu, "The Anti-Party Anti-People Nature of Hu's Thought on Literature and Art 胡风文艺思想反党反人民的实质," *People's Daily*, April 13, 1955.

68. Shu Wu said in his 1997 essay, "The series of revision that turned 'Materials on the Hu Small Clique' to 'Materials on the Hu Counterrevolutionary Clique' was not something I had expected." See Shu Wu, "Postscript to *Return to 'May Fourth'* " 〈回归 "五四"〉后序," *Historical Data of New Literature*, no. 2 (1997).

69. See Lin, "The Ins and Outs of the Hu Incident," 25 (my emphasis). Later, in the same interview, Lin blamed Shu Wu for the "accidental" creation of the case of Hu. "Why the criticism of Hu changed from an issue of ideology in literature and art to a political issue was closely related to Shu Wu's turning over of that batch of letters. Before reading this batch of letters, for more than ten years, in areas under GMD's control, Hong Kong, as well as in postliberation Beijing, we had always believed that the argument with Hu was simply a difference of opinion about literature and art theory and that we were identical politically. . . . Neither had Chairman Mao regarded him as counterrevolutionary until Shu Wu handed over Hu's letters. He had only declared Hu's thinking to be anti-Party and anti-Marxist. Our criticism was limited to the ideological field. However, [the Hu letters] provoked Chairman Mao's suspicions and indignation. I believe the letters were detrimental and contributed to Mao's determination to brand the Hu small group as a 'counterrevolutionary group.' " Lin, "The Ins and Outs of the Hu Incident," 27.

70. See Lin, "The Ins and Outs of the Hu Incident," 25.

71. Ba Jin, "Remembering Hu Feng 怀念胡风," in *Free Thoughts: A Collection of Untitled Essays* 随想录: 无题集 (Beijing: Renmin wenxue chubanshe, 2000), 746–747.

EPILOGUE

1. Raymond Williams, "Alignment and Commitment," in *Marxism and Literature* (Oxford: Oxford University Press, 1977), 200.

2. In the foreword to Liu Binyan's *China's Crisis, China's Hope*, Merle Goldman regarded Liu as "the conscience of China." The CCP expelled Liu in 1957 only to rehabilitate him in 1979, after having imprisoned and exiled him for twenty-two years. In his capacity as "special correspondent" for the *People's Daily* between 1979 and 1987, he published a series of "exposés," investigative essays exposing the CCP's "corrupt practices and suppression of the people's rights." This led to Liu's loss of Party membership for the second time. He left the PRC for the United States in March 1988. See Merle Goldman, foreword to *China's Crisis, China's Hope*, by Liu Binyan, trans. Howard Goldblatt (Cambridge, MA: Harvard University Press, 1990), vii–xii. See also Harrison E. Salisbury's chapter on Liu in *Heroes of My Time* (New York: Walker and Company, 1993), 163–172. Goldman's use of the phrase "the conscience of China" to describe Liu reminded me of the Dreyfus Affair that took place in France in the late nineteenth century. In January 1898, Émile Zola (1840–1902) published an open letter titled "J'accuse" in a newspaper, protesting against the French police's infringement of justice in the Dreyfus Affair. Zola's intervention, which led to worldwide condemnation of French anti-Semitism, evidenced "a moment in the conscience of humanity." As Zola's letter became a manifestation of the French intellectuals' new power in shaping public opinion, critics referred to those who defended Dreyfus as "public intellectuals." See Habermas, *The New Conservatism: Cultural Criticism and the Historians' Debate*, ed. and trans. Shierry Weber Nicholsen (Cambridge, MA: MIT Press, 1990), 72–73.

3. Zeng Huiyan, "A Special Birthday Party: Celebrating Liu Binyan's 80th Birthday and 65th Anniversary of Literary Career—個溫馨特別的祝壽會: 慶祝劉賓雁80壽辰暨文學寫作65周年," *World Journal* 世界週刊, March 13, 2005. Unfortunately, this has not happened. In place of this hoped-for statue is the English PEN Award won by Gregor Benton for his English translation of Mei Zhi's memoir.

4. Wang Wenzheng, "Do Not Forget Him—'A Comrade from Suzhou': The Fiftieth Anniversary of the Case of the 'Hu Counterrevolutionary Clique' 别忘记了他: 苏州一同志—〈胡风反革命集团〉案五十年祭," a transcript written by Shen Guofan, *Ming Pao Monthly* 明报月刊, August 2005, 104. Elsewhere, at a conference jointly organized by the Literature Division of the Academy of Social Sciences and the editors of the *Literature Review* in 1988, Liu Zaifu talked about Hu in similar terms. After asserting Hu's achievement in literary criticism and literature, Liu said, "Hu's problem is not a personal one. It is rooted in the development of socialist literature and art in China. . . . The Hu Incident has affected at least two generations of Chinese writers and intellectuals . . . and their attitude toward culture." Liu's speech was first published in the *Literary Gazette*, July 16, 1988. The papers delivered at the conference were collected in no. 5 of the *Literature Review* (1988) under the title "Reconsidering Hu's Thought on Literature and Art 关于胡风文艺思想的反思."

5. Sheila Melvin, "In Praise of Hu Feng," Caixin Online, December 12, 2014. http://english.caixin.com/2014-12-26/100768519.html.

6. Blackmur, "The Critic's Job of Work," 372–395.

7. Blackmur, "The Critic's Job of Work," 372.

8. Edward W. Said, *Representations of the Intellectual* (New York: Knopf Doubleday, 2012), 98.

9. Leszek Kolakowski, "The Concept of the Left," in *Toward a Marxist Humanism: Essays on the Left Today*, trans. Jane Zielonko Peel (New York: Grove Press, 1968), 71.

10. See Mao Zedong, "Sixty Points on Working Methods—A Draft Resolution from the Office of the Centre of the CPC, January 31, 1958," in vol. 8 of *Selected Works of Mao Tse-tung*, https://www.marxists.org/reference/archive/mao/selected-works/volume-8/mswv8_05.htm.

11. Mao, "Sixty Points on Working Methods."

12. Lu, "Hu Feng and Me," 574.

13. The Chinese here is *pengdang* 朋党, which refers to political coalitions in traditional China among officials who shared a common background or political viewpoint. The term is derived from *The Book of Warring States* 战国策, in the section on the state of Zhao.

14. The term *stalls*, originally *tanzi* 摊子 in Chinese, indicates the appearance of factions in public. The term, which originated from the practice of hawkers displaying their merchandise on the ground along much-traveled pedestrian thoroughfares, often has a derogatory connotation.

15. The "question of the *Literary Gazette*" refers to the uproar that the editorial collective of the *Literary Gazette* caused in the controversy over the interpretation of the novel *The Dream of the Red Chamber*. From the end of October to the beginning of December 1954, the presidiums of the China Federation of Literary and Art Circles and the Writers Union held enlarged joint meetings to examine the mistakes of the *Literary Gazette* in suppressing criticism by young writers. Hu believed that his opportunity had come and he began attacking Zhou in the meetings.

16. Mao Zedong, "Editor's Comment to the Second Collection of Materials on the Hu Counterrevolutionary Clique," 568.

17. Zhenyin Lu 鲁贞银, "Record of Conversations concerning 'Hu Feng's Editorial Activities and Editorial Thought': Conversations with Niu Han, Lu Yuan, Geng Yong, Luo Luo, Shu Wu 关于〈胡风编辑活动和编辑思想〉访谈录: 访谈牛汉, 绿原, 耿庸, 罗洛, 舒芜," *Historical Data of New Literature*, no. 4 (1999): 147–172.

18. See Geng Yong, "Memories Bristling with Profusions and Complications," in vol. 2 of *Hu Feng in My Eyes*, ed. Xiaofeng, 642.

19. Lu, "Hu Feng and Me," 595.

20. Dialectics, as conceptualized by Lenin when he was reading chapter 3 ("The Absolute Idea") of Hegel's *The Science of Logic*, is the study of "the identity of opposites," "the recognition (discovery) of the contradictory, *mutually exclusive*, opposite tendencies in all phenomena and processes of nature (including mind and society). . . . The splitting of a single whole and the cognition of its contradictory parts . . . is the *essence* . . . of dialectics. . . . In social science: the class struggle."

See vol. 38 of V. I. Lenin, *Collected Works*, 45 vols. (Moscow: Foreign Languages Publication House, 1960–70), 221–222 (emphasis in original).

21. For example, from Yang Tianzhen, a Chinese Communist and the closest of friends who led Hu to participate in underground revolutionary activities, which made him feel like "a girl falling in love for the first time." From Yang, Hu learned that truth could be neither compromised by friendship nor regarded in a nonserious manner. See Hu, "Requiem," 189–190.

22. Hu, "Annotations of 'Passenger,' " 591.

23. Hu, afterword to *Collected Critical Essays* by Hu Feng, 623 (my emphasis).

24. Jean-Paul Sartre, *Between Existentialism and Marxism* (London: New Left Books, 1974), 13–14.

25. Hu, "Man and Poet," 74.

26. Hu, "Man and Poet," 74.

27. The line "I am not guilty; yet I carry the guilt" described Ah-long's state of mind when he decided to join the Chinese Revolution in the role of a revolutionary, an outlaw living under the rule of the GMD.

28. Ah-long, "Leaving the Country 去国" (May 2, 1947)," in *White Flower*, ed. Lu Yuan and Niu Han, 27–28.

29. Edward W. Said, "Presidential Address 1999: Humanism and Heroism," *PMLA* 115, no. 3 (May 2000): 290.

30. Said, "Presidential Address 1999," 290.

31. Said, "Presidential Address 1999," 287.

32. Said, "Presidential Address 1999," 290.

33. Said, "Presidential Address 1999," 290.

BIBLIOGRAPHY

WORKS BY HU FENG

Collected Criticism of Hu Feng 胡风评论集. 3 vols. Beijing: Renmin wenxue chubanshe, 1984–85.

Collected Letters of Hu Feng 胡风书信集. Edited by Xiao Feng. Tianjin: Baihua wenyi chubanshe, 1989.

Collected Essays of Hu Feng 胡风杂文集. Beijing: Shenghuo, dushu, xinzhi sanlianshudian, 1987.

Collected Translations of Hu Feng 胡风译文集. Beijing: Renmin wenxue chubanshe, 1986.

Complete Poems of Hu Feng 胡风诗全编. Edited by Niuhan and Lu Yuan. Hangzhou: Zhejiang wenyi chubanshe, 1992.

Complete Works of Hu Feng 胡风全集 (abbreviated to *HFQJ* throughout). 10 vols. Wuhan: Hubei People's Publishing House, 1999.

Hu Feng and Lu Ling's Literary Correspondence 胡风路翎文学书简. Edited by Xiao Feng. Hefei: Anhui wenyi chubanshe, 1994.

Hu Feng on Lu Xun 胡风论鲁迅. Edited by Chen Mingshu and Liu Xiangfa. Zhengzhou: Huanghe wenyi chubanshe, 1985.

Hu Feng on Poetry 胡风论诗. Guangzhou: Huacheng chubanshe, 1988.

Hu Feng's Poetry 胡风的诗. Edited by Xiao Feng. Beijing: Zhongguo wenlian chubangongsi, 1987.

A Memoir of Hu Feng 胡风回忆录. Beijing: Renminwenxue chubanshe, 1993.

Posthumous Works of Hu Feng 胡风遗稿. Jinan: Shandong youyi chubanshe, 1998.

Selected Letters of Hu Feng 胡风书话. Selected by Xiao Feng. Edited by Jiang Deming. Beijing: Beijing chubanshe, 1998.

Selected Works of Hu Feng 胡风选集. Edited by Xiao Feng. 2 vols. Chengdu: Sichuan People's Publishing House, 1996.

Selected Works of Hu Feng in His Late Years 胡风晚年作品选. Guilin: Lijiang chubanshe, 1987.

BIOGRAPHIES OF HU FENG

Boorman, Howard L. *Biographical Dictionary of Republican China*. Vol. 2, 155–158. Vol. 4, 210–211. New York: Columbia University Press, 1967.

Dai Guangzhong 戴光中. *A Biography of Hu Feng* 胡风传. Yinchuan: Linxia People's Publishing House, 1994.

Fang Han 方翰 [He Dinghua 何定华]. "Hu Feng in His Adolescence 胡风的青少年时期." *Hubei Writers*, no. 1 (1987): 33–54.

Gibbs, Donald A., ed. "Dissonant Voices in Chinese Literature: Hu Feng." *Chinese Studies in Literature*, no. 1 (1979–80): 3–89.

Klein, Donald W., and Anne B. Clark, eds. *Biographic Dictionary of Chinese Communism 1921–1965*. 2 vols. Vol. 1, 377–379. Cambridge, MA: Harvard University Press, 1971.

Li Hui 李辉. *The Unjust Case of the Hu-Feng Clique from the Beginning to the End* 胡风集团冤案始末. Hong Kong: Xiangjiang, 1989.

Lin Xi 林希. *Looting the White Flower* 白色花劫. Wuhan: Changjiang wenyi chubanshe, 1999.

Liu Xuewei 刘雪苇. "Details of My Relation with Hu Feng 我和胡风关系的始末." In vol. 1 of *Hu Feng in My Eyes: Thirty-Seven Reminiscences of the Hu-Feng Incident* 我与胡风：胡风事件三十七人回忆, edited by Xiao Feng, 64–73. 2 vols. Yinchuan: Ningxia People's Publishing House, 1993.

Lu Xin 路莘. *Thirty Years [for] Three-Hundred Thousand Words: A Side Account of the "Hu Feng Case" 1955–1985* 三十万言*30*年：*1955–1985* "胡风案" 侧记. Yinchuan: Ningxia People's Publishing House, 2007.

Ma Tiji 马蹄疾. *A Biography of Hu Feng* 胡风传. Chengdu: Sichuan remin chubanshe, 1989.

Mei Zhi 梅志. *An Account of Keeping a Prisoner Company* 伴囚记. Beijing: Gongren chubanshe, 1988.

———. 1989. *Past as Smoke: A Memoir of Hu Feng's Prison Years* 往事如烟：胡风沉冤录. Beijing: Ke xue.

———. 1998. *A Biography of Hu Feng* 胡风传. Beijing: Beijing shiyue wenyi chubanshe.

———. 2013. *F: Hu Feng's Prison Years*. Edited and translated by Gregor Benton. London: Verso.

Peng Xiaolin 彭小莲, and S. Louisa Wei, directors. *Storm under the Sun* 红日风暴, a documentary film. World Distribution: Blue Queen Cultural Communication, 2009.

Qian Yanbin 钱雁宾. "Anecdotes of Hu Feng's Adolescent Life 胡风的青少年时期生活琐记." *Hubei Writers*, no. 3 (1989).

Wan Jiaji 万家骥, and Zhao Jinzhong 赵金钟. *A Critical Biography of Hu Feng* 胡风评传. Chongqing: Chongqing chubanshe, 2001.

Xi Chun 奚纯. "The Publication of the First Collection of Materials on Hu Feng 第一批胡风材料发表前后," an interview with Shu Wu. In vol. 1 of *Celebrities and Unjust Cases: True Accounts of Literary Circles in China* 名人与冤案－中国文坛档案实录, edited by Hu Ping and Xiao Shan, 264–287. 3 vols. Beijing: Qunzhong chubanshe, 1998.

Xiao Feng 晓风, ed. *Hu Feng in My Eyes: Thirty-Seven Reminiscences of the Hu-Feng Incident* 我与胡风: 胡风事件三十七人回忆. 2 vols. Yinchuan: Ningxia People's Publishing House, 1993.

———. 1996. *Forever Unregretful: A Biography of Hu Feng* 九死未悔: 胡风传. Taipai: Yeqiang.

———. 2001. Xiao Shan 晓山, and Xiao Gu 晓谷. *My Father Hu Feng* 我的父亲胡风. Shenyang: Chunfeng wenyi chubanshe.

PERIODICALS

The Compiled Volume of Les Contemporains 现代合订本. 8 vols. Shanghai: Shanghai shudian, 1984.

China Youth 中国青年. Edited by the League of Chinese Communist Youth 共青团中央, 1923–.

Creation Monthly 创造月刊. Shanghai: Chuangzaoshe chubanbu, 1926–1928.

Historical Data of New Literature 新文学史料. Beijing: Renmin wenxue chubanshe, 1994.

Hubei Writers 湖北作家论丛. (June 1987–).

Les Contemporains 现代. Shanghai, May 1932–May 1935.

Liberation Daily 解放日报. Shanghai: Jiefang ribao she, 1949–.

Literary Battlefield 文艺阵地. (April 1938–November 1942). Shanghai: Shanghai shudian, 1983.

Literary Criticism 文学评论. Beijing: Renmin wenxue chubanshe, 1959–.

Literature and Art for the Masses 大众文艺丛刊. Hong Kong: Dazhong wenyi congkan she, March–July 1948.

The Literary Events I Experienced 我亲历的文坛往事. Beijing: Renmin wenxue chubanshe, 2004.

Material for Lu Xun Research 鲁迅研究资料. Tianjin: Tianjin People's Publishing House, 1979–.

People's Daily 人民日报, overseas edition. Beijing: Renminribao chubanshe, 1985–.

The Pioneer 先驱. Shanghai, January 1922–August 1923.

Publication Archives 出版史料. Shanghai: Xuelin chubanshe, 1982–.

Records of the National Congress of Literary and Art Workers 中华全国文学艺术工作者代表大会纪念文集. Beijing: Xinhua shudian, 1950.

Research on Mao Zedong Thought 毛泽东思想研究. Beijing: Zhongguo renmin daxue shubao ziliao zhongxin, 1987–2000.

Times Literary Supplement (TLS). London: TLS Education.
Wenhui Post 文汇报. Shanghai: Wenhuibao she, 1938–.

WORKS CITED

A Compilation of Critical Essays on Hu Feng's Literary Thought 胡风文艺思想批判论文汇集. 6 vols. Beijing: Zuojia, 1955–.

Adorno, Theodor W. *Philosophy of Modern Music*. New York: Seabury Press, 1973.

———. 1998. *Critical Models: Interventions and Catchwords*. Translated by Henry W. Pickford. New York: Columbia University Press, 1998.

Ah-long 阿龙. "White Flower 白色花" (September 9, 1944). In *White Flower* 白色花, edited by Lu Yuan and Niu Han, 1944, 21.

———. 1947. "Leaving the Country 去国" (May 2, 1947). In *White Flower* 白色花, edited by Lu Yuan and Niu Han, 27–28.

Ai Keyen 艾克恩. "The Historical Record of the Yan'an Literary Rectification Campaign 延安文艺运动纪实." *Historical Data of New Literature*, no. 3 (1992): 193–222.

Ai Qing 艾青. "A Few Comments on Contemporary Literature and Art 我对于目前文艺上几个文题的意见," a speech first given at the "Yan'an Forum" on April 23, 1942. *Liberation Daily*, May 15, 1942.

———. 1952. "Beggar 乞丐." In *Selected Works of Ai Qing* 艾青选集, 84–85. Beijing: Kaiming shudian.

Alber, Charles J. *Embracing the Lie: Ding Ling and the Politics of Literature in the People's Republic of China*. Westport, CT: Praeger, 2004.

Anderson, Marston. *The Limits of Realism: Chinese Fiction in the Revolutionary Period*. Berkeley: University of California Press, 1990.

Apter, David, and Tony Saich. *Revolutionary Discourse in Mao's Republic*. Cambridge, MA: Harvard University Press, 1994.

Archive Research Office, CCP's Central Committee 中共中央文献研究室, ed. *Selected Important Documents of the PRC* 建国以来重要文献选编. Beijing: Zhongyang wenxian chubanshe, 1993.

Arendt, Hannah. "Martin Heidegger at Eighty." In *Heidegger and Modern Philosophy*, edited by M. Murray, 295–298. New Haven, CT: Yale University Press, 1978.

———. 1981. *The Life of the Mind*. Vols. 1–2. New York: Harcourt.

———. 1993. Preface to *Between Past and Future: Eight Exercises in Political Thought*. Harmondsworth, Middlesex: Penguin.

Auerbach, Erich. "Philology and Weltliteratur." Translated by Maire and Edward Said. *Centennial Review* 13, no. 1 (Winter 1969): 1–17.

Ba Jin 巴金. "My Self-Defense 我的自辩," first published in *Les Contemporains* 2, no. 5 (March 1933). In *The Compiled Volume of Les Contemporains*, 706–746.

———. I 2000. "Remembering Hu Feng 怀念胡风," first published in *Dagong bao* 大公报, Hong Kong, September 21–28, 1986. In *Free Thoughts* 随想录, 732–747. Beijing: Renminwenxue chubanshe.

Ba Ren 巴人. *Treatise on Literary Theory* 文学论稿. Shanghai: Xinwenyi chubanshe, 1954.

Bakhtin, Mikhail. *The Dialogic Imagination*. Edited by Michael Holquist, translated by Caryl Emerson and Michael Holquist. Austin: University of Texas, 1981.

Barlow, Tani E., ed. *New Asian Marxisms*. Durham, NC: Duke University Press, 2002.

Bellow, Saul. *To Jerusalem and Back: A Personal Account*. New York: Penguin, [1976] 1998.

Benenson, Peter. *Persecution 1961*. Harmondsworth, Middlesex: Penguin, 1961.

Benton, Gregor. "The Yenan Literary Opposition." *New Left Review*, no. 92 (July–August 1975): 93–106.

———. 1996. *China's Urban Revolutionaries: Explorations in the History of Chinese Trotskyism, 1921–1952*. Atlantic Highlands, NJ: Humanities Press.

Berman, Paul. *Power and the Idealists*. New York: W. W. Norton, 2005.

Berninghausen, John, and Ted Huters, eds. *Revolutionary Literature in China: An Anthology*. White Plains, NY: M. E. Sharpe, 1976.

Birch, Cyril. "Literature under Communism." Chapter 11 in vol. 15 of *The Cambridge History of China: The People's Republic, Part 2: Revolutions within the Chinese Revolution 1966–1982*, edited by Roderick MacFarquhar, John K. Fairbank, and Denis Twitchett, 743–814. Cambridge: Cambridge University Press, 1991.

Blackmur, R. P. *Language as Gesture: Essays in Poetry*. New York: Columbia University Press, 1981.

Bodde, Derk. *Peking Diary: A Year of Revolution*. New York: Henry Schuman, 1950.

Børdahl, Vibeke. *Along the Broad Road of Realism: Qin Zhaoyang's World of Fiction*. London: Curzon Press, 1990.

Bowie, Robert R., and John K. Fairbank, eds. and trans. *Communist China 1955–1959: Policy Documents with Analysis*. Cambridge, MA: Harvard University Press, 1962.

Breines, Paul. "Marxism, Romanticism, and the Case of Georg Lukács: Notes on Some Recent Sources and Situations." *Studies in Romanticism* 16, no. 4 (Fall 1977): 473–489.

Butler, Marilyn. *Romantics, Rebels, and Reactionaries: English Literature and Its Background 1760–1830*. Oxford: Oxford University Press, 1981.

Camus, Albert. *L'Homme révolté*. Paris: Gallimard, Folio, 1951.

Cao Guofei 曹国辉. "The First Edition of the 'Talks' and Yi Da 〈在延安文艺座谈会上的讲话〉第一个版本与尹达." *Publication Archives*, no. 1 (2004): 42–43.

Central Studies Committee, CCP's Central Committee 中央总学委. "Instruction on Studies of Mao Zedong's 'Talks at the Yan'an Forum on Literature and Art'

中央总学委关于学习毛泽东〈在延安文艺座谈会上的讲话〉的通知." *Liberation Daily*, October 22, 1943.

Chang Hao 张灏. *Liang Qichao and Intellectual Transition in China, 1890–1907* 梁启超与中国思想的过渡, *1890–1907*. Nanjing: Jiangsu People's Publishing House, 1993.

Cheek, Timothy. "The Fading of Wild Lilies: Wang Shiwei and Mao Zedong's Yan'an Talks in the First CPC Rectification Movement." *Australian Journal of Chinese Affairs*, no. 11 (January 1984): 25–38.

Chen Baida 陈百达. "After Wang Shiwei's 'A Short Discussion of National Forms' 写在王实味同志〈文艺的民族形式短论〉之后." *Liberation Daily*, July 3 and July 4, 1942.

Chen Duxiu 陈独秀. "On Literary Revolution 文学革命论," first published in *New Youth* 新青年 2, no. 6 (February 1, 1917): 1–4. In vol. 2 of *New Youth*, 487–490. 14 vols. Tokyo: Daian, 1962.

Chen Qingquan 陳清泉, and Song Guangwei 宋廣渭. *A Biography of Lu Dingyi* 陆定一传. Beijing: Zhonggong dangshi chubanshe, 1999.

Chen Sihe 陈思和. "The Value System of Contemporary Intellectuals 当代知识分子的价值规范." *Literature in Shanghai* 上海文学 (July 1993): 64–71.

Chen Xiaoquan 陈孝全. *A Biography of Zhu Ziqing* 朱自清传. Beijing: Beijing shiyue wenyi chubanshe, 1991.

Chen Xuezhao 陈学昭. "Accounts of My Two Trips to Yan'an [continued] 两次去延安的前后[续]." *Historical Data of New Literature*, no. 2 (1980): 49–64.

Cheng Ching-mao. "The Impact of Japanese Literary Trends on Modern Chinese Writers." In *Modern Chinese Literature in the May Fourth Era*, edited by by Merle Goldman, 63–88. Cambridge, MA: Harvard University Press, 1977.

Cheng Fangwu 成仿吾. "From a Literary Revolution to a Revolutionary Literature 从文学革命到革命文学." *Creation Monthly* 1, no. 9 (February 1928). In *Revolutionary Literature in China: An Anthology*, edited by John Berninghausen and Ted Huters, translated by Michael Gotz, 33–36. White Plains, NY: M. E. Sharpe, 1976.

Chow, Rey. "Pedagogy, Trust, Chinese Intellectuals in the 1990s—Fragments of a Post-Catastrophic Discourse." *Dialectical Anthropology*, no. 16 (1991): 191–207.

Christenson, Reo et al. *Ideologies and Modern Politics*. London: Nelson, 1972.

Cotton, James. "Intellectuals as a Group in the Chinese Political Process." In *Groups and Politics in the People's Republic of China*, edited by David S. G. Goodman, 176–195. Cardiff: University College Cardiff Press, 1984.

Dai Guangzhong 戴光中. *A Biography of Hu Feng* 胡风传. Yinchuan: Linxia renmin, 1994.

Dai, Qing. *Wang Shiwei and "Wild Lilies": Rectification and Purges in the Chinese Communist Party, 1942–1944*. Edited by David E. Apter and Timothy Cheek, translated by Nancy Liu and Lawrence R. Sullivan. Armonk, NY: M. E. Sharpe, 1994.

Dai Ying 代英. "Literature and Revolution 文学与革命." *China Youth*, no. 31 (May 1924).

Dante, Alighieri. *The Divine Comedy: Purgatorio*. Translated by Charles S. Singleton. Princeton, NJ: Princeton University Press, 1989–91.

Denton, Kirk A., ed. *Modern Chinese Literary Thought: Writings on Literature 1893–1945*. Stanford, CA: Stanford University Press, 1996.

———. 1998. *The Problematic of Self in Modern Chinese Literature: Hu Feng and Lu Ling*. Stanford, CA: Stanford University Press.

———. 2003. "Literature and Politics: Mao Zedong's 'Talks at the Yan'an Forum on Art and Literature.'" In *The Columbia Companion to Modern East Asia Literature*, edited by Joshua S. Mostow, 463–469. New York: Columbia University Press.

———. 2008. "The Hu Feng Group: Genealogy of a Literary School." In *Literary Societies of Republican China*, edited by Kirk A. Denton and Michel Hockx, 413–466. Lanham, MD: Lexington Books.

Denton, Kirk A., and Michel Hockx, eds. *Literary Societies of Republican China*. Lanham, MD: Lexington Books, 2008.

Dirlik, Arif. "Revolutionary Hegemony and the Language of the Revolution: Chinese Socialism between Present and Future." In *Marxism and the Chinese Experience*, edited by Arif Dirlik and Maurice Meisner, 27–39. Armonk, NY: M. E. Sharpe, 1989.

———. 1991. *Anarchism in the Chinese Revolution*. Berkeley: University of California Press.

———. 1996. "Mao Zedong and Chinese Marxism." In *Marxism beyond Marxism*, edited by Saree Makdisi, Cesare Casarino, and Rebecca Karl, 119–148. New York: Routledge.

Dirlik, Arif, and Maurice Meisner, eds. *Marxism and the Chinese Experience*. Armonk, NY: M. E. Sharpe, 1989.

Dittmer, Lowell. "Thought Reform and Cultural Revolution: An Analysis of the Symbolism of Chinese Polemics." *American Political Science Review* 71, no. 1 (March 1977): 67–85.

Eastman, Max. *Artists in Uniform: A Study of Literature and Bureaucratism*. London: George Allen and Unwin, 1934.

Editorial Board of the *People's Daily*, ed. *Collection of Materials on the Hu-Feng Counterrevolutionary Clique* 关于胡风反革命集团的材料. Beijing: People's Publishing House, 1955.

Egan, Michael. "Yu Dafu and the Transition to Modern Chinese Literature." In *Modern Chinese Literature in the May Fourth Era*, edited by Merle Goldman, 309–324. Cambridge, MA: Harvard University Press, 1977.

Endrey, Andrew. "Hu Feng: Return of the Counter-Revolutionary." *Australian Journal of Chinese Affairs*, no. 5 (January 1981): 73–90.

Engels, Frederick. "The Role of Force in History." In vol. 26 of *Marx and Engels Collected Works*, 455–510. Charlottesville, VA: InteLex Corp., [1895] 2001.

Eyerman, Ron. *Between Culture and Politics: Intellectuals in Modern Society*. Cambridge: Polity Press, 1994.

Fairbank, John K. *Chinabound: A Fifty-Year Memoir*. New York: Harper and Row, 1982.

Fairbank, John K., Edwin O. Reischauer, and Albert Craig. *East Asia: Tradition and Transformation*. Boston: Houghton Mifflin, 1965.

Fan Jiyan 范际燕, and Qian Wenliang 钱文亮. *Hu Feng: His Views on Culture and Literature* 胡风论: 对胡风的文化与文学阐释. Wuhan: Hubei People's Publishing House, 1999.

Fan Zhongyan 范仲淹. *An Account of Yueyang Tower* 岳阳楼记. Hong Kong: Commercial Press, 2002.

Fang Fanren 方凡人. *A Biography of Ba Ren* 巴人传. Changsha: Hunan wenyi chubanshe, 1997.

Fang Han 方翰 [He Dinghua 何定华]. "Hu Feng in His Adolescence 胡风的青少年时期." *Hubei Writers*, no. 1 (1987): 33–54.

Feis, Herbert. *The China Tangle: The American Effort in China from Pearl Harbor to the Marshall Mission*. Princeton, NJ: Princeton University Press, 1953.

Feng, Chi-tsai. *Ten Years of Madness: Oral Histories of China's Cultural Revolution*. San Francisco: China Books, 1996.

Feng Guanglian 冯光廉, and Liu Zengren 刘增人, eds. *The History of the Development of Chinese New Literature* 中国新文学发展史. Beijing: Renminwenxue chubanshe, [1991] 1994.

Feng Xuefeng 冯雪峰. "Concerning the 1936 Activities of Zhou Yang and Others and the 'Mass Literature in the National Revolutionary War' Slogan Put Forth by Lu Xun 有关一九三六年周扬等人的行动以及鲁迅提出〈民族革命战争大众文学〉口号的经过." *Historical Data of New Literature*, no. 2 (1979): 247–258.

———. 1980. "Feng Xuefeng Talks about the Left-league 冯雪峰谈左联." Transcript edited by Feng Xiaxiong. *Historical Data of New Literature*, no. 1: 1–11.

Feuerwerker, Yi-tsi. *Ideology, Power, Text: Self-Representation and the Peasant "Other" in Modern Chinese Literature*. Stanford, CA: Stanford University Press, 1998.

Figes, Orlando. *A People's Tragedy: The Russian Revolution, 1891–1924*. London: Jonathan Cape, 1996.

FitzGerald, Carolyn. *Fragmenting Modernisms: Chinese Wartime Literature, Art, and Film, 1937–49*. Leiden: Brill, 2013.

Fokkema, D. K. *Literary Doctrine in China and Soviet Influence 1956–1960*. The Hague: Mouton, 1965.

Foucault, Michel. "Truth and Power." In vol. 3 of *Essential Works of Foucault 1954–1984: Power*, edited by James D. Faubion, translated by Robert Hurley et al., 111–133. New York: New Press, [1979] 2000.

———. 1982. "The Subject and Power." *Critical Inquiry* 8, no. 4 (Summer): 777–795.

———. 2003. *"Society Must Be Defended": Lectures at the College de France, 1975–1976*, edited by Mauro Bertani and Alessandro Fontana, translated by David Macey. New York: Picador.

Froissart, Chloé. "Xu Youyu, or How to Write the History of the Cultural Revolution So as to Set China on the Right Future Path?" *China Perspectives*, no. 42 (July–August 2002): 15–23.

Fromm, Erich. *Beyond the Chains of Illusion: My Encounter with Marx and Freud*. New York: Continuum, 2001.

Fu, Qilin. "The Reception of Mao's 'Talks at the Yan'an Forum on Literature and Art' in English-Language Scholarship." *CLCWeb: Comparative Literature and Culture* 17.1 (2015). http://dx.doi.org/10.7771/1481-4374.2567.

Gálik, Marián. *Mao Tun and Modern Chinese Literary Criticism*. Wiesbaden: Franz Steiner Verlag, 1969.

Gao Hua 高华. *The Rise of the Red Sun: The Cause and Effect of the Rectification Movement in Yan'an* 红太阳是怎样升起的: 延安整风运动的来龙去脉. Xianggang: Zhongwen daxue chubanshe, 2000.

Geng Yong 耿庸. "Memories Bristling with Profusions and Complications 枝蔓丛丛的回忆." In vol. 2 of *Hu Feng in My Eyes: Thirty-Seven Reminiscences of the Hu-Feng Incident* 我与胡风: 胡风事件三十七人回忆, edited by Xiao Feng, 634–663. 2 vols. Yinchuan: Ningxia People's Publishing House, 1993.

Geuss, Raymond. "Dialectics and the Revolutionary Impulse." In *The Cambridge Companion to Critical Theory*, edited by Fred Rush, 103–138. Cambridge: Cambridge University Press, 2004.

Gogol, Nikolai Vasilievich. *Dead Souls*. Translated by George Reavey. London: Hamish Hamilton, 1948.

Goldman, Merle. "Hu Feng's Conflict with the Communist Literary Authorities." *Harvard Papers on China*, no. 11 (1957): 149–191. Reprinted in the *China Quarterly*, no. 12 (December 1962): 102–138.

———. 1967. *Literary Dissent in Communist China*. Cambridge, MA: Harvard University Press.

———. 1977. ed. *Modern Chinese Literature in the May Fourth Era*. Cambridge, MA: Harvard University Press.

———. 1990. Foreword to *China's Crisis, China's Hope*, by Liu Binyan. Translated by Howard Goldblatt. Cambridge, MA: Harvard University Press.

Goldman, Merle, Timothy Cheek, and Carol Lee Hamrin, eds. *China's Intellectuals and the State: In Search of a New Relationship*. Cambridge, MA: Council on East Asian Studies, Harvard University, 1987.

Goldman, Merle, and Leo Ou-fan Lee, eds. *An Intellectual History of Modern China*. Cambridge: Cambridge University Press, 2002.

Goodman, David S. G. *Groups and Politics in the People's Republic of China*. Cardiff: University College Cardiff Press, 1984.

Gorky, Maxim. "Anton Chekhov: Fragments of Recollections" (1899). In *Reminiscences of Anton Chekhov, Maxim Gorky, Alexander Kuprin, and I. A. Bunin*, translated by by S. S. Koteliansky and Leonard Woolf. New York: B. W. Huebsch, 1921. http://www.eldritchpress.org/ac/gorky.htm.

Gramsci, Antonio. *Selections from the Prison Notebooks of Antonio Gramsci*. Edited and translated by Quintin Hoare and Geoffrey Nowell Smith. London: Lawrence and Wishart, 1971.

Grieder, Jerome B. *Intellectuals and the State in Modern China: A Narrative History*. New York: Free Press, 1981.

Gruner, Fritz. "Some Remarks on the Cultural-Political Significance of the Chinese League of Left-Wing Writers at the Beginning of the 1930s." In *Search for Identity: Modern Literature and the Creative Arts in Asia*, edited by A. R. Davis, 203–244. Sydney: Angus and Robertson, 1974.

Guo Moruo 郭沫若. "The Social Mission of Literature 文艺之社会使命" (1924). In vol. 10 of *Literary Works of Guo Moruo*, 83–88. 17 vols. Xianggang: Sanlian shudian, 1957–63.

———. 1926. "Revolution and Literature 革命与文学," first published in *Creation Monthly* (May 1926). In vol. 10 of *Literary Works of Guo Moruo*, 312–323. 17 vols. Xianggang: Sanlian shudian, 1957–63.

———. 1928. "The Heroic Tree 英雄树," first published in *Creation Monthly*, no. 1 (1928). In vol. 10 of *Literary Works of Guo Moruo*, 324–330. 17 vols. Xianggang: Sanlian shudian, 1957–63.

———. 1936. "An Inspection of the Military Exercise 搜苗的检阅." *The Literary World* 文学界 1, no. 4 (September 10).

———. 1940. "Discussing the Problem of 'National Forms' 民族形式〈商兑〉," first published in *Dagong bao*, June 9, 10, 1940. In vol. 19 of *Complete Works of Guo Moruo*, 31–47. Beijing: Renmin wenxue chubanshe, 1982–92.

———. 1957–. *Literary Works of Guo Moruo* 沫若文集. 17 vols. Xianggang: Sanlian shudian, 1957–63.

———. 1982–. *Complete Works of Guo Moruo* 郭沫若全集. Beijing: Renmin wenxue chubanshe, 1982–92.

Guo Yushi. "Revision of the 'Talks': From the First Edition to the Standard Edition 谈〈在延安文艺座谈会上的讲话〉从原本到今本的增删修改." *Theoretical Studies in Literature and Art* 文艺理论研究, no. 4 (1992): 77–80.

Habermas, Jürgen. *The Theory of Communicative Action: Reason and Rationalization of Society*. Translated by Thomas McCarthy. Boston: Beacon Press, 1984.

———. 1989. *The Structural Transformation of the Public Sphere: An Enquiry into a Category of Bourgeois Society*. Translated by Thomas Burger. Cambridge, MA: MIT Press.

———. 1990. *The New Conservatism: Cultural Criticism and the Historians' Debate*. Edited and translated by Shierry Weber Nicholsen. Cambridge, MA: MIT Press.

Haft, Lloyd, ed. *A Selective Guide to Chinese Literature, 1900–1949: The Poem*. Vol. 3 of 4 vols. Leiden: E. J. Brill, 1989.

Hao, Zhidong. *Intellectuals at a Crossroads: The Changing Politics of China's Knowledge Workers*. Albany: State University of New York Press, 2003.

He, Henry Yuhuai. *Dictionary of the Political Thought of the People's Republic of China*. Armonk, NY: M. E. Sharpe, 2000.

He Qifang 何其芳. "An Ordinary Story 一个平常的故事." In vol. 2 of *The Collected Essays of He Qifang* 何其芳文集. 6 vols. Beijing: Renmin wenxue chubanshe, 1982.

———. 1949. "Preface to Realism 〈关于现实主义〉的序." In vol. 2 of *A Compilation of Critical Essays on Hu Feng's Literary Thought* 胡风文艺思想批判论文汇集, 22–48. 6 vols. Beijing: Zuojia, 1955–.

Herdan, Innes. *The Pen and the Sword: Literature and Revolution in Modern China*. London: Zed Books, 1992.

Ho Kan-chih 何干之. *A History of the Modern Chinese Revolution* 中国现代革命史. Translated by the English faculty of the Western Languages Department, Peking University. New York: AMS Press, [1959] 1979.

Hockx, Michel. "Review of *The Problematic of Self in Modern Chinese Literature*, by Kirk A. Denton." *China Quarterly*, no. 160 (December 1999): 1086–1088.

Hollander, Paul. *Political Pilgrims*. Lanham, MD: University Press of America, 1990.

Holm, David. "The Literary Rectification in Yan'an." In *Essays in Modern Chinese Literature and Literary Criticism: Papers of the Berlin Conference 1978*, 272–308. Bochum, West Germany: Studienverlag N. Brockmeyer, 1982.

Hong Zicheng 洪子诚. *History of Contemporary Chinese Literature* 中国当代文学史. Beijing: Beijing daxue chubanshe, 1999.

———. 2009. *History of Contemporary Chinese Literature*. Translated by Michael M. Day. Leiden: Brill.

Horkheimer, Max. "The Authoritarian State." In *The Essential Frankfurt School Reader*, edited by A. Arato and E. Gebhardt, 95–117. New York: Continuum, [1982] 1987.

Hoston, Germaine A. *The State, Identity, and the National Question in China and Japan*. Princeton, NJ: Princeton University Press, 1994.

Hsia, C. T. *A History of Modern Chinese Fiction*. New York: Columbia University Press, 1971.

———, ed. 1971. *Twentieth-Century Chinese Stories*. New York: Columbia University Press.

Hsia, T. A. *The Gate of Darkness: Studies on the Leftist Literary Movement in China*. Seattle: University of Washington Press, 1968.

Hu Ping 胡平, and Xiao Shan 晓山, eds. *Celebrities and Unjust Cases: True Accounts of Literary Circles in China* 名人与冤案－中国文坛档案实录. 3 vols. Beijing: Qunzhong chubanshe, 1998.

Hu Sheng 胡绳. "A Critique of Lu Ling's Short Stories 评路翎的短篇小说," first published in *Literature and Art for the Masses*, no. 1 (March 1948). In vol. 1 of *A Compilation of Critical Essays on Hu Feng's Literary Thought* 胡风文艺思想批判论文汇集, 96–115. 6 vols. Beijing: Zuojia, 1955–.

———. 1948. "The Development of Lu Xun Thought 鲁迅思想发展的道路," first published in *Literature and Art for the Masses*, no. 1 (March). In vol. 1 of *A Compilation of Critical Essays on Hu Feng's Literary Thought* 胡风文艺思想批判论文汇集, 116–135. 6 vols. Beijing: Zuojia, 1955–.

Hua, Shiping. "One Servant, Two Masters: The Dilemma of Chinese Establishment Intellectuals." *Modern China* 20, no. 1 (January 1944): 92–121.

Huang Changyong 黄昌勇. "Events before and after 'Wild Lilies' 〈野百合花〉 的前前后后." *Historical Data of New Literature*, no. 3 (2000): 42–57.

Huang Qiaosheng 黄乔生. *Lu Xun and Hu Feng* 鲁迅与胡风. Shijiazhuang: Hebei People's Publishing House, 2003.

Huters, Theodore D. "Hu and the Critical Legacy of Lu Xun." In *Lu Xun and His Legacy*, edited by Leo Ou-fan Lee, 129–152. Berkeley: University of California Press, 1985.

Imai, Tadashi, dir. *Takiji Kobayashi: The Life of a Communist Writer*. 1 hr. 59 min. Japan: Takiji, 1974.

James, Crowley. *Japan's Quest for Autonomy: National Security and Foreign Policy, 1930–1938*. Princeton, NJ: Princeton University Press, 1966.

Jameson, Fredric. *Marxism and Form: Twentieth-Century Dialectical Theories of Literature*. Princeton, NJ: Princeton University Press, 1971.

———. 1986. "Third-World Literature in the Era of Multinational Capitalism." *Social Text*, no. 15 (Autumn): 65–88.

Ji Xianlin 季羡林, Niu Han 牛汉, and Deng Jiuping 邓九平, eds. *Memories Bristling with Profusions and Complications* 枝蔓丛丛的回忆. Beijing: Beijing shiyue wenyi chubanshe, 2001.

Jia Zhifang 贾植芳. "Fragments of Memory 片断的回忆." *Historical Data of New Literature*, no. 4 (1987): 70–73.

———. 1992. "In This Complex World—A Memoir 在这个复杂的世界里—生活回忆录." *Historical Data of New Literature*, no. 1: 43–56.

———. 2004. Jia Zhifang 贾植芳. "Life: A Prose-Poem 人生赋" (1936–46). In *Collected Works of Jia Zhifang: Creative Writing* 贾植芳文集: 創作卷, 1–90. Shanghai: Shanghai shehui kexueyuan chubanshe.

Jiang Guangci 蒋光慈. "The October Revolution and Russian Literature 十月革命与俄罗斯文学." *Creation Monthly*, April 1928.

Jiang Jian 姜建, and Wu Weigong 吴为公. *A Chronicle of Zhu Ziqing* 朱自清年谱. Hefei Shi: Anhui jiaoyu chubanshe, 1996.

Jiang Zuquan 蒋祖权. "Analysing the Cultural Revolution through the Hu Incident 透过胡风事件剖析文革." In *Red Disaster: A Collection of Academic Papers on the 50th Anniversary of the Cultural Revolution* 红祸: 文革五十周年 (*1966–2016*) 论文集, edited by Wu Chengmou 吴称谋, 131–141. Taipei: World Chinese Publishing, 2016.

Jin Ding 金丁. "Memories of the 'Left-league' 有关 〈左联〉 的一些回忆." In *The Past and the Man of Culture* 往事与文化人, 5–20 Beijing: Zhongguo renmin daxue chubanshe, 1988.

Jin Hongyu 金宏宇. "Editions and Revisions of the 'Yan'an Talks on Literature and Art' 〈在延安文艺座谈会上的讲话〉 的版本与修改." *Modern Chinese Literature Studies* 中国现代文学研究丛刊, no. 6 (2005): 76–84.

Jin Yaoji 金耀基. *Politics and Culture in China* 中国政治与文化. Hong Kong: Oxford University Press, 1997.

Jin Yi 靳以. "Life: To My Young Friends 生存 — 献给忘年的朋友." In vol. 4 of *Selected Works of Jin Yi* 靳以选集, 689–690. 5 vols. Chengdu: Sichuan People's Publishing House, 1983–84.

Johnson, Chalmers, ed. *Ideology and Politics in Contemporary China*. Seattle: University of Washington Press, 1973.

Kang Zhuo 康濯. "The *Literary Gazette* and the Wrongful Case of Hu Feng 《文艺报》 与胡风冤案." In *Memories Bristling with Profusions and Complications* 枝蔓丛丛的回忆, edited by Ji Xianlin, Niu Han, and Deng Jiuping, 511–559. Beijing: Beijing shiyue wenyi chubanshe, 2001.

Keaveney, Christopher T. *Beyond Brushtalk: Sino-Japanese Literary Exchange in the Interwar Period*. Hong Kong: Hong Kong University Press, 2008.

Kelly, David. "The Emergence of Humanism: Wang Ruoshui and the Critique of Socialist Alienation." In *China's Intellectuals and the State: In Search of a New Relationship*, edited by Merle Goldman, Timothy Cheek, and Carol Lee Hamrin, 159–182. Cambridge, MA: Council on East Asian Studies, Harvard University, 1987.

Kennedy, Michael D., and Ronald Grigor Suny. Introduction to *Intellectuals and the Articulation of the Nation*, edited by Ronald Grigor Suny and Michael D. Kennedy, 1–51. Ann Arbor: University of Michigan Press, 1999.

Kolakowski, Leszek. *Toward a Marxist Humanism: Essays on the Left Today*. Translated by Jane Zielonko Peel. New York: Grove Press, 1968.

Kondo, Tatsuya. "Notes on Hu [1]" 胡风研究札记1. *Hubei Writers*, no. 1 (1987): 55–84.

———. 1997. "The Transmission of the *Yenan Talks* to Chungking and Hu Feng: Caught between the Struggle for Democracy in the Great Rear Area and Maoism." *Acta Asiatica*, no. 72: 81–105.

Kuriyagawa, Hakuson. *Symbols of Anguish* 苦闷的象征. Translated by Lu Xun. Beijing: Renmin wenxue, 1988.

Kuskowski-Pieroni, Theresa. "The Writings of a Poet-Warrior: Hu Feng's Vision of Realism in China (1928–1948)." PhD diss., University of Wisconsin, Madison, 1987.

Larson, Wendy. *Literary Authority and the Modern Chinese Writer: Ambivalence and Autobiography*. Durham, NC: Duke University Press, 1991.

———. 2001. "Review of *The Problematic of Self in Modern Chinese Literature*, by Kirk A. Denton." *China Journal*, no. 45 (January): 218–220.

Lee, Leo Ou-fan, ed. *Lu Xun and His Legacy*. Berkeley: University of California Press, 1985.

———. 1987. *Voices from the Iron House: A Study of Lu Xun*. Bloomington: Indiana University Press.

———. 1999. *Shanghai Modern: The Flowering of a New Urban Culture in China 1930–1945*. Cambridge, MA: Harvard University Press.

Lenin, V. I. "Party Organization and Party Literature," first published in Russian in Moscow 1905. In vol. 10 of *Lenin Collected Works*. Moscow: Progress Publishers, 1965.

———. 1927. "Party Publication and Literature 论党的出版物与文学." Translated from the Russian into Chinese. China Youth, no. 144.

Lethen, Helmut. *Cool Conduct: The Culture of Distance in Weimer Germany*. Translated by Don Reneau. Berkeley: University of California Press, 2002.

Li Guangtian 李广田. *Gravitation* 引力. Shanghai: Chenguang chubangongsi, 1947.

Li Hui 李辉. *The Unjust Case of the Hu-Feng Clique* 胡风集团冤案始末. Hong Kong: Xiangjiang, 1989.

———. 1998. *A Tragedy of the Literary Circle* 文坛悲歌. Guangzhou: Huacheng chubanshe.

———, ed. 1998. *The Swaying Swing: Zhou Yang's Rights and Wrongs* 摇荡的秋千: 是是非非说周扬. Shenzhen: Haitian chubanshe.

Li Xiang 项黎. "On the Attitude toward Art and Life 论艺术态度和生活态度." In vol. 1 of *Literature in the Rear Areas during the Years of War against Japan* 中国抗日战争时期大后方文学书系, edited by Lin Mohan et al., 697–698. Chongqing: Chongqing chubanshe, 1989.

Li Xin 黎辛. "The 'Yan'an Forum on Literature and Art,' the Writing and Publication of the 'Talks' and Forum Participants 关于〈延安文艺座谈会〉的召开、〈讲话〉的写作、发表和参加会议的人." *Historical Data of New Literature*, no. 2 (1995): 203–210.

———. 2001. "On the Case of 'the Hu-Feng Counterrevolutionary Clique' 关于〈胡风反革命集团〉案件." *Historical Data of New Literature*, no. 2: 83–112.

Li Yang 李扬. *The Predestination of Resistance: Research on Socialist Realism 1942–1976* 抗争宿命之路: 社会主义现实主义 1942–1976 研究. Changchun: Shidai wenyi chubanshe, 1993.

Li Zhi 黎之. "Memory and Thoughts: From 'An Intellectual Meeting' to 'A Meeting for Propaganda Work' (January 1956–March 1957) 回忆与思考: 从〈知识分子会议〉到宣传工作会议 (1956年1月–1957年3月)." *Historical Data of New Literature*, no. 4 (1994): 102–124.

Lieberthal, Kenneth. *Governing China: From Revolution through Reform*. New York: W. W. Norton, 1995.

Lilla, Mark. *The Reckless Mind: Intellectuals in Politics*. New York: New York Review of Books, 2001.

Lin Mohan 林默涵. "Individual Emancipation and Collectivism 个性解放与集体主义," first published in the *Wenhui Post*, 1948. In vol. 1 of *A Compilation of Critical Essays on Hu Feng's Literary Thought* 胡风文艺思想批判论文汇集, 136–142. 6 vols. Beijing: Zuojia, 1955.

———. 1989. "The Ins and Outs of the Hu Incident 胡风事件的前前后后." *Historical Data of New Literature*, no. 3: 4–28.

Lin Mohan et al., eds. *Literature in the Rear Areas during the Period of War of Resistance against Japan* 中国抗日战争时期大后方文学书系. 10 vols. Chongqing: Chongqing chubanshe, 1989.

Lin Xi 林希. *Looting the White Flower* 白色花劫. Wuhan: Changjiang wenyi chubanshe, 1999.

Lin Xianzhi 林贤治. *The Case of the Hu-Feng Clique: A Political and Intellectual Incident in Twentieth-Century China* 胡风集团案: 二十世纪中国的政治事件和精神事件. Xianggang: Shanghai shuju, 1998.

Lin, Yü-sheng. *The Crisis of Chinese Consciousness: Radical Antitraditionalism in the May Fourth Era*. Madison: University of Wisconsin Press, 1979.

Liu, Binyan 刘宾雁. *China's Crisis, China's Hope*. Translated by Howard Goldblatt. Cambridge, MA: Harvard University Press, 1990.

Liu, Kang, and Xiaobing Tang, eds. *Politics, Ideology, and Literary Discourse in Modern China: Theoretical Interventions and Cultural Critique*. Durham, NC: Duke University Press, 1993.

———. 1993. "Subjectivity, Marxism, and Cultural Theory." In *Politics, Ideology, and Literary Discourse in Modern China: Theoretical Interventions and Cultural Critique*, edited by Liu Kang and Tang Xiaobing, 23–55. Durham, NC: Duke University Press.

———. 2002. "Aesthetics and Chinese Marxism." In *New Asian Marxisms*, edited by Tani E. Barlow, 173–204. Durham, NC: Duke University Press.

Liu Xiaobo 刘晓波. *Contemporary Chinese Politics and Chinese Intellectuals* 中国当代政治与中国知识分子. Taipai, Taiwan: Tonsan Books, 1990.

Liu Xiaoqing 刘小清. *The Red Hurricane: A Historical Record of the Left-league* 红色狂飙: 左联实录. Beijing: Renminwenxue chubanshe, 2004.

Liu Zaifu 刘再复. "Reconsidering Hu Feng's Thought on Literature and Art 关于胡风文艺思想的反思." *Literature Review*, no. 5 (1988): 4–6.

Lou Shiyi 楼适夷. "About the Rally against War in the Far East 关于远东反战大会." *Historical Data of New Literature*, no. 2 (1984): 45–49.

———. 1987. "Reminiscences of Hu Feng 回忆胡风." *Historical Data of New Literature*, no. 4: 58–62.

Lu Ling 路翎. "The Friend and Teacher Who Goes through Hardship Together with Me 一起共患难的友人和导师." In vol. 2 of *Hu Feng in My Eyes: Thirty-Seven Reminiscences of the Hu-Feng Incident* 我与胡风: 胡风事件三十七人回忆, edited by Xiao Feng, 708–740. 2 vols. Yinchuan: Ningxia People's Publishing House, 1993.

———. 2004. *Children of the Rich* 财主底儿女们. 2 vols. Beijing: Renminwenxue chubanshe.

Lu Xun 鲁迅. 1922. Preface to *Call to Arms* 〈呐喊〉 序言. In vol. 1 of *Selected Works of Lu Hsun*, translated by Yang Xianyi and Gladys Yang, 1–7. 4 vols. Beijing: Foreign Press, 1956–60.

———. 1925a. Preface to *Hot Wind* 〈热风〉 序言. In vol. 1 of *Complete Works of Lu Xun* 鲁迅全集, 291–294. 16 vols. Beijing: Renmin wenxue chubanshe, 1981.

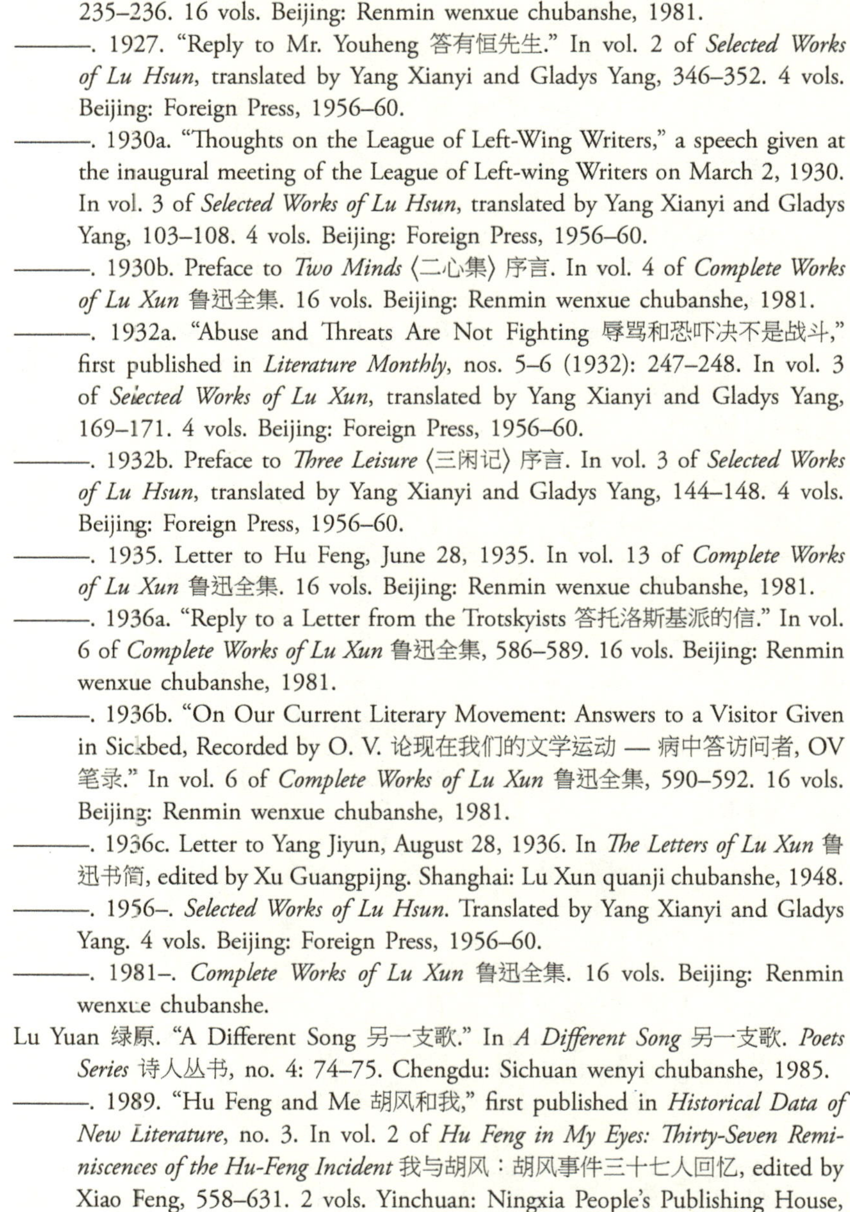

———. 1925b. Preface to *Kumon no shocho* 〈苦闷的象征〉 序言 (*Symbols of Angst*), by Hakuson Kuriyagawa. In vol. 10 of *Complete Works of Lu Xun* 鲁迅全集, 235–236. 16 vols. Beijing: Renmin wenxue chubanshe, 1981.

———. 1927. "Reply to Mr. Youheng 答有恒先生." In vol. 2 of *Selected Works of Lu Hsun*, translated by Yang Xianyi and Gladys Yang, 346–352. 4 vols. Beijing: Foreign Press, 1956–60.

———. 1930a. "Thoughts on the League of Left-Wing Writers," a speech given at the inaugural meeting of the League of Left-wing Writers on March 2, 1930. In vol. 3 of *Selected Works of Lu Hsun*, translated by Yang Xianyi and Gladys Yang, 103–108. 4 vols. Beijing: Foreign Press, 1956–60.

———. 1930b. Preface to *Two Minds* 〈二心集〉 序言. In vol. 4 of *Complete Works of Lu Xun* 鲁迅全集. 16 vols. Beijing: Renmin wenxue chubanshe, 1981.

———. 1932a. "Abuse and Threats Are Not Fighting 辱骂和恐吓决不是战斗," first published in *Literature Monthly*, nos. 5–6 (1932): 247–248. In vol. 3 of *Selected Works of Lu Xun*, translated by Yang Xianyi and Gladys Yang, 169–171. 4 vols. Beijing: Foreign Press, 1956–60.

———. 1932b. Preface to *Three Leisure* 〈三闲记〉 序言. In vol. 3 of *Selected Works of Lu Hsun*, translated by Yang Xianyi and Gladys Yang, 144–148. 4 vols. Beijing: Foreign Press, 1956–60.

———. 1935. Letter to Hu Feng, June 28, 1935. In vol. 13 of *Complete Works of Lu Xun* 鲁迅全集. 16 vols. Beijing: Renmin wenxue chubanshe, 1981.

———. 1936a. "Reply to a Letter from the Trotskyists 答托洛斯基派的信." In vol. 6 of *Complete Works of Lu Xun* 鲁迅全集, 586–589. 16 vols. Beijing: Renmin wenxue chubanshe, 1981.

———. 1936b. "On Our Current Literary Movement: Answers to a Visitor Given in Sickbed, Recorded by O. V. 论现在我们的文学运动 — 病中答访问者, OV 笔录." In vol. 6 of *Complete Works of Lu Xun* 鲁迅全集, 590–592. 16 vols. Beijing: Renmin wenxue chubanshe, 1981.

———. 1936c. Letter to Yang Jiyun, August 28, 1936. In *The Letters of Lu Xun* 鲁迅书简, edited by Xu Guangpijng. Shanghai: Lu Xun quanji chubanshe, 1948.

———. 1956–. *Selected Works of Lu Hsun*. Translated by Yang Xianyi and Gladys Yang. 4 vols. Beijing: Foreign Press, 1956–60.

———. 1981–. *Complete Works of Lu Xun* 鲁迅全集. 16 vols. Beijing: Renmin wenxue chubanshe.

Lu Yuan 绿原. "A Different Song 另一支歌." In *A Different Song* 另一支歌. *Poets Series* 诗人丛书, no. 4: 74–75. Chengdu: Sichuan wenyi chubanshe, 1985.

———. 1989. "Hu Feng and Me 胡风和我," first published in *Historical Data of New Literature*, no. 3. In vol. 2 of *Hu Feng in My Eyes: Thirty-Seven Reminiscences of the Hu-Feng Incident* 我与胡风：胡风事件三十七人回忆, edited by Xiao Feng, 558–631. 2 vols. Yinchuan: Ningxia People's Publishing House, 1993.

———. 1992. "Editor's Postscript Talk 编余对谈录." In *Complete Poems of Hu Feng* 胡风诗全编, edited by Niu Han and Lu Yuan. Hangzhou: Zhejiang wenyi chubanshe.

———. 2003. "To Try Knocking on the Door of Fate: Remembering and Reflecting on the '300,000-Character Report' 试叩命运之门: 关于〈三十万言〉的回忆与思考, Preface to '300,000-Character Report 胡风三十万言书,'" by Hu Feng. Wuhan: Hubei People's Publishing House.

Lu Yuan, and Niu Han, eds. *White Flower* 白色花. Beijing: Renmin wenxue chubanshe, 1981.

Lu Zhenyin 鲁贞银. "Record of Conversations concerning 'Hu Feng's Editorial Activities and Editorial Thought': Conversations with Niu Han, Lu Yuan, Geng Yong, Luo Luo, Shu Wu 关于〈胡风编辑活动和编辑思想〉访谈录: 访谈牛汉, 绿原, 耿庸, 罗洛, 舒芜." *Historical Data of New Literature*, no. 4 (1999): 147–172.

Ma, Shuyun. "Clientelism: Foreign Attention, and Chinese Intellectual Autonomy." *Modern China* 24, no. 4 (1998): 445–471.

Ma Tiji 马蹄疾. *A Biography of Hu Feng* 胡风传. Chengdu: Sichuan remin chubanshe, 1989.

Makdisi, Saree, Cesare Casarino, and Rebecca E. Karl, eds. *Marxism beyond Marxism*. New York: Routledge, 1996.

Mao Dun 茅盾. "Struggle of Revolutionary Literature under Reactionary Opposition 在反动派压逼下斗争的革命文艺" (1922). In vol. 2 of *A Compilation of Critical Essays on Hu Feng's Literary Thought* 胡风文艺思想批判论文汇集, 1–21. 6 vols. Beijing: Zuojia, 1955–.

———. 1938a. "Story of the First Stage 第一阶段的故事," first published under the title "To Where Can You Run? 你往那里跑?," *Literary Battlefield*, October 12.

———. 1938b. "Literature and Art for the Masses and the Use of Traditional Forms 大众化与利用旧形式," first published in *Literary Battlefield* 文艺阵地 1, no. 4, June 1. In *Modern Chinese Literary Thought: Writings on Literature, 1893–1945*, edited by Kirk Denton, 433–435. Stanford, CA: Stanford University Press, 1996.

———. 1981–. *The Path I Walked Past* 我走过道路. 3 vols. Hong Kong: Sanlian shudian, 1981–89.

Mao Zedong 毛泽东. "Analysis of the Classes in Chinese Society 中国社会各阶级的分析" (December 1, 1925). In vol. 1 of *Selected Works of Mao Tse-tung*, 13–22. 5 vols. Peking: Foreign Languages Press, 1965–77.

———. 1937a. "On Lu Xun 论鲁迅," a speech given at the memorial meeting at the North Shaanxi Public School on the first anniversary of Lu Xun's death on October 19, 1937. In vol. 4 of *Mao Zedong's Road to Power: Revolutionary Writings, 1912–1949*, edited by Stuart R. Schram, 96–98. 4 vols. Armonk, NY: M. E. Sharpe, 1992–2004.

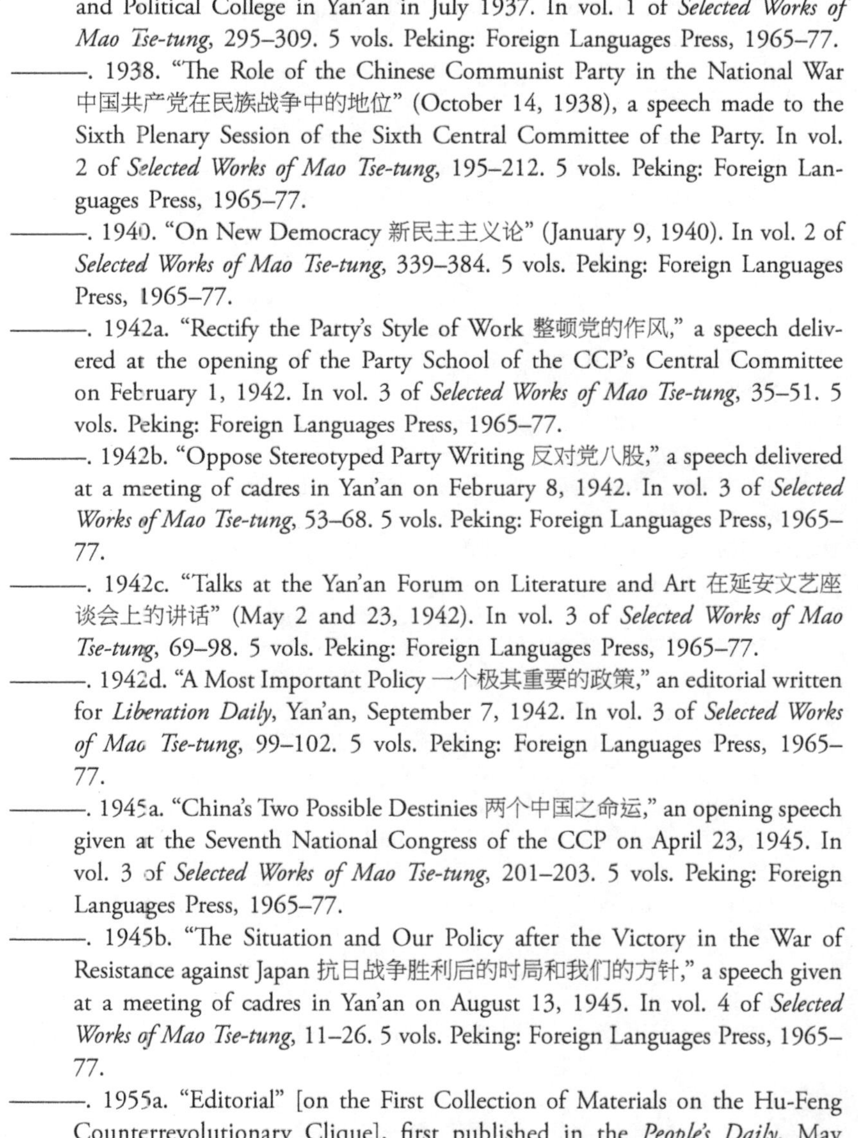

———. 1937b. "On Practice 实战论," a lecture given at the Anti-Japanese Military and Political College in Yan'an in July 1937. In vol. 1 of *Selected Works of Mao Tse-tung*, 295–309. 5 vols. Peking: Foreign Languages Press, 1965–77.

———. 1938. "The Role of the Chinese Communist Party in the National War 中国共产党在民族战争中的地位" (October 14, 1938), a speech made to the Sixth Plenary Session of the Sixth Central Committee of the Party. In vol. 2 of *Selected Works of Mao Tse-tung*, 195–212. 5 vols. Peking: Foreign Languages Press, 1965–77.

———. 1940. "On New Democracy 新民主主义论" (January 9, 1940). In vol. 2 of *Selected Works of Mao Tse-tung*, 339–384. 5 vols. Peking: Foreign Languages Press, 1965–77.

———. 1942a. "Rectify the Party's Style of Work 整顿党的作风," a speech delivered at the opening of the Party School of the CCP's Central Committee on February 1, 1942. In vol. 3 of *Selected Works of Mao Tse-tung*, 35–51. 5 vols. Peking: Foreign Languages Press, 1965–77.

———. 1942b. "Oppose Stereotyped Party Writing 反对党八股," a speech delivered at a meeting of cadres in Yan'an on February 8, 1942. In vol. 3 of *Selected Works of Mao Tse-tung*, 53–68. 5 vols. Peking: Foreign Languages Press, 1965–77.

———. 1942c. "Talks at the Yan'an Forum on Literature and Art 在延安文艺座谈会上的讲话" (May 2 and 23, 1942). In vol. 3 of *Selected Works of Mao Tse-tung*, 69–98. 5 vols. Peking: Foreign Languages Press, 1965–77.

———. 1942d. "A Most Important Policy 一个极其重要的政策," an editorial written for *Liberation Daily*, Yan'an, September 7, 1942. In vol. 3 of *Selected Works of Mao Tse-tung*, 99–102. 5 vols. Peking: Foreign Languages Press, 1965–77.

———. 1945a. "China's Two Possible Destinies 两个中国之命运," an opening speech given at the Seventh National Congress of the CCP on April 23, 1945. In vol. 3 of *Selected Works of Mao Tse-tung*, 201–203. 5 vols. Peking: Foreign Languages Press, 1965–77.

———. 1945b. "The Situation and Our Policy after the Victory in the War of Resistance against Japan 抗日战争胜利后的时局和我们的方针," a speech given at a meeting of cadres in Yan'an on August 13, 1945. In vol. 4 of *Selected Works of Mao Tse-tung*, 11–26. 5 vols. Peking: Foreign Languages Press, 1965–77.

———. 1955a. "Editorial" [on the First Collection of Materials on the Hu-Feng Counterrevolutionary Clique], first published in the *People's Daily*, May 13, 1955. In vol. 1 of *The Writings of Mao Zedong 1949–1976: September 1949–1955*, 559–564. 2 vols. Armonk, NY: M. E. Sharpe, 1986.

———. 1955b. "Editor's Comments to the Second Collection of Materials on the Hu-Feng Counterrevolutionary Clique," first published in *Liberation Daily*, May 24, 1955. In vol. 5 of *Selected Works of Mao Tse-tung*, 178–179. 5 vols. Peking: Foreign Languages Press, 1965–77.

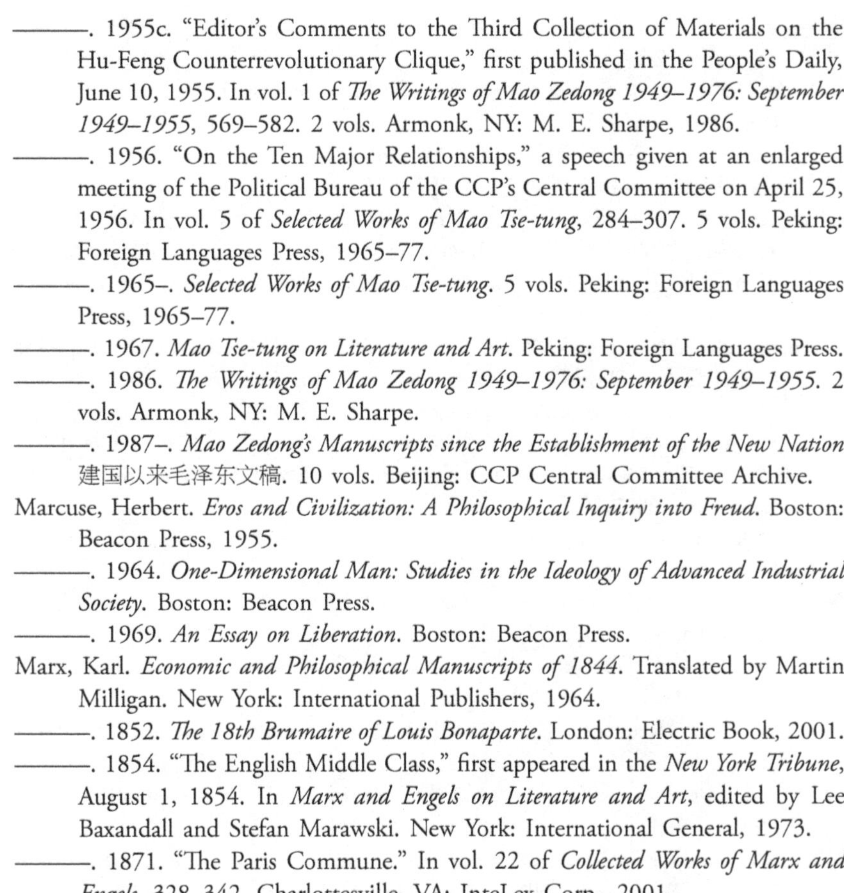

———. 1955c. "Editor's Comments to the Third Collection of Materials on the Hu-Feng Counterrevolutionary Clique," first published in the People's Daily, June 10, 1955. In vol. 1 of *The Writings of Mao Zedong 1949–1976: September 1949–1955*, 569–582. 2 vols. Armonk, NY: M. E. Sharpe, 1986.

———. 1956. "On the Ten Major Relationships," a speech given at an enlarged meeting of the Political Bureau of the CCP's Central Committee on April 25, 1956. In vol. 5 of *Selected Works of Mao Tse-tung*, 284–307. 5 vols. Peking: Foreign Languages Press, 1965–77.

———. 1965–. *Selected Works of Mao Tse-tung*. 5 vols. Peking: Foreign Languages Press, 1965–77.

———. 1967. *Mao Tse-tung on Literature and Art*. Peking: Foreign Languages Press.

———. 1986. *The Writings of Mao Zedong 1949–1976: September 1949–1955*. 2 vols. Armonk, NY: M. E. Sharpe.

———. 1987–. *Mao Zedong's Manuscripts since the Establishment of the New Nation* 建国以来毛泽东文稿. 10 vols. Beijing: CCP Central Committee Archive.

Marcuse, Herbert. *Eros and Civilization: A Philosophical Inquiry into Freud*. Boston: Beacon Press, 1955.

———. 1964. *One-Dimensional Man: Studies in the Ideology of Advanced Industrial Society*. Boston: Beacon Press.

———. 1969. *An Essay on Liberation*. Boston: Beacon Press.

Marx, Karl. *Economic and Philosophical Manuscripts of 1844*. Translated by Martin Milligan. New York: International Publishers, 1964.

———. 1852. *The 18th Brumaire of Louis Bonaparte*. London: Electric Book, 2001.

———. 1854. "The English Middle Class," first appeared in the *New York Tribune*, August 1, 1854. In *Marx and Engels on Literature and Art*, edited by Lee Baxandall and Stefan Marawski. New York: International General, 1973.

———. 1871. "The Paris Commune." In vol. 22 of *Collected Works of Marx and Engels*, 328–342. Charlottesville, VA: InteLex Corp., 2001–.

———. 1906. "The Fetishism of Commodities." In vol. 1 of *Capital: A Critique of Political Economy*, edited by Frederick Engels, translated by Samuel Moore and Edward Aveling. Moscow: Progress Publishers, 1999.

Marx, Karl, and Frederick Engels. *The German Ideology*. London: Lawrence and Wishart, 1974.

McDougall, Bonnie S. "The Impact of Western Literary Trends." In *Modern Chinese Literature in the May Fourth Era*, edited by Merle Goldman, 37–62. Cambridge, MA: Harvard University Press, 1977.

———. 1980. *Mao Zedong's "Talks at the Yan'an Conference on Literature and Art": A Translation of the 1943 Text with Commentary*. Ann Arbor: Center for Chinese Studies, University of Michigan.

Mei Zhi 梅志. *An Account of Keeping a Prisoner Company* 伴囚记. Beijing: Gongren chubanshe, 1988.

———. 1989. *Past as Smoke: A Memoir of Hu Feng's Prison Years* 往事如烟: 胡风沉冤录. Beijing: Ke xue chubanshe.

———. 1995. "The Lasting Influence of Scholarship 书香余韵." In *Wild Peppers Turn Red* 花椒红了, 168–174. Beijing: Zhongguo huaqiao chubanshe.

———. 1998. *A Biography of Hu Feng* 胡风传. Beijing: Beijing shiyue wenyi chubanshe.

Melvin, Sheila. "In Praise of Hu Feng." December 12, 2014. Caixin Online. http://english.caixin.com/2014-12-26/100768519.html.

Miao Junjie 缪俊杰. "Zhou Yang and the Chinese Style of Literary Criticism 周杨与中国式的文艺批评." In *Reminiscences of Zhou Yang* 忆周杨, edited by Wang Meng and Yuan Ying, 315–331. Huhehaote: Nei Menggu People's Publishing House, 1998.

Minnich, Elizabeth Kamarck. "ARENDT, HEIDEGGER, EICHMANN: Thinking in and for the World." *Soundings: An Interdisciplinary Journal* 86, nos. 1–2 (2003): 103–17. http://www.jstor.org/stable/41179087.

Molnar, Thomas. *The Decline of the Intellectual.* Cleveland: Meridian Books, 1961.

Moody, Peter. *Conservative Thought in Contemporary China*. Lanham, MD: Lexington Books, 2007.

Mostow, Joshua S., ed. *The Columbia Companion to Modern East Asia Literature.* New York: Columbia University Press, 2003.

Nathan, Andrew J. "A Factionalism Model for CCP Politics." *China Quarterly*, no. 53 (January–March 1973): 34–66.

Nietzsche, Friedrich. *The Will to Power*. Translated by Walter Kaufmann and R. J. Hollingdale. New York: Vintage Press, 1968.

Niu Han 牛汉. "Reunion 重逢." In vol. 2 of *Hu Feng in My Eyes: Thirty-Seven Reminiscences of the Hu-Feng Incident* 我与胡风: 胡风事件三十七人回忆, edited by Xiao Feng, 812–823. 2 vols. Yinchuan: Ningxia People's Publishing House, 1993.

O'Brien, Conor Cruise. Introduction to *Power and Consciousness*, edited by Conor Cruise O'Brien and William Dean Vanech. London: University of London Press, 1969.

Okano, Susumu. "The Revolutionary Struggle of the Toiling Masses of Japan," a speech given before the Thirteenth Plenum of the Executive Committee of the Communist International, Moscow, December 1933. New York: Workers Library Publishers, 1934.

Pang Yanjiao 彭燕郊. "Quanlin: A Communist Saint 荃麟-共产主义的圣徒." *Historical Data of New Literature*, no. 2 (1997): 83–95.

Pocha, Jehangir S. "Ex-Red Guards Come to Grips with Maoist Tumult: Revisiting China's Cultural Revolution." *Boston Globe*, August 31, 2006.

Pollock, Friedrich. "Technological Trends and National Policy." In *Studies in Philosophy and Social Science* 9, 483–489. New York: Institute of Social Research, 1940.

Propaganda Department, CCP Central Committee. "Decision on the Execution of Party Cultural Policy 关于执行党的文艺政策的决定." *Liberation Daily*, November 8, 1943.

Průšek, Jaroslav. *The Lyrical and the Epic: Studies of Modern Chinese Literature.* Bloomington: Indiana University Press, 1980.

Qian Liqun 钱理群, Wen Rumin 温儒敏, and Wu Fuhui 吴福辉. *Modern Chinese Literature in Thirty Years* 中国现代文学三十年. Beijing: Beijing daxue chubanshe, 1998.

Qian Yanbin 钱雁宾. "Anecdotes of Hu's Adolescent Life 胡风的青少年时期生活琐记." *Hubei Writers*, no. 3 (1989).

Qiao Guanhua 乔冠华 [Qiao Mu 乔木]. "Literary and Artistic Creation and Subjectivity 文艺创作与主观." *Literature and Art for the Masses*, no. 2 (May 1948): 8–19.

———. 1989. [Yu Chao 于潮]. "When Fang Sheng Lay Dying 方生未死之间." In vol. 1 of *Literature in the Rear Areas during the Period of War of Resistance against Japan* 中国抗日战争时期大后方文学书系, edited by Lin Mohan et al. 10 vols. Chongqing: Chongqing chubanshe.

———. 1997. *Those Gone-with-the-Wind Years* 那随风飘去的岁月. Shanghai: Xuelin chubanshe.

Qin Zhaoyang 秦兆阳. *On Formulism, Abstract Generalization* 论公式化，概念化. Beijing: Renminwenxue chubanshe, 1953.

Qiu Shi 秋士. "To the Young Students Studying Literature 告研究文学的青年." *The Pioneer* (February 1922).

Qu Qiubai 瞿秋白. "Political Movement and the Learned Class 政治运动与知识阶级" (January 31, 1923). In *The Guide Weekly* 向导周报. Tōkyō: Kabushiki Gaisha Daian, 1963.

———. 1932a. [Shi Tieer 史铁儿]. "Practical Problems of Proletarian Art and Literature 普罗大众文艺的现实问题," first published in *Literature* 文学 1, no. 1 (April 1932). In *The Birth and Development of Chinese Revolutionary Literature* 中国革命文学的产生和发展, part 1 of vol. 1 of *Reference Material of Modern Chinese Literary History* 中国现代文学史参考数据, edited by the Chinese Department of Beijing Normal University, 305–323. Beijing: Gaodeng jiaoyu chubanshe, 1959.

———. 1932b. [Song Yang 宋阳]. "The Question of Popular Literature and Art 大众文艺的问题." *Literature Monthly* 文学月报 6, no. 10 (1932). In *Revolutionary Literature in China: An Anthology*, edited by John Berninghausen and Ted Huters, translated by Paul Pickowicz, 47–51. Armonk, NY: M. E. Sharpe, 1976.

"Review of *Dead Souls*, by Nikolai Gogol, trans. by David Magarshack." May 3, 2002. Accessed 2007. http://www.geocities.com/athens/academy/6422/rev1081.html.

Sabu, Kohso. "A Brief History of Japanese Anarchism." [1998] 2006. http://www.ne.jp/asahi/anarchy/anarchy/english/history1.html.

Said, Edward W. *Representations of the Intellectual: The 1993 Reith Lecture.* New York: Vintage Books, 1996.

———. 2000. "Presidential Address 1999: Humanism and Heroism." *PostModern Language Association* 115, no. 3 (May): 285–291.

Sakai, Hiroshi. "Hu as Found in Oda Takeo's *Memoir Bungaku seishun gunzo* 小田岳夫回忆录《文学青春群像》中的胡风." *Studies of Lu Xun Monthly* 鲁迅研究月刊, no. 1 (2003): 28–31.

Salisbury, Harrison E. *Heroes of My Time*. New York: Walker and Company, 1993.

Sartre, Jean-Paul. *What Is Literature?* Translated by Bernard Frechtman. London: Routledge, 1993.

Scalapino, Robert A. *The Japanese Communist Movement: 1920–1966*. Berkeley: University of California Press, 1967.

Schwartz, Benjamin. *In Search of Wealth and Power: Yen Fu and the West*. Cambridge, MA: Belknap Press of Harvard University Press, 1964.

Seybolt, Peter J. "Terror and Conformity: Counterespionage Campaigns, Rectification, and Mass Movements, 1942–1943." *Modern China* 12, no. 1 (January 1986): 39–73.

Shang Yanlin 尚延龄, and Shang Ying 尚缨. "The First and Last Song of the New Republic: Hu's *Time Has Begun* 开国的绝唱—论胡风〈时间开始了〉." *Hexi University Post* 河西学院学报 22, no. 1 (2006): 63–67.

Shao Quanlin 邵荃麟. "Views on the Current Literature and Art Movement 对于当前文艺运动的意见." *Literature and Art for the Masses*, no. 1 (March 1948): 4–18.

———. 1948. "The Question of Subjectivism 论主观问题," first published in *Literature and Art for the Masses*, no. 1 (March 1948). In vol. 1 of *A Compilation of Critical Essays on Hu Feng's Literary Thought* 胡风文艺思想批判论文汇集, 63–95. 6 vols. Beijing: Zuojia, 1955–.

Shi Yun 史云, ed. *A Historical Account of Zhang Chunqiao Yao Wenyuan: Autobiography, Diary, and Testimony* 張春橋姚文元實傳: 自傳、日記、供詞. Xianggang: Sanlian shudian (Xianggang) youxian gongsi, 2012.

Shu Wu 舒芜. "Hu's Anti-Marxist Thought on Literature and Art 反马克思主义的胡风文艺思想," first published in China Youth (April 1954). In vol. 3 of *A Compilation of Critical Essays on Hu Feng's Literary Thought* 胡风文艺思想批判论文汇集, 147–164. 6 vols. Beijing: Zuojia, 1955–.

———. 1955. "The Anti-Party Anti-People Nature of Hu's Thought on Literature and Art 胡风文艺思想反党反人民的实质." *People's Daily*, April 13, 1955.

———. 1997. "Postscript to Return to 'May Fourth' 〈回归'五四'〉后序." *Historical Data of New Literature*, no. 2: 126–141.

———. 2001. *Collected Works of Shu Wu* 舒芜集. 8 vols. Shijiazhuang: Hebei People's Publishing House.

Siu, Helen F., ed. *Furrows: Peasants, Intellectuals, and the State, Stories and Histories from Modern China*. Stanford, CA: Stanford University Press, 1990.

———. 1990. Introduction to *Furrows: Peasants, Intellectuals, and the State: Stories and Histories from Modern China*, edited by Helen F. Siu, 1–28.

Snell, William. "Bertrand Russell at Keio University, July 1921." *Modern Japan Study (Kindai Nihon Kenkyu)*, no. 14 (1997): 171–192.

Solomon, Richard H. "From Commitment to Cant: The Evolving Functions of Ideology in the Revolutionary Process." In *Ideology and Politics in Contemporary China*, edited by Chalmers Johnson, 47–77. Seattle: University of Washington Press, 1973.

Spence, Jonathan. "On 'Chinese Revolutionary Literature.'" In "Literature and Revolution," special issue, *Yale French Studies*, no. 39 (1967): 215–225.

Su Wen 苏文. "Critical Theory and Practice 批评之理论与实践," first published in *Les Contemporains* 2, no. 5 (March 1933). In vol. 2 of *The Compiled Volume of Les Contemporains* 现代合订本, 695–705. 8 vols. Shanghai: Shanghai shudian, 1984.

Sullivan, Lawrence, and Richard H. Solomon. "The Formation of Chinese Communist Ideology in the May Fourth Era: A Content Analysis of Hsin ch'ing nien." In *Ideology and Politics in Contemporary China*, edited by Chalmers Johnson, 117–160. Seattle: University of Washington Press, 1973.

Sun Guolin 孙国林. "Editions of the 'Yan'an Talks on Literature and Art' 在延安文艺座谈会上的讲话的版本." *China Reading Weekly* 中华读书报, May 15, 2002.

Swearingen, Rodger, and Paul Langer. *Red Flag in Japan: International Communism in Action 1919–1951*. Cambridge, MA: Harvard University Press, 1952.

Tagore, Amitendranath. *Literary Debates in Modern China: 1918–1937*. Tokyo: Centre for East Asian Cultural Studies, 1967.

Tang Zong 唐纵. *The Eight Years with Jiang Jieshi* 在蒋介石身边八年: 侍从室高级幕僚唐纵日记. Edited by the Ministry of Public Security Archives. Beijing: Qunzhong chubanshe, 1991.

Therborn, Göran. *The Ideology of Power and the Power of Ideology*. London: Verso, 1980.

Times Literary Supplement (TLS). London: TLS Education.

Tong, Q. S. "Review of *The Problematic of Self in Modern Chinese Literature*, by Kirk A. Denton." *Journal of Asian Studies* 58, no. 2 (May 1999): 484–486.

Tong, Q. S. 童庆生. "Towards a Common Literature 走向共同的文学." In *The Meaning of the Chinese Language: Philology, World Literature, and the Western Idea of the Chinese Language* 汉语的意义: 语言学、世界文学和西方汉语观, 313–346. Beijing: Shenghuo, dushu, xinzhi sanlianshudian, 2018.

Trotsky, Leon. *Literature and Revolution*. Ann Arbor: University of Michigan Press, 1966.

———. 1999. "The Dustbin of History." In *The Penguin Book of Twentieth-Century Speeches*, edited by Brian MacArthur, 65. London: Penguin Books.

Tsu, Jing. *Failure, Nationalism, and Literature: The Making of Modern Chinese Identity, 1895–1937*. Stanford, CA: Stanford University Press, 2005.

Twitchett, Denis Crispin, and John King Fairbank, eds. *The Cambridge History of China*. Cambridge: Cambridge University Press, 1978–.

"Victims of the Powers That Be." *Times Literary Supplement* 3123, January 5, 1962.

Wagner, Rudolf G. *Inside a Service Trade: Studies in Contemporary Chinese Prose.* Cambridge, MA: Council on East Asian Studies, Harvard University, 1992.

Wan Jiaji 万家骥, and Zhao Jinzhong 赵金钟. *A Critical Biography of Hu Feng* 胡风评传. Chongqing: Chongqing chubanshe, 2001.

Wan Tonglin 万同林. *Martyrs: Hu and His Fellow Travelers* 殉道者: 胡风及其同仁们. Jinan: Shandong huabao chubanshe, 1998.

Wang Chuanyong 王昌勇. "Events before and after 'Wild Lilies' 〈野百合花〉的前前后后." *Historical Data of New Literature,* no. 3 (2000): 42–58.

Wang, David Der-wei. *The Lyrical in Epic Time: Modern Chinese Intellectuals and Artists through the 1949 Crisis.* New York: Columbia University Press, 2015.

Wang Ginshan 王景山. "Two or Three Things about Ba Jin the Senior 巴金老学长二三事," 2003. Accessed March 2005. http://www.people.com.cn/GB/14738/14759/21864/2227809.html.

Wang, Jing. *High Culture Fever: Politics, Aesthetics, and Ideology in Deng's China.* Berkeley: University of California Press, 1996.

Wang Kang 王康. "My Participation in the Investigation of the Hu Incident 我参加审查胡风案的经历." *Hundred Year Tide* 百年潮, no. 12 (1999).

Wang Lili 王丽丽. *Between Literature and Ideology: A Study of Hu Feng* 在文艺与意识形态之间: 胡风研究. Beijing: Zhongguo renmindaxue chubanshe, 2003.

Wang Meng 王蒙, and Yuan Ying 袁鹰, eds. *Reminiscences of Zhou Yang* 忆周杨. Huhehaote: Nei Menggu People's Publishing House, 1998.

———. 1998. "Zhou Yang's Eyes 周扬的目光." In *Reminiscences of Zhou Yang* 忆周杨, edited by Wang Meng and Yuan Ying, 407–413. Huhehaote: Nei Menggu People's Publishing House.

Wang Shengyun 汪圣云. "The Yan'an Rectification Movement's Contribution to the Establishment of Mao Zedong Thought 论延安整风对毛泽东思想确立的促进作用." *Research on Mao Zedong Thought* 20, no. 6 (November 2003): 14–16.

Wang Shiwei 王实味 et al. *Wild Lilies* 野百合花. Edited by Shen Mo. Guangzhou: Huacheng chubanshe, 1992.

Wang Wenzheng 王文正. "Do Not Forget Him—'A Comrade from Suzhou': The Fiftieth Anniversary of the Case of 'Hu Counterrevolutionary Clique' 别忘记了他: 〈苏州一同志〉—胡风反革命集团〈案五十年祭〉," a transcript written by Shen Guofan. *Ming Pao Monthly* 明报月刊 (August 2005): 100–104.

———. 2007. *The Hu Incident as I Experienced It: An Oral History of Judge Wang Wenzheng* 我所亲历的胡风案: 法官王文正口述. Beijing: Zhongguo dangshi chubanshe.

Wang Yunsheng 汪云生. "Why Did Intellectuals of the 1930s Go to Yan'an? 20世纪30年代知识分子为何走向延安?" *Beijing Daily* 北京日报, September 25, 2006. Accessed June 2007. http://epaper.bjd.com.cn/rb/20061107/200609/t20060925_93489.htm.

Wen Rumin 温儒敏. "Memories of and Reflections on the Eight Years 八年的回忆与感想." In *Eight Years in the United Universities* 联大八年. Chengdou: Xinian lianda xuesheng chubanshe, 1946.

———. 1993. *The History of Modern Chinese Literary Criticism* 中国现代文学批评史. Beijing: Beijing daxue chubanshe.

Wen Yiduo. "Memories of and Reflections on the Eight Years 八年的回忆与感想." Manuscript written by Ji Kan. In *Eight Years in the United Universities* 联大八年. Chengdou: Xinan lianda xuesheng chubanshe, 1946.

Wen Zhenting 文振庭, and Fan Jiyan 范际燕, eds. *Collected Essays on Hu Feng* 胡风论集. Beijing: Zhongguo shehuikexue, 1991.

Wiggershaus, Rolf. *The Frankfurt School: Its History, Theories, and Political Significance*. Translated by Michael Robertson. Cambridge, MA: Harvard University Press, 1994.

Williams, Raymond. *Marxism and Literature*. Oxford: Oxford University Press, 1977.

Wong, Wang-chi. *Politics and Literature in Shanghai: The Chinese League of Left-wing Writers, 1930–36*. Manchester: Manchester University Press, 1991.

Wu Chengmou 吴称谋, ed. *Red Disaster: A Collection of Academic Papers on the 50th Anniversary of the Cultural Revolution* 红祸: 文革五十周年(1966–2016)论文集. Taipei: World Chinese Publishing, 2016.

Wu Xiru 吴奚如. "Remembering Lu Xun the Great *Master* 回忆伟大大师鲁迅." In *Material for Lu Xun Research*, no. 5 (1980): 179–192.

———. 1993. "The Hu Feng I Knewg 我所认识的胡风." In vol. 1 of *Hu Feng in My Eyes: Thirty-Seven Reminiscences of the Hu-Feng Incident* 我与胡风: 胡风事件三十七人回忆, edited by Xiao Feng, 13–32. 2 vols. Yinchuan: Ningxia People's Publishing House.

Wu Yongping 吳永平. "The First National Congress of Literature and Art Workers and Hu." In *News of the Communist Party of China*, people.com.cn 人民網, November 12, 2006. Accessed March 20, 2009. http://cpc.people.com.cn/BIG5/64162/64172/64915/5028110.html.

Wylie, Raymond F. "Mao Tse-tung, Ch'en Po-ta and the 'Sinification of Marxism,' 1936–38." *China Quarterly*, no. 79 (September 1979): 447–480.

Xi Chun 奚纯. "The Publication of the First Collection of Materials on Hu 第一批胡风材料发表前后," an interview with Shu Wu. In vol. 1 of *Celebrities and Unjust Cases: True Accounts of Literary Circles in China* 人与冤案－中国文坛档案实录, edited by Hu Ping and Xiao Shan, 264–287. 3 vols. Beijing: Qunzhong chubanshe, 1998.

Xia Yan 夏衍. *Old Dreams Recollected at Leisure* 懒寻旧梦录. Beijing: Shenghuo, dushu, xinzhi sanlianshudian, 2000.

Xiao Feng 晓风, ed. *Hu Feng in My Eyes: Thirty-Seven Reminiscences of the Hu-Feng Incident* 我与胡风: 胡风事件三十七人回忆. 2 vols. Yinchuan: Ningxia People's Publishing House, 1993.

———. 1996. *Forever Unregretful: A Biography of Hu Feng* 九死未悔: 胡风传. Taipai: Yeqiang.

Xiao Gu 晓谷. "Indelible Memories 没有忘却的记忆." In *My Father Hu Feng* 我的父亲胡风, by Xiao Feng, Xiao Shan, and Xiao Gu, 199–225. Shenyang: Chunfeng wenyi chubanshe, 2001.

Xiao Jun 肖军. "A Collection of Random Notes on 'Random Notes on Literature and Life' and Discussions with Comrade Zhou Yang 〈文学与生活漫谈〉读后漫谈集录并商榷于周扬同志." In *Literature Monthly*, no. 8 (1941).

———. 1942. "My Views on Contemporary Literature and Art 对于目前文艺诸问题我见," a speech first given at the "Yan'an Forum" on April 23, 1942. *Liberation Daily*, May 14, 1942.

———. 2000, ed. *If He Were Still Alive: Late-Generation Pupils Remembering Lu Xun* 如果现在他还活着: 后期弟子忆鲁迅. Shijiazhuang: Hebei jiaoyu.

Xiao Shan 晓山. "Fragments of Memory 片段的回忆." In *My Father Hu Feng* 我的父亲胡, by Xiao Feng, Xiao Shan, and Xiao Gu, 1–162. Shenyang: Chunfeng wenyi chubanshe, 2001,.

Xu Maoyong 徐懋庸. *Memoirs of Xu Maoyong* 徐懋庸回忆录. Beijing: Renminwenxue chubanshe, 1982.

Xu Qingquan 徐庆全. "Kang Zhuo's Editor's Comment on Hu's 'My Self-Criticism' Newly Discovered 新发现的康濯为胡风〈我的自我批评〉起草的按语." *China Reading Weekly* 中华读书报, August 13, 2003.

Xu Shoushang 许寿裳. *The Lu Xun I Knew* 我所认识的鲁迅. Beijing: Renmin wenxue chubanshe, 1978.

Yan Jiayan 严家炎. "A Lesson: There Should Be 'Fair Play' in the Academic Arena 教训: 学术领域应该〈费厄泼赖〉." *Literary Criticism*, no. 5 (1988): 4–23.

Yang, I-fan. *The Case of Hu Feng*. Hong Kong: Union Research Institute, 1956.

Yang Mo 杨沫 (1958). *The Song of Youth* 青春之歌. Beijing: Renmin wenxue chubanshe, 2013.

———. 1978. *The Song of Youth*. Translated by Nan Ying. Peking: Foreign Languages Press.

Yang Shangkun 杨尚昆. *Diary of Yang Shangkun* 杨尚昆日记. Beijing: Zhongyang wenxian chubanshe, 2001.

Yao Wenyuan 姚文元. "Distinguish Right and Wrong, Mark Out the Boundary! 分清是非, 划清界限!" first published in the Literary Gazette, May 1954. In vol. 3 of *A Compilation of Critical Essays on Hu Feng's Literary Thought* 胡风文艺思想批判论文汇集, 56–62. 6 vols. Beijing: Zuojia, 1955–.

———. 1955a. "Clear Out the Hidden Double-Dealing Counterrevolutionary Elements 彻底清除隐藏的两面派反革命分子." *Youth Post*, June 14.

———. 1955b. "Hu's Three Ways to Distort Marxism 胡风歪曲马克思主义的三套手段." *Literature and Art Monthly* 文艺月报, no. 3 (March).

———. 1955c. "Marxism or Anti-Marxism? Review of a Few Points in Hu's 'Report on Literary and Artistic Practice since the Liberation' to the Central

Committee 马克思主义还是反马克思主义? —评胡风给当中央报告中关于文艺问题的几个主要观点." *Liberation Daily*, March 15.

———. 1955d. "The Reactionary Nature of Hu's Literary Thought 胡风文艺思想的反动本质." *Wenhui Post*, March 28.

———. 1955e. "Hu Feng Denies the Objective Rules of Historical Development—a Critique of Hu's Subjective Historicism (1) 胡风否认历史发展的客观规律性—批判胡风唯心主义历史观之一." *Liberation Daily*, May 7.

———. 1955f. "Hu Feng's Reactionary Views That Belittle the Working Masses—a Critique of Hu's Subjective Historicism (2) 胡风污蔑劳动人民的反动观点—批判胡风唯心主义历史观之二." *Liberation Daily*, May 9.

———. 1955g. "Crush the Hu Counterrevolutionary Clique with the Strongest Determination 用最大的决心粉碎胡风反党集团案." *News Daily*, May 27.

———. 1955h. "Hu Feng Opposes Organized Class Struggles—A Critique of Hu's Subjective Historicism (3) 胡风反对有组织有领导的阶级斗争—批判胡风唯心主义历史观之三." *Liberation Daily*, May 11.

———. 1955i. "Identify the Enemy and Destroy Hu Feng's Anti-Party and Counterrevolutionary Basis 认清敌人, 把胡风反党反革命的毒巢彻底捣毁." *Wenhui Post*, May 29.

———. 1955j. "To Counterattack Decisively Hu Feng's Double-Dealing Tactics 给胡风的两面派手腕以十倍还击." *Liberation Daily*, May 17.

———. 1955k. "Hu Feng's Double-Dealing Counterrevolutionary Clique Is the Diehard Enemy of the Revolution 胡风的反革命两面派是革命的死敌," first published in the *People's Daily*, June 1, 1955. Reprinted in *Liberation Daily*, June 3.

———. 1955l. "We Need a Hardened Heart to Combat the Enemy 要用铁的心肠消灭敌人." *News Daily*, June 18.

———. 1967. "Zhou Yang's Counterrevolutionary Dealings and Double-Sidedness 评反革命两面派周扬," first published in *Red Flag*, no. 1 (1967). In *The Swaying Swing: Zhou Yang's Rights and Wrongs* 摇荡的秋千：是是非非说周扬, edited by Li Hui. Shenzhen: Haitian chubanshe, 1998.

Ye Yao 叶遥. "Remembering 'The First Materials' Related to the Unjust Case of Hu Feng 我所记得的有关胡风冤案〈第一批材料〉及其它," first published in the *Literary Gazette*, November 29, 1997. In vol. 1 of *Celebrities and Unjust Cases: True Accounts of Literary Circles in China* 人与冤案－中国文坛档案实录, edited by Hu Ping and Xiao Shan, 253–263. 3 vols. Beijing: Qunzhong chubanshe, 1998.

Ye Yonglie 叶永烈. *A Biography of Yao Wenyuan* 姚文元传. Changchun: Shidai wenyi chubanshe, 1993.

Yeh, Michelle. *Modern Chinese Poetry: Theory and Practice since 1917*. New Haven, CT: Yale University Press, 1991.

Yi Ding 一丁 [Lou Zichun 楼子春]. "Lu Xun and the Chinese Communist Party 鲁迅与中国共产党." *Open Magazine* 开放 (1995).

Yu Dafu 郁达夫. *Sinking* 沉沦. Translated by Joseph S. M. Lau. In *Twentieth-Century Chinese Stories*, edited by C. T. Hsia, 1–33. New York: Columbia University Press, 1971.

Yu Guangyuan 于光远. *Zhou Yang and Me* 周扬和我. Xianggang: Shidai guoji chuban you xiangongsi, 2005.

Yuan Shuipai 袁水拍. "The Bankruptcy of Hu Feng's Theory as Seen from His Creative Work 从胡风的创作看他的理论破产." In *Critical Essays on Hu Feng* 胡风文艺思想批判, edited by the Association of Chinese Writers, 94–111. Shanghai: Xinwenyi chubanshe, 1955.

Ze Min 泽民. "The Youth and Literary Movements 青年与文学运动." *The Pioneer*, February 1922.

Zeng Huiyan 曾慧燕. "A Special Birthday Party: Celebrating Liu Binyan's 80th Birthday and 65th Anniversary of Literary Career—個溫馨特別的祝壽會: 慶祝劉賓雁80壽辰暨文學寫作65周年." *World Journal* 世界週刊, March 13, 2005.

Zhang Guangnian 张光年. "Remembering Zhou Yang 回忆周扬." In *Reminiscences of Zhou Yang* 忆周杨, edited by Wang Meng and Yuan Ying, 1–21. Huhehaote: Nei Menggu People's Publishing House, 1998.

Zhang Guotao. "Is China Now Safe from International Aggression? 中国已脱离了国际侵略的危险吗?" *The Pioneer Weekly* 先导周报, no. 6, October 18, 1922.

Zhang Renguang 张刃光. "The Literary Writers China Needs 中国所要的文学家." *The Pioneer*, February 1922.

Zhang Zhongxiao 张中晓. *Complete Set of the Dreamless Tower* 无梦楼全集. Edited by Lu Xin. Wuhan Shi: Wuhan chubanshe, 2006.

Zhao Haosheng 赵浩生. "Zhou Yang Talks about Historical Achievements and Mistakes 周杨笑谈历史功过." *Historical Data of New Literature*, no. 2 (1979): 228–242.

Zhao Shuli 赵树理. *Young Blacky Gets Married* 小二黑结婚. In *Complete Novels of Zhao Shuli* 赵树理小说全集, 67–82. Changchun: Shidai wenyi chubanshe, 1997.

Zheng Boqi 郑伯奇. "Random Memories of the Left-league 左联回忆散记." *Historical Data of New Literature*, no. 1 (1982): 14–23.

Zheng Chaolin 郑超麟. "A Response to Hu's 'Mr. Lu Xun' 读胡风《鲁迅先生》长文有感." *Studies of Lu Xun Monthly* 鲁迅研究月刊, no. 10 (1993): 48–50.

Zhi Kejian 支克坚. *On Hu Feng* 胡风论. Nanning: Guangxi jiaoyu chubanshe, 2000.

———. 2004. *On Zhou Yang* 周扬论. Kaifeng: Henan daxue chubanshe.

Zhou Erfu 周而复. "Remembering Comrade Shao Quanlin 回忆荃麟同志." In vol. 1 of *Collected Essays of Zhou Erfu* 周而复散文集, 277–290. 4 vols. Beijing: Huaxia chubanshe, 1999.

Zhou Yanfen 周燕芬. *Chance Encounter: July School, Hope School, and Related Literary Schools* 因缘际会: 七月社、希望社及相关现代文学社团研究. Wuhan shi: Wuhan chubanshe, 2011.

Zhou Yang 周扬. "Who Forgoes Truth, Forgoes Literature? 到底是谁不要真理, 不要文艺么?," first published in *Les Contemporains*, 1, no. 6 (October 1, 1932).

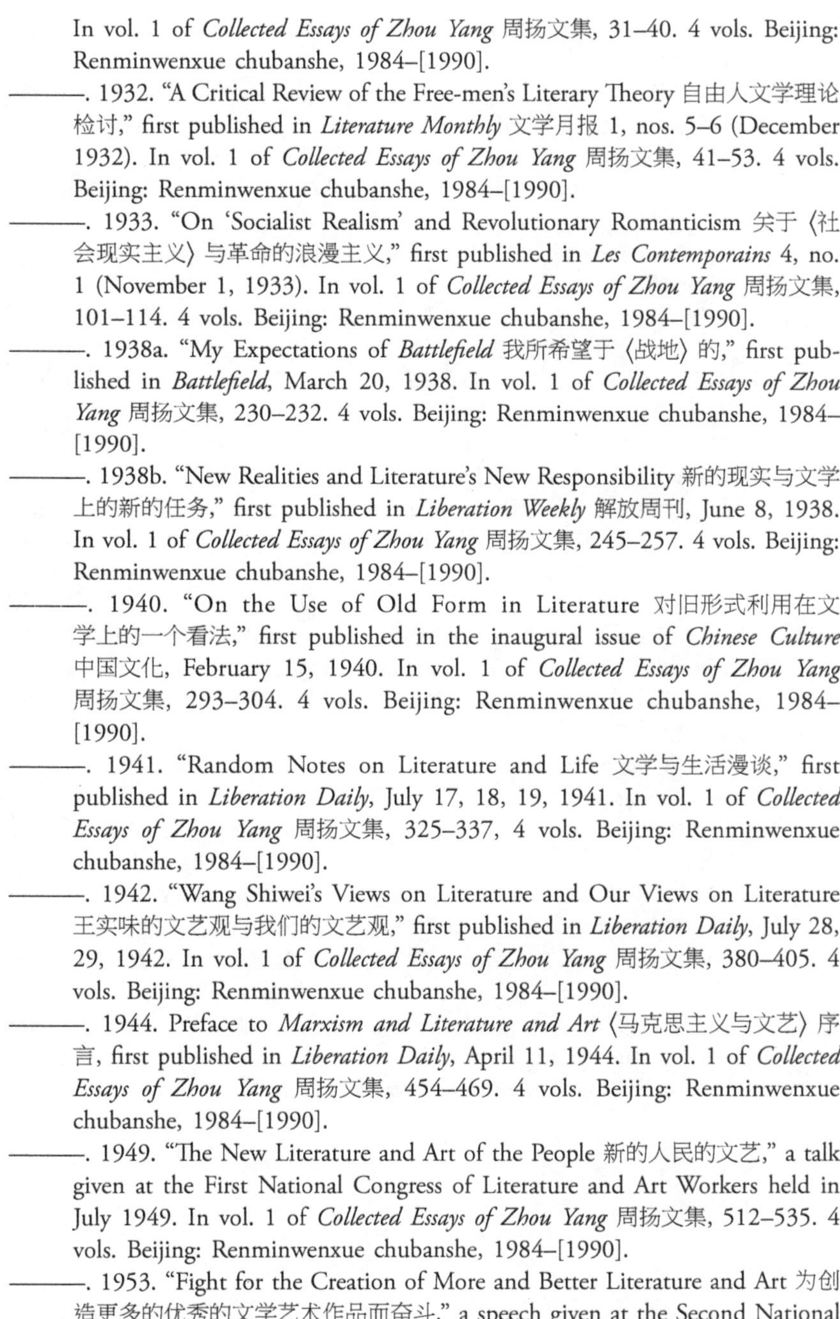

In vol. 1 of *Collected Essays of Zhou Yang* 周扬文集, 31–40. 4 vols. Beijing: Renminwenxue chubanshe, 1984–[1990].

———. 1932. "A Critical Review of the Free-men's Literary Theory 自由人文学理论检讨," first published in *Literature Monthly* 文学月报 1, nos. 5–6 (December 1932). In vol. 1 of *Collected Essays of Zhou Yang* 周扬文集, 41–53. 4 vols. Beijing: Renminwenxue chubanshe, 1984–[1990].

———. 1933. "On 'Socialist Realism' and Revolutionary Romanticism 关于〈社会现实主义〉与革命的浪漫主义," first published in *Les Contemporains* 4, no. 1 (November 1, 1933). In vol. 1 of *Collected Essays of Zhou Yang* 周扬文集, 101–114. 4 vols. Beijing: Renminwenxue chubanshe, 1984–[1990].

———. 1938a. "My Expectations of *Battlefield* 我所希望于〈战地〉的," first published in *Battlefield*, March 20, 1938. In vol. 1 of *Collected Essays of Zhou Yang* 周扬文集, 230–232. 4 vols. Beijing: Renminwenxue chubanshe, 1984–[1990].

———. 1938b. "New Realities and Literature's New Responsibility 新的现实与文学上的新的任务," first published in *Liberation Weekly* 解放周刊, June 8, 1938. In vol. 1 of *Collected Essays of Zhou Yang* 周扬文集, 245–257. 4 vols. Beijing: Renminwenxue chubanshe, 1984–[1990].

———. 1940. "On the Use of Old Form in Literature 对旧形式利用在文学上的一个看法," first published in the inaugural issue of *Chinese Culture* 中国文化, February 15, 1940. In vol. 1 of *Collected Essays of Zhou Yang* 周扬文集, 293–304. 4 vols. Beijing: Renminwenxue chubanshe, 1984–[1990].

———. 1941. "Random Notes on Literature and Life 文学与生活漫谈," first published in *Liberation Daily*, July 17, 18, 19, 1941. In vol. 1 of *Collected Essays of Zhou Yang* 周扬文集, 325–337, 4 vols. Beijing: Renminwenxue chubanshe, 1984–[1990].

———. 1942. "Wang Shiwei's Views on Literature and Our Views on Literature 王实味的文艺观与我们的文艺观," first published in *Liberation Daily*, July 28, 29, 1942. In vol. 1 of *Collected Essays of Zhou Yang* 周扬文集, 380–405. 4 vols. Beijing: Renminwenxue chubanshe, 1984–[1990].

———. 1944. Preface to *Marxism and Literature and Art* 〈马克思主义与文艺〉序言, first published in *Liberation Daily*, April 11, 1944. In vol. 1 of *Collected Essays of Zhou Yang* 周扬文集, 454–469. 4 vols. Beijing: Renminwenxue chubanshe, 1984–[1990].

———. 1949. "The New Literature and Art of the People 新的人民的文艺," a talk given at the First National Congress of Literature and Art Workers held in July 1949. In vol. 1 of *Collected Essays of Zhou Yang* 周扬文集, 512–535. 4 vols. Beijing: Renminwenxue chubanshe, 1984–[1990].

———. 1953. "Fight for the Creation of More and Better Literature and Art 为创造更多的优秀的文学艺术作品而奋斗," a speech given at the Second National Congress of Literature and Art Workers in September 1953, published in the *Literary Gazette*, no. 19 (September 1953). Translated into English in

China's New Literature and Art: Essays and Addresses, 1–51. Peking: Foreign Languages Press, 1954.

———. 1954. "We Must Fight 我们必须战斗," first published in the *People's Daily*, December 10, 1954. In vol. 2 of *Collected Essays of Zhou Yang* 周扬文集, 306–327. 4 vols. Beijing: Renminwenxue chubanshe, 1984–[1990].

———. 1961a. "On the Editorial Work of High-School Textbooks 关于高校教材的编写工作," a speech given on May 15, 1961. In vol. 3 of *Collected Essays of Zhou Yang* 周扬文集, 323–332. 4 vols. Beijing: Renminwenxue chubanshe, 1984–[1990].

———. 1961b. "Talks to the Editorial Board of *The History of Chinese Literature* 对〈中国文学史〉编写组的讲话," a speech given on August 14, 1961. In vol. 4 of *Collected Essays of Zhou Yang* 周扬文集, 67–71. 4 vols. Beijing: Renminwenxue chubanshe, 1984–[1990].

———. 1977. "Defend Mao Zedong Thought on Literature and Art, Rebuke 'Totalitarian Talks about the Literary and Artistic Black Line' 捍卫毛泽东文艺思想, 驳斥〈文艺黑线专政论〉," a speech given at a symposium on December 30, 1977. In vol. 1 of *Zhou Yang's Essays on Literature in the New Era* 周扬新时期文稿, edited by Xu Qingquan. 2 vols. Shanxi: Shanxi People's Publishing House, 2004.

———. 1983. "Respecting History and Evaluating Historical Figures Fairly 尊重历史, 给历史人物以应有评价," first published in *People's Daily*, August 30, 1983. In *Recent Work of Zhou Yang* 周揚近作, 260–265. Beijing: Zuojia chubanshe, 1985.

———. 1984–. *Collected Essays of Zhou Yang* 周扬文集. 4 vols. Beijing: Renminwenxue chubanshe, 1984–[1990].

Zhu Huijun 朱辉军. "A Study of the Zhou Yang Phenomenon 周扬现象初探." In *Reminiscences of Zhou Yang* 忆周杨, edited by Wang Meng and Yuan Ying, 642–653. Huhehaote: Nei Menggu People's Publishing House, 1998.

Zhu Ziqing 朱自清. "The Government Head's Massacre 执政府屠杀记." In vol. 3 of *Complete Prose of Zhu Ziqing* 朱自清散文全集, edited by Zhu Qiaosen, 182–190. 3 vols. Nanjing: Jiangsu jiaoyu chubanshe, 1996.

Zola, Émile. "J'accuse." *Paris Daily (L'Aurore)*, January 13, 1898. Reprinted in Émile Zola, *The Dreyfus Affair: "J'accuse" and Other Writings*, edited by Alain Pagès, translated by Eleanor Levieux. New Haven, CT: Yale University Press, 1996.

INDEX

Ah-long (Chen Shoumei), 160–161, 167, 222
Ai Qing, 74, 127, 167, 177, 209, 227
Ai Siqi, 68, 128, 177
Alber, Charles J., 223
anarchism, 197
Anderson, Marston, 124, 224, 226
Apter, David, 86, 211
Arendt, Hannah, 45, 199
Arishima Takeo, 10, 25, 192
Association of Chinese Writers and Artists, 67, 166, 169, 177, 204
Auerbach, Erich, 45, 131, 198

Ba Jin (Sun Shuxun), 24, 57, 67, 150, 163, 190
Bakhtin, M. M., 40, 197
Ba Ren (Wang Renshu), 177
Bai Lang, 177
Beijing Daily, 211
Bellow, Saul, 222
Benenson, Peter, 9, 184
Benton, Gregor, 184, 202
Bi Lei, 177, 200
Birch, Cyril, 207
Bodde, Derk, 217
Breines, Paul, 193
Børdahl, Vibeke, 187

Camus, Albert, 30, 193
Cao Baohua, 177
Cao Guofei, 213
Chinese Communist Party (CCP), 1, 202, 210, 212, 225; Central Committee, 6, 51, 62, 78, 105, 139, 142, 145–149, 165, 168, 171–172, 174–175, 188, 213–215, 221
Cheek, Timothy, 184, 210
Chekhov, A. P., 10, 183
Chen Baida, 210
Chen Duxiu, 21, 177
Chen Huangmei, 78, 177
Chen Jiakang, 84, 86, 177, 215
Chen Shoumei, 177
Chen Xuezhao, 77, 177, 211
Chen Zhuyin, 177
Cheng Fangwu, 21, 177, 189
China Youth, 177, 189–190, 197
Chinese Revolution, 3, 15, 17, 22, 25, 40, 45, 47, 50, 70–71, 74, 77, 82–83, 93–95, 97, 100–101, 103, 110, 129–130, 137–138, 140, 150–151, 154, 156–157, 183, 191, 197, 207, 210, 212, 222, 227
Cotton, James, 184
Creation Monthly, 21, 177, 193
Creation Society, 28, 196
Cultural Revolution, 2–3, 8, 12, 16, 42, 55, 74–75, 95, 140–142, 144, 173, 184, 190, 213, 227

Dagong bao, 177
Dai Qing, 210
Dai Ying, 190
Dante, Alighieri, 221
Deng Xiaoping, 218
Denton, Kirk, 10, 98, 186, 204, 212, 217, 222, 226
Dickens, Charles, 29
Ding Ling, 6, 38, 53, 61, 78, 100, 165, 167, 171, 194, 208, 210, 212, 223
Dirlik, Arif, vii, 197, 226
Dong Biwu, 58, 85, 164, 167, 177, 215

Eguchi Kiyoshi, 27, 34, 164, 192
Endrey, Andrew, 184
Engels, Frederick, 225
expository essay, 78, 208, 210, 235

Fairbank, John K., 203, 207
Fan Zhongyan, 177
Fang Han (Sun Kang), 33, 165, 177, 193
Fang Juehui, 177
Fang Ran, 222
Feng Naichao, 100, 169, 177, 198, 207
Feng Xuefeng, 33, 38, 55, 57, 67, 86, 95, 166, 178, 195–196, 198, 201–205, 216
Feuerwerker, Yi-tsi, 136
Figes, Orlando, 209
FitzGerald, Carolyn, 227
formulism, 83, 99, 103, 123–125, 129, 180, 187, 220, 222, 224
Foucault, Michel, 16, 133, 188, 227
Frankfurt School, 93, 203, 219
Freud, Sigmund, 162, 247
Fu Guoquan, 178

Gálik, Marián, 189
Gang of Four, 140, 142
Gaskell, Elizabeth, 29
Geng Yong, 44, 158, 178, 198
Goldblatt, Howard, 235
Goldman, Merle, 184, 189, 202, 211, 216, 224
Gorky, Maxim, 10, 183, 192; *Dead Souls*, 107, 221
Gramsci, Antonio, 11, 187
Grieder, Jerome B., 186, 198
Guidance, 13, 100, 130, 178, 213
Guo Moruo, 21, 28, 68, 100, 127–128, 164, 169–170, 178, 189, 192–193, 205, 207, 226
Guomingdang, 178, 196

Habermas, Jürgen, 16, 187–188
Hai Rui, 16, 173
Hakuson Kuriyagawa, 200
He Dinghua, 177, 193
He Ganzhi, 68, 178
He Manzi, 158, 178
He Qifang, 61, 77–78, 86, 98, 172, 178, 205, 211, 217
Hegel, Georg Wilhelm Friedrich, 236
Heidegger, Martin, 45, 199
Heine, Heinrich, 162
Herdan, Innes, 184
heroism, 146
Historical Data of New Literature, 188, 195, 201, 204–205, 209–211, 217
Hockx, Michel, 186, 222
Hong Cuie, 163–164, 178
Hong Lingfei, 178, 205
Hope, 10, 24, 32, 41, 45, 52, 76–77, 94, 96, 125–126, 129, 143, 146, 169, 172, 186, 200, 217, 220
Horkheimer, Max, 219
Hsia, C. T., 218
Hsia, T. A., 4, 183, 187, 203, 204, 211
Hu Feng, i, iii, v–viii, 1–2, 4, 6, 8, 10, 12, 14, 16, 20, 22, 24, 26, 28, 30, 32, 34, 36, 38, 40, 42, 44, 46, 48, 50, 52, 54, 56, 58, 60, 62, 66, 68, 70, 72, 74, 76, 78, 80, 82, 84, 86, 88, 90, 92, 94,

96, 98, 100, 102, 104, 106, 108, 110, 112, 114, 116, 118, 120, 122, 124, 126–128, 130, 132–151, 154–156, 158, 160, 162–175, 178, 180–181, 183–207, 209–210, 214–217, 220–227; "Hu Feng counterrevolutionary clique," 69, 123, 140, 143, 144, 145, 157, 173, 188, 203, 206, 216, 232, 233, 234, 235, 236; Hu Feng Incident, v, 1, 133, 135, 137, 139, 141, 143, 145, 147, 149, 151, 153–155, 185; Hu Feng *pai*, 44, 158
Hu Jiansan, 178
Hu Qiaomu, 61–62, 78, 80, 171, 178, 207, 223
Hu Sheng, 92, 100, 102, 178, 216, 218
Hu Zhimin, 178
Huang Yaomian, 169, 178
Huang Yuan, 67, 178
humanism, 30, 37, 47, 50, 131, 162, 184, 190, 202
Huters, Theodore D., 45, 187, 198

Jameson, Fredric, 11, 187
Japan, 13–14, 21, 26–41, 47, 66, 68, 96, 111, 159, 164, 166, 168–169, 189, 191–195, 209–210, 214, 216, 220; Japanese Communist Party, 3, 192, 195
Ji Fang, 168, 222
Ji Xianlin, 203
Jia Zhifang, 34, 75, 178, 194, 209
Jiang Chunzhu, 178
Jiang Guangci, 178, 189
Jiang Jieshi, 74, 178, 208
Jiang Qing, 141, 173, 178
Jiang Zuquan, 227
Jin Ding, 205
Jin Hongyu, 213
Jin Yaoji, 184
Jin Yi, 75, 178, 209
Johnson, Chalmers, 183, 211
July, 10, 26–27, 109, 128–131, 153, 166–175, 186, 188

Kang Sheng, 78, 178
Kang Zhuo, 148–149, 178
Keio University, 27, 164, 191
Kelly, David, 7, 184
Kobayashi Takiji, 32, 119, 164, 165, 192
Kurahara Koreto, 27, 164
Kuriyagawa Hakuson, 10, 50, 200

Langer, Paul, 37, 191
Larson, Wendy, 186
League of Left-wing Writers, 4, 34, 165, 177, 196, 205
Lee, Leo Ou-fan, 198, 201–203
Lenin, Vladimir Ilyich, 43, 190, 197, 209, 236
Les Contemporains, 178
Li Fenglian, 119, 178
Li Guangtian, 76, 178, 210
Li Lisan, 178
Li Weihan, 178
Li Xiang, 85, 178, 214
Li Xin, 80, 147, 178, 211
Li Xiuzhen, 119, 178
Liberation Daily, 80, 85, 141–142, 168, 208, 210–211, 214
Lilla, Mark, 81, 213
Lin Biao, 140, 178
Lin Mohan, 61, 69, 100–101, 145, 149, 172, 178, 205–206, 214, 218
Lin Yutang, 179
Literary Gazette, 123, 148, 171–173, 179, 187–188, 207, 224
Literature and Art for the Masses, 99–101, 104–105, 170, 179, 218, 226
Literature and Art Monthly, 179
Literature Monthly, 165, 179, 195–196
Literature Review, 179, 221
Liu Baimin, 102, 179, 219

Liu Baiyu, 78, 86, 179
Liu Binyan, 179
Liu Qing, 179
Liu Shaoqi, 179
Liu Xuewei, 43, 179, 198
Liu Zaifu, 179
Lou Shiyi, 165, 179, 194–195, 204
Lou Zichun, 181, 202
Lu Dingyi, 146, 179
Lu Ling, 10, 75, 92, 102, 129, 167–169, 172, 179, 185–186, 189, 200, 209, 216, 218, 222–223, 226
Lu Xun, 10–15, 23, 43–70, 73, 80, 84, 88, 92–93, 95, 119, 127–128, 154, 156, 159, 163–167, 174, 179, 187, 190, 191, 195, 196, 198, 199, 200, 201, 202, 203, 204, 205, 207, 213, 215, 218, 210; Lu Xun *pai*, 44
Lu Yuan, 14, 90, 118, 122, 157–158, 179, 185, 188, 203, 215–216, 222–224, 227
Lukács, Georg, 10, 193
Luo Feng, 179

Ma Shuyun, 184
Ma Tiji, 185
Mao Dun, 53, 67, 76, 81, 100, 128, 170, 179, 201, 204, 226–227
Mao Zedong, 1, 5–6, 39, 65–66, 68–70, 74, 77, 85, 93, 97, 113, 115–116, 119, 133, 135–136, 157, 166–167, 172, 179, 183–184, 188, 198, 206, 208, 212, 224–227; Mao Zedong thought, 5–6, 39, 66, 70, 85, 93, 97, 135, 157
Marco Polo Bridge Incident, 74, 166
Marcuse, Herbert, 105, 221
Marx, Karl, 20, 162, 189, 193–194, 216, 219, 225
Marxism, 2–6, 8, 10, 12, 15, 19–23, 25, 28–32, 34–35, 38, 54–56, 65–66, 69, 71–72, 81, 83, 85–87, 89, 97–98, 105–106, 124–125, 128–129, 131–132, 135, 138–139, 141–142, 147–148, 150, 160, 186, 193, 199–200, 214, 224–227
Marxist-Leninism, 72, 85, 128, 214, 226
Marxist literary theory, 39
May Fourth, 4, 6, 12, 21–22, 25, 44, 47–48, 50, 54, 68, 75, 77, 83, 85, 88, 92–93, 125, 127–128, 130–131, 154–155, 157, 163, 189, 191, 208, 211, 215–216, 218, 226; May Fourth literature, 12, 125, 127, 128, 226
McDougall, Bonnie S., 189, 213
Mei Zhi, 6, 24, 28, 59, 70, 90, 155, 165, 173–174, 179, 184–186, 190, 197, 206, 221–222, 224
Melvin, Sheila, 155
modern Chinese intellectuals, 76, 191, 225
modern Chinese literature, 12, 17, 21–22, 93, 154, 175, 186, 189–191, 196, 212–214, 217–218
modern Chinese poetry, 227
modernism, 3, 128, 130, 226
modernist poetry, 227
Morning Flower Society, 179
Morning Post, 48, 163, 179
Mu Mutian, 39, 196

Nameless Society, 179
National Daily: Awakenings, 23, 179
national literature, 10, 128
naturalism, 191, 222
New China, 38, 85, 101, 167–168, 179, 206, 218
New Life, 179
new literature, 2, 14, 21–22, 43–44, 49, 62, 74, 79, 85, 89, 93, 96–97, 125, 127–128, 131, 163, 188–189, 195, 197, 199, 201, 204–211, 216–217, 220
New Youth, 179, 189

New Zhanchun, 179
News Daily, 179
Nie Gannu, 96, 179, 217
Nietzsche, Friedrich, 201
Niu Han, 118, 179, 203, 221, 224, 227

O'Brien, Conor Cruise, 193
objectivism, 99, 107, 124–125, 179, 187, 217, 222
Oda Takeo, 191

Pan Hannian, 179
Pang Yanjiao, 217
Peng Yanjiao, 179
People's Daily, 37, 117, 141, 143–145, 148, 150, 171–173, 175, 188, 206, 216
Pioneer, 39, 116, 173
Pollock, Friedrich, 219
proletarian literature, 42, 164
Propaganda Department, 38–39, 84, 142, 145–148, 165, 205, 214–215

Qian Liqun, 214
Qian Mu, 179, 219
Qian Shibo, 180
Qian Yanbin, 23, 180, 190
Qiao Guanhua, 20, 84, 104, 180, 189, 215, 218, 220
Qiao Mu, 104, 180, 218
Qiu Dongping, 119, 167, 180
Qiu Shi, 189
Qu Qiubai, 21, 81, 166, 180, 183, 198
Qu Yuan, 180

realism, 10, 12, 49–50, 54, 57, 63, 83–84, 103, 105, 123–124, 130–131, 147, 160, 166, 170, 172, 187, 202, 211, 215, 217, 220–222, 224–227
rectification, 8, 55, 78, 85, 87, 95, 140, 143, 151, 169, 171, 185, 210–212, 215, 220
Report, 300,000-Character, 14, 62–63, 66, 69, 83, 86, 105, 142, 158, 172–173, 188, 203–205, 214–215, 224
reportage literature, 167
Restoration Society, 180
revolutionary new literature, 2, 14, 21, 22, 43, 49, 62, 74, 79, 85, 89, 93, 96, 97, 125, 127, 128, 131, 163
revolutionary romanticism, 5, 8, 16, 56, 77, 133, 211
Rising Point, 180, 224
Rolland, Romain, 10, 11, 51, 189, 200
romanticism, 5, 7–8, 16, 31, 42, 51, 56, 75, 77, 121, 133, 193, 211
Rong Guanxiu, 119, 180
Russell, Bertrand, 26, 191

Said, Edward W., 156, 162
Sartre, Jean-Paul, 42, 160, 197
Sha Ting, 180, 197
Shan, Ouyang, 166
Shao Quanlin, 88, 98, 100, 170, 180, 218–219
Shi Yun, 216
Shiping Hua, 184
Shu Qun, 180
Shu Wu, 85, 87, 98, 123, 143–145, 149–150, 168–169, 171, 180, 207, 215, 217, 220, 224
sinification, 225
Sino-Japanese War, 4–5, 8, 32, 41, 47, 57, 65, 67, 75, 78, 100, 137, 169, 197, 220
Siu, Helen F., 219
Snell, William, 27, 191
socialist realism, 10, 12, 63, 83, 130–131, 160, 166, 211, 222
Su Wen, 195
subjective combative spirit, 12, 49–51, 62, 72, 90, 92–93, 95–97, 99, 103, 107, 109, 125–126, 154, 159, 168, 180, 227

subjective-formulism, 99, 103, 124–125, 180, 222
subjectivism, v, 3, 8, 10, 17, 20–21, 50–51, 56, 66, 69, 85–95, 97–101, 103, 105, 107–109, 118, 122–123, 133, 143, 157, 159–160, 169, 215, 217–218, 220
Sullivan, Lawrence, 211
Sun Guolin, 213
Susumu Okano, 194
Swearingen, Rodger, 37, 191

Tadashi Imai, 192
Tagore, Amitendranath, 183
Talks at the Yan'an Forum on Literature and Art, 14, 56, 71, 73, 79–86, 88, 94–96, 98–99, 102, 124, 138, 167–169, 171, 184, 195, 204–208, 210–214, 219
Tang Tao, 180
Thackeray, William Makepeace, 29
The Mainland, 180, 220
Therborn, Göran, 81, 213
"third-category" man, 29, 195
Tian Han, 53, 180, 205
Tian Jian, 76, 125–126, 166–167, 180, 210–211, 225
Tian Jiaying, 180, 213
Time Has Begun, v, vii, 8, 14, 109, 111, 113, 115, 117–119, 121–123, 125, 127, 129, 131, 170, 188, 222–224
Times Literary Supplement, 186
Today, 2, 8, 53, 79, 82, 124, 154–155, 157, 207, 225, 227
Tolstoy, Aleksey Nikolayevich, 10, 56
Tong, Q. S., 186, 226
Trotsky, Leon, 56, 202, 209

Wagner, Rudolf, 185
Wan Jiaji, 190
Wan Tonglin, 136, 214
Wan Xiyan, 119, 180
Wang Chengzhi, 33, 165, 180
Wang, David Der-wei, 127, 225
Wang Ginshan, 190
Wang Jing, 187
Wang Lili, 185
Wang Meng, 70, 206
Wang Ruowang, 180
Wang Shengyun, 212
Wang Shiwei, 77–78, 180, 206, 210–211
Wang Wenzheng, 154, 180, 214
Wen Rumin, 214
Wen Yiduo, 76, 180, 208, 210
Wen Zhenting, 185
Wenhui Post, 142, 180
Wiggershaus, Rolf, 61, 203
Wild Lilies, 77, 208, 210–211
Williams, Raymond, 9, 47, 186, 199
Writers Monthly, 180
Wu Fuhui, 214
Wu Han, 173
Wu Tiehan, 119, 180
Wu Xiru, 15, 165–167, 180, 188, 196
Wu Yongping, 207
Wuchang, 22, 48, 163, 180

Xi Zhongxun, 172, 180, 188
Xia Yan, 40, 67, 100, 180, 196, 198, 204–205
Xiang Linbing (Zhao Jibin), 128, 180
Xiao Feng, 25, 180, 185–186, 188, 196, 198, 221
Xiao Hong, 166–167, 222
Xiao Jun, 57, 73, 78, 166–168, 181, 206, 208, 212, 222
Xiao Gu, 206
Xiao Shan, 181
Xiong Zimin, 6, 72, 140, 167, 181, 194
Xu Bingzhi, 181
Xu Fuguan, 181
Xu Maoyong, 57, 67, 181, 204, 213, 218
Xu Shaochang, 181

Xu Zhimo, 198

Yan Ao, 181
Yan Jiayan, 221
Yan Wenjing, 78, 181
Yan'an, 14–15, 55–56, 58–59, 65–66, 68–69, 74, 77–89, 91–92, 95–96, 99–100, 102, 106–107, 115, 117, 124, 136, 138, 140, 155–157, 167–168, 171, 181, 206–208, 210–215, 219–220, 226; Yan'an Forum, 14–15, 65–66, 68, 74, 78–82, 84, 86, 88, 102, 138, 157, 168, 171, 206, 208, 211–214, 219; Yan'an rectification movement, 55, 85, 87, 95, 220; Yan'an Talks on Literature and Art, 124, 210, 213–214
Yang Chao, 163–164, 181
Yang Hansheng, 67, 181, 202
Yang, I-fan, 184
Yang Mo, 181, 191
Yang Tianzhen, 23, 119, 181
Yao Pengzi, 102, 181
Yao Wenyuan, 16, 134, 140, 143, 173, 181, 216
Ye Yiqun, 181, 220
Yi Ding, 181, 202
Youth Post, 181
Yu Chao, 180, 220
Yu Dafu, 181, 198
Yu Guangyuan, 206
Yuan Shuipai, 172
Yuan Xiyan, 23, 163, 181
Yuan Ying, 206

Zang Kejia, 181, 223
Ze Min, 190
Zhang Chunqiao, 140, 142, 181, 216
Zhang Guangnian, 181, 206
Zhang Guangren, 34, 163, 181
Zhang Guotao, 137, 181
Zhang Mingshan, 181
Zhang Pijie, 181, 219
Zhang Renguang, 190
Zhang Tianyi, 25, 164, 166, 181, 227
Zhang Zhongxiao, 91, 181, 214, 216
Zhao Haosheng, 204
Zhao Shuli, 181, 191
Zheng Boqi, 181, 198–199, 205
Zhi Kejian, 14, 98, 185, 207
Zhou Enlai, 15, 23, 58–59, 62, 99, 166–169, 171, 173, 181, 203, 215
Zhou Erfu, 100, 181, 219
Zhou Libo, 181
Zhou Yanfen, 186
Zhou Yang (Zhou Qiying), 5, 13, 33, 38–39, 53, 61–62, 78, 81, 90, 95, 98, 165–167, 172, 181, 184, 187, 198, 201–203, 205–208, 212–213, 216
Zhou Zouren, 181
Zhu Qixia, 28, 56, 164, 181, 193–194, 202
Zhu Yifu, 181
Zhu Ziqing, 76, 181, 208–209

www.ingramcontent.com/pod-product-compliance
Lightning Source LLC
LaVergne TN
LVHW040159080826
844660LV00001B/35

* 9 7 8 1 4 3 8 4 7 9 5 3 8 *